A Guide to the
STONE CIRCLES
of Britain, Ireland and Brittany

A Guide to the
STONE CIRCLES
of Britain, Ireland
and Brittany

Aubrey Burl

Yale University Press
New Haven and London

Set in Linotron Sabon by Best-set Typesetter Ltd, Hong Kong
Printed in Hong Kong through World Print

Library of Congress Cataloging-in-Publication Data

Burl. Aubrey.
    Stone Circles: a guide to the megalithic rings of Britain.
Ireland, and Brittany / Aubrey Burl.
        p.   cm.
    Includes index.
    ISBN 0-300-06331-8
    1. Stone circles—Great Britain—Guidebooks.   2. Stone circles—
Ireland—Guidebooks.   3. Stone circles—France—Brittany—
Guidebooks.   4. Great Britain—Antiquities—Guidebooks.
    5. Ireland—Antiquities—Guidebooks.   6. Brittany (France)—
Antiquities—Guidebooks.   I. Title.
GN805.B8698   1995
914.104′859—dc20   94-23685
                                                              CIP

To my wife
JUDITH,
whose ability to read maps,
determination to ignore bad weather,
meticulous recording of details,
and whose insistence in the twilight
that the programme took precedence over pints
added many lonely circles to this Guide

CONTENTS

A NOTE ON COMMERCIAL MAPS

The usefulness of published maps varies considerably from country to country. For the United Kingdom the Ordnance Survey 1:50,000 maps, including those for Northern Ireland, provide a scale and a grid system that makes it easy to locate any site by its grid reference even if the site itself is not shown. For Jersey in the Channel Isles there is an excellent Ordnance Survey map at a scale of 1:25,000.

For Brittany matters are less simple. The French Government has discontinued publication of the Serie Orange 1:50,000 maps. The 1:100,000 Serie Verte is at a scale too small for anything but the most general of directions. For obscure sites one should use the detailed Serie Bleue 1:25,000 maps whose scale of 4cm to a kilometre is sufficiently detailed for most cromlechs to be shown. Fortunately, the majority of Breton rings in this Guide, such as those around Carnac, are close to roads and are not difficult to find.

'For the Republic of Ireland there is now an extensive series of 1:50,000 maps in the Discovery Series published by the Ordnance Survey of Ireland. On them the names of many archaeological sites are clearly printed in red. By the end of 1997 nearby sixty of the eighty-nine projected sheets were available. They may be obtained from: Map Sales, Ordnance Survey Office, Phoenix Park, Dublin.

Visitors should be warned, however, that in the countryside there are few signposts but there are usually people. Almost invariably a polite enquiry will be rewarded with the famous Irish courtesy and helpfulness. I have been taken by tractor to an obscure site and led for several miles by car through a spider's web of lanes. Ask.

Maps for all the countries in the Guide can be ordered from the very efficient Map Shop, 15 High Street, Upton-upon-Severn, Worcestershire WR8 0HJ (01684-593146).

ACKNOWLEDGEMENTS

For their guidance and information I am very grateful to the following: Mr Stan Beckensall; Mr Paul Devereux; Mr James Dyer; Dr Alex Gibson; Ms Wendy Horn and Ms Wendy Thirkettle, the Manx Museum; Mr Jonathan Jackson, Sennybridge Training Unit; Mr Roger Mercer; Mr Leslie Myatt; Dr Sean O'Nuallain; Miss Hazel Simons; Professor Derek Simpson; Mr Jack Stevenson; Mr Homer Sykes; Dr F.J. Wray.

Many institutions have provided me with references, photo-copies and books: Birmingham Reference Library; the Borthwick Institute, York; the Library of Birmingham University; Hereford Reference Library; The Map Shop, Upton-upon-Severn; Northallerton Reference Library; the Library of the Society of Antiquaries of London; the Library of the Society of Antiquaries of Scotland.

In conclusion I wish to express my continuing gratitude to John Nicoll, my editor of long standing, and Sally Salvesen, without whose keen eye, sympathetic pencil and persuasive tongue this book would have been very much the worse.

PHOTOGRAPHS

The photographs are the author's except for those taken by: Mr Philip Abramson, 116; Ms Isabel Churcher, 354, 366, 367, 368; Mr A.E.P. Collins, 268; Crown copyright. Reproduced with the permission of the Controller of HMSO, 267, 272, 284; Andrew Johnson, Courtesy of Manx National Heritage, 266; Dr Graham Ritchie, 182; Mr Alastair Service, 125, 190; Mr Mick Sharp, 130g; Professor Derek Simpson, 185.

Julie McManus developed the author's photographs with her customary expertise, and I am very grateful for the care with which she treated them.

PREFACE

Writing this Guidebook has been a particular pleasure. Like looking through old diaries one is reminded of the discoveries, sometimes the failures, the obstacles of unstable drystone walls, of bogs, brambles, bulls and barbed-wire. There were also gentle strolls on days of John Aubrey's 'delicate freshness'. Stone circles are one of the enticements of prehistory. And one of the frustrations.

It is the emptiness and the mystery that lures visitors, the weathered stones, the whimsicalities of petrified giants and dancing girls, druids, fairy gold, witches and sacrifice, the awareness that each ring is unique. Some have central pillars that are not central. Others have rings within rings, or a recumbent block, rubble banks, entrances, outliers, avenues and lines of standing stones that diminish across the moorland. Every region is different in its architecture, content and age.

The circles tempt even in poor weather. I have been lost in instant fog at Whiteholm Rigg (145), drenched at Temple Wood (125), struggled shin-deep in snow at Ninestones Close (34), shivered at Drumskinny (272), suffered everything – rain, frost, mist, snow and sleet at Arbor Low (27). But I have also had the delight of a sudden funnel of sunshine falling goldenly through black, swirling clouds onto the stones at Castlerigg (18), lighting them radiantly against a sky ominous enough for King Lear. I have also known the rarity of an un-Hebridean heat-wave at Callanish (185).

Not every ring survives in open countryside. Sandy Road, Scone (214), is in a housing estate. So is Aviemore's ring-cairn (149). In Perthshire Ardblair (193) has a busy road racing through it. Grey Croft (21) is overlooked by the Sellafield nuclear power station. Moncreiffe (209) was moved to make room for a motorway. Tossen-Keler in Côtes-du-Nord (369) was shifted kilometres to the harbour of Tréguier and prettily planted with shrubs and bushes. Incongruous lawns and flowers surround Harestanes (191) and Tigh-na-Ruaich (216) in their private gardens.

The book is concerned with these oddities. It is not concerned with fakes and follies like Auldgirth in Dumfriessshire, and the nineteenth century 'Druid's Temple' at Ilton in Yorkshire. It excludes modern Welsh gorsedds, such as the one erected in 1908 outside the 'small, gloomy mansion', as George Borrow described it, at Plas Newydd, home of two eccentric Irish ladies in Llangollen. Novelties like these are omitted whereas others, because of their uncertain age or unsure status as stone circles, are given entries: the reconstructed Blakeley Raise in Cumberland (15), and Ysbyty Cynfyn near Aberystwyth (238) whose suspicious stones edge a circular churchyard.

All the expected warhorses are here: Stonehenge (84) , Castlerigg (18), Callanish (185), Beaghmore (284), Newgrange (363), Carnac and Er-Lannic (379) in Brittany, but there are also over five hundred more modest rings for the curious: White Moor Down's fine circle on Dartmoor (56); Glenquickan, Kirkcudbright (179), with its great central stone; the group of four dissimilar rings at Cong in Co. Mayo (359); the little circle with its entrance at Broughderg SW, Co. Tyrone (285); Brittany's greatest and most neglected megalithic horseshoe at Kergonan, Morbihan (383); the Four Stones, Powys (253), a 'Scottish' Four-Poster in Wales; and Ville-ès-Nouaux (265), an 'Irish' recumbent stone circle in Jersey. Little known they may be, but they are delights. Like so many others they intrigue.

Visitors should ask what use there was for an outlying stone less than 3ft (89cm) high and in line with no astronomical event at the Nine Ladies (33) in the Peak District; should look at the ingenious choice of naturally-but helpfully-shaped blocks to act as lunar foresights in the Scottish recumbent stone circles; puzzle over the medley of cupmarks on a slab at Beltany Tops (340) and argue about patterns; remark upon taller stones, of pointed and flat-topped partners; question why over 4,000 years ago people cut a shelf into a hillside to create a level platform for the circle at Berrybrae (95).

It is not only the stones of a circle that should be looked at. Observe how they stand on a hill-shoulder or on a terrace with long views down a valley or glen, near water, by a cemetery of round cairns or against a chambered tomb. Even the name can be informative. Rollright (70), *hrolla-landriht*, 'the land-holding of the Saxon Hrolla'. Or Pobull Fhinn (190), 'the holy people', or the contradictory Nine Stones at Ilderton (67) where five stones remain of an original fifteen or sixteen.

It has been hard pleasure to see so many fine circles in western Europe. They are of one family, now dispersed, a megalithic confusion of parents, children, nieces and nephews, in-laws, second cousins, even some dubious offspring at the farthest edge of acceptability such as the Carrowmore chambered tombs-cum-kerbed cairns-cum-boulder circles-cum-stone circles. They fascinate and perplex. Enjoy them.

It is only to be expected that these great megalithic monuments of a prehistoric age should excite the wonder and stimulate the imagination of those who see them. In all countries and at all times they have been centres of story and legend, and even at the present day many strange beliefs concerning them are to be found.

T.E. Peet. *Rough Stone Monuments and their Builders*, 1912, 10

INTRODUCTION

This Guidebook is intended to give as much help as possible for visitors to a stone circle. It contains not only the expected information about (1) the location and condition of a site; (2) the best approach to it; (3) its known archaeology, but it also offers (4) suggestions for making surveys of a circle's shape, size and possible astronomy. Such non-destructive work can add much to the understanding of almost any megalithic ring.

The Guide is arranged by country and province in the order: – Great Britain (England; Scotland; Wales); the remainder of the United Kingdom (Channel Isles; Isle of Man; Northern Ireland); Republic of Ireland; and Brittany. Within these groupings an alphabetical order is followed for the counties of Britain and Ireland, for the départements of Brittany, and for the sites in them.

For ease of cross-reference the circles are numbered in sequence from the first, (1), Boscawen-Un, Cornwall, England, to the last, (390), Puy de Pauliac, Aubazines, Corrèze, in central France.

Where there are several rings in a complex they are subdivided a, b, c, such as the five on Burn Moor, Cumberland: Brat's Hill (16a), and the pairs at White Moss (16b), and Low Longrigg (16c).

Location and Condition
At the head of the entry for each circle is its number, its name and its rating in terms of condition from 1 to 6.

(1) Good. Worth visiting
(2) Also good but restored
(3) Ruined but recognisable
(4) Badly ruined
(5) Uncertain status
(6) Possibly a fake or folly

Only the most significant grade 4 rings are described, such as the Lochmaben Stane, Dumfriess (141), with its vital C-14 date, or Killycluggin, Co. Cavan (300), possibly associated with St Patrick. Most others have been excluded. They offer little except for the keenest researcher for whom details are available in the gazetteers of Burl (1976, 1985), Barnatt (1989) and O'Nuallain (1984a,b).

References to circles examined by Alexander Thom are given in square brackets with Thom's name for the ring if this differs from the traditional one. The circle's latitude has been decimalised to facilitate astronomical calculations on site. As an example, the 53° 15′ 21″ of the Druids' Circle (245c), Penmaenmawr, Wales, becomes 53°.3. For sites in Britain and Ireland the grid reference is cited at the end of the heading.

A typical entry is:

(219) BURGH HILL (3) [G9/15. Allan Water] Lat: 55°.3 NT 470 062

Approach

Following the name and grid reference, the distances from the nearest towns are given. Then, under the heading, Walk, what is believed to be the best way of reaching a site is suggested. Distances are given with an indication of the ease or difficulty of the walk. Most of these routes have been used by the writer. Finally, the map in the Guide on which the site is shown is indicated.

It must be emphasised that the approaches cannot be guaranteed. There may be better, untried ways. On the other hand, new roads, fences, conversion of pasture into arable, afforestation, closing of footpaths, a change of ownership, all can transform last year's pleasant stroll into this year's frustration. If in doubt enquire locally.

A warning has to be given about access. Sites are not always and inevitably open to the public, even sites in State Care. A few years ago a part of Avebury (82) was temporarily closed. Stonehenge (84) is roped-off. Stanton Drew (75) is always shut on Sundays and, temporarily, on weekdays also. Heavily-worn sections of the Carnac rows are surrounded by wire-netting.

The laws of trespass, moreover, differ in Britain, Ireland and Brittany and wherever possible it is better to obtain permission beforehand. That splendid archaeologist and fieldwalker, Leslie Grinsell, writing of barrows in north Devon thanked 'the various landowners and tenants on whose land he has trespassed on many occasions'. Honest and grateful but not to be recommended.

It must be stressed that proper equipment is vital: an Ordnance Survey map; stout clothing and footwear; and a reliable compass such as those made by Silva. Even for sites near a road all these are necessary. When the writer was visiting Whiteholm Rigg (145), only 150 yards (137m) from the car, a dense fog descended on the moor. It was only by a considerable act of will-power that trust in the compass overcame the instinct to go in another – and wrong – direction.

Archaeology

What is known about the site is offered in some detail, its size, height of stones, architectural features, possible age. Results of excavations and the whereabouts of any finds are provided where known. C-14 dates and their laboratory references are quoted followed by their calibration into 'real years'. For Barbrook Centre (29) in the Peak District of Derbyshire this appears as 1500 ± 150 bc (BM-197), c.1800 BC. The approximate dates of prehistoric periods are:

Early Neolithic	4500 BC –
Late Neolithic	3500 BC –
Early Bronze Age	2200 BC –
Middle Bronze Age	1750–1000 BC

These vary somewhat from region to region in western Europe.

Extra sources are supplied for readers seeking more information although, because of space, the majority of sites have only one or two bibliographical references. Even a small and little-known ring such as Kealkil in Co. Cork (323) has received at least eight reports from 1897 to 1984 and a famous circle such as the Rollright Stones in Oxfordshire (70) has been written about by dozens of visitors from the fourteenth century onwards. Readers wishing to learn more about a stone circle will usually find extra works listed within the references cited here.

For Britain more comprehensive gazetteers can be found in Burl (1976, to be updated in 1996) and Barnatt (1989). Irish sites are also cited in Burl (1976). More details for south-west Ireland occur in O'Nuallain (1984a,b). For Brittany there is partial coverage in Burl (1985) and Bender (1986). A full gazetteer and bibliography will be published in Burl (1996).

Where particular aspects of a ring, such as architecture and astronomy, have been analysed by different scholars further data are given.

Books containing descriptions of many circles are quoted by author only (e.g. Grimes, 1963), the title and date being given in full in the Bibliography. For single sites the best account is given in full either by author and title (e.g. G. and M. Ponting, *The Standing Stones of Callanish*, 1977); or by the name and date of the journal in which the report was published (e.g. for Arbor Low, Derbyshire: *Arch. 58*, 1903, 461–98).

An explanation must be given for the use of the new and old Welsh names. Sites are quoted under the names of the new, such as Dyfed or Gwynedd but for each site entry the old name is also given. As an example, Dyfed is composed of three old counties: Cardigan, Carmarthen and Pembrokshire. Three of the site entries in Dyfed are listed as:

> Dyffryn, Syfynwy, Pembrokeshire (235)
> Meini-gwyr, Llandyssilio, Carmarthen (237)
> Ysbyty Cynfyn, Ponterwyd, Cardigan (238)

The system tells which old county to look for in early reports.

For England and Scotland the historic names for counties have been preferred to the administratively imposed but confusing hybrids such as

Avon (north Somerset and south Gloucestershire) and Grampian (Aberdeenshire, Banff, Kincardine and Moray).

It has not been possible to provide plans except for complex sites and circles of especial architectural or archaeological importance. To compensate for this lacuna a note is given of where reliable surveys exist elsewhere.

Practical Work on Site
Visits to stone circles do not have to be only a few minutes' inspection of the stones. Longer stays can include photography, painting and recording.

The making of a plan often deepens one's appreciation of the ring. Equipment for the professional archaeologist is expensive and operated by trained technicians. For one or two circle-lovers, a school party, or group of students, the kit need consist of no more than one or two 66ft (20m) tapes, a 6ft (2m) flexitape, some probes, a compass, a pocket calculator with sine and cosine, a piece of white chalk, and writing material to record results.

A. *Shape and Size* The quickest, easiest and often surprisingly accurate method of discovering the dimensions of a ring is by pacing. Using the compass to establish directions, four angled crossings of the circle will give an indication of its diameter/s and shape.

Better results can be obtained by use of a tape to measure to each stone from the approximate centre of the ring. Attach the tape's metal clip to a thin, short pin, such as a meat skewer. Bayonets, ranging-poles and long, thick probes can damage material below ground. When measuring take compass-bearings. Repeating the same system at other sites, perhaps starting at the north and working clockwise – *never* widdershins for fear of rousing the Devil – should overcome possible confusion in one's notes.

A very reliable method uses two fixed points. Placing two pins north-south orientated, 10ft (3m) apart, inside the ring, one can first measure from the north probe and then from the south. The triangulated distances and the compass-bearings of the stones, should result in a good plan.

The width, thickness and height of an individual stone can be obtained through the flexitape. If a pillar is more than 6ft (1.8m) high a light chalk mark at that height enables the upper part of the stone to be measured from it.

B. *The Population and Area of a Ring* The minimum and maximum numbers of people who used a ring can be deduced within wide limits by calculating its area. For circles the well-known πr^2 is the formula. For ovoids and ellipses it is $\frac{1}{4}\pi \times$ the product of its axes.

As examples from Cornwall, the elegant Merry Maidens (8) is a true circle 78ft (23.8m) in diameter, $\pi \times 39^2 = 4778$ square feet (444m^2). Two miles to the north-west the fine ring of Boscawen-Un (1) is an ellipse about 83ft by 73ft (25.2 × 22.3m). Its area is $\frac{1}{4}\pi$ × 83 × 73 = 4759 s.ft (442m²), very similar to the Merry Maidens.

If people had stood packed shoulder to shoulder and chest to back in these rings, each occupying about 6 s.ft (0.6m²), they could have numbered about 800 men, women and children. It is more feasible, though utterly beyond proof, that the participants had a comfortable body-space of some 28 s.ft (2.6m²). Anthropological parallels suggest that only half the ring would be taken up by the watchers, whether standing around the perimeter or to one side, the remainder of the space being allotted to the officiants or priests. Such a disposition would reduce the assembly to about eighty-five.

It can be assumed that 800 is the maximum congregation. In theory it is also possible to discover the minumum number by working out how many labourers were needed to erect the heaviest stone. When a slab being pulled upright reached an angle of 70° from the horizontal it exerted a pull of one-fifth its dead weight. A strong and fit adult could haul about 100 lbs for a short while.

Boscawen-Un's tall, off-centre granite pillar is about 10ft 3ins long, 2ft 7ins wide and 1ft 5ins thick (3.1 × 0.8 × 0.4m). It weighs around 2½ tons. The equation for the necessary work-force is

$$\frac{5600 \text{ lbs}}{5} \div 100 = 11 \text{ to } 12 \text{ workers.}$$

Even if the hypothetical population of eighty-five was reduced to a fifth by discounting the aged, the very young, females and cripples, this would still leave an available work-force of seventeen, quite sufficient for the task of elevating the stone. What one does not know is who was allowed to participate, and whether neighbouring communities gave assistance when some especially demanding project, such as Avebury or Stonehenge, was planned.

For those interested in pursuing this demographic will o'the wisp the average weights of different kinds of stone and timber are given. Weights are expressed in terms of specific gravity, their density related to that of water. One cubic foot of water weighs 62.3 lbs. Granite, with an average specific gravity of 2.6 × 62.3, weighs 162 lbs per cubic foot.

Igneous rocks	Specific gravity	Average weight of a cubic foot
Plutonic		
Granite.	2.5–2.7	162 lbs
Syenite	2.6–2.8	168 lbs
Diorite	2.7–2.8	171 lbs
Gabbro	2.95–3.0	185 lbs
Fine-grained		
Rhyolite	2.5–2.6	159 lbs
Quartz	2.65	165 lbs
Basalt	2.83–3.3	191 lbs
Dolerite	2.8–3.3	190 lbs

Sedimentary [Conglomerate and breccia, varying according to pebble content]

Sandstone	2–2.5	140 lbs
Millstone Grit	Variable	138 lbs
Sarsen	2.47	154 lbs
Shale	Variable	172 lbs
Limestone	2.6–2.8	168 lbs

Metamorphic

Gneiss	2.55–3.0	173 lbs
Schist	Soft and variable	165 lbs
Slate	2.752	172 lbs

Timber

Oak		52 lbs
″	If green	67 lbs
Elm		34 lbs
Ash		47.5 lbs

Other material

Clay		125 lbs
Chalk		110 lbs when moist

Nearly all the stones in a circle are local and seldom come from more than a mile or two away. Inspection of drystone walls in the vicinity of a ring gives an indication of how close the source was. Such walls were customarily built of stones dragged off fields in the immediate neighbourhood.

Useful books for the prospective surveyor and experimental archaeologist are listed in the bibliography.

c. *Astronomy* More and more firm evidence has become available to prove that prehistoric societies in western Europe built astronomical alignments into some of their ritual monuments. The lines were imprecise. But they exist and can be recovered. They are concerned with the sun, the moon and with cardinal points, usually to north or south, less commonly to east or west. To be sure that an alignment was intended there are three requirements: a backsight where the observer stood and a manmade foresight in line with a celestial target.

The backsight is a difficulty. It is popularly assumed to be the centre of a ring but such an unmarked position is very susceptible to misjudgement. Equally valid backsights are distinctive features such as the smallest stone, a decorated slab, a boulder of a different colour or texture. Of a shining quartz block at the wsw of Boscawen-Un (1), visually conspicuous among its grey granite partners, Sir Norman Lockyer commented that 'from it the May sun was seen to rise over the centre of the circle.'

The foresight has to be artificial. A tempting notch in a hillside is unacceptable because it cannot be proved to have mattered to the builders of a megalithic ring. The fact that the sun rose or the moon set in it might be no more than coincidence. Today's observer must use something made by man and very noticeable, such as the tallest stone, or a slab deliberately laid flat, an entrance, or a cupmarked pillar. Subjectivity affects these choices. One can only be honest.

A compass-bearing, technically known as the azimuth, must be taken, ideally by a theodolite. This will be impracticable for most visitors but the alternative, the handheld compass, will be reliable only to a degree or two. It is also affected by magnetic variation and this must be allowed for. At Land's End in 1986 magnetic north was some 5° to the west of True North, decreasing by about $\frac{1}{2}$° every three years. Information about the amount of divergence is provided on Ordnance Survey maps.

Reassuringly, for the interested but uncommitted surveyor a feeling of discouragement is unnecessary. An error of a degree or two does not invalidate the deduced sightline, because prehistoric designers were not much concerned with astronomical niceties. As William Stukeley observed in 1743 about the plan of Avebury (82), 'This is done with a sufficient, tho' not a mathematical exactness, where preciseness would have no effect.' Only those intending to publish their results should be more fastidious.

Having obtained an azimuth it is possible to analyse its relevance to a celestial target. Solar orientations will be to the solstitial risings or settings at midsummer and midwinter, to the equinoxes and to early May and November, the prehistoric festivals of Beltane and Samain. For the moon sightlines will generally be to its four extreme, or major, positions in the north and south quadrants.

With its regular cycle the sun is easy. At midsummer it is rising and setting at the north-east and north-west, and for the succeeding six months it moves steadily southwards to its midwinter extremes. These positions vary slightly according to the latitude. In Scotland the winter hours of daylight are shorter and summer hours longer than in England. The varying daylight hours are:

Latitude		Midsummer Sun		Daylight Hours	Midwinter Sun		Daylight Hours
		Rise	Set		Rise	Set	
50°	Land's End	51°	309°	16½	129°	231°	6¾
55°	S.W. Scotland	45°	315°	18	135°	225°	6
60°	Shetlands	35°	325°	19¼	145°	215°	4½

One has to know the latitude of a circle. The Guidebook provides this for each site.

The sun is simple, the moon is not. It moves along the skyline as the sun does but whereas the sun takes a year to complete its cycle from north-east to south-east back to north-east the moon takes only a month, the time it takes to circle the earth. It swings swiftly from one extreme to another, waxing and waning from left-facing crescent to full moon to right-facing crescent and then invisibility before reappearing, its rapid transformations perhaps seeming magical to the prehistoric mind. It has advantages. It is conspicuous in the night sky and it can be looked with the naked eye. It also has a considerable disadvantage. Unlike the metronomic sun with an identical cycle year in, year out, the moon's extreme positions at both north and south open and close over 18.61 years like heavenly fans.

As an example, one year at the central latitude of Britain, 55°, an observer would have seen the moon rise at its southernmost around 148°. This was not a constant. Successively, year by year, the moon rose ever farther to the north of 148° until after nine years it was rising no nearer to south than 124°, its minor standstill. In that year the full moon rose there at midsummer, setting at 236°. At midwinter it rose at 56° and set at 304°. Then it began its slow return to its major positions when its midsummer and midwinter arcs were from 148° to 212° and from 32° to 328° respectively.

Astronomically there is a further complication. These solar and lunar azimuths are correct only when the skyline is level with the eye of the observer. A hill or a valley will affect the places where the rising sun and moon first appear and where their settings vanish. It is essential to know the horizon's altitude. The combination of latitude, altitude and azimuth is known as the *declination*, which for the sun and moon has remained almost unaltered over the centuries.

BC	Approx bc	Sun	Major Moon	Minor Moon
4000	3200	24°.112	29°.262	18°.962
3500	2775	24°.072	29°.222	18°.922
3000	2325	24°.027	29°.177	18°.877
2500	2000	23°.979	29°.129	18°.829
2000	1625	23°.928	29°.078	18°.778
1500	1200	23°.873	29°.023	18°.723
1000	825	23°.816	28°.966	18°.666

For the Beltane and Samain festivals of early May and November the solar declinations will be about ±16° respectively (see Thom, 1967, 110; Epochs 4, 6, 10, 12).

Daunting though these permutations once were, with Sir Norman Lockyer's assistants working laboriously with slide-rules, today with a pocket calculator the declination is easily computed. If the skyline is level with the site then the declination is calculated by cos Lat × cos Az = sin Decl. If the sightline is towards the north the declination will be +, if to the south, −.

If, as is the usual case, the skyline is higher or lower than the circle the formula is: (sin Lat × sin Alt) + (cos Lat × cos Alt × cos Az) = sin Decl. For those people wishing to recover more clearcut alignments consideration must then be given to the effects of refraction for the sun and moon and parallax for the moon. Methods of calculating these are given in:

A. Thom. *Megalithic Sites in Britain*, Oxford, 1967, 26, 118.

P. Duffet-Smith. *Practical Astronomy with Your Calculator*, Cambridge, 1979, 40–3, 100–1.

These are highly technical. A less demanding work is John Edwin Wood's *Sun, Moon and Standing Stones*, Oxford, 1978, 63, 64.

The innumerate or unambitious may prefer the writer's even more elementary *Prehistoric Astronomy and Ritual*, Princes Risborough, 1983.

The splendid stone circle of Loch Buie (182) on the island of Mull, latitude 56°.4, shows how a declination is obtained. The ring has an azimuth of 150°.8 towards an outlying stone. Beyond it a mountain ridge 1½ miles away is some 710ft (216m) higher than the ring. To determine the angle of the horizon altitude use the Pythagorean formula for a right-angle triangle: base^2 + height^2 = $\sqrt{\text{hypotenuse}}$. $7920^2 + 710^2 = \sqrt{7952}$.

The horizon angle is inv. sin $\dfrac{710}{7952}$ = 5°.1. Refraction changes this to 4°.84. The formula for declination is:

Decl. = (sin 56.4 × sin 4.84) + (cos 56.4 × cos 4.84 × cos 150.8)
x inv sin = −24°.3, that of the midwinter sunrise.

This does not imply that the circle and its outlying stone were erected before 4000 BC. The extreme positions of the sun and moon have shifted hardly at all over thousands of years and the slightest surveying error will create a chronological inaccuracy of several centuries. Loch Buie's declination of −24°.3 means only that the outlier was standing in line with the midwinter sunrise at some time in the Late Neolithic/Early Bronze Age between 3500 and 1750 BC.

Alignments to cardinal points are uncomplicated and easily recovered even with a handheld compass. These lines are accurate to no more than ±5°. The fault does not lie with the Pole Star which did not reach its present position until about AD 200. Nor was it a blunder by prehistoric people. It appears that they were concerned not with true north or south but with the points midway between the sun's or moon's risings and settings. It was a ritualistic sightline that was desired, not a scientific alignment for the prediction of eclipses by astronomer-priests.

The method had a built-in flaw. With a level horizon, halfway between north-east and north-west would be true north. If, however, the skyline were higher to east or west this would 'pull' the midpoint away from north because the rising sun would appear behind the hills later, and the setting sun would descend a little earlier to the west of its theoretical position. These effects can be confirmed on site simply by observing the unevenness of the horizon.

This Introduction has been written to add to the pleasure and interest of the visit to a stone circle. It is hoped that it succeeds.

On your visits please do observe the sensible Country Code of closing gates, avoiding crops and doing no damage to hedges and walls.

THE MAPS

Following the base map there are four small-scale maps showing the numbered whereabouts of the circles in this Guide. They are (1) Scotland; (2) Ireland; (3) England and Wales; (4) Brittany. On these maps there are shaded blocks covering those areas where stone circles are dense. These areas are given largescale maps in the relevant places in the text. From north to south they are:

A. North-east Scotland, p. 92; B. Central Scotland, p. 154; C. Northern Ireland, p. 190; D. North-west England, p. 39; E. The Peak District, Derbyshire, p. 50; F. South-west Ireland, p. 210; G. Dartmoor and Bodmin Moor, p. 54.

For reasons of space the Shetland Isles have been omitted. The grid-references to the three sites there should be sufficient for the rings to be found.

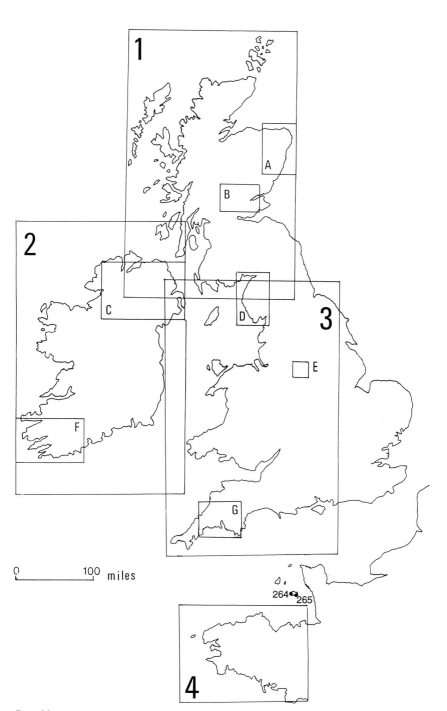

1

A

B

2

C

D

3

E

F

G

0   100 miles

264 265

4

Base Map

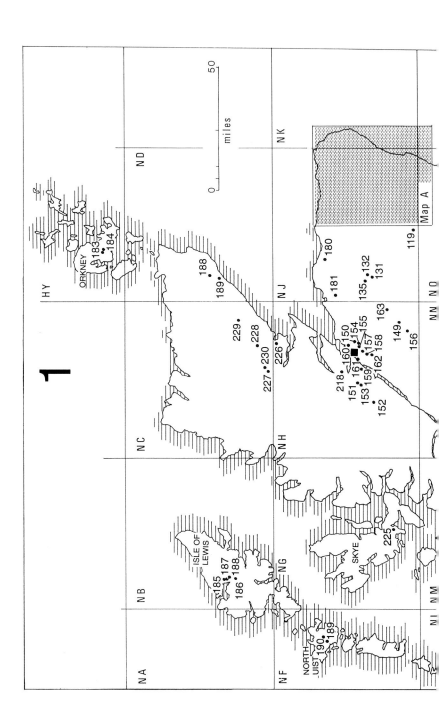

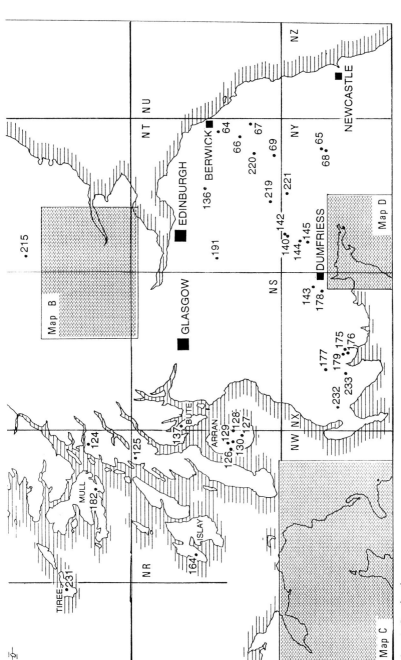

Map 1, Scotland

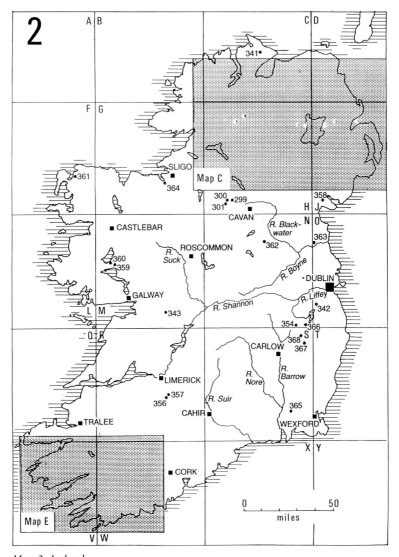

Map 2, Ireland

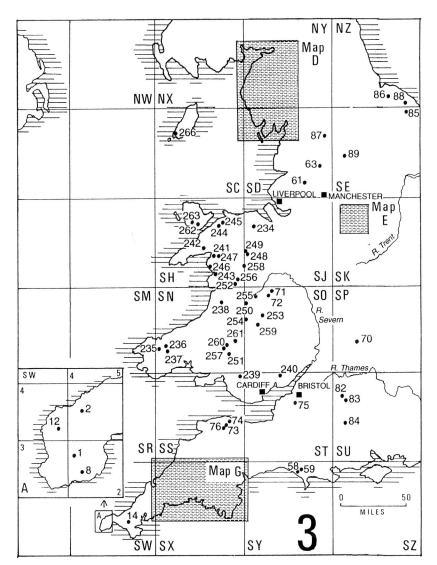

Map 3, England

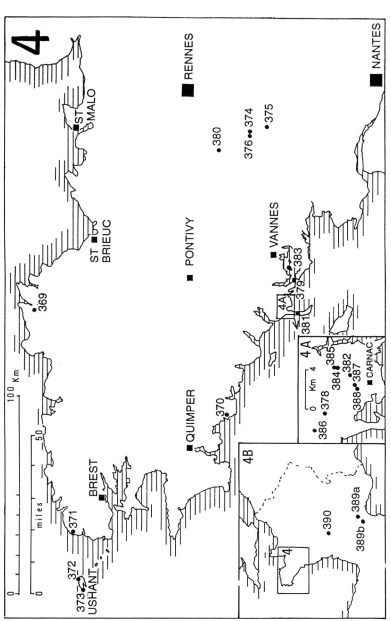

Map 4, Brittany

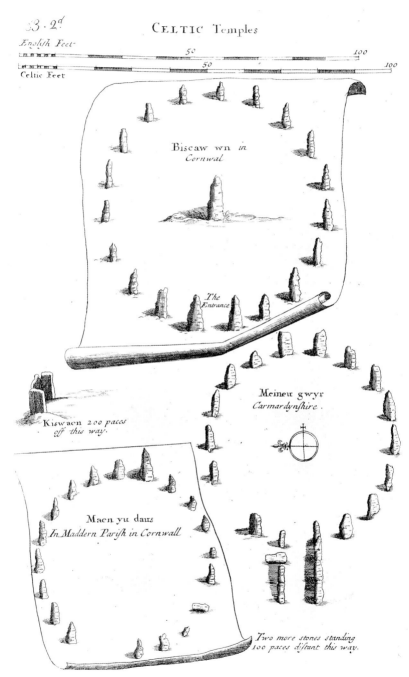

William Stukeley's sketch of Boscawen-Un [Biscaw-wm], Cornwall (1); Merry Maidens, Cornwall (8) and Meini-gwyr (237)

Britain

England   Scotland   Wales

ENGLAND

Avon, see Somerset

CORNWALL
The county contains fine open circles probably of a period towards the end of the Late Neolithic and after, 2700 BC –

Altarnun, see Nine Stones

1 Boscawen-Un, Land's End (1) [S1/13]
Lat: 50°.1   SW 412 274
4 miles sw of Penzance, 1 mile n of St Buryan. Walk. From A30 at SW 410 276, ¹/₄ mile to s across gorse. Fairly easy. Map 3A
Despite its neglect Boscawen-Un, 'the house of the elder tree', is one of the most evocative megalithic rings in western Europe. In late summer and autumn usually half-concealed in summer bracken, this fine stone 'circle' is actually an oval 82ft 7ins SE-NW by 73ft 2ins (25.2 × 22.3m). It contains nineteen regularly-spaced stones, a number common to several Land's End circles, and has a wide gap at the west. The number of stones and the 'entrance' at a cardinal point make an interesting architectural parallel to the Merry Maidens (8) only 2¹/₄ miles to the sse.

The pillars range in height from 3ft

to 5ft (1–1.2m). They are of local granite except one of quartz at the wsw which has been thought to be a backsight for observing the May Day sunrise.

There is a controversial pillar at the centre of the ring. Although 8ft 3ins (2.5m) long it leans so badly that its tip is only 6ft 6ins (2m) above ground. About 1864 the Penzance Natural History and Antiquarian Society trenched across the circle but found nothing. They also dug down to the base of the central stone 'and found that it was carefully placed in its leaning position'.

Other strange claims have been made for the site. In the eighteenth century Stukeley stated that the 'famous Druid temple call'd *Biscawoon*' was the first circle to be built in Britain, erected by the proto-Christian, Tyrian Hercules. In the Welsh triads 'Beisgowan' was one of the three great *gorsaddau* of Britain, and may have been the moot or judicial assembly-place of West Wales down to AD 926.

W. Stukeley. *Stonehenge*, 1740, 54; Barnatt, 1982, 159–62, *Plan*

2 Boskednan (3) [S1/11. Nine Maidens, Ding Dong]
Lat: 50°.6   SW 436 351
1¹/₄ miles s of Porthmeor. Via Carfury to Boskednan farm, SW 444 348. Walk. ³/₄ miles nw. Easy. Map 3A
The ruined ring, also known as the Nine Maidens, stands on moorland. The tall stones of local granite have their

smoother faces towards the interior of the ring, a characteristic they share with the Merry Maidens and Boscawen-Un. Originally there may have been twenty-two stones in a circle 71ft 7ins (21.8m) across. Today only six remain erect and much of the northern arc is missing. The average height is 4ft (1.2m) but one at the north, now broken, was over 6ft (2m) high.

A round barrow was erected on the SSE perimeter. On 26 July 1872, an excavation found a rifled cist at its centre. An earlier investigation had come upon sherds of a Cornish ribbon-handled urn, known as Trevisker ware, near it. There were no bones or ashes in the cist and 'it may reasonably be supposed that the vessel, originally interred in the kist [sic] had been broken by the workmen who discovered it, and the pieces carelessly thrown aside'.

North-west of Boskednan, at SW 432 353, is a ruinous ring termed a 'stone circle' but in reality its stones are the tall kerbs of a low and overgrown round barrow. In the eighteenth century there was an outlying stone 400ft (120m) to the west. A fragment remains at SW 433 351.

W.C. Borlase. *Naenia Cornubiae*, 1872, 280–3; TTB, 92, *Plan*

3 DULOE (1) [S1/3. Duloo]
Lat: 50°.4   SX 235 583
4 miles s of Liskeard, 1½ miles NNW of Sandplace on the B3254. Walk. Immediately w of the road and easily found in the field behind the farm. Map G
Standing on a ridge between the rivers East and West Looe, Duloe is aptly named, 'two Looes'. It is an attractive ring, 39ft N-S by 35ft (12 × 11m), of eight large and shiningly white quartz stones. The highest, 8ft 6ins (2.6m) tall, is at the south. It weighs about twelve tons and must have needed some fifty workers to erect it.

The majority of circles in Cornwall are of local granite but there is a source of quartz close to the farm confirming that prehistoric people used what stone

there was to hand. Bits of quartz can still be found near Dupath holy well east of Callington.

When an intrusive hedge was uprooted in 1861 Duloe was clumsily restored, breaking the north stone, and leaving only the stump of the south-eastern block. By the NNE pillar a Bronze Age ribbon-handled urn, smashed by the labourers, was dug up, filled with human bones that 'crumbled in the air'. 'A considerable quantity of charcoal was found within the enclosure when the bisecting hedge was removed ... and much still remains beneath the turf.'

Barnatt, 1982, 192–5, *Plan*, 192

4 FERNACRE, Bodmin Moor (3) [S1/7. Rough Tor] Lat: 50°.6   SX 144 799
3¼ miles SE of Camelford. It is now possible to approach this circle from a road 1¼ miles NE of St Breward at SX 109 784. Drive ENE for 3 miles. Walk. ¼ mile N across moor. Easy. Map G
A. On a boggy slope ½ mile south of Rough Tor this is a very large stone circle, an attribute it shares with other Bodmin Moor rings: Stannon (10) a mile to the west, Craddock Moor, Goodaver (5), the three Hurlers (6), Leaze (7), the Stripple Stones (11) and the Trippet Stones (13), their average diameter of just over 120ft (37m) being almost twice that of the national mean. Only the Nine Stones (9), Altarnun, at the far north-east corner of the moor is small.

Fernacre's spacious flattened ring has diameters of 151ft NW-SE by 142ft (46 × 43m). Like its neighbour, Stannon (10), it is composed of many stones, over seventy *in situ*, of which some forty stand. The stones appear small but they are deeply sunk in the peat and when first set up must have appeared quite imposing.

The circle is enclosed on all sides by tors and hills but there are many hut-circles to east and north on the southern slopes of Rough Tor and their presence may explain the choice of site.

B. Midway between Fernacre and Stannon are the ruins of a third large

Duloe, Cornwall (3), from the south.

ring at SX 132 794.

Barnatt, 1982, 170–2; Thom, 1967, 57, *Plan*

5 GOODAVER, Bodmin Moor (2 or 6) [S1/17. Trezibbet]
Lat: 50°.5   SX 208 751
10 miles ENE of Bodmin. Walk. Difficult. Either overgrown footpath at SX 205 745, or via Trezibbett farm, turning E at the farm, Barbed-wire and fences on the 1/2+ mile walk uphill. Hard. Map G
On a level hilltop, and now in good condition except for long summer grass, the ring was re-erected under the direction of the Rev. A.H. Malan in 1906. Doubts have been expressed about its authenticity but its size, 106ft (32.3m), circular shape, number of stones, twenty-five but probably twenty-eight or twenty-nine originally, and close spacing, 12ft (3.7m), indicate that it is a genuine member of the Bodmin Moor group of big rings. That there are gaps still existing at the NNE, ENE and south-east testifies to the integrity of the restoration.

The reconstruction, however, did have faults. Although the stoneholes were located quite accurately, inspection shows several stones are either upside down or with their faces reversed, rough face inwards, smooth outside. The south-west quadrant is very suspect.

Barnatt, 1982, 187–90; TTB, 102, *Plan*

6 HURLERS, Bodmin Moor (3) [S1/1]
Lat: 50°.5   SX 259 714
4 1/4 miles NE of Liskeard, 1 1/2 miles W of Upton Cross. At SW end of Minions village is a carpark to the N (Rt). Walk. 200 yds (180m). Easy. Map G
Three large stone circles stand in a NNE-SSW line on Bodmin Moor. Unlike most circles the stones of local granite have been shaped. A. *The north circle*, 114ft (34.8m) across has retained sixteen of a possible twenty-eight stones. B. *The central ring*, slightly oval, 137ft SSE-NNW by 133ft (41.8 × 40.5m) has seventeen of twenty-eight, the tallest, 5ft 10ins (1.8m) high; and C. *The southern ring*, almost demolished by a cart-track, has only nine, mostly prostrate, of a probable twenty-six. The tallest stones are at the south in the two northernmost circles.

The 1935 excavation, never fully published, revealed that the northern ring was paved with granite and the interior of the middle circle was thickly strewn with crystals, probably débris from the hammer-dressing of the uprights. The two rings were linked by a 6ft (1.8m) wide granite pathway along their common axis. Like other composite settings circle may have been added to circle here although in what sequence cannot be determined. In the northern ring there is a questionable carving of a triple concentric ring on the inner face of a stone that stands at the WNW against a large fallen slab.

320ft (98m) to the WSW of the central circle are two upright stones, the Pipers WSW-ENE of each other, 7ft (2.1m) apart. The western stone is 5ft 5ins high, its partner 4ft 9ins (1.7, 1.5m). Legend claims that they were musicians turned into stone for playing on the Sabbath.

The circles were more plebeian, being men transformed on the Lord's Day for their dangerously rough struggle to grab a wooden ball from their opponents, hurling it from team-mate to team-mate until an unchallenged player could carry it off. As late as the nineteenth century similar games were played between teams of forty to sixty men, the object being to take the ball to the winning side's village. Significantly, such matches were usually played on a Sunday afternoon.

At SX 260 719 ¼ mile to the north is the ravaged Rillaton round barrow from whose cist a handled gold beaker, a bronze dagger and faience beads were found in 1818. They are in the British Museum.

Craddock Moor fallen stone circle, SX 248 718, is ¾ mile north-west of the Hurlers.

PPS 4, 1938, 319; Barnatt, 1982, 180–7; TTB, 74, *Plan*

7 LEAZE, Bodmin Moor (3) [S1/6]
Lat: 50°.6   SX 137 773
2¹/₂ miles E of St Breward. Walk. From the village take the NE lane for 1¹/₂ miles to Middle Candra, SX 120 780. The

circle is one mile ESE. Pass King Arthur's Hall at SX 129 776. Fair. Map G
A. This *badly-damaged ring* has a mouldering stone wall passing through it. Of local granite, the site may once have had twenty-eight stones in a true circle 82ft (25m) across. Of these sixteen survive, ten of them erect with an average height of 3ft 6ins (1.1m).

B, C. A nearby pair of *ruined circles*, one about 82ft (25m) in diameter, have been discovered on King Arthur's Down, SX 134 775.

Barnatt, 1982, 172–4; TTB, 84, *Plan*
D. The embanked rectangle of *King Arthur's Hall*, SX 129 776, is ¹/₂ mile to the WNW. Measuring 154ft N-S by 66ft (47 × 20m) its thick, heavy earthen bank has a south-west entrance. Its sunken interior is lined with standing stones up to 5ft (1.5m) high. Its plan has strong affinities with rectangles such as Crucuno in Brittany (378).

Johnson and Rose, 28–9, *Plans*

8 MERRY MAIDENS, Land's End (2) [S1/14] Lat: 50°.1   SW 433 245
4 miles SW of Penzance, In a field against the B3315. Easy. Map G
The Merry Maidens stone circle, restored in the 1860s, is one of the most perfect in Cornwall. Nineteen stones stand on the perimeter of a perfect circle 78ft (23.8m) in diameter. Each is about 4ft (1.2m) high. Because of their regular spacing about 12ft (3.7m) apart, a much wider 20ft (6.1m) gap at the east may be a cardinal point entrance. The ring is sometimes known as the Dawn's Men, a corruption of 'Dans Maen' or 'the stone dance' after the belief that the stones were girls transmogrified for dancing on the sabbath.

A second circle, destroyed in the nineteenth century, is thought to have existed to the WSW near the Merry Maidens at, or close, to SW 431 244. Paired rings are not uncommon in Cornwall, others being known at the Hurlers (6) on Bodmin Moor, at Wendron (14) and at Tregeseal (12), Land's End.

Across the road from the Merry

The Hurlers, Cornwall (6), the northern arc of the central ring. Stones of the north circle can be seen in the background.

Nine Stones, Altarnun, Cornwall (9), from the south-west.

Maidens is a holed stone at SW 432 246. It has been re-used as a gatepost.

Nearly $^1/_4$ mile to the north-east is the pair of stones known as the Pipers. The north-east pillar is 15ft (4.6m) high, the tallest stone in Cornwall. Its partner, 317ft (97m) to the south-west is 13ft 6ins (4.2m) high, but the stones are not visible from the ring. A dig in 1871 produced no finds.

The cupmarked chambered tomb of Tregiffian stands by the road a little way downhill just west of the circle.

Barnatt, 1982, 155–9; TTB, 98, *Plan*

9 NINE STONES, Altarnun (2) [S1/2] Lat: 50°.6   SX 236 781
7 miles SW of Launceston. Walk. From the unfenced lane at SX 238 772 $^1/_4$ mile N over the hill and down. Not steep. Map G
Just SSE of Altarnun village with its lovely fifteenth-century church, 'the Cathedral of the Moors', the Nine Stones ring, a perfect circle 50 ft (15.2m) across of eight stones with a ninth near its centre, is an evocative site. Isolated, it is the smallest, neatest ring on Bodmin Moor. Erected in a slight hollow seven stones stand with one fallen at the north-east. A gap at the north like an entrance is probably the site of a missing stone. The ring was reconstructed in the nineteenth century but there is no record of excavation.

The stones are local granite. The tallest, at the north-west, is just over 4 ft (1.2m) high. One a little lower stands just south of the ring's centre. The Stripple Stones (11) circle-henge, six miles WSW, also has a central stone.

A row of small stones, probably marking a mediaeval boundary, runs ENE from the ring towards a nearby ridge on which there are cairns. There are hut-circles 600 yards (550m) north-east of the ring at SX 240 784. There is another to the south at SX 234 776.

Tregelles, *VCH Cornwall I*, 1906, 396–7; TTB, 76, *Plan*

10 STANNON, Bodmin Moor (1) [S1/8. Dinnever Hill] Lat: 50°.6   SX 126 800

$2^1/_2$ *miles SE of Camelford. From the B3266 $^1/_4$ mile SE of Michaelstow take the SE (Lt) lane becoming a track by the Stannon china clay tips, SX 125 801. The ring is visible to the S. Walk. 50 yds (46m). Map G*
Like its neighbour, Fernacre (4), to the east, this is a big ring, roughly circular with diameters of about 140ft E-W by 133ft (43 × 41m). Also like Fernacre it is composed of many stones, irregularly spaced and most of them low, the tallest, 3ft 9ins (1.1m) high at the south. Some hardly appear above the long grass.

'A hint that areas of land [were] set aside for ceremonial sites is clearly seen at the Stannon Circle, which was built between two streams; the surrounding land is unenclosed and has no sign whatsoever of houses or fields, only a boundary reeve [sic] crosses the area well south of the circle. This area of "sacred land" appears to be no less fertile than others, and is midway between extensive settlements to the ENE/NW and WSW.' Many hut-circles and enclosures can be seen half a mile to the east below Loudon Hill.

Barnatt, 1982, 167–70, *Plan*

11 STRIPPLE STONES, Bodmin Moor (4) [S1/4] Lat: 50°.6   SX 144 752
$6^3/_4$ *miles NE of Bodmin. At SX 135 736 on the A30 take NW lane. In $^1/_4$ mile turn E (Rt). The Trippet Stones are visible 200 yards (180m) to the N. Walk. The Stripple Stones are $^3/_4$ mile ENE across the moor. Fair, but make a detour around cattle pens. Map G*
On the south-eastern slope of Hawk's Tor is the ruination of a circle-henge once of twenty-eight stones but now of fifteen including a fallen pillar near the middle of a ring 147ft (44.8m) in diameter. The circle stood inside a henge 224ft (68.3m) across with an entrance 15ft (4.6m) wide at the WSW. Despite two field-walls for which some stones were split in the late 1880s and despite reeds and undergrowth three bulging semi-circular apses can be detected in the bank at the NNE, east and WNW.

Like two other Cornish henges, Castilly (SX 031 627) and Castlewitch (SX 371 685) the Stripple Stones circle-henge lies near an ancient trackway down the 'spine' of the county. The meaning of the name is unknown, but is blatantly suggestive, bearing in mind the legends of other girls ossified for their brazen misbehaviour.

Only four stones stand. The excavation of 1905 discovered that despite their size, up to 6ft (1.8m) high, almost every one had been set up in a very shallow and inadequate hole no more than 1ft 6ins (45cm) deep. The only finds were three flint flakes, a burnt flint, a fragment of ox bone and some bits of wood in the ditch.

Paradoxically, the prostrate 'central' pillar, 12ft (3.7m) long, was set up 14ft (4.3m) SSE of the middle of the ring. Three postholes just to its east and a fourth to its west may have been trial pits made by workers wanting a precise position for the stone.

The stonehole finally chosen was in line with the entrance and the Trippet Stones to the WSW, but, as that ring was out of sight, this could be coincidental. Instead, the entrance and the stone may have been arranged to be in view from the direction of the easiest approach to the circle.

There is an alternative, more exotic possibility. The pillar could have acted as a backsight from which an observer looking towards the sides of the three apses would have seen the major northern moonrise at the NNE, the equinoctial sunrise at the east, and the May Day sunset at the WNW.

Such complicated astronomy involving three diffuse alignments demanded a very well-judged location for a backsight. An error of even 2ft (0.6m) would alter the angle of sight by over a degree, a problem made three-fold by the inclusion of three independent sightlines. Using the excavator's largescale plan the hypothesis works neatly in the study and has the merits of explaining the 'inexplicable' apses, the four postholes and the eccentric placing of the 'centre'

stone. A rigorous site-survey would check its validity.

There are more prosaic explanations-sheer incompetence on the part of the workers, or their indifference to exactness. Prehistoric societies were rarely dedicated to the minutiae of design.

Arch 61, 1908, 1–60; TTB, 80, Plan

12 TREGESEAL EAST, Land's End (2) [S1/16. Botallack]
Lat: 50°.1   SW 387 324
1¼ miles NE of St Just. From Tregeseal take E road and follow lanes to SW 386 324. Walk. A footpath for 200 yards (180m). Easy. Map 3A
Standing on an open common below the jagged crest of Carn Kenidjack is a splendid ring, the survivor of a pair of which the western (SW 386 323), already badly wrecked by 1905, was finally destroyed in February 1961 when the land was cleared and ploughed. The eastern, threatened by a small quarry in the mid-nineteenth century, had several stones re-erected in 1932 'by persons unknown'.

The eastern ring is 72ft (22m) across but is flattened at the north where its diameter is reduced to 69ft (21m). Like several other Land's End circles it consisted of about nineteen stones, suggesting that such a number was intended. Whether this was to record the 18.61 years of the lunar cycle is little more than a guess.

Aerial photography recorded what may be the site of a third ring to the west of the field, SW 385 322, on the same axis as the others.

The ring is known as the Dancing Stones, impious young girls changed into stone for engaging in round dances on the sabbath.

Barnatt, 1982, 162–5; TTB, 100, *Plan*

13 TRIPPET STONES, Bodmin Moor (3) [S1/5. Treswigger]
Lat: 50°.5   SX 131 750
6 miles NNE of Bodmin. For directions see the Stripple Stones. Map G
This very attractive circle stands on

Trippet Stones, Bodmin Moor, Cornwall (13), *from the south-east.*

open moorland to the west of Hawk's Tor and the Stripple Stones (11). Its stones of local granite are 4ft to 5ft 2ins (1.2–1.6m) high, taller than the average in Cornwall. There may once have been twenty-eight of them in a circle 108ft (32.9m) across but stonebreakers have damaged or removed some and today only eight remain standing.

Like many other rings the stones appear to have been set up in opposing pairs from north-east to south-west. They are also quite evenly spaced about 12ft (3.7m) apart around the circumference.

From the circle the Stripple Stones are visible on the skyline to the ENE but the reverse is not true.

The name of the Trippet Stones is yet another example of the belief that the stones are the petrified bodies of girls punished for dancing on the Sabbath.

> Come, and trip it as you go
> On the light fantastic toe.
> *L'Allegro*, John Milton

Barnatt, 1982, 174–7; TTB, 82, *Plan*

14 WENDRON, Land's End (3) [S1/10.

Nine Maidens] Lat: 50°.2   SW 683 365
1¹/₂ miles SE of Troon. Walk.
Immediately by the B3297 ¹/₂ mile S of its junction with the B3280. Easy. Map 3
This damaged ring is the remnant of a pair of circles NE-SW of each other and about 62ft (19m) apart on Wendron Moor. The northernmost, of ten stones up to 4ft 2ins (1.3m) high, was about 60ft (18m) across. Its partner, of which only five stones on the southern arc survive, has a diameter of 54ft (16.5m). Many of its stones have been taken for the field-wall hard by to the north.

G.F. Tregelles, *VCH Cornwall, I*, 1906, 388–9; TTB, 90, *Plan*

CUMBRIA, see Cumberland, Lancashire, Westmorland

CUMBERLAND
The central region has large open circles, some with entrances. Late Neolithic. Smaller Bronze Age rings with internal cairns occupy the edges of the Lake District

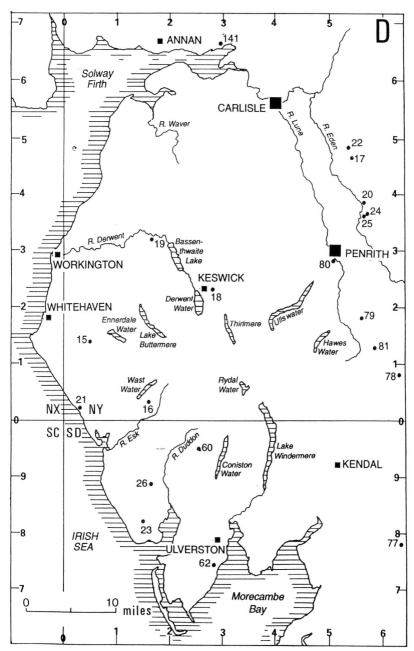

Map D, The Lake District

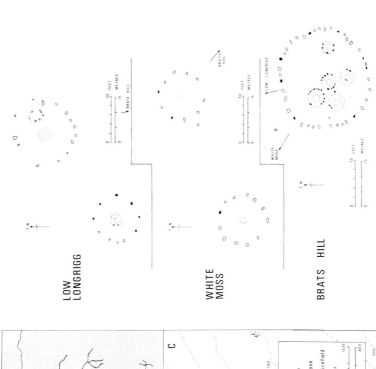

Burn Moor, Cumberland (16)

Blakeley Raise, Cumberland (15), from the east.

15 BLAKELEY RAISE, Cumbria (2) [L1/16.
Blakeley Moss]
Lat: 54°.5   NY 060 140
*3¹/₂ miles NE of Egremont, 1¹/₂ mile S of
Ennerdale Bridge, immediately E of the
lane. Walk. 10 yds (9m). Easy. Map D*
This ring of eleven small stones is about
54ft 9ins (16.7m) in diameter. The
stones are set in concrete, having been
re-erected by Dr Quine in 1925. Quine
wrote only of 'partial restoration'
which suggests that the majority of the
stones are in their original positions.
Another report says the ring once
consisted of thirteen stones, eight of
which were removed for a gateway and
that it was these that were replaced.

The stones, quite regularly spaced
14ft (4.3m) apart, range in height from
a broken stump to the two tallest, 3ft
3ins and 3ft 8ins (1, 1.1m) standing
astride a 20ft (6.1m) gap at the south,
possibly an embryonic entrance.

Waterhouse, 68–70; TTB, 52, *Plan*

16 BURN MOOR, Eskdale (1) [L1/6A–E]
Lat: 54°.4   NY 173 023
*12¹/₂ miles W of Ambleside, 6¹/₂ miles NE
of Ravenglass. Walk. Steep ³/₄ mile from
Boot, NY 177 010, at a gradient of 1*

*in 5 up an old stream bed on hillside.
Hard going but rings are worth it. Map
D*
There are five stone circles on Burn
Moor, the largest a single ring at Brat's
Hill, [L1/6E], NY 173 023, with two
outlying pairs, one at White Moss, [L1/
6C, D], NY 172 023, and another at
Low Longrigg, [L1/6A, B], NY 172
028.

A. *Brat's Hill* is a flattened ring
measuring 104ft 6ins ENE-WSW by 97ft
(31.9 × 29.6m). Its stones are local
granite. Although they are low this is
an attractive ring. The tallest stone, 3ft
4ins (1m) is at the south, a
characteristic Cumbrian preference for
a cardinal point.

Five cairns, each with fourteen
kerbstones, lie inside the ring, four of
them crowded into the western half of
the interior. An excavation in 1827
discovered that two had crude cists
with 'the remains of burnt bones with
fragments of the horns of the stag and
other animal remains.' The fifth cairn,
isolated at the east, was surrounded by
a 'parallelogram of stones [about 33ft
by 26ft (10 × 7.9m)] similar to that in
the Keswick circle', an intriguing

comment considering Thom's observation that the plans of Brat's Hill and Castlerigg (18) are exceptionally similar, almost overlapping in design. Nothing of the rectangle remains. (Thom, 1967, 60, *Plan*)

PSAL 3, 1856, 225–6; Dymond, 55–7, *Plan*, 48

B. *White Moss* From Brat's Hill, 100 yards (90m) north-west. On a level stretch of moorland the rings stand on a wsw-ene axis 100ft (31m) apart, their stones of local granite. Both are ruinous, the wsw ring about 54ft 6ins (16.6m) in size, its partner slightly smaller, 52ft (15.9m) across. They have central cairns. (TTB, 38, *Plan*)

C. *Low Longrigg* 420 yards (385m) north of White Moss and 500 yards (455m) NNW of Brats Hill are two paired rings. They stand 67ft (20m) apart on a sw-ne axis. Their stones are a mixture of local and nearby porphyritic granite.

The south-west ring is about 50ft (15m) in diameter and has a low cairn at its centre. The north-east ring, 70ft (21.3m) across, is ruinous. Inside are two overgrown cairns.

Immediately to the south-east of these rings are a score or more of small cairns. Excavation of one by the writer in the wet summer of 1974 found no human remains or cist and it is likely that it, like the other low mounds, was a clearance cairn, evidence of settlement on this high plateau in the Bronze Age. (TTB, 36, *Plan*)

D. 700 yards (640m) NNE of the rings near Boat How there are the remains of an unenclosed platform settlement and a droveway.

Burl, 1976, 93–7, *Plan*, 94; Waterhouse, 53–61

17 BROOMRIGG PLANTATION, Ainstable (4) Lat: 54°.8   NY 548 467

10½ miles N of Penrith, 3½ miles N of Kirkoswald. Walk. In a dense plantation immediately E of the lane. For the hardy, determined and fanatical. Included for its variety. Before the conifers were planted here

this was a fascinating complex of stone circles, cairn- and kerb-circles and a henge. It is now more akin to a Transylvanian forest. Almost lost among the trees are the fragmentary remains of four rings of local red sandstone.

A. SD 548 467 Once this was an immense stone circle some 180ft (55m) in diameter with the suspicion of a wide avenue approaching from the north-west. A few low stones of the ring's north arc can still be seen. An excavation in 1950 found nothing.

B. SD 548 466 110 yards (100m) to the south is a ruinous cairn-circle of which four stones survive of an original seven. Measuring about 11ft (3.4m) across it was excavated in 1950. A rifled central pit was discovered. Just to the east was a tiny kerb-circle.

C. SD 548 465 Even more difficult to see is a neat circle 110 yards (100m) SSW of B. The ring, some 55ft (16.8m) in diameter has a damaged north-western arc and a displaced run of stones at the south-west that may be the relics of an earlier circle.

Deposits of burnt human bone, v-perforated jet buttons, a collared urn and a small pygmy cup of the Early Bronze Age suggest a date in the early second millennium BC for the ring. The finds are now in the Tullie House Museum, Carlisle.

D. 200 yards (180m) ENE of C at SD 550 466 is the wreckage of a kerb-circle excavated in 1960. Known as the Wallmoor ring the oval setting, 18ft by 15ft (5.5 × 4.5m), yielded nothing.

Waterhouse, 107–13, *Plans*

E. At SD 549 466 is the worndown bank and internal ditch of a henge about 167ft N-S by 163ft (51 × 50m). At the eastern side of its south-east entrance is a large stone.

TCWAAS 35, 1935, 174–5, *Plan*

18 CASTLERIGG, Keswick (1) [L1/1. Castle Rigg] Lat: 54°.6   NY 291 236 *1½ miles E of the centre of Keswick. Signposted. Layby. Walk. 100 yds (90m). Easy. In State care, no charge. Map D*

This may be one of the earliest circles in Europe, its stones raised around 3200 BC. It is often called the 'Carles' as though the stones were husbandmen petrified for some forgotten sin but the nickname came from a misreading of Stukeley who, after visiting the ring in 1725, wrote, 'They call it the Car∫les, and corruptly I suppose, Ca∫tle-rig. There seemed to be another larger circle in the next pasture toward the town.' If it ever existed this second ring, whether a stone circle or an earthen henge, has disappeared.

Castlerigg is spectacularly situated among the mountains and the surroundings of this numinous ring evoked an admiring respect from that stone circle enthusiast, A.L. Lewis who thought it the 'grandest position in which I have ever seen a circle placed.' A hundred years earlier John Keats dyspeptically referred to it as a 'dismal cirque of Druid stones upon a forlorn moor'.

The ring stands on a level stretch of ground on Chestnut Hill at the heart of the Lake District. Of local metamorphic slate the thirty-eight survivors of the original forty-two stones are 3ft to 5ft (1–1.5m) high and stand on the perimeter of a flattened ring 107ft NNW-SSE by 96ft 9ins (32.6 × 29.5m). The heaviest, weighing about sixteen tons, stands radially to the circumference at the south-east. There is a wide entrance at the north formed by two tall stones respectively 5ft 8ins and 5ft 6ins (1.73, 1.68) high.

At the ESE is an internal rectangular setting of low stones, 29ft by 15ft (8.8 × 4.6m), maybe akin to the controversial 'parallelogram' at Brat's Hill (16a). It had no internal cairn but an excavation in 1882 discovered a pit at its west containing charcoal. The tall radial pillar 8ft 3ins (2.5m) high at its south-east corner stands in line with the November or Samain sunrise.

A stone 3ft (0.9m) high stands 296ft (90m) to the south-west by the hedge. From the many plough-marks on one of its sides it probably once lay shallowly buried in the field, damaging ploughs as

they passed over it. Removed to the hedgerow it was used as a stile for many years until it was set upright around 1913.

Evidence of later activity can be seen in the faint outlines of round cairns, smoothed down by cultivation in recent centuries, lying inside the ring as though later people had buried their dead in a long-hallowed sanctuary.

One of Castlerigg's many functions may have been to act as an emporium connected with the Neolithic stone axe industry in the Langdales. The mountainous source of the epidotised tuff used for the axes was only a few miles to the south along a pass between the steep mountainsides. In 1875 an unpolished stone axe was found inside the ring itself, and in 1901, in the peat at Portinscale 2½ miles to the west, four roughed-out and one polished axe were found near a pile of chippings and a thick log stump with a battered top, a collection thought to have been an axe-maker's workshop.

The ring, acting as a social and trading centre, quite feasibly was the focus of seasonal ceremonies, their occasions determined by the important risings and settings of the sun and moon.

Dymond, 50–5, *Plan*, 42; *TCWAAS 34*, 1934, 91–100

19 ELVA PLAIN, Setmurthy (3) [L1/2]
Lat: 54°.7   NY 176 317
3½ miles ENE *of Cockermouth, At Elva Plain farm, NY 175 314,* WNW *of Bassenthwaite Lake. Walk. ⅓ mile along farm track. Easy. Map D*
The stones of local volcanic ash lie inconspicuously on a gentle southern slope. Fifteen survive of some thirty, none of them big in a circle 113ft (34.4m) across. The largest lies at the west, 3ft 6ins (1m) long. Those at the east and north are noticeably smaller. There was once a small outlier 182ft (56m) to the south-west.

The site was known as Elfhow in 1488. This may be a corruption of 'elfshot', an old term for a prehistoric axe. As the circle does lie near a trackway along which such axes may have been transported westwards from the Langdales this is a possibility.

Equally, 'elfhow' may be derived from *elfhaugr*, 'the hill of the malignant elves', an Old Norse or Viking name for Elva Hill, 788ft (240m) high, on whose lower slopes the uncanny stone circle lies.

Waterhouse, 74–6; TTB, 32, *Plan*

20 GLASSONBY, Lazonby (3) [L1/9] Lat: 54°.75   NY 575 393
6¹/₂ miles NNE of Penrith, 600 yds (550m) down a field. Easy. Map D
This cairn-circle, once of some thirty stones was excavated in 1900. So disrupted and overgrown is the site that Thom thought it a true circle with a diameter of 47ft (14.3m). It had, however, been an oval 51ft SSW-NNE by 46ft 3ins (15.6 × 14m). Its low stones had been concealed under a huge mound.

The excavators found a neatly rectangular but empty cist of red sandstone at the south-east and an isolated blue faience bead at the north-west. A cremation under an inverted Early Bronze Age collared urn was buried just outside the ring at the south-west. The urn and the bead are now in the Tullie House Museum, Carlisle.

As at Long and Little Meg (24, 25) there were decorated stones at Glassonby. The southernmost of a run of six stones from east to south-east has a faint set of concentric circles surmounted by two groups of semi-circles like the ears of a Mickey Mouse. Another stone with cup-and-ring markings has been lost.

Not on the short WSW-ENE axis but a few degrees away, 230°–50° in a straight line, was a red sandstone slab at the south-west of the ring, a burnt patch inside at the north-east and a second cremation outside at the north-east. With the fells rising beyond the cremation the 'alignment' was close to the place of the midsummer sunrise.

TCWAAS 1, 1901, 295–9; Waterhouse, 105–6, *Plan*; Beckensall, *Cumbrian Prehistoric Rock Art*, 1992, 16–19

21 GREY CROFT, Gosforth (2) [L1/10. Seascale] Lat: 54°.4   NY 034 024
2 miles WSW of Gosforth, Walk. At Seascale take the footpath E of the golf-course ENE for ¹/₂ mile. The circle is

Grey Croft, Cumberland (21), from the west. The outlier is at the extreme left.

visible to NW. *Barbed-wire between.*
Easily seen. Difficult to visit. Map D
Attractively situated within ¹/₂ mile of
the sea to the west this ring is about
89ft (27m) in diameter. Ten of an
original twelve stones are of local
volcanic lava and average 4ft 3ins
(1.3m) in height. None weighs more
than four tons. In 1820 a tenant farmer
buried many but they were dug up and
re-erected in 1949. A small outlying
stone 68ft 10ins (21m) to the north was
also set upright.

Within the ring a central kerbed
cairn, 22ft by 15ft (6.7 × 4.6m)
contained traces of charcoal, bone
fragments, flint flakes, a scraper, and an
Early Bronze Age jet or lignite pulley-
ring. The presence of grass or bracken
and hawthorn berries showed that the
burial had taken place in the autumn.
Close to the disturbed hole of the
eastern stone there was a broken Group
VI stone axe from the Langdales, a
'factory' that had been abandoned
around 1800 BC (c.2200 BC). The circle
probably dates to the centuries around
2500 BC.

Its location is ironical. Two sources
of power are juxtaposed here. One is
the Bronze Age stone circle.
Immediately to its north are the
dominating towers of the Sellafield
nuclear power station partly hidden
behind two monstrous, ugly banks of
waste. The stone circle is lovelier.
TCWAAS 57, 1957, 1–8, Plan;
Waterhouse, 63–5

22 GREY YAUDS, Newbiggin (4)
Lat: 54°.8   NY 545 487
1 mile WSW *of Newbiggin. Walk. ¹/₂ mile*
W *opposite lane to Newbiggin. Fair.*
Completely ruined but once important.
Map D
Once one of the great Cumbrian rings
the 'grey mares', standing on 'a lean,
desolate and hungry country', according
to Camden, this was a circle, of eighty-
eight 'pretty, large' stones, 156ft
(47.6m) across. Today all that survives
is a lonely outlier known as 'King
Harry's Stone', 4ft 8ins high by 4ft
wide (1.4 × 1.2m) that had stood about

16ft (5m) to the north-west of the ring.

The remainder of the stones were
taken and broken up for walls and
rubble for roads in the nineteenth
century. 'So dull is the mind of the
average rustic, and so wanting in
imagination, that he actually appraises
these venerable relics of a bygone age at
their value for road metal.'
TCWAAS 7, 1907, 67–71. No plan

23 LACRA, A, B, C, D, Millom (3, 1, 5,
3) [L1/12. A, C.] Lat: 54°.2 SD 150 814
1¹/₂ miles WNW *of Millom. From*
Millom, notice Kirksanton pair of
standing stones in field to W, *SD 136*
811. Walk. At SD 149 826, Po House.
A good track leads windingly SSW *uphill*
for ³/₄ mile. Not very steep. Map D
These rings are for the true enthusiast
and well worth the uphill walk. Their
condition, size and date are typical of
the majority of stone circles.

Close in miles but distant in years
from the great Cumbrian stone circles
they lie high on Lacra Fell overlooking
the sea to their west. Although only
thirteen miles south of Brat's Hill and
less than five miles from Swinside they
are Bronze Age bread and butter to
those vintage Late Neolithic sites and
separated from them by as many as a
thousand years. Four circles have been
claimed but there are only three, the
fourth being a short row of standing
stones.

A. *Lacra A* (3) At the crest of the hill
120 yards (110m) ESE of ruined farm
buildings are the vestiges of a small
stone circle about 53ft (16.2m) across.
Only two of six small stones, all local
volcanic ash, stand at the east and
south.

B. *Lacra B* (1) 370 yards (338m) to
the south is the best of the complex, a
circle once of about eleven stones of
which six survive, three standing 3ft
6ins (1.1m) high in a good circle 50ft
(15m) in diameter. Gaps in the ring
may show where others were dragged
away to facilitate ploughing.
Excavation in 1947 uncovered a kerbed
central mound, 32ft (10m) across
concealing a kerbed ring with cremated

bone on the old land surface surrounded by ash and maybe birch charcoal.

C. *Lacra C* (5) Thought to be the wreckage of a ring once 70ft (21m) across this is a Three-Stone row 39ft (12m) long, SW-NE and graded up to the north-east stone 3ft 6ins (1.1m) high. Between it and its neighbour is a space through which ridge-and-furrow passes. It may be the position of a missing fourth stone.

D. *Lacra D* (3) 320 yards (295m) to the NNE is a very ruinous oval about 60ft N-S by 51ft (18 × 16m). A large and heavy slab, 8ft by 6ft (2.4 × 1.8m), like the others of volcanic ash, lies near the centre. No other central features were recognisable.

Buried by the north-west stone was an inverted overhanging-rim urn of the late Early Bronze Age, its base shattered by the plough. Charcoal of oak and some hazel lay in and under it. The urn is now in Barrow-on-Furness Museum. If the deposition of the urn were contemporary with the erection of the ring, maybe as a foundation offering, the circle is unlikely to be much earlier than 2000 BC.

Possible but virtually unrecognisable avenues have been claimed to lead to the ring from the north-east and south-west but they are almost impossible to make out in the scatter of boulders and stones.

E. *Lacra E* A very uncertain ring can be imagined 25ft (8m) to the north-west. Lacra D is 150 yards (137m) ESE of Lacra A.

TCWAAS 48, 1948, 1–22, Plans

24 LITTLE MEG, Little Salkeld (3) [L1/8]
Lat: 54°.7   NY 576 374
6 miles NE of Penrith. NNE of Little Salkeld, NY566 362. Go past the signposted lane to Long Meg. Little Meg is another ¹/₂ mile. Walk. Just inside a field on the W of the lane. Easy.
Map D
This ruined and diminutive kerb-circle, also known as the Maughanby circle, is about 20 ft (6.1m) in diameter. It is much disturbed and the largest stone,

now near the centre, was obviously placed there in historic times as it is plough-marked.

There were once about twelve disproportionately tall kerbstones around a low barrow containing a cist with an urned cremation. Alongside the tallest stone, 3ft 6ins (1.1m) high, lies a slab with concentric circles carved on it. Another stone with more elaborate carvings is now in Tullie House Museum, Carlisle. The only stone circles to be decorated in Cumbria are very close together, Little Meg, Long Meg (25), and Glassonby (20), NY 573 393, just over a mile to the north. Little Meg lies about 650 yards (600m) ENE of Long Meg.

Waterhouse, 102–4, *Plan*; S. Beckensall. *Cumbrian Prehistoric Rock Art*, 1992, 14–15

25 LONG MEG AND HER DAUGHTERS,
Little Salkeld (1) [L1/7]
Lat: 54°.7   NY 570 372
For directions, see Little Meg (24).
Map D
This is the sixth biggest of all stone circles, some 359ft E-W by 305ft (109.4 × 93m). Its internal area of about 86,000 sq.ft (7,989m²) is greatly exceeded only by the enormous outer ring at Avebury (82), whose interior is 5¹/₂ times larger. Other circles such as Stanton Drew (75), the Ring of Brodgar (183) and Newgrange (363) exceed Long Meg but only marginally so. One assumes that these vast enclosures were for huge assemblies.

The ring at Long Meg was built on a considerable slope down to the north and it has been suggested that this was because the ring was erected alongside an earlier earthwork. It is equally possible that the circle was set up to be close to the tall pillar of Long Meg, a thin red sandstone already standing on the south-west skyline 82ft (25m) away and possibly brought 1¹/₂ miles from the Eden valley.

In the eighteenth century an attempt was made to destroy the ring by blasting, but thunderstorms and superstitious fears caused the work to

Long Meg and Her Daughters, Cumberland (25), *from the west. Long Meg is in the foreground.*

be abandoned and some of the stones were replaced. Seventy local porphyritic boulders remain in the circle which has a flattened northern arc. The cardinal points are stressed in the ring. Two massive blocks stand almost at the exact east and west.

Two further large slabs at the south-west define an entrance, outside which two extra stones stand as external portals. From the ring's centre the two western portals stand in line with the tapering outlier whose south-east face has several carvings of rings and spirals on it. The stone stands in line with the midwinter sunset and the carvings may reflect this. The sun's shadow casts clockwise spirals on its northward journey towards midsummer, anti-clockwise as it moves back towards midwinter. The spiral on Long Meg is an anti-clockwise one. Despite claims to the contrary the decorated side does not face the circle, another reason for believing that the outlier and the ring are not contemporary.

In the mid-seventeenth century John Aubrey reported that there were two large cairns inside the ring covering a

'Giants bone, and Body' but by Stukeley's time they had been removed. Stukeley did, however, notice a small stone circle, about 50 ft (15m) in diameter in the field to the ssw. It has since disappeared.

Long Meg was a witch of unknown origins, who probably got her name from 'as long as Meg of Westminster', a saying that Thomas Fuller in his *History of the Worthies of Britain* (1662), wrote was 'applyed to persons very tall, especially if they have *Hop-Pole-heighth* wanting *breadth* proportionable thereunto.' Such a description certainly fits the outlier, a scrawny pillar at least 12ft high but never more than 3ft 6ins wide (3.7 × 1.1m). According to the traveller Celia Fiennes in 1698 the stones were not Meg's daughters but her 'Sisters, the story is that these soliciting her unto an unlawfull love by an enchantment are turned with her to stone . . .', adding that 'Mag' was 'much bigger and have some forme like a statue or figure of a body'.

To a correspondent writing to the *Gentleman's Magazine* in 1752 this was

Swinside, Cumberland (26), from the north-west. The tallest stone at the north is one the left, the entrance is at the far side of the ring.

preposterous. 'The vulgar notion that the largest of these stones has breasts and resembles the remainder of a female statue is caused by the whimsical irregularity of the figure, in which a fervid imagination may discover a resemblance of almost anything.'

The stone was supposed to bleed if a piece were broken from it. The stones of the circle could not be counted.

Dymond, 40–7, *Plan*, 41; S. Beckensall. *Cumbrian Prehistoric Rock Art*, 1992, 7–14; Burl, 1994

Low Longrigg, Eskdale see Brat's Hill (16A)

26 Swinside, Swinside Fell (1) [L1/3. Sunken Kirk] Lat: 54°.6   SD 171 882 *5 miles N of Millom. No parking unless at the far end of the rough farm track. Walk. From Broad Gate, SD 18.86. In ¹/₂ mile N turn NW along track. Circle is ³/₄ mile. Fairly easy. Worth the effort. Map D*

Also known as Sunkenkirk this well-preserved ring is one of the finest stone circles in western Europe. It stands in the south-west corner of the Lake

District twenty-three miles SSW of Castlerigg. The stones of porphyritic slate came from the adjacent fells where they are plentiful. Locally they are known as 'grey cobbles'.

The ring is about 93ft 8ins (28.6m) in diameter. Of a possible original sixty stones some fifty-five remain, thirty-two still standing, quite closely set about 5ft (1.5m) apart. The tallest, a tapering pillar 7ft 6ins (2.3m) high, stands almost exactly at the north, a cardinal position common to several large Cumbria stone circles. Despite its height, it is elegantly slender and weighs only about five tons.

There is a well-defined entrance, 7ft (2.1m) wide, at the south-east created by both a wide gap and the presence of two portal stones outside the circumference, another characteristic of early Cumbrian rings such as Long Meg and Her Daughters (25).

In 1901 an excavation at Swinside took place from midday on Tuesday, 26 March, to the evening of the following day. Two crosstrenches, only 18 inches (45cm) wide, NW-SE, SW-NE, were dug with others across the south, a total length of 360ft (110m). The area uncovered was hardly one-thirteenth of the interior. The only finds were a small lump of charcoal and a fragment of decayed bone. Interestingly, however, the site had been levelled by cutting into the slope before the erection of the stones. Its counterpart, Ballynoe in Ireland, had also been levelled by the construction of an earthen platform.

An alignment from the centre of Swinside across the line of the two southernmost portal stones has an azimuth of 134°.5 and a declination of −24°.6, very close to the midwinter sunrise. A similar phenomenon has been noticed at Long Meg and Her Daughters where the thin outlier, apparently a midwinter sunset marker, is not framed in the middle of the wide entrance but stands nicely in line with the two western portal stones.

In the 1806 edition of Camden's *Britannia* there is a report of a central stone at Swinside but no one before or since has remarked upon such a feature.

The circle is sometimes known as Sunkenkirk because at night the Devil is reputed to have pulled down the stones of a church that was being built during the day. The same story occurs at the Scottish ring of Chapel o'Sink.

Dymond, 47–50, *Plan*, 48; *TCWAAS*

2, 1902, 53–63

WHITE MOSS, Eskdale see Brat's Hill (16A)

DERBYSHIRE
The majority of Peak District rings are Bronze Age. They are small, embanked, and often contain cairns, They lie on the millstone grit plateau east of the River Derwent. Larger Neolithic rings are to the west on the limestone

27 ARBOR LOW, Middleton (3)
Lat: 53°.2   SK 160 636
5 miles SW of Bakewell, Walk. From SK 159 639, 500 yds (460m) S on track and field. In State care, entrance Fee at farm. Map E
Magnificently situated at 1230ft (375m) O.D. this great circle-henge, 'the Stonehenge of the North', commands superb views. It may be a hybrid monument of four long-drawn-out phases: first a Cove; then a henge; a ring of standing stones; until, finally, a round barrow was built on top of the henge bank.

The site was constructed on a pronounced slope down to the west and was, perhaps, meant to be seen and approached from there. It is dramatically conspicuous on the skyline from the head of a ridge half a mile

Arbor Low, Peak District, Derbyshire (27), from the north-west. Stone 16 leans deeply on the right. The fallen Cove is at the centre of the ring. An Early Bronze Age round barrow built on the bank rises in the background.

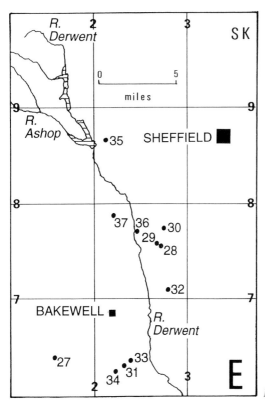

Map E, The Peak District

Arbor Low, Derbyshire (27), from the south entrance. The leaning stone 16 is conspicuous against the ditch.

away in that direction.

Unlike the majority of Derbyshire rings which are of Bronze Age date and erected on the harsh millstone grits east of the River Derwent Arbor Low, *eordburgh-hlaw*, 'the earthwork mound', was built on the richer limestone plateau to the west. It is probably a Late Neolithic monument of about 3000 BC.

The rubble quarried from a 30ft wide, 6ft deep (9 × 2m) ditch was heaped up to make a massive outer bank, sub-circular, 259ft SE-NW by 246ft (79 × 75m) and 7ft (2.1m) high, broken by two entrances at the north-west, 324°, 30ft (9m) wide, and SSE, 157°, 20ft (6m) across.

The henge enclosed a central platform some 171ft by 131ft (52 × 40m). On it lie the slabs of an irregular circle, once egg-shaped, about 143ft SE-NW by 122ft (43.6 × 37.2m). It contains forty-six large stones, up to 13ft (4m) long, and thirteen smaller, some of which are fragments broken from the former. Arguments that the stones never stood are confuted both by stone 16 at the WSW which still leans, by the upright stumps of others at the north and by the obvious breaks in others when the pillars were blown down by the tempestuous winds howling in from the north. The stones themselves reveal this, lying inwards at the north, outwards at the south.

They came not from the ditch but from a nearby source of limestone different from that at Arbor Low itself. It introduces the possibility that the ring was an addition to the henge. Unusually, the builders chose to set the blocks up with the weathered side facing inwards lining the interior of the ring. It was not particularly spacious, around 13,700 s.ft (1,273m²), and was diminished further by the presence of a Cove at its centre. A congregation of no more than two hundred and fifty participants might be imagined.

The three-sided Cove is now prostrate, two huge sides tumbled outwards, a long low stone on edge like a sill or septal slab between them at the

east and other little stones nearby. A skeleton of a man about 5ft 5ins (1.65m) tall was buried against the eastern corner. Immediately to the east was a deep pit with a human armbone in it. 'It is possible', wrote the excavator, 'that a skeleton or skeletons may have been removed from here'.

The Coves of other circles and henges such as Stanton Drew (75), Avebury (82) and Cairnpapple have been likened to the chambers of megalithic tombs and the connection with death is manifest at Arbor Low suggesting funerary rites and rituals of fertility. The north-east facing Cove may have been aligned on the major northern moonrise. There is also the chance that it was the very first structure here, standing remote and gaunt on its hillside.

Excavations in 1901 and 1902 made few finds, two arrowheads and other flints, ox bones and antlers but little to indicate the purpose of the place. Later prehistoric people dug out stretches of the bank against the eastern side of the SSE entrance to construct a big round barrow in which human bones, flints and two Early Bronze Age food-vessels were found. What appears to be the beginnings of an earthen avenue curves away from the entrance, turning towards the mound of Gib Hill 330 yards (300m) west of Arbor Low.

That the circle-henge was the sub-tribal focus of a well-populated countryside, usurping the roles of earlier family shrines, seems indisputable. It lies at the heart of a landscape of eight Early Neolithic chambered tombs including Five Wells, Brushfield and Harborough Rocks. In turn, it became the centre of dozens of Bronze Age cairns. It is one of the wonders of megalithic Britain.

Arch 58, 1903, 461–98, Plan 461

28 BARBROOK I, SOUTH (1) [D1/7]
Lat: 53°.3   SK 278 755
4¹/₂ miles SE of Hathersage, 2¹/₂ miles NE of Baslow. Walk. A footpath at SK 281 751 leads to the ring ¹/₄ mile NW. Easy. Map E

Standing on a gentle slope on Ramsley Moor this is a typical Peak District embanked circle. The twelve low stones are embedded in a worn bank, 10ft (3m) wide, around an area 44ft (13.4m) across. The tallest stone, 3ft 3ins (1m) high, is at the south-west.

Before 1939 two trenches were dug across the ring by the Duke of Rutland's gamekeeper but the only finds were three flints. The ditches have been re-excavated to recover environmental evidence.

Barbrook II (Centre) is 660 yards (600m) to the NNW and Barbrook III is nearly $^1/_4$ miles to the NNE.

Thom, 1967, *Plan*, 66; Barnatt, 1989, II, 365–6

29 BARBROOK II, CENTRE (2)

Lat: 53°.3   SK 277 758
2$^3/_4$ miles NE of Baslow. Walk. 660 yards (600m) across the moor NNW of Barbrook I. Easy. Map E
This ring has been restored but imperfectly. Its rubble bank, 66ft (20m) across externally and 11ft (3.4m) wide, is held in place by low kerbing. The interior is lined with a ring, 44ft (13.4m) in diameter, of nine or ten standing stones interspersed with drystone walling. The tallest pillar is at the WSW.

An excavation in 1966, not fully published, found that the probable NNE entrance had been covered by a cairn beneath which was a stone-filled pit. A cupmarked stone lay nearby. Inside the ring at the south-west was a small cairn, 7ft 6ins (2.5m) across, 'retained by selected kerbstones', one of them cupmarked. Under the cairn a pit held an overhanging-rim urn, a cremation, two flint scrapers and a knife, all of them burnt. On the ground under the cairn was a broken shale ring. Charcoal gave a radiocarbon date of 1500 ± 150 bc (BM-197), the approximate equivalent of 1800 BC, quite late in the Early Bronze Age. Near the cairn was a third pit with a cremation. The sequence of events had been strange. 'There was clear evidence that a ritual fire had been lit *after* the burial of the

burnt bones.'

To the south-east a tiny cist with a cupmarked capstone had been disturbed. In the same quadrant was another pit with an urn in it. The finds are in Sheffield Museum, Weston Park.

Barnatt, 1978, 111, *Plan*; Barnatt, 1989, II, 366

30 BARBROOK III, NORTH-EAST (3) [D1/8. Owler Bar]

Lat: 53°.3   SK 283 772
2$^1/_4$ miles WNW of Froggatt, Walk. A footpath off the A621 at SK 289 772 leads W for $^1/_4$ mile. The ring is 200 yards (180m) E of the reservoir. Easy. Map E
The twenty-one low stones stand in a bank about 96ft (29m) in diameter and 6ft to 10ft (2 − 3m) wide. There may be a south-west entrance. The 'circle' is flattened to the ENE and measures 86ft SSW-NNE by 74ft (26.2 × 22.6m). There is no surviving central mound.

Barnatt, 1978, 114, *Plan*; Barnatt, 1989, II, 366–7

31 DOLL TOR, Birchover (3)

Lat: 53°.2   SK 238 628
$^1/_2$ mile N of Birchover. At N end of a plantation on W side of Birchover to Stanton-in-the-Peak lane, SK 242 628. Walk. Circle is 300 yards (275m) to W in front of a second plantation. Easy. Map E
This is a site of at least two phases: the first a stone circle 23ft (7m) in diameter with its slightly taller (5ft (1.5m) high) and heavier stones at the west. Of the six two are fallen. Drystone walling linked them.

Its date is unknown but in the Early Bronze Age people filled it with rubble converting it into a kerb-cairn. In 1852 William Bateman found three or four collared urns of Pennine type and the same number of incense cups. Excavations in 1931–3 discovered five more burials, some with urns. They are now in Sheffield Museum.

A sub-rectangular mound was added to the east side of the kerb-cairn. It contained four cremations at its east, three with collared urns, one with a star-shaped faience bead. At the centre, covered by a heavy capstone, was a pit holding the cremated bones of a young woman with a segmented faience bead. At the north-west corner of the extension were the bones of a young girl with another urn.

DAJ 13, 1939, 116–25, *Plan*, fig. 1; Barnatt, 1989, II, 367–8

32 GIBBET MOOR NORTH, Bunker's Hill

(5) Lat: 53°.2   SK 282 708
2¹/₄ miles NNE of Beeley, Walk. A footpath opposite Stone Low tumulus, SK 286 708, leads SW for ¹/₂ mile. Turn S over the moor for 550 yards (500m). Fair. Map E
On a north-facing slope of moorland are three stones of local gritstone, about 2ft (60cm) high, at the corners of a rectangle roughly 13ft (4m) square. A fourth has been removed. It is possible that the site is a unique Peak District example of a 'Scottish' Four-Poster stone 'circle'. If so, its nearest counterparts are the Druid's Altar near Grassington sixty miles to the NNW and the High Bridestones on the Yorkshire Moors ninety miles to the NNE.

Barnatt, 1989, II, 369. *No plan*

33 NINE LADIES, Birchover (1) [D1/3]

Lat: 53°.2   SK 247 634
3¹/₂ miles SE of Bakewell, At SK 241 626 there is a convenient layby on the W of the lane from Birchover to Stanton-in-the-Peak. Walk. Follow the footpath east past the Cork Stone, 150 yards (137m) to second turning on the north (Lt), 375 yards (340m). to the circle in ¹/₂ mile. Pleasant because of the other sites on the way. Map E
Pass through a cairn cemetery with three large ring-cairns to the west from which cremations and collared urns were recovered.

Among airy trees the Nine Ladies is 330 yards (300m) NNE of the Reform Tower. Once enclosed in a low modern wall it is now untrapped and has become prey to vandalism. It is a typical Peak District small Bronze Age ring, its low stones set in a rubble bank and enclosing a central burial mound.

Of local millstone grit the nine stones, a tenth being a recent intrusion, stand in a circle 35ft 6ins (10.8m) across. The tallest 3ft (0.9m) is at the north-east. The bank seems to have entrances at the north-east and south-west. The outlying King Stone is 130ft (40m) to the WSW.

At Birchover is the Druid Inn. At the bottom of the village are the Rowtor Rocks with mythical druidical associations.

TTB, 16 *Plan*; Barnatt, 1989, II, 370

34 NINE STONE CLOSE, Harthill Moor

(3) Lat: 53°.2   SK 225 625
1¹/₂ miles SE of Youlgreave, Visible to the E of the lane from Elton to Alport. Walk. 200 yards (180m) Easy. Map E
Even in ruin this is an impressive site. Its four remaining stones are the tallest in Derbyshire. Standing on the eastern rim of a circle once 45ft (13.7m) in diameter they range in height from 4ft (1.2m) to a giant at the south, 7ft (2.1m) high but 11ft 6ins (3.5m) long before its re-erection in 1936. Both it and its northern partner are set in concrete. 250 yards (230m) to the north-west in a field is a long, prostrate stone.

Seven stones still stood in 1847 when Bateman dug there finding 'several fragments of imperfectly baked pottery accompanied by flint both in a natural and calcined state.' In 1877 William Greenwell and Llewellyn Jewitt dug at the base of the second highest stone and in the centre of the circle but found nothing.

A third of a mile to the SSW the gritstone crag of Robin Hood's Stride rises jaggedly with two stubby piles of boulders jutting up at either end of its flat top like the head and pricked-up ears of a wrinkled hippopotamus. From the circle the major southern moon sets between the ears and this may be the reason for the situation of the ring.

The site is also known as the 'Grey Ladies' who are supposed to dance at midnight and also, so it is said, at midday.

The writer has seen the stones in

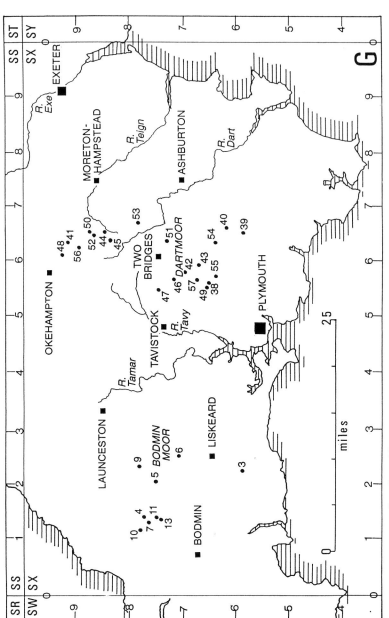

Map G, Dartmoor and Bodmin Moor

deep twilight, in heavy rain, in snow, and not at all in fog. It is hoped that the reader will be more fortunate.

DAJ 13, 1939, 127, *Plan*; Barnatt, 1989, II, 370

35 Seven Stones of Hordron (3) [D1/ 9. Moscar Moor]
Lat: 53°.4   SK 215 868
4¹/₂ miles NE *of Castleton and 2 miles* NNE *of Bamford. Walk. At SK 216 874 go* S *for 600 yds (550m). Pleasant views. Map E*
Known also as Hordron Edge this is an unusual Peak District ring. It has no bank or central mound, simply ten stones of millstone grit, seven still standing, the survivors of an original twenty-six or more. They enclose an area about 54ft ESE-WNW by 49ft (16.5 × 15m). A visit in summer can be frustrating because of head-high bracken.

Barnatt, 1978, 175, *Plan*; Barnatt, 1989, II, 371

36 Stoke Flat, Froggatt Edge (3)
Lat: 53°.3   SK 249 768
1¹/₂ miles NE *of Stoney Middleton, Walk. At SK 254 776 at a bend in the B6054 1 mile* N *of Froggatt a footpath leads* S *for ¹/₄ mile. Fair. Map E*
Dilapidated and often lost in bracken at the steep western edge of Froggatt bank this is a circular rubble bank, 7ft (2.1m) wide and about 47ft (14.3m) across. It has five standing stones on its outer perimeter and six more inside in a ring about 37ft (11.3m) in diameter. The tallest is at the south-west, 3ft 7ins (1.1m) high. It stands with two others like gateposts at the corners of a SSW entrance 6ft (1.8m) wide. There is a questionable entrance at the north which may have been blocked up.

Before 1939 the Duke of Rutland had the ring examined. There is a vague report of an urned cremation being found.

Barnatt, 1978, 95, *Plan*; Barnatt, 1989, II, 372–3

37 Wet Withens, Eyam Moor (3) [D1/ 2. Wet Withers]

Lat: 53°.3   SK 225 789
1³/₄ miles NNE *of Eyam, Walk. Where the lane from Eyam to Grindleford Bridge turns sharply* E *at SK 224 780, a footpath to the* NE *leads ¹/₄ mile. The circle is 600 yards (550m) to* W *(Lt). Hard walking if the heather is thick. Map E*
On a slope 7ft (2.1m) higher on one side than the other this site stands at a height of 1050ft (320m) O.D. It should be visited when the heather is low. Otherwise, tiring.

Wet Withens, 'the wet land where willows grew' (O.E. *widign*), has ten or eleven low stones standing inside a wide overgrown bank about 116ft (36m) from crest to crest. Originally the ring may have consisted of sixteen stones. The tallest 2ft 4ins, (0.7m) is at the north-east, widening to a flat top and with a low projection near its bottom. It 'stands perpendicularly, and is shaped like a chair'. The others, on edge, all of local millstone grit, lean inwards in a circle according to Thom 96.9 ± 0.5ft (29.5 ± 0.2m) in diameter. On average they are an inconspicuous 1ft 9ins (53cm) high.

There are old, and probably illusory, reports of the vestiges of an avenue to the south-west, and of a large central stone, possibly a cist cover. It has gone and may even have been a mistaken reference to the cist discovered by roadworkers in June 1759, at the 'Round Hillock', a large cairn 60ft (18m) to the NNE. From it came a cremation in a badly-fired urn, a small incense cup, amber beads, a perforated jet pendant and a flint arrowhead.

Barnatt, 1978, 120, *Plan*; Barnatt, 1989, II, 383

DEVON
The large open circles are at the edges of Dartmoor, especially the north-east. The smaller Bronze Age rings, often with stone rows and internal cairns, occupy more central areas

Belstone, see Nine Stones

38 Brisworthy, Ringmoor Down (2)
[S2/3] Lat: 50°.5   SX 565 655
*3 miles ESE of Yelverton. From Cadover
Bridge, SX 555 647, take road N for ¹/₂
mile, turn E (Rt) to Brisworthy Farm, ¹/₂
mile. Walk. Take NE path through
fields, over stile. Circle ¹/₄ mile. Easy.
Map G*
This splendid circle, 81ft 5ins (24.8m)
in diameter stands on a gentle south-
east slope. It is one of the great
Dartmoor rings but being at the south-
west of the moor it is remote from the
others. An adjacent field wall accounts
for gaps in the south arc.

Once of some forty-two local granites
6ft (1.8m) apart, twenty-four survive,
the tallest at the north, 3ft 8ins (1.1m)
high, the apex of a ring graded
upwards from the south. Two others,
about 3ft (0.9m) high straddle the east
point. Only three stones stood before
the circle was manually reconstructed in
1909 under the direction of the Rev.
H.H. Breton of Sheepstor. The heaviest
stone weighed about ¹/₂ ton and
required the use of sheer-legs. A dozen
prehistoric workers would have
managed better.

A limited excavation uncovered
charcoal inside the ring. Evidence of fire
has been noticed in other large
Dartmoor rings like the Grey Wethers
(45) and Fernworthy (44), a circle
cardinally graded like Brisworthy.

A complex of four pounds, one
within the other and with at least ten
hut-circles lies on Legis Tor ¹/₂ mile to
the east, a settlement from which the
ring is visible. Ringmoor cairn-circle
(49) is NNW of Brisworthy, ¹/₄ mile
uphill.

TTB, 108, *Plan*; H.H. Breton, *The
Forest of Dartmoor*, *II*, 1931, 23–4

39 Butterdon, Weatherdon Hill (4)
Lat: 50°.4   SX 656 588
*2 miles NE of Ivybridge. Walk. From
Bittaford, SX 666 570, take NE lane by
the Post Office and inn for ¹/₂ mile to a
copse. Continue up hillside for ³/₄ mile.
A long, steep climb but worth the
effort. Map G*
Among a cemetery of at least sixteen

cairns on Butterdon Moor is an
unimpressive cairn-circle and a very
impressive stone row, the second
longest on Dartmoor. The circle is
small, no more than 36ft 5ins (11.1m)
in size with only one of eleven stones
standing. Nothing is known of the
contents of its ravaged 20ft (6m) cairn.

The attraction is the row, graded in
height up to the ring but extending
2095 yards (1916m) northwards to a
tall re-erected terminal, the Longstone,
8ft 6ins (2.6m) high. Suggesting that
this is a multi-phase complex, the row
does not point to the stone circle's
centre but to its western side.

Worth, 1967, 229–31; Butler, 1993,
24–7, *Plan*

40 Corringdon Ball (3)
Lat: 50°.4   SX 666 612
*2 miles WNW of South Brent. From Aish,
SX 692 607, do not take the lane SW to
Owley nor the NW to Badworthy but the
one between. Walk. Go W along lane,
track, footpath and moor for 1³/₄ miles
W to a chambered tomb. Rows are ¹/₄
mile to the W. Long, often steep. Map G*
The humpy outline of a plundered
megalithic tomb slumps on the eastern
skyline. On the moorland below,
several rows of minute stones creep
uphill towards the sides of a cairn-
circle. Worth planned the rows as two
sets of treble lines, but in dry weather
more can be seen. The circle, in ruin,
appears to be ovate, 41ft 4ins (12.6m)
WSW-ENE by 35ft 7ins (10.9m). Six
more unencircled cairns lie just to its
south-west.

Worth, 1967, 231; Butler, 1993, 91–
3, *Plan*

41 Cosdon, Cawsand Hill (2)
Lat: 50°.7   SX 643 916
*1 mile SSW of South Zeal. From South
Zeal take the lane S towards
Throwleigh. In ⁵/₈ mile a bridlepath to
W (Rt) is signposted 'Nine Stones'.
Walk. Follow SW, becoming steeper and
degenerating into a rough stream-bed
before the end of field-walls, ¹/₂ mile.
Ring is ¹/₄ mile SW. Steep, hard. Map G*
On one of the highest hills on
Dartmoor one of the three rows

approaching a stone circle is taller and heavier than its partners, and is likely to have been an addition to them, just as the avenue itself may have been erected against an older ring. Restored in 1897 the complex had suffered prehistoric depredation. About 120 yards (110m) to the south is a Bronze Age reave. Large stones can be seen in it, probably taken from the convenient rows and circle.

The circle, now with only five stones, was about 19ft (5.8m) in diameter. It surrounded a disturbed kerbed cairn, 15ft (4.6m) across. Remarkably. inside are the disturbed sideslabs of not one but two rectangular cists side by side, aligned SE-NW.

Just over the brow of the hill was another stone circle, now destroyed. Known as Sticklepath or Eight Rocks

the stones danced when they heard the bells of South Tawton two windy miles away.

Butler, 1991, 204–6, *Plan*

42 DOWN TOR, Hingston Tor (1)
Lat: 50°.5   SX 587 694
7 miles ESE of Tavistock, 4 miles ENE of Yelverton. Approach from the NE end of Burrator Reservoir, SX 568 693. Walk. 1¼ miles to E. Sometimes rough going. Map G
This is a splendid cairn-circle, one of the best on Dartmoor. its twenty-five stones of local granite forming a ring 36ft (11m) in diameter. The stones are low, averaging 1ft 7ins (48cm) in height. Inside is a low, ransacked cairn 28ft (8.5m) across.

Extending south-westwards towards the circle from a terminal stone 5ft

Down Tor, Dartmoor, Devon (42), from the north-east. The terminal stone stands at right-angles to the row which curves to the stone circle up the hillside.

(1.5m) high is a well-preserved stone row. After the stones were 'tampered with' in 1880 the damaged stretches were re-erected in 1894. Some 1145ft (349m) long and concave as though of two phases of construction the row has pillars that rise in height as they approach the ring, the closest being 9ft 6ins (2.9m) high. Weighing about five tons, at least twenty-four workers were needed to erect it.

East of the terminal stone are cairns and a pound with worn-down hut-circles from which the stone circle is visible on the far slope.

Worth, 1967, 212; Butler, 1994, 71–4, 'Hingston Hill', *Plan*

43 DRIZZLECOMBE, Dartmoor (1)

Lat: 50°.5   SX 592 671
4¹/₂ miles E of Yelverton, From Sheepstor go ESE and in ¹/₂ mile take the left fork. Drive ¹/₂ mile along track. Walk. Beyond coppice just to E circles and rows are 1 mile SE. Quite easy.
Map G

Overlooked by the crowded settlement of hut-circles on Whittenknowles Rocks and within yards of the River Plym is one of the most elegant arrangements of tiny stone circles, long rows, standing stones, cists, cairns and pounds in western Europe. It is also one of the most tantalising. There is so much that one can almost see the people. Almost. There is only the river, the grass and the stones.

Although very small the circles are the major elements of the complex. Three encircled cairns lie in a 160ft (48.8m) long SW-NE line.

A. *The south-east ring*, 34ft (10.4m) across has thirteen low stones. From it a line of small stones extends south-west for 296ft (90m) culminating in a great terminal stone, the most spectacular of three towering pillars at Drizzlecombe. When measured in July 1893, it was found to be 17ft 10ins long and 4ft wide at its base (5.4 × 1.2m), seven tons of pointed granite, 'the largest recorded on Dartmoor'. After re-erection it loomed 14ft (4.3m) high, 'by far the finest in the West of

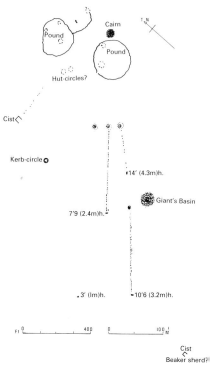

Drizzlecombe, Dartmoor, Devon (43)

England'.

To its south is a small round cairn, lacking a circle, but with a row 488ft (149m) long, ending in a south-western terminal 10ft 6ins (3.2m) high and set at right-angles to the row like a blocking stone.

B. *The central cairn-circle*, about 80ft (24m) from the first is 29ft (8.8m) in diameter and has twelve stones imaginatively inclined outwards like a coronet and packed round with small stones 'to ensure that although leaning they shall not fall'. From it a row stretches south-westwards for some 491ft (150m) to a terminal 7ft 9ins (2.4m).

C. *The north-west cairn-circle*, 30ft (9.1m) across, is surrounded by nine short pillars. Unlike its partners it has no row, only the 'ghost' of one. There is no high terminal, just a 3ft (1m) long block 963ft (294m) to the south-west, almost lost in the grass and about 330ft (100m) north-west of the most southerly terminal. If it had any purpose it was that of a marker-stone to indicate where an impressive stone should stand at the end of an intended row.

Connected with this intriguing ritual complex are two great cairns, one of them the Giant's Basin, an enormous but assaulted mound 71ft across and 10ft high (21.6 × 3m). There are three cists, one a little to the west of the cairn-circles with a splendid capstone. There is a ruinous kerb-circle west of the marker-stone. And there are two pounds to the north of the circles, hut-circles in both of them and so temptingly close to the rings that their inhabitants would not only have known them but may well have raised them.

The south-east cairn-circle may be the earliest. Although it has the shortest row it has the tallest terminal. Its cairn, though small, only six paces across, retains the traditional stone circle, a diminished version of the fine Down Tor ring a mile and a half away. The alignment of the row is close to the moon's most northerly rising.

All this is megalithic splendour but there is more. Examination of the complex reveals an unexpected symmetry. The layout of the circles, cairns, rows and terminals forms an enormous trapezoid in which the narrow north-east head, wider base and long sides were proportional to each other. The base, between the southern terminal and the 'marker-stone' is twice the length of the line of three stone circles at the top of the plan. The sides are six times as long. The distances are not precise. Pacing or using a measuring-rod across yards of coarse, uneven grassland inevitably caused errors. But about 160ft (49m) for the barrows, 330ft (101m) for the base, and 947ft and 963ft (289, 294m) for the sides gives ratios of 1:2.1:5.9 and 6, too close to multiples of each other for coincidence.

How long Drizzlecombe was in the making, who lived in the huts, why two

of the single rows were being converted into doubles but abandoned, these are questions that serve only to remind us that the ruins at Drizzlecombe are, in Bacon's words, 'some remnants of history which have casually escaped the shipwreck of time.'

Worth, 1967, 212–16, *Plan*; Burl, 1993, 113–16

44 FERNWORTHY, Fernworthy Forest, Dartmoor (1) Lat: 51°.0   SX 655 841
3¹/₂ miles SW of Chagford; carpark at end of Fernworthy Reservoir road. Walk. ¹/₂ mile WNW along a rising E-W track. Ignore an early track to the N (Rt). Ring is in clearing just N of track. Map G

In a clearing on Forestry Commission land the ring, 65ft (19.8m) across and slightly flattened E-W, has twenty-seven local granite blocks graded in height up to the south where the tallest is about 4ft (1.2m) high. Architecturally it is similar to Brisworthy on the far side of the moor. The circle is also unhappily known as Froggymead.

Excavated in 1897 the interior was full of charcoal fragments. 'In fact, fires seem to have been kindled all over the circle, for every scoop of the pick and shovel which was removed from the floor displayed charcoal.' There were no other finds.

Just to the south and east of the ring are inconspicuous burial-cairns against this established ritual centre, 'the important and predominant feature of a group of sepulchral remains, and it is very probable that we can now see in this the crematorium of the site of the funeral feasts or both.'

Ten yards (9m) south of the ring is a tiny, ransacked cairn to which a low and ragged avenue, once 230ft (70m) long, extends from the far side of the track where a wall accounts for the sudden absence of stones. From there 56ft (17m) to the south-east is a second robbed cairn and 84ft (25.6m) ESE of it are the slabs of a cist that contained a mass of cremated bone and charcoal. The eye of faith will make out the stutter of an avenue between it and the

Grey Wethers, Dartmoor, Devon (45), from the south-west. Fernworthy Forest is in the background.

cairn.

In the trees 56 yards (51m) east of the cist is a third cairn, 19ft (5.8m) across that once stood inside a stone circle 38ft (11.6m) in diameter. Below the heavy, hand-sized cairnstones was a central pit, 3ft (1m) deep, in which was the remnant of a bronze knife whose wooden scabbard had decayed. Below were the crushed sherds of a fine S2/W beaker, now in Plymouth Museum, and a v-shaped perforated button of Kimmeridge shale. A flint knife lay alongside it.

Fernworthy is not well looked after but is interesting for the diversity of its monuments. A hundred yards north of the circle is a good double row, 110 yards (100m) of minute stones extending to an overgrown circular mound.

Westwards through the forest and then south across the shabby moor are the Grey Wethers stone circles.

TDA 30, 1898, 97–115; Butler, 1991, 162–5, *Plan*

45 GREY WETHERS, Fernworthy Forest, Dartmoor (2) [S2/1]
Lat: 50°.9   SX 638 832
2½ miles N *of Postbridge. Walk. From Fernworthy stone circle continue* W *for ³/4 mile along track to end of forest. Turn* S. *Circles are ³/4 mile uphill. Tedious but rewarding. Map G*

Typical of multiple rings in the south-west peninsula of England the arrangement of these two finely restored circles reveals that considerable care was taken in their layout. They stand almost exactly N-S (182°–358°) of each other, 15ft (4.6m) apart, the north 107ft 2ins (32.7m) in diameter, the south 107ft 10ins (32.9m). Erected just below the crest of a north-facing slope they were excavated in 1898 and restored in 1909. This may explain the slight discrepancy in their sizes. In 1879, however, Lukis surveyed the tumbled sites and recorded their dimensions as 103ft 6ins (north) and 116ft 6ins (31.6, 35.5m). Thom recorded 104ft 6ins and 108ft 9ins (31.9, 33.2m).

Like Fernworthy their interiors were strewn with charcoal, their floors 'deep in ashes'. Charcoal also filled the pits beneath two small cairns still visible just south of the southern ring.

The crystalline granite stones, probably from the clitter of Sittaford Tor to the west, are regular in shape, flat-topped, ranging from 4ft to 4ft 6ins (1.2, 1.4m) in height. They are so symmetrical geologically that they appear to have been shaped by man. On the tor there is a natural 'rocking-stone' which caused Crossing to remark that 'it is a pity the Druidophiles were unaware of this'.

Put up in a pass between the hills, the elegant Grey Wethers may have acted as assembly places for communities from north and south. There are hut-circles a mile to the south.

TDA 71, 1939, 326–8; Butler, 1991, 165–6, *Plan*

46 HARTOR NORTH, Meavy, Dartmoor (3) Lat: 50°.5 SX 577 717
1¹/₂ miles ssw of Princetown. Walk. From unfenced B3212 at SX 570 718 go E for ¹/₂ mile. The River Meavy between can be fast and deep. Map G
Of the fourteen stones of this 30ft (9m)

diameter circle seven stand, two lean and five are fallen. The tallest is 3ft 2ins (1m) high but one prostrate at the north is 4ft 9ins (1.5m) long and may have stood about 3ft 7ins (1.1m) high. Inside the ring is a low cairn 21ft (6.4m) across.

An avenue of stones leads to the ring from the wsw. About 450ft (137m) long it is incomplete and many of its stones are embedded in deep peat. There is a single row, 165ft (50m) in length to the south. It has a cairn but no circle at its eastern end.

Worth, 1967, 213, no. 22, *Plan*

47 MERRIVALE, N, S, Dartmoor (1) [S2/2] Lat: 50°.6 SX 553 746
3¹/₄ miles W of Two Bridges. Walk. 200 yds (180m) S of the A384, Easy. Map G
Merrivale, 'the pleasant valley', is a

Merrivale, Dartmoor, Devon (47)

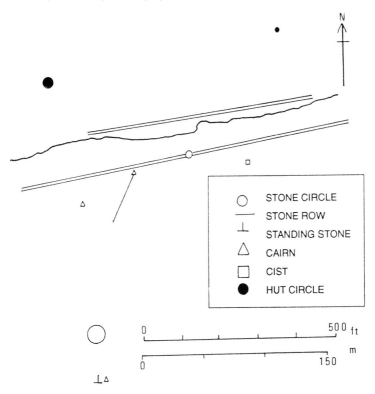

○	STONE CIRCLE
—	STONE ROW
⊥	STANDING STONE
△	CAIRN
☐	CIST
●	HUT CIRCLE

0   500 ft

0   150 m

complex of two stone circles, an avenue, a double row, a single row, a large despoiled cist, standing stones and hut-circles. This splendid complex deserves a lengthy visit. It was first described in 1802.

From the main road pass through an extensive group of over twenty hut-circles, a spacious pound with walls unusually of upright stones, and a broken apple-crusher that romantics thought was a druidical sacrificial altar. A nineteenth-century excavation of some huts uncovered hearths, charcoal and flint flakes.

The settlement, presumably of the Bronze Age, is known locally as the 'Plague Market' or 'Potato Market'. It was there in 1625 that in exchange for money farmers left food for the inhabitants of Tavistock during an outbreak of bubonic plague when 575 deaths were recorded in the town.

A hundred or so yards (c. 90m) south of the farthest hut is a double row aligned almost E-W, 596ft long but only 3ft 6ins wide (182 × 1m). It has paired terminals at its west and a triangular stone at its east. Some 80ft (24m) to its south, across a defective leat that often turns the ground into a morass, is an impressive avenue.

A. *North circle* The avenue is 865ft (264m) long but less than 3ft (0.9m) wide, hardly adequate for any dignified procession. Contrary to casual belief it is not parallel to the northern row but is aligned 2° farther to the north, 82°–262°. It terminates at its western end with a paired pillar and slab. At its east is a big triangular stone set solidly across the line. Not quite at the centre of the avenue is a minute circle only 11ft 8ins (3.6m) across, its seven stones enclosing a rifled barrow.

There is more. About 280ft (85m) west of the triangular blocking-slab and 15 or so yards (14m) south of the avenue is a magnificent cist, 7ft long, 3ft wide and 3ft 6ins deep (2.1 × 1 × 1.1m). The central section of its tremendous covering slab was cut out by a stonemason for a gatepost in 1860. Excavation recovered a good flint

scraper, a flake and a small whetstone.

Just south of the avenue and 135ft (41m) west of the stone circle an unspectacular single row, with 'all the appearance of an afterthought', 139ft (42.4m) long, creeps from the SSW towards a cairn. Hardly 100ft (30m) to the west is a larger, even more ruinous cairn.

Suggestions of astronomical alignments in the rows and avenue to stars such as the Pleiades and Arcturus and of arcane geometrical layouts for the prediction of the moon's movements are unconvincing.

B. *South circle*. In the vicinity, but separated from the rows to its north by 350ft (107m) of moorland, and 590ft (180m) south-west of the cist, there is a second stone circle. Eleven stones, 1ft to 1ft 6ins (30–45cm) high, of local granite dragged from the clitter of King's Tor to the south enclose a flattened ring 67ft 5ins E-W by 58ft 5ins (20.6 × 17.8m). Twenty yards (18m) to the north-east is a small stone but to the south of the circle is a tall, slender standing stone 10ft 4ins (3.2m) high. Near it is a low cairn and three very little stones to its south. Nearby is a second stone, 6ft 10ins (2.1m) long. It was re-erected in 1895 but has fallen again. Several pits were dug into near the circle but only one flint flake was found.

Cardinal-point alignments seem to have been desired. The axis of the ring is 88°–268° and the outlier stands 182° from the centre.

There is a line of late seventeenth-century trackway markers starting 330 yards (300m) south-east of the avenue, the western faces of the tall stones deeply carved with 'T' for Tavistock, and 'A' for Ashburton on the other side.

Worth, 1967, 196, *Plan*

48 NINE STONES, Belstone, Dartmoor (3) Lat: 50°.7   SX 612 928 *2¹/₂ miles WSW of South Zeal. In Belstone drive SW past church. Walk. Go S along lane that shortly peters out into moor. ¹/₂ mile circle is visible on*

the E (Lt) Easy. Map G
Despite its name eleven closely-set
stones stand with others prostrate in a
ring 25ft 8ins (7.8m) across. There are
gaps at the north-east, south and south-
west and originally the circle may have
had as many as forty stones. None is
more than 3ft (1m) high and some have
been damaged by geological hammers.
Upheaval inside the ring is all that is
left of a robbed cairn and its lost cist.

Standing on ground falling to the
west the stones are outlined on the false
crest from that direction and the site
may have been chosen to be
conspicuous from an ancient hollow
way.

The stones are said to be petrified
girls who dance at noon 'when the
conditions are favourable' and it is
noticeable that heat-haze, although
unusual for Dartmoor, does give the
impression of movement. Paradoxically,
the circle is also known as the
Seventeen Brothers.

Butler, 1991, 208–9, *Plan*

49 RINGMOOR, Dartmoor (2) [S2/4]
Lat: 50°.5   SX 563 658
*2³/4 miles ESE of Yelverton. Walk. To N
of Brisworthy circle. Map G*
330 yards (300m) uphill north of
Brisworthy stone circle (38) is a cairn-
circle with a small kerb-circle 260 yards
(240m) to its north-west. Both are in
fair condition.

A. *The kerb-circle*, only 12ft 8ins
(3.9m) across originally was lined with
about twenty almost contiguous slabs
sunk low in the turf. It has been
suggested that being bluish and with
quartz veins they may not be local.

B. *The cairn-circle*, 41ft 9ins (12.7m)
in diameter, was re-erected in 1909.
Five of its eleven tallish but untidy
stones were plucked shamelessly from
the moor to complete the ring. It
surrounds a disrupted cairn, a
characteristic Dartmoor combination.

Climbing uphill from the SSW is
something of an avenue, 1740ft (530m)
long but often merely of a single line of
stones. Near the circle an overgrown
reave, probably of the later Bronze Age,

passes through the line showing that
the 'avenue' must be earlier.

*TDA 73, 1941, 234–5; TTB, 110,
Plans*

50 SCORHILL, Dartmoor (3)
Lat: 50°.7   SX 654 873
*3 miles W of Chagford. Walks. Either
leave car at Batworthy corner, SX 662
865, ³/4 mile walk NW via clapper bridge
over River North Teign; or at small
carpark, SX 661 877, ¹/2 mile walk SW.
Map G*
Despite the enthusiastic words of the
Rev. Samuel Rowe in 1848 that 'the
sacred circle of Scorhill . . . is by far the
finest example of this rude kind of relic
in Devonshire', the ring has been too
accessible to have avoided pillage,
chiefly before 1800.

Of an original sixty-five to seventy
stones only thirty-four survive, twenty-
five standing in a circle 88ft (26.8m)
across. Yet, even with two horrible
cart-tracks lurching through it, the ruin
retains a bleak grandeur, its peaked
pillars conspicuous on the hillside. The
tallest of these unevenly spaced uprights
rises 8ft 2ins (2.5m) at the north-west.
There is a comparable massive slab, 6ft
3ins long and 5ft wide (1.9 × 1.5m)
slumped at the SSW.

The north-west stone is in line with
no significant landmark and it may be
no more than chance that from the
centre of the circle an observer would
have seen the most northerly moon set
over its tip. But the fact that it is set
radially to the circumference, like the
great pillar at Castlerigg (18) in the
Lake District, adds interest to this
supposition.

Worth, 1967, 247–54, *Plan*; Butler,
1991, 192–3

51 SHERBERTON, Dartmoor. (3)
Lat: 50°.6   SX 639 732
*2¹/4 miles ESE of Two Bridges. Walk. ¹/2
mile WSW of Sherberton Farm. Easy.
Map G*
On a commanding site with fine views
from the crest of its ridge this once-
great circle has been partly
incorporated in an old field-wall. Today

it consists of seven standing stones, mainly in the NW-E arc of a ring about 98ft (29.9m) in diameter. Originally there may have been as many as thirty stones, possibly graded in height towards the south like Brisworthy (38) and Fernworthy (44). The stones at the north are slight, averaging some 2ft (60cm) in height but there are two prostrate monsters at the SSE, 7ft 4ins and 8ft 8ins (2.2, 2.6m) long. A slab at the north-west, 4ft 10ins high and 4ft 6ins wide (1.5 × 1.4m), was reset to fit into the line of the wall.

Worth, 1967, 248, 254–6, 260, *Plan*

52 SHOVEL DOWN, Dartmoor (3)
Lat: 50°.7   SX 659 861
3 miles WSW of Chagford. Walk. ¹/₂ mile SW of Batworthy Corner. Easy. Map G
This avenue and circle is less than a mile from Scorhill (50) at the north-east. As Batworthy Corner is roughly midway between them a visit can be combined to both circles.

The avenue of parallel lines on Shovel Down, sometimes called Shuggledown, 596ft (182m) long and 3ft 6ins (1m) wide, climbs southwards up an easy slope to an unusual stone circle. The ring, no more than 28ft 8ins (8.7m) across, encloses three others, the innermost a mere 8ft (2.4m) in diameter. This multiple stone circle is one of ten recorded on Dartmoor, one at Yellowmead (57), several others being covered by low cairns for which the rings acted as stabilisers.

Although some of the avenue stones are little more than 4ins (10cm) high, they are architecturally interesting. They rise unsteadily in height until, abutting the circle, they end in two monsters, both fallen, one a wide flat-topped block, 7ft 4ins (2.2m) long, its partner a long slim column a full 11ft 6ins (3.5m) in length. When erect they would have formed a majestic portal to the ring. Such a pairing of a pillar and a lower, broader block is reminiscent of the 'male and female' stones of the Kennet Avenue in Wiltshire.

There are several stone rows near the circle, a double immediately to the west, a second just west of the ring and running south-east. Two hundred yards (180m) to the south is a third arranged N-S. Further south still is the fine menhir of the Long Stone, 10ft 5ins (3.2m) and, nearing Thornworthy Corner, is the leaning survivor of the Three Boys.

The hut-circles, droveway and the Round Pound of the Late Bronze Age settlement of Kestor, SX 665 867, lie on either side of the lane just before Batworthy Corner.

Worth, 1967, 219–22, *Plan*; Burl, 1993, 51–2, 80, 229

53 SOUSSONS COMMON, Dartmoor (1)
[S2/8] Lat: 50°.6   SX 675 786
1³/₄ miles E of Postbridge. No walk. By a forest plantation. Map G
Lying in a neat clearing against the lane this cairn-circle is in fine condition. Almost touching each other twenty-two low slabs on edge, up to 4ft (1.2m) long but varying in height from about 2ins to 4ins (5–10cm) surround a smoothly domed cairn, hardly 3ft (1m) high but measuring 28ft 6ins ESE-WNW by 27ft 5ins (8.7 × 8.4m). Two long slabs, parallel, lying SSE-NNW and 4ft 6ins and 5ft 2ins (1.4, 1.6m) long are the remains of a central rifled cist. The heavier kerbstones are in the north-west quadrant. A 7ft (2.1m) gap at the south-west may be an original entrance.

Returning for ¹/₄ mile north-west along the lane, a track leads ¹/₂ mile north and then north-east (fork right) to four cairns just in the trees on the left (W). Lying N-S the two northern were empty, small cairns but the two barrows to the south were more productive. In 1901–2, they yielded pits with flint flakes, burnt bone, bits of bronze and fragments of a human skull.

TDA 35, 1903, 142; Worth, 1967, 182–3, *Plan*

54 STALL MOOR, Dartmoor (3)
Lat: 50°.5   SX 635 644
3¹/₂ miles NE of Cornwood. Start from Harford, SX 638 595. Long 3 mile walk, Slopes, valleys, streams. Rewarding. Map G

Deep in the moor this ring merits a visit both for the achievement of reaching it and because of the variety of monuments passed on the way.

At Harford go west over the bridge of the River Erme and turn north (Rt) along a sometimes muddy footpath for half a mile to Tristis Rock. Just to the west on Burford Down is a single row, 1650ft (503m) long, N-S, with a wrecked stone circle at its southern end. From there the line of pillars at Staldon is another mile past pounds and hut-circles, up slopes to a single row, 1643ft (501m) formed of the tallest stones on Dartmoor.

A further mile and a quarter north is the stone circle known as The Dancers or Kiss-In-The-Ring. It overlooks the west bank of the Erme. Around the remnants of a cairn the circle, 54ft (16.5m) across, has twenty-six stones between 2ft 6ins to 3ft (0.8–1m) high but with one much taller, 5ft 4ins (1.6m) high, at its NNW.

The pillar is not in line with an incredible row attached to the ring from the north, its other end terminating at a small barrow on Green Hill. Between it and the circle are two and a quarter miles of small, determined stones. In 1879 the Rev. William Collings Lukis declared the line to be 11,239ft 8ins (3425.89m) long! R.H. Worth amended this to 11,150ft (3399m), but subtracted nothing from the fanaticism that created such a prehistoric maverick. The row wanders minilithically. It drops to the Erme, uneasily climbs Green Hill and becomes a staccato of gaps and groups veering from NNW to north before stopping at an isolated stone about 200ft (60m) south of a tiny, savaged barrow whose cist and kerbstones lie in tumbled disorder around it.

It is possible that the 'row' is a multi-phase structure, its southern end leading to the circle, its western to the barrow, the gap between them across the low, wet reaches of the Erme being an improvised afterthought.

Worth, 1967, 204–5; Butler, 1993, 74–7, *Plan*; Burl, 1993, 94–6

55 TROWLESWORTHY WARREN, E, W, Dartmoor (3) [S2/5]

Lat: 50°.5   SX 577 640
4 miles SE of Yelverton. 1 mile SE of Cadover Bridge. Drive SE down quarry road to car-park at SX 568 632. Walk. 1/2 mile NNE. Easy. Map G
Because of the deliberate introduction of rabbits in the thirteenth-century AD – hence the 'Warren' – many of the pounds and hut-circles at Trowlesworthy Warren are in poor condition. The ground was further disturbed by the digging out of a leat, a canal-like flume of water, to drive the wheel of the Lee Moor china clay works a mile to the south.

A. *East ring* Despite this the 22ft 4ins (6.8m) circle, 'The Pulpit', of eight stones, 2ft 3ins to 4ft 2ins (0.7–1.3m) high, still stands as does the 426ft (130m) of its 4ft 6ins (1.4m) wide avenue which marches up the slope to it from the south. Although slightly damaged by labourers in 1859 who removed some stones and blasted others before being stopped by the Rev. Coppard of Plympton and despite being interrupted by the deep, fast-flowing leat it is a good ring. The tallest stone stands where the avenue joins the circle. It is set radially to the circumference like one side of an embryonic entrance.

B. *West ring* 350ft (107m) to the west, via a slab across the leat, is a once-double but now single stone row, ENE-WSW, 254ft (77.4m) long with a fragmentary stone circle at its end. To the north on the gentle hillsides are the walls of eight pounds, two conjoined, with hut-circles still noticeable in them.

Worth, 138–9, 209, *Plan*; Burl, 1993, 52–4, 229, 233

56 WHITE MOOR DOWN, Dartmoor (2)

Lat: 50°.7   SX 634 896
3¼ miles SSW of South Zeal. Walk. Either approach as for Cosdon. Steep, sometimes unpleasant climb. 2¼ mile walk. Or carpark, SX 661 877. 2¼ mile walk NW. Difficult. Map G
This little-known but fascinating site is

recommended to the enthusiast. It stands in a saddle about ¼ mile south of Little Hound Tor. But from whichever direction it is approached, take care over the morass of Raybarrow Pool, ½ mile long, ¼ mile wide, SX 640 905 to SX 638 894, a nuisance in dry weather, positively dangerous in wet, 'an extensive mire', wrote William Crossing, a veteran of Dartmoor, 'one of the worst in the moorland region'.

The ring is one of Dartmoor's great circles, 66ft (20m) across, of eighteen impressive stones, sixteen erect, one leaning, one fallen. There was a probable nineteen, the pit of the missing one still visible at the east. By the late nineteenth century the ring was badly damaged, robbed by stonemasons, plundered by farmers for gateposts, its surface stripped by turfcutters. Three stones were reduced to stumps. Only one stone remained standing.

The site was reconstructed in 1896 and is a megalithic splendour. Its gruff stones average about 3ft (1m) in height but there are two much bigger opposite each other, the north, 4ft 2ins (1.3m) high and south, 4ft 5ins (1.4m), the former a broad, sharp-topped slab, the latter a higher, thinner, flat-topped pillar.

There is a wider gap at the north-west but no stonehole was discovered during the reconstruction and the space may be an original entrance facing the direction of the modern trackway.

An outlying stone leans 520ft (159m) to the south-east. Although 'playing-card' in shape, its longer sides are not aligned on the circle. Standing as it does close to the South Tawton-Throwleigh boundary its function is debateable. To the writer it appears to be a marker stone that acted as a guide to the ring itself.

White Moor Down is the most northerly of a line of great stone circles on north-eastern Dartmoor: Butterdon (39); Scorhill (50); Fernworthy (44); extending to the Grey Wethers (45) four miles to the south, a distribution

suggesting the existence of former territories some one to two miles across. In his study of Bronze Age reaves Andrew Fleming speculated that one land-holding may have been bounded by the Taw and Whitemoor Marshes. It is the area of the pre-existing stone circle.

TDA 28, 1896, 181–2; *ibid* 29, 147–8; Butler, 1991, 203–4 'Little Hound Tor', *Plan*

57 YELLOWMEAD, Dartmoor (2)
Lat: 50°.5   SX 575 678
3 miles E of Yelverton. ³/₄ NE of Sheepstor. Walk. From SX 580 673 ¹/₂ mile NW. Easy. Map G
This is one of several multiple rings on Dartmoor, Shovel Down (52), thirteen miles to the NNE, being another. Once almost lost in peat, its stones displaced and fallen, Yellowmead was discovered during a prolonged drought in 1921 when the heather was burned off. It was dug out and re-erected in the autumn of that year by the Dartmoor Preservation Society employing farmworkers under the direction of the Rev. H. Breton.

It is one of the many megalithic puzzles of prehistory. None of its four rings is concentric with another and only the innermost is a true circle. It may therefore be a monument of several phases.

A. *The outer ring (D)* an ellipse 66ft 2ins SSW-NNE by 63ft (20.2 × 19.2m), has twenty-four stones surviving of a possible thirty-seven. They are heavy slabs on edge, the biggest, at the south-east, 4ft 3ins high and 5ft 6ins long (1.3 × 1.7m). The ring is incomplete with a great gap at the north-east where stones were robbed for a wall to the north and a bridge to the north-west.

B. *The second ring (C)* an ellipse with a centre 3ft (90cm) west of D's, measures 50ft 6ins SSE-NNW by 46ft 4ins (15.4 × 14.1m) has kept twenty-eight of its probable forty-two stones, smaller than those of D and very regularly set at east and south.

C. *The third ring (B)* is also an ellipse

but with a centre 2ft (60cm) west of C's. 39ft 6ins N-S by 37ft 2ins (12 × 11.3m) it has thirty-one of approximately forty-two stones on its circumference.

D. Within it is *ring A*, a circle 21ft 10ins (6.7m) in diameter, with a centre identical to that of C making it likely that they rings were contemporary. The stones of A are virtually contiguous, thick, ponderous kerbs for the cairn that once filled it.

This strange site, visually attractive, has a possible avenue, short and aligned not to the centre of the circle but towards its eastern side. An adjacent arc of three low stones, however, and two other slabs at the southern edge of the ring suggests that the Yellowmead 'avenue' may instead be the first stages of a complex of multiple rows. This is made likely by the comments of the discoverers of several other multiple rings that such sites are linked with internal cairns and strongly associated with stone rows. They are 'a distinct sub-group of Dartmoor prehistoric

cairns'. Visit one.

H.H. Breton, *The Forest of Dartmoor*, II (1932), 55–9; Worth, 1967, 188–9, *Plan*; *PDAS 44*, 1986, 166–70

DORSET
The rings here are small, plain and mostly damaged

58 HAMPTON DOWN, Portesham (5) [S4/3] Lat: 50°.7   SY 596 865
1¹/₂ miles NE of Abbotsbury, ¹/₂ mile NW of Portesham. Just S of a minor lane. Walk. From SY 601 869 a by-lane leads SW. The ring is 700 yds (640m) on the S side. No distance. Map 3
From its position on a hillside this disturbed and perplexing site offers a splendid view of the sea to the south. But far from being an orthodox stone circle it has been a megalithic chameleon. In 1939 sixteen stones were recorded, the same as shown in a photograph of 1908. But by 1964 there were twenty-eight.

Stukeley's sketch of the Nine Stones, Winterbourne Abbas, Dorset (59). It shows the ring more completely than is possible today.

A Celtic Temple at Winterburn 22. Aug. 1723.
10. *stones of a very hard sort full of flints, the tallest to W. 8 f h. the N. 7 broad 6 high.*

Excavation the following year produced more problems, not the least being that the stones were in the wrong place. Originally they had stood to the west but had been moved to make way for a banked hedge. The ring, if it had been that, never had sixteen or twenty-eight stones but no more than eight or nine in an ellipse about 20ft SE-NW by 19ft (6.1 × 5.8m). The stones at the north and south had been set in individual holes whereas those at east and west had stood in stretches of V-shaped ditches. Whether in holes or ditches all were close-set.

A narrow trackway, 4ft (1.2m) wide had approached this setting from the north. Such avenues are known to lead to round barrows at Poole some twenty miles to the east and it may be that the Hampton Down 'stone circle' was in reality the disrupted kerbstones of a similar burial-place.

Ant 13, 1939, 152; *PDNHAS 88*, 1967, 122–7, *Plan*

59 NINE STONES, Winterbourne Abbas
(1) [S4/1] Lat: 50°.7   SY 611 904
5 miles w of Dorchester and immediately s of the A35. No walk. Map 3
This petite ring should be a delight to see. Instead, it is a frustration. Hard against the road it huddles among obstructive trees that are so many and so near that photography is difficult and concentration still more so.

It is a small ellipse about 30ft N-S by 25ft 6ins (9.1 × 7.8m) of stones grossly disproportionate in height. Of them seven are less than 3ft (90cm) high but at the north-west are two monsters, a thin pointed pillar at the WSW 7ft (2.1m) high, its partner 11ft (3.4m) to the north-west a 6ft high by 6ft broad (1.8m square) smooth-topped slab. Conjunctions of stones different in height and shape are becoming commonly recognised as intentionally chosen, perhaps as a form of sexual symbolism. The lowest stones of the ring are opposite the pair. John Aubrey vividly described the mineralogy as 'petrified clumps of Flints'. Until the

nineteenth century there may have a little stone between the two pillars.

Aubrey mentioned the existence of a second circle where 'in this road, halfe a mile farther westwards, stand three stones . . . fower foot hight'. They have gone.

The best intepretation of the distorted Nine Stones is that it is of south-west Scottish influence. There, rings such as the Loupin' Stanes, Dumfriess-shire (142), and Ninestane Rigg (221) and Burgh Hill (219) in Roxburghshire, share the feature of having two much taller stones on their perimeters. Emphasising the likelihood of such a far-flung connection there is a 'south-west Scottish' chambered tomb of Clyde-Solway tradition at the Grey Mare and Her Colts, SY 583 871 only 2½ miles south-west of the Nine Stones. The collapsed chamber and standing stones of its typically crescentic forecourt survive in overgrown confusion.

Aubrey, I, 106–7; TTB, 118, *Plan*

LANCASHIRE
The rings, particularly in the Pennines, are small, embanked, and frequently contain cremation cairns

60 BLEABERRY HAWS, Torver (3)
Lat: 54°.3   SD 264 946
3 miles sw of Coniston, 1¼ w of Torver. Walk. Steep slopes and valleys. Best found by walking about 220 yards (200m) sw of a prominent cairn on the hilltop. Hard going. Map D
This tiny ring, one of the smallest of many in the Bronze Age Pennines, lies at 1060ft (323m) O.D. close to the ramparts of a camp. About 17ft NE-SW by 13ft (5.2 × 4m) its seven small stones enclose a cobbled area that may once have covered a burial. Such funerary 'paving' is common to many of the late rings in the north-west.

Arch 53, 1893, 419; Waterhouse, 39–41, *Plan*

61 CHEETHAM CLOSE, Chapeltown (3, 4)
Lat: 53°.6   SD 716 159

4³/₄ miles wsw of Ramsbottom, 1¹/₄ w of Chapeltown. Walk. There is a curious approach from Turton Towers Museum, SD 732 151, through a coal-depot, across a railway line and a ³/₄ mile walk NW uphill across Turton Moor. Fair. Map 3

Near the hilltop are two unobtrusive rings, both almost demolished, within 60ft (18m) of each other. The south-west, a version of a ring-cairn, 72ft (22m) in diameter, was enclosed in a 4ft (1.2m) wall of closely-set little stones within whose rubble-laid central space was a small circular cairn. The site is severely damaged.

To its north-east is a true stone circle, 50ft (15.2m) across. Once of seven stones from 1ft to 4ft 8ins (0.3 – 1.4m) high, the tallest at the south-east, the ring has an outlier 115ft (35m) to the south-east, silhouetted against the hillcrest. A second peeps 82ft (25m) to the ssw. There are magnificent views from the WNW.

Before 1893 a tenant farmer deliberately smashed some of the stones of this 'Druidical circle' to discourage trespassers. Fortunately a fair plan of the settings had already been made in 1871.

TLCAS. 12, 1894, 42–51, Plan

62 DRUID'S TEMPLE, Birkrigg Common (1) [L5/1] Lat: 54°.2   SD 292 739
2¹/₂ miles s of Ulverston, 1 mile w of Morecambe Bay. Turn w from A 5087 at SD 296 737. ¹/₄ mile, circle visible on heath to N. No walk. Map D

Summer is the worst time to visit this interesting concentric ring because bracken conceals much of the outer circle.

The stones of local limestone, probably from an outcrop just to the NNW, are low, the least conspicuous being those of the spacious outer circle which is about 87ft (26.5m) in diameter. Shrunken inside it the inner ring is only 27ft 8ins (8.4m) across but has two taller stones 4ft (1.2m) high at the south-west and another at the north.

Excavations in 1911 and again in

1921 showed that the rings stood on a rough, cobbled platform. Characteristically, the inner ring contained burials. Under a layer of blueish stones brought in from some distance away were five cremations in a pit, one of them, thought to be of a man, in a small collared urn, 6ins (15cm) high, its deep collar neatly impressed with a lattice pattern of whipped cord. The urn is in Carlisle Museum.

Other finds included a lump of red ochre, perhaps for body-painting as part of the funerary rites, a sandstone disc of a kind often found with burials, a stone knife and a grain-rubber. Such objects reveal the site's affinities with other sepulchral circles in the region such as Oddendale (81) and Gunnerkeld (79).

But, demonstrating links with Lake District traditions such as the sightline at Swinside (26) earlier than those Bronze Age rings, the taller triangular-topped stone of the south-western pair at the Druid's Temple stood in line with the midwinter sunset. It is a use of the side of an entrance to define a celestial event already noticed at great Neolithic rings such as Long Meg (25).

TCWAAS 12, 1912, 262–74; ibid 22, 1922, 346–52; Waterhouse, 35–8, Plan

63 MOSLEY HEIGHT, Worsthorne Moor (3) Lat: 53°.8   SD 881 302
3 miles SE of Burnley, ¹/₂ mile NE of Walk Mill. Walk. ¹/₄ mile E of road from Mere Clough to Hebden Bridge. Fair. Map 3

A. Lying only about 100 yards (90m) from the Long Causeway, possibly a Bronze Age trackway, this broken ring of eighteen stones standing in a low bank 42ft (12.8m) across enclosed a paved area of stones and cobbles.

Excavations in 1950 uncovered three small pits just inside the perimeter of the bank. They contained an assortment of domestic equipment: grain rubbers, broken querns, stone hammers, a stone pestle, flint scrapers and arrowheads and, significantly, two funerary sandstone discs like that at the Druid's

Temple (62) forty-four miles north-west across Morecambe Bay. The finds may have been the possessions of the people buried at the centre of this embanked stone circle.

Near its middle was an irregular line of four rough cists in which there were cremations with upright and inverted Bronze Age Pennine urns and what may have been a food-vessel. The primary cremation in a cist surrounded by small stones seemed to be that of a woman. The urns are now in Towneley Hall Museum, Burnley.

B. Five miles to the south-east is the Blackheath, Todmorden ring-cairn at SD 945 255. The bank, 3ft high and 90ft across (1 × 27.4m), is still visible. An excavation in 1898 found cremations and urns.

TLCAS. 62, 1950–1, 204–8, Plan

NORTHUMBERLAND
The rings are a cosmopolitan collection of influences from the Lake District, Scotland and the Pennines. Everything from great circles to tiny Four-Posters

64 DUDDO FIVE STONES, Felkington (2?, 3) [L3/1] Lat: 55°.7   NT 931 437
7 miles SW of Berwick, ¹/₄ mile NNW of Duddo village. Walk. At NT 939 426 a lane and footpath go N for ¹/₄ mile to copse. Turn NW for 700 yds (640m). Fair. Map 1

Standing on at the top of a large knoll near the River Tweed this small ring, 32ft (9.8m) in diameter, consists of five heavy, weatherworn stones deeply runnelled by rain. All of coarse local sandstone they stand up to 7ft 6ins (2.3m) high. Of the present stones the ENE was re-erected after 1903 explaining why the circle was known as the 'Four Stones' in the nineteenth century. The site is conspicuous and the stones stand sharply against the skyline.

It is almost certain that several other stones had fallen and been set upright. They do not stand circumferentially as is customary but are at eccentric angles to the perimeter of the ring. Low stones between them are unlikely to be original. All move if gently pushed.

About 1890 a somewhat undisciplined dig found two stoneholes

Duddo Five Stones, Northumberland (64), from the south.

in a gap at the north-west. There was a wide central pit with 'much charcoal and bone'. No trace was discovered of a reputed outer ring.

TBFC. 28, 1932, 84–6; TTB, 66, Plan

65 GOATSTONES, Bellingham (1)

Lat: 55°.1   NY 829 748
9 miles NW of Hexham, 5¼ miles S of Bellingham. Walk. At NY 832 751 take track S by Ravensheugh Crags. Ring is ¼ mile. Easy. Map 1
This is the southernmost of a pair of 'Scottish' Four-Posters in Northumberland, the other being the Three Kings (69) sixteen miles to the north.

The four plump stones were erected on a spur by Ravensheugh Crags from which there are long views. Three stand with one fallen at the south. None is more than about 2ft (0.7m) high. Although they are placed at the corners of a fairly good rectangle, like other Four-Posters the stones were arranged around the circumference of a true circle, in this case one with a diameter of 17ft 2ins (5.2m). The interior is slightly domed, suggesting it contains a low cairn.

On the top of the ENE stone are sixteen well-preserved cupmarks.

There is no record of an excavation but the centre has been disturbed since 1930 when there were 'no signs that any sacrilegious hand has ever disturbed the bones of the dead man who was honoured with this simple monument.'

The name of Goatstones may be a corruption of *gyet-stanes*, 'wayside stones', the ring standing close to an old droveway.

PSAN 5, 1932, 304–6; Burl, 1988, 66–7, Plan

66 HETHPOOL, College Burn Valley (3, 4, 5)

Lat: 55°.6   NT 892 278
6½ miles W of Wooler, ½ mile SW of Hethpool. Walk. At S end of Hethpool village footpath leads S for ¼ mile. Easy. Map 1
This is a problematical site. Its stones

lie on a low knoll between a steep fall to a burn on the east and a steepish hillside to the west. All the blocks are fallen except for one at the south that leans. Eight stones measure between 5ft 6ins and 6ft 6ins (1.7, 2m) in length. There are others, half-buried, to the north-east.

In 1935 the setting was interpreted as a vast horseshoe with a long axis 200ft (61m) from open end to its north-eastern head and with a narrow straight base 90ft (27.4m) across.

The ground has been so disturbed by ploughing that nothing can be certain, but a survey by Peter Topping indicates that there may have been two rings here, a northern so damaged that no dimensions can be recovered and a southern, 70 yards (64m) away, measuring about 200ft E-W by 140ft (61 × 42.7m).

This would be one of the largest rings in northern Britain. It is interesting, therefore, that it is only four miles west of the group of Milfield henges.

PSAN 6, 1935, 116–17; Northern Archaeology 2 (2), 1981, 3–10, Plan

67 ILDERTON, Threestone Burn (3) [L3/4]

Lat: 55°.5   NT 971 205
5 miles SSW of Wooler, near nowhere. Walk. To reach this remote ring take car to NU 012 196 where the lane remains driveable for the steady-nerved. Abandon car after 1¼ miles W. Then a walk of 1½ miles WNW. The site is almost worth the effort. Fair. Map 1
Of its thirteen remaining stones five stand – with ominously hollowed bases – in a spacious ring 118ft E-W by 96ft (36 × 29.3m). Ranging from 1ft 9ins to 5ft 6ins in height at the north (0.5–1.7m) there is a hefty block at the south-west. A report of 1862 recorded that digging had unearthed charcoal inside the ring.

The site itself is odd, with a fall of some 8ft (2.4m) from north to south.

TBFC 4, 1856–62, 450–3; TTB, 68, Plan

68 SIMONBURN, Haughton Common (3)
Lat: 55°.0   NY 802 712
5 miles NW of Haydon Bridge. At NY
813 699 follow track across line of
Hadrian's Wall. At NY 811 711 track
swings N. Walk. WNW for 1/2 mile. Only
fair. Map 1
Less than three miles SSW of the
Goatstones 65 and 1 1/2 miles north of
the course of Hadrian's Wall, the
overgrown stones lie on moorland at
the top of a steepish scarp that drops
northwards down to the tree-lined
Halleypike lough. Experience warns
that cars can become bogged down in
the wet ground before reaching the
ring.

Eleven stones are just visible here on
a shallow platform that may have been
artificially levelled. A survey by Martin
Taylor produced a plan of a ring 29ft
3ins WSW-ENE by 25ft 7ins (8.9 ×
7.8m). Two of the tallest, some 4ft
(1.2m) high at the south-west may have
acted as portals.

There are possible hut-circles a
hundred yards (90m) to the east.

O.S. Southampton, *Plan*

69 THREE KINGS, Kielder Forest (3)
Lat: 55°.3   NT 774 009
4 miles NW of Rochester and
Bremenium Roman fort. 8 miles NW of
Otterburn battlefield, 1388. 1/2 mile W
of the A68 across the River Rede.
Walk. From A68, at NT 782 014,
follow winding track across river, Map
essential. Ring in trees, 1 mile.
Concentrate. Map 1
On a hillside in Forestry Commission
land overlooking a valley to the east
three stones and one fallen are the
weathered remains of a second Four-
Poster in Northumberland (see
Goatstones, 65). Known as the 'Three
Kings of Denmark' the four were set up
on the circumference of a circle 14ft
4ins (4.4m) in diameter. The tallest
stands 4ft 8ins (1.4m) high at the SSW.
From the depth of its hole the long,
fallen stone at the ESE, now 7ft 6ins
(2.3m) long, would have stood about
4ft 6ins (1.4m) high. Excavated by the
writer in 1971, a central, ruined cairn

covered a ransacked pit, in which a
solitary flint scraper survived.

The name comes from the belief that
the stones marked the graves of kings
killed in some forgotten battle. Eleven
miles to the east is the Five Kings stone
row, (NT 955 015), presumably other
slaughtered royalty.

The Three Kings Four-Poster is a
Bronze Age burial-place. 'The men who
raised the stones have utterly vanished,
even their ghosts have gone . . . Great
hunters they were, and nature-
worshippers, the star circles they made
we have, and here and there on the
moorlands their confused forts and
villages . . . These stone fingers . . . have
a significance we shall never be able to
understand, and a forgotten message we
shall never read.' The present writer is
as romantically-minded but not so
despondent.

PSAN 5, 1911–12, 234–7; *Arch Ael*
50, 1972, 1–14; Burl, 1988, 68–9, *Plan*

OXFORDSHIRE
One splendid 'Cumbrian' circle. Late
Neolithic

70 ROLLRIGHT STONES, Chipping Norton
(1) [S6/1] Lat: 52°.0   SP 296 309
2 1/2 miles NNW of Chipping Norton. 1 3/4
W of Great Rollright, immediately to S
of lane to Little Rollright. Entrance
Fee. Easy. Map 3
The evocative stone circle of the
Rollright Stones stands on a prehistoric
trackway at the edge of a ridge falling
steeply to the north. The perfect circle
is 104ft (31.7m) in diameter. Its
weathered stones of local oolitic
limestone were vividly described by
Stukeley as 'corroded like worm-eaten
wood, by the harsh jaws of time.' The
name derives from *Hrolla-landriht*, 'the
land of Hrolla'.

Until recently it was believed that the
circle consisted of no more than
twenty-two stones, well-spaced 15ft
(4.6m) apart, pieces between them
being fragments broken from their tops.
It is now known that originally there
were some eighty pillars, virtually
shoulder to shoulder except at the

Three Kings Four-Poster, Northumberland (69), from the north. The author's excavation of 1971.

south-east where there is an entrance. The weathered bank in which the stones stand is broken here.

Across the lane, 230ft (70m) NNE of the ring, is a distorted outlier, the King Stone, 8ft 2ins (2.5m) high. Its east side was hacked into by nineteenth-century Welsh drovers who believed chippings from it would act as amulets.

Excavations in the 1980s indicated that the pillar could have been a marker stone for a prehistoric burial mound. A round cairn, 56ft (17m) across, was discovered just to the NNW of the stone. Radiocarbon assays of 1420 ± 40 bc (BM-2427), and 1540 ± 70 bc (BM-2430), about 1800 BC, are of Early Bronze Age date. A small round barrow to the west of the King Stone, covering an infant's cremated bones and a collared urn, gave comparable 'dates' of 1370 ± 90 bc (BM-2429) and 1530 ± 50 bc (BM-2428), about 1770 BC. If the King Stone was erected even some centuries before this, it might have been later than the erection of the circle by as much as a thousand years. Equally, however, it may have become the focus

for later burials, having originally been set up as a outlier to guide wayfarers to the ring.

The skeleton of a megalithic tomb, the Whispering Knights, rises bleakly 380 yards (348m) ESE of the Rollright Stones. The rectangular ruin of five large slabs is the denuded chamber of a portal dolmen facing south-eastwards down a gradual slope. A 'portion of a human left cheekbone' was discovered inside the setting.

In the stone circle the entrance at the south-east is formed by two outlying portals, one now fallen. As with other stone circles with a pair of external stones, such as the Cumbrian rings of Swinside (26) and Long Meg and Her Daughters (25), the builders created an unequivocal astronomical sightline through the use of a pair of stones forming one side of the entrance, here the two on its north. At this latitude with an azimuth of 142.5° and a horizon of −0°.03 the declination is −29°.3, very close to the major rising of the southern moon at midsummer.

In its size, shape, closely-set stones and 'astronomical' entrance the

Rollright Stones is a Midlands counterpart of stone circles in the Lake District such as Swinside, and one of its functions may have been to act as a depot from which Cumbrian stone axes were exchanged.

There is indirect confirmation of its early date. About nineteen miles to the SSW the once-great circle-henge of the Devil's Quoits, SP 411 048, has been robbed, wrecked and vandalised. Assays from the ditch of 2060 ± 120 bc (HAR-1887) and 1640 ± 70 bc (HAR-1888) suggest occupation from late in the Neolithic to well into Early Bronze Age times, perhaps from as early as 3000 BC to as late as 1800 BC. Discovery of Late Neolithic grooved ware in a posthole fits well with this time-span.

Many legends are attached to the Rollright Stones. A king and his army were turned to stone after a witch had tricked them. The Whispering Knights, traitors, were similarly petrified. Witches also prevented anyone form counting the stones.

Nothing has been discovered inside the circle. John Aubrey wrote that 'Ralph Sheldon, of Beoley Esq, my honoured Friend, told me, he was at some charge to digge within this Circle, to try if he could find any Bones: but he was sure that no body was buried there: but had he digged without the circle, and neer to it; it is not unlikely he mought have found bones there.' Sheldon seems not to have done so.

Long Compton, down the hill, was a stronghold of witches. When a miller from the village dragged a stone from the circle to dam a stream for his waterwheel, every night the water drained away. Although it had taken three horses to drag the stone down the hill it took only one to return it. The resentful and fearful miller believed that malicious witches in the village had cast a spell on it.

T.H. Ravenhill, *The Rollright Stones and the Men who Erected Them*, Birmingham, 1932; G. Lambrick, *The Rollright Stones*, London, 1988, *Plan*

SHROPSHIRE
Two open rings near Corndon. Probably Early Bronze Age

71 HOARSTONES, Shelve (3) [D2/2. Black Marsh] Lat: 52°.6   SO 324 999
7 miles N of Bishop's Castle, 1 mile NW of Shelve. Walk. 250 yds (230m) W of lane from Black Marsh. Easy. Map 3
Overlooked to the east by the long quartzite ridge of the Stiperstones with its grotesquely weathered crags, the highest known as the Chair in which the Devil sits for shelter during storms and blizzards, the ring, also known variously as Black Marsh, Hemford and Marsh Pool lies in flat and sometimes wet ground.

Somewhat elliptical it measures 76ft 6ins N-S by 69ft 2ins (23.3 × 21.1m), but, despite its above average size, its stones are small. They are local dolerites probably from Stapeley Hill nearby. Just south of the ring's centre is a stone about 3ft (1m) high, but its prehistoric ancestry is questionable. A gap at the east may be a original entrance.

Thin, tubular holes can be found in some of the stones. They are the results of wedding celebrations when miners would drill into the boulders and fill them with gunpowder. The explosions caused accidents but, by report, no fatalities.

TSANHS 10, 1926, 247–53; TTB, 26, Plan

72 MITCHELL'S FOLD, Corndon (3, 4) [D2/1] Lat: 52°.6   SO 305 983
6 miles N of Bishop's Castle, 1 mile N of Corndon Hill. Where lane to Priestweston turns sharply N then W at SO 302 977 drive N up track for 500 yds (450m). Walk. N for 300 yds (270m). Easy. Map 3
At a height of 1083ft (330m) O.D. this ring stands in dry heathland at the south-west end of Stapeley Hill within a few miles of the Late Neolithic-Early Bronze Age picrite stone axe factory of Cwm-Mawr. It is only 1½ miles south-west of Hoarstones stone circle (71). The name may derive from 'micel' or

'mycel', O.E. for 'big', referring to the size of this large circle.

Its doleritic stones came from Stapeley Hill. Many of them are now missing and others are fallen. In the beginning there may have been some thirty pillars. The survivors that stand range in height from 10ins to 6ft 3ins (0.3 – 1.9m), and stand in an ellipse 89ft NW-SE by 82ft (27.1 × 25m). The tallest is at the south-east end of the major axis, standing, perhaps by coincidence, close to the line of the major southern moonrise. This pillar and a companion have been taken to flank an entrance about 6ft (1.8m) wide. About 77 yards (70m) to the south-east is a weathered cubical block on a small cairn.

There was a claim for a central stone and a very dubious eighteenth-century report that 'there was a stone across your two Portals, like those at Stonehenge, and that the stone at eighty yards distance was the altar.' The probability of a trilithon, otherwise unique to Stonehenge, at Mitchell's Fold, like an identical claim for Kerzerho in Brittany, should be regarded as rumour rather than reality.

An intriguing fact does exist however. Aerial photographs have revealed mediaeval ridge-and-furrow ploughmarks not only running up to the ring but also through it as though this 'prehistoric' megalithic ring might postdate the Middle Ages! It does not.

A third stone circle, the Whetstones, was less than half a mile to the east, SO 305 976, but nearly all its stones were blown up in the 1860s. Now there is only a collapse of stones. When the last stone was uprooted around 1870 charcoal and bones were seen in its hole.

Huddling as they do around the axe-factory it is likely that all three rings were connected with the distribution of Early Bronze Age perforated shafthole axes, many of which have discovered in Wessex. They may have been exchanged for flint, which is not indigenous to Shropshire, but which is prevalent in Wiltshire.

Legend says that the circle was used by a giant whose cow gave unceasing milk until tricked by a witch who used a sieve to drain the animal dry. The cow fled to Warwickshire where it became the Dun Cow. The witch,

Mitchell's Fold, Shropshire (72), from the south-east showing a vandalised stone in the foreground, toppled in June 1994.

deservedly, was turned to stone. What became of the milkless giant is not known.

The nineteenth-century Middleton-in-Chirbury church a mile to the west of the ring has a carving of the cow legend on the capital of a column on the north side of the nave. The font, benches and choir-stalls also are carved with flowers, dragons, animals, bonneted women, grim men, laughing men and men in medieval caps. They are the work of a former parson, Waldegrave Brewster.

Grimes, 1963, 125–7; TTB, 24, *Plan*

SOMERSET

A strange mixture in age and plan. An enigmatic site, two ruinous rings, probably Early Bronze Age, and a Late Neolithic triumph ·

73 ALMSWORTHY, Almsworthy Common, Exmoor (5)
Lat: 51°.2   SS 844 417
4¼ miles sw of Porlock, 2¼ miles NNW of Exford. Walk. From the unfenced road at SS 848 417 less than ½ mile w. Easy. Map 3
Speculatively named 'Stone Circle' on the Ordnance Survey map. When the conglomeration of poky stones on the common was discovered in 1931 after heather-burning it was interpreted as three damaged ovals, one inside the other, measuring 129ft by 94ft (39.3 × 28.7m). This was probably mistaken. There is little conformity to an ellipse in the disposition of the fourteen blotchy-red sandstones and the site, lying near an elaborate field-system, has been re-identified as the wreckage of six stone rows.

An eye of faith is needed to see either a ring or a set of rows. One observable fact is that the tallest stone, a sharp-cornered, flat-topped cube, no more than 1ft 10ins (56cm) high, stands at right-angles like a blocking-stone at the ESE lower end of the longest 'line'. But others on this quiet slope twist in a confusion of directions unlike most other rows. The eccentric disposition, however, may be the result of soil

slipping down the slope and moving the little, slight stones.

PSNHAS 77, 1931, 78–82, *Plan*; Burl, 1993, 118, 121, 241

74 PORLOCK, Exmoor (3)
Lat: 51°.2   SS 844 447
2¼ miles sw of Porlock. 1 mile s of the A39 immediately to the w (Rt) of the lane going s to Exford. Easy. Map 3
This once-fine circle, 80ft (24.4m) in diameter, has been persistently despoiled since the beginning of this century. In 1928 ten of its twenty-one stones were erect, the survivors of a possible forty to forty-five uprights. Today there are fourteen, five of them standing. Expectedly for Exmoor, except for a prostrate block at the SSE, 6ft 3ins by 2ft 2ins (1.9 × 0.7m), all the stones are small, no more than 2ft 7ins to 3ft 3ins (0.8–1m) in height. 83ft (25.3m) to the north-east is a low circular mound. A little stone used to stand at its north-west edge.

PSNHAS 74, 1928–9, 71–7, *Plan*

75 STANTON DREW, Chew Magna (3)
[S3/1] Lat: 51°.4   ST 601 631
6 miles S of Bristol. Circles. Open to the public. Honesty box at the entrance. Signpost in village. By church. Easy. Cove is s of the Druid's Inn. Easy. No charge. Map 3
This is one of the wonders, and perplexities, of megalithic Britain, a marvel of landscaping that included a gigantic central ring with two large rings to north-east and ssw of it, two avenues, a Cove and an outlier.

The stone circles, on a singularly bent NE-SSW axis, stand by the River Chew. Their unworked stones are mostly pustular breccia but some are of oolitic limestone perhaps from Dundry Hill four miles to the north-west. The two outer rings have been called ellipses but Dymond's surveys of 1872 and 1894 showed them to be true circles. They are not evenly spaced. The north-east ring and Great Circle are 145ft (44.2m) apart but 450ft (137.2m) separates the ssw from the Great Circle.

A. *The north-east ring*, 97ft (29.6m)

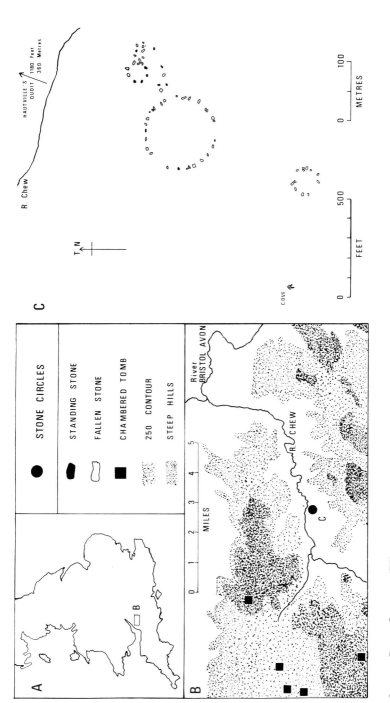

Stanton Drew, Somerset (75)

Stanton Drew, Somerset (75), the north-east ring from the east. The leaning stone on the right is part of the avenue.

in diameter, once had eight massive stones, up to 9ft 8ins (3m) high and weighing fifteen tons or more, the biggest of the entire complex.

B. *The Great Circle*, 368ft (112.2m) across, of some thirty-six smaller stones, is the largest of all rings after Avebury's Outer Circle.

C. *The ssw ring*, 145ft (44.2m) across, badly ruined and on higher ground, once had twelve stones. The numbers eight, twelve and thirty-six may be evidence of a society using an elementary counting-base of four.

Had the builders used a unit of measurement a little over 3ft (92cm) long, a pace, there would have been thirty-two units in the diameter of the north-east ring and forty-eight in the ssw, both of them multiples of four. But Dymond's diameter of 368ft (112.2m) for the Great Circle produced 122 units, maybe an intended 120 by careless planners, or an error by Dymond, or simply a revelation that the unit never existed. Thom, unsure of the size of the damaged ring, offered a tentative 372ft 3ins (113.5m), 122.9 units, quite close to 124. In 1740 John

Wood, the Bath architect, recorded 378ft (115.2m), 124.8 units; so did Philip Crocker, Hoare's surveyor, in 1826. An 'in-between' 376ft (114.6m) would fit 124 units exactly, a number again a multiple of four.

Two wrecked avenues extend eastwards towards the river from the north-east ring and the Great Circle. Seven stones survive of four pairs in the north-east avenue, 34ft (10.4m) wide and about 96ft (29.3m) long. The remains of a second avenue extend ENE from the Great Circle, 161ft long and 34ft wide (49 × 10.4m). The avenues, if continued, would have joined 330ft (100m) from the Great Circle.

D. *The Cove*, a three-sided unroofed setting open to the south-east, of two sideslabs and a backstone, is behind St Mary's church 988ft (300m) south-west of the Great Circle. Inevitably, it stands against the Druid's Inn. Its sideslabs stand 10ft (3m) apart, the west stone 10ft 3ins (3.1m) high. Its counterpart is only 4ft 6ins tall (1.4m), a squarish fragment broken from the bottom corner of its partner. The backstone, 14ft 6ins long and 8ft 8ins wide (4.4 ×

2.6m) has fallen outwards. It has a natural cleavage through it, identical in outline to the shapes of the two sideslabs, and the three may once have been one enormous, naturally fracturing block.

Unlike the stones of the circles the Cove is formed of dolomitic breccia suggesting that it had a different origin and may be of an earlier date from the rings. With a bearing of about 147°, looking towards a gentle rise, this imitation of a Neolithic megalithic chamber may have been planned to face the most southerly moonrise.

E. *The Outlier* On a high ridge 1856ft (566m) NNE of the circles a sandstone slab lies inside a farm hedge by the Pensford-Chew road, shamefully neglected and overgrown. Known as Hautville's Quoit it was already prostrate in the seventeenth-century, measuring 10ft 6ins long and 6ft 6ins in width (3.2 × 2m). It is shorter today.

It must be asked why the three rings do not stand in a straight line like the Priddy henges just to their south, or the Hurlers (6) on Bodmin Moor or the Thornborough henges in Yorkshire. The answer to this gives an insight into the ritual planning of their builders.

Over two centuries ago John Wood noticed that a line passing through the centres of the north-east circle and Great Circle pointed accurately to the Cove, and that a second line from the SSW ring through the Great Circle was aligned on the Quoit. To this subtle landscaping can be added an astronomical calculation by Alexander Thom that there is a third orientation from the centre of the north-east circle through the SSW ring. Looking towards that ring's 7ft (2.1m) high stones standing on ground 46ft (14m) above the north-east circle, observers would have seen the southern moon setting between the pillars blackly silhouetted against the skyline.

As an hypothesis it may be speculated that the Great Circle was the first of the three rings, erected on spacious level ground near a clutter of local stones. The north-east circle followed, built inconveniently close to the Great Circle because the ground fell sharply to its east preventing it from being erected any farther away. Its position was also chosen to be where its centre and that of the Great Circle formed a line towards the Cove. It meant, however, that a second line from its centre to the SSW ring 920ft (280m) away had to pass between stones on the extreme east of the Great Circle. Otherwise, the midsummer lunar alignment between the two smaller rings would have been imprecise.

The complications were considerable. The SSW circle contained not one but two sightlines, one through the centre of the Great Circle to the outlying Quoit, the other from the north-east circle to the major southern moonset. Had it been as close to the Great Circle as the north-east ring this would have altered the bearing between the two smaller circles from 211° to 218°, badly misaligned on the southern moonset. As it was, the development was a triumph of design. Midsummer processions and ceremonies may be imagined, rituals by moonlight celebrated by hundreds of people from the countryside, assembling for reasons long forgotten but preserved silently in the stones themselves.

Other assemblies are associated with the circles. The rings have been known as The Weddings because they were supposedly the petrified remains of merrymakers who revelled too long on the Saturday and were turned to stone for impiety on the Sunday. The avenue stones are the Fiddlers, and the Cove is the upstanding Bride and Groom and the drunken Parson flat on his back.

Hautville's Quoit is said to have been thrown there by the crusader, Sir John Hauteville, 1216–72, from over a mile away. An oak effigy in the church of Chew Magna, assigned to him but in anachronistic plate armour, is probably that of John Wych a century later.

C.W. Dymond, *The Ancient Remains at Stanton Drew . . .* , 1896, *Plan*, 41; L.V. Grinsell, *The Folklore of Stanton Drew*, Bristol, 1973

76 WITHYPOOL, Withypool Hill (3)

Lat: 51°.1   SS 838 343
2³/₄ miles ssw of Exford, just sw of the summit of Withypool Hill. Walk. At SS 846 338 take footpath wnw for ¹/₂ mile. Ring is 200 yds (180m) to n. Easy. Map 3

Despite the 119ft 6ins (36.4m) diameter of this large circle its stones are so hidden in the long grass that it was only discovered by accident in 1898. Some of its pale, grey grits and quartz stones have been removed for repairing roads half a mile away. Originally, the ring contained perhaps a hundred spaced about 3ft 6ins (1m) apart. In 1906 there were only thirty-seven. By 1989 there were twenty-seven standing and three fallen. 'Standing' is a misleading term. On average these miniscule slabs are only 4ins high, 1ft wide and 4ins thick (0.1 × 0.3 × 0.1m) and weigh no more than 15 to 20lbs.

There are conspicuous round barrows, including the Brightworthy cemetery with its Wessex bell-barrow, visible in all directions.

PSNHAS, 1906–7, 42–50, Plan

WESTMORLAND

A mélange of Early Bronze Age concentric stone circles at the edge of the Lake District, an embanked ring to its south and a great Late Neolithic circle-henge

77 CASTERTON (3)

Lat: 54°.2   SD 640 799
2 miles ne of Kirkby Lonsdale, ³/₄ mile e of Casterton. From farm lane at SD 643 799. Walk. 200 yds (180m) w up slope. Fair. Map D

Composed of small stones in spite of plentiful large boulders on the nearby hillside, this is probably an embanked stone circle 62ft 4ins (19m) in diameter. Its well-spaced stones jut shyly from a flat-topped platform that may have been cut into the hillslope. At the north some stones are hardly visible whereas at the south and south-west they are up to 1ft 6ins (46cm) high. The heights

vary so much, however, that it would be wrong to suggest careful grading.

On the north-west perimeter are the remains of a possible secondary cairn from which, in 1828, a bronze spearhead, a flint arrowhead and perhaps a late beaker may have been recovered. They cannot be securely dated to the first use of this flimsy 'Druid's Temple', presumably the ritual centre of a small community.

Waterhouse, 86–8, *Plan*

78 GAMELANDS, Orton (3) [L2/14.

'Orton'] Lat: 54°.0   NY 640 082
6¹/₂ miles se of Shap, 1¹/₄ miles e of Orton. There is a farm lane at NY 639 080. Ring is immediately to its e. Easy. Map D

The ruined ring, 146ft ene-wsw by 123ft (44.5 × 37.5m), lies on level ground, the majority of its stones fallen. Except for a single limestone boulder they are reddish, coarse granite erratics plentiful in the vicinity. Of an original forty-two stones or so some have been taken for a wall to the south and, around 1862 when the area was ploughed, other stones were buried or blasted. There are reports of a probable cist-slab and of two flints being unearthed.

With its low bank and numerous stones the ring has affinities with early Lake District circles and with the Druids' Circle (245c) on Penmaenmawr, North Wales.

TCWAAS 6 (O.S.), 1881–2, 183–5; ibid 64, 1964, 408; TTB, 64, Plan

79 GUNNERKELD, Shap (3) [L2/10]

Lat: 54°.6   NY 568 178
1¹/₂ miles n of Shap, 330 yds (300m) sw of Gunnerwell Farm. Walk. ¹/₂ mile along track from NY 572 184. Easy. Map D

The names of both the ring and the adjacent farm share the same Old Norse meaning, 'the spring of Gunnarr'. The circle, now incongruously close to the M6, consists of two concentric rings on a slight ridge. The outer ring, badly pillaged at the north and with flattish prone slabs at the south, is about 104ft 4ins N-S by 95ft 6ins (31.8 × 29.1m) in size. Whether of granite or limestone all the stones are local glacial erratics.

The inner ring is much smaller, only 50ft (15.2m) across but built of almost contiguous, boulderish kerbs to a low mound in which there were the remains of a cist. Architecturally it is very like Oddendale (81) 3½ miles to the SSE.

A tall stone, 5ft 4ins (1.6m) high rises at the SSW of the outer ring. Two others, 4ft 6ins and 5ft 6ins (1.4, 1.7m) high stand just outside the circle at the precise north like portals to an entrance about 5ft (1.5m) wide. Waterhouse has drawn attention to the likeness of the proportions of Gunnerkeld to the magnificent circle of Castlerigg (18) eighteen miles to the WNW which measures 32.6m by 29.5m, a ratio of 1:0.98 between the rings. Both have entrances at the north but there was probably a difference of many centuries between them.

Gunnerkeld is a wreck but it does exist, a future improbable in 1844 when it was threatened by the laying of the Lancaster and Carlisle railway line. Being on the land of the Earl of Lonsdale, wrote 'Druid', 'I am surprised that the noble earl should permit such barbarity.' Thankfully, he did not.

TCWAAS 4 (O.S.), 1878–9, 537–40; Waterhouse, 127–9, Plan

80 MAYBURGH, Eamont Bridge (4)
Lat: 54°.7   NY 519 284
1 miles SSE of Penrith, ¼ mile SW of Eamont Bridge, between the rivers Eamont and Lowther. From A592 turn WNW at the Crown Inn. Entrance to the ring is 300 yds (275m) on side road to the N. Easy. Map D
All that remains of this controversial stone circle is one graceful pillar of local volcanic ash, 9ft 2ins (2.8m) high. It stands just north-west of the centre of a monumental henge, 383ft (117m) from crest to crest of a bank 15ft (4.6m) high and awesomely composed of hundreds of thousands of river-washed cobbles. There is one entrance at the exact east. The central plateau is

gently dished like an upturned saucer where soil was scraped up around its rim for the creation of an earthen marker core upon which the stones of the bank were piled. Such a technique, creating a henge lacking a quarry ditch, was one widely practised by the builders of Irish henges.

According to Camden there were once four stones at the corners of a rectangle 60ft N-S by 53ft (18.3 × 16.2m) in the middle of the earthwork with four others lining the corners of the entrance. 'Circles' of four stones, Four-Posters, are known in central Scotland and it is possible that an aggrandised version of one, twenty times the average in size, was erected inside Mayburgh's henge. If it was a genuine Four-Poster then, like others, its stones would have been placed on the circumference of a circle, in this case one with a diameter of 80ft (24.4m).

The henge itself, standing at the mouth of the pass into the heart of the Lake District, may have been connected with the trade in Neolithic stone axes. A broken Cumbrian axe was found in the entrance late in the nineteenth century and, suggesting some continuity of tradition, Stukeley recorded that 'in ploughing at Mayborough they dug up a brass celt', most probably an Early Bronze Age bronze axe.

When he saw the henge in 1725 its interior was already under cultivation and stones 'were blown to pieces with gunpowder; one now stands ten foot high . . . another lies along . . . and some more lie at the entrance within side, others without, and fragments all about.'

The destruction led to tragedies. 'These smaller stones were blasted and removed . . . one of the men employed in the work having hanged himself, and the other turning lunatic, has given a fair opening to vulgar superstition, to impute these misfortunes to their sacrilege in defacing what they suppose was formerly a place of eminent sanctity.'

The Yorkshire-type henge of King

Arthur's Round Table, lopped off on its north by a lane and briefly converted into a tea-garden, lies 330 yards (300m) to the east against the A6, the Penrith-Shap road.

Aubrey, I, 112–13; *TCWAAS 11 (O.S.)*, 1890–1, 191–200; Burl, 1988, 58–9, *Plan*

81 ODDENDALE (3) [L2/13]
Lat: 54°.5   NY 593 129
2¹/₂ miles SE of Shap, 2¹/₄ SW of Crosby Ravensworth. From Shap take the lane E towards Crosby Ravensworth. In 1¹/₂ miles turn S (Rt) before a plantation. Drive 1¹/₂ miles to Oddendale farm. Walk S for ¹/₄ mile. Easy. Map D
Like Gunnerkeld (79) this is a concentric stone circle. It lies on a level terrace on the moor, the ground falling away to the west. The outer ring of thirty-four closely-spaced stones, all local limestone, is about 86ft (26.2m) in diameter with its heaviest, biggest stones concentrated at the east. There is no sign of an entrance but a small, isolated and unexplained stone stands halfway between the rings at the ESE.

The inner ring is a kerbed cairn, also noticeably graded to the east. The stone-lined mound, 25ft (7.6m) across was dug into before 1862. It had previously been disturbed and any cobbled paving had been thrown aside but charcoal was discovered and traces of a cremation.

Such composite rings, peripheral to the great Neolithic circles of the Lake District, share the same Bronze Age attribute of combining a burial-place with a stone circle as those of Dartmoor. As well as Gunnerkeld and another at Knipe Scar, in 1882 the Rev. Canon Simpson recorded a third at Penhurrock, NY 629 104, on the same moor as Oddendale. 'There still exists one of those stone circles, within which, at no distant period, there was a large barrow.' When it was levelled burnt bone was found in a rock-cut cist. The site is now no more than a dishevelled mound and a scatter of boulders.

PSAS 4, 1860–2, 445; *TCWAAS 6 (O.S.)*, 1882, 178–9; TTB, 62, *Plan*

WILTSHIRE
The county has the two most famous of all megalithic rings

82 AVEBURY (3) [S5/3]
Lat: 51°.4   SU 103 700
7 miles NE of Devizes, 5¹/₂ miles W of Marlborough. Two car-parks. Easy. In State care, no charge. Map 3
This is an amazing collection of monuments, all of them excessive in size. There is a colossal earthwork enclosure with four entrances; the largest stone circle in western Europe surrounding the remains of the fifth and seventh biggest rings; and the remnants of two Coves, a holed stone and two avenues.

A series of C-14 determinations published in 1993 suggest that the earthwork was constructed in the centuries between 2690 ± 70 bc (Har-10325) and 2210 ± 90 bc (Har-10326), c.3400–2850 BC. The later date is more likely. Stoneholes of the great Outer Circle, contemporary with it, gave 'dates' of 2180 ± 90 bc (Har-10062) and 1920 ± 90 bc (Har-10327), c.2800–2400 BC. A feasible though as yet unproveable sequence would have the inner North and South Circles erected around 2800 BC, the Outer Circle and earthwork around 2600 BC and the two avenues later still, about 2400 BC.

The complex is so vast that a systematic tour is recommended. (1) Walking westwards from the Red Lion Inn at the heart of Avebury pass the Post Office and Henge Shop on the left. In a few yards, well before the church, turn right down a roughish track. Had you gone straight on you would have passed through the demolished WSW entrance of the earthwork just before the school on the left.

The track soon swings to the left. There is a short flight of steps on the right. You will need these. (2) First, however, looking to the left (W), there is the National Trust shop on the left, the Stones Restaurant on the right, the Great Barn with its Wiltshire bygones beyond it, and, straight on, a round

Avebury, Wiltshire (82), the south-west arc of the Outer Circle. The sarsen at the front is the Barber's Stone.

pigeon-house on the left, the cause of a seventeenth-century lawsuit. Avebury's small museum is directly ahead. With its evocative displays of prehistoric material, including models, skeletons, pottery and tools, postcards and booklets – it should be visited. Entrance Fee.

(3) Return to the steps for a clockwise tour of Avebury. In this north-west quadrant some great stones of the Outer Circle still stand, with their smoother faces inwards as usual. It is an deformed ring some 1100ft (335m) across at its widest, its ninety-eight stones ranging in height from 7ft to a maximum of 18ft (2.1–5.5m) at the entrances.

Some sarsens or sandstones were piously buried in the fourteenth century. Others were commercially heated and broken up for houses in the eighteenth in an unlucky enterprise. Some of the buildings burned down and the speculator was bankrupted. Nor were the residences desirable. Sarsen, observed Stukeley, is 'always moist and dewy in winter, which proves damp and unwholsom, and rots the furniture.' The places of stones demolished for this futile exercise are marked today by unsightly concrete obelisks. Where occasional fragments were excavated they were reassembled whenever possible, sometimes grotesquely.

To the west of the stones is the ditch from which chalk was quarried to make the bank. The trench is now two-thirds full of silt and rubble but was once sheer-sided and 30ft (9m) deep, its bottom littered with lumps of solid chalk crumbling from the sides. To fall into it would have been the equivalent of tumbling from the roof of a house onto a jagged pile of bricks. When sections of the ditch elsewhere were excavated early in the twentieth century unused antler picks and human jawbones were uncovered near the bottom, bones that may have slipped from mortuary scaffolds around the rim of the central plateau.

Outside the ditch is a bank, once 20ft (6m) high, its serpentine outline showing where workgangs had piled up heaps of chalk side by side. In this quadrant a long stretch was levelled in the late seventeenth century to make room for a barn. The downcast was used for a causeway, the one still there by the steps, for carts crossing the ditch.

(4) At Avebury's NNW entrance against the road looms the gigantic sarsen lozenge called the Swindon, or, more descriptively, the Diamond Stone, its height and bulk typical of the monsters that dominated the entrances. 14ft 9ins (4.5m) high and as wide across its waist, some forty tons in weight, it was dragged like all the stones from the upper downs visible on the eastern horizon. The causewayed enclosure of Windmill Hill can be seen a mile away to the north.

The Diamond Stone is said to cross the road when the clock strikes midnight. It may be searching for its even heavier but lost partner whose doom Stukeley recorded. It was 'of a most enormous bulk, fell down, and broke in the fall. It measured full 22 feet [6.7m] long.' When he saw it three wooden wedges had been driven in to 'break it in pieces'. Nothing remains of the gargantuan block.

(5) Notice the arc of three concrete obelisks by the Diamond Stone. They show where stones of an intended third inner circle were erected before being withdrawn when the project was abandoned to enable the defensive earthwork to be raised.

Turning from the entrance follow the footpath south and before reaching the corner and the inn cross the road – taking great care – through gates that provide access to the north-east quadrant. (6) Facing you are two tremendous stones, the back- and south sideslab of a three-sided Cove whose second sideslab fell and later was broken up in 1713. The seemingly inexplicable design of the Cove is best explained as an aggrandised imitation of the chambers in early Neolithic megalithic tombs such as West Kennet 1¼ miles to the south. If the Cove had

any astronomical significance it may have been aligned on the most northerly moonrise. Several excavations have found nothing of importance within the setting.

(7) Around the Cove, 160ft (48.8m) both to north-east and east are two standing and two prostrate stones which traditionally have been considered the survivors of a concentric North Circle, 320ft and 170ft (97.5, 51.8m) across of twenty-seven and twelve stones. Recent resistivity surveys suggest that they may instead be the relics of a spacious horseshoe or semi-circle 230ft deep and 345ft wide (70 × 105m) across its open SSW mouth. The Cove stood at its heart. With Avebury's South Circle only about 100ft (30m) away it is a conjunction of a megalithic horseshoe and circle well-known in Brittany at sites such as Er-Lannic (379) and is comparable to the horseshoe of five trilithons inside the sarsen ring of Stonehenge (84) eighteen miles to the south. John Aubrey's 1663 plan of Avebury shows just such a horseshoe.

Little remains of the Outer Circle in this quadrant but the expanse of featureless grass conceals the postholes of a concentric timber building 165ft (50.3m) across that was detected 280ft (85m) north-east of the Cove, perhaps one of a number of dwellings in a settlement protected by the earthwork. Beyond it is Avebury's eastern entrance with a track leading up to the downs. A massive slab lies by the opening.

(8) Leaving the Cove and walking south to a gate between some buildings notice the chapel on the far side of the road. It was built in 1670 of shattered sarsen from the circles at a time when damage was increasing from casual destruction to persistent eighteenth-century demolition. (9) West of the chapel, before the busy Swindon-Devizes road bends sharply to the left, a gate opens onto the south-east quadrant with the South Circle, once 336ft (102m) across and of thirty stones 9ft to 13ft 6ins (2.7, 4.1m) high. The ring still has a good run of stones in its south-west quadrant. A broad and

high slab at its wsw has a notched top like a gunsight. Skull and rib fragments were found at its base. Sandstone discs discovered in other areas of Avebury are, like others elsewhere, associated with death.

(10) At the middle of this despoiled ring was a tall pillar, now marked by a heavy concrete obelisk. Immediately around it concrete roundels show where pits filled with fertile brown earth had been dug into the chalk, presumably to receive offerings. Around the Obelisk may have stood a rectangle of smaller sarsens of which only the west side, known as the Z Stones, has been disinterred.

(11) Just to the sse is a shattered stump overlooked by most visitors but once an important pillar in line with the north and south ring centres. 'Not of great bulk', wrote Stukeley. 'It has a hole wrought in it, and probably was design'd to fasten the victim, in order for slaying it. This I call the *ring-stone*.' Before the bank was raised, this sarsen, chosen for the small natural perforation at its top corner, stood as an outlier to the South Circle.

(12) At the sse entrance two astonishing slabs stand, the one nearer the road known as the Devil's Chair because it has a flat cavity near the base of its outer side, a natural seat smoothed by the bottoms of countless visitors posing for photographs. Before leaving the earthwork by the sse entrance look down into the eastern (left) side of the ditch. There, right against the entrance, the skeleton of a female dwarf was discovered in a shallow grave, maybe a sacrifice to strengthen the power of the enclosure.

In the eighteenth century the entrance was widened to enable stagecoaches to cope more easily with a sudden bend in the road, and then later further disfigured for material to raise the road. (13) Walking carefully through a few trees on its east side, avoiding their exposed roots, one can cross the lane and come to the beginning of the Kennet Avenue. Many of its buried stones were dug up and re-erected in

the 1930s and it is now possible to walk along the 900 yards (825m) of the reconstituted section, preferably southwards along its eastern side, then northwards along its west.

The ground rises gently and at the head of the slope the first pairs of stones can be seen. A single tall stone just outside the entrance is aligned upon them. But to its west there is a run of low obelisks 45ft (14m) apart extending southwards away from the stone and the sarsens visible on the skyline.

One is probably looking at three distinct phases of construction. (14) The first stone, 4B, 9ft 8ins (2.9m) high, may be the sole survivor of an initial short avenue of three or four pairs outside the entrance. (15) This was later dismantled and replaced by the south stretch, about 250ft (76m) long and laid out at a sharp angle to the entrance. The change may have ensured that the interior of Avebury was hidden from view until one was almost at the earthwork.

(16) Stage by stage further sections were added, the first some 500ft (150m) long up to the brow of the rise. All its stones have gone, neither broken nor buried, simply removed for walls and buildings, leaving only empty holes.

As it lengthened the avenue widened from 45ft to 80ft (13.7, 24.4m). Although its stones diminished in height they were of selected types. Unshaped thin, flat-topped columns alternate with peaked, broad lozenges along each side and also stand opposite each other. Such coupling is particularly obvious in the fifth and twelfth pairs from the far end of the avenue. Sexual symbolism has been proposed. As comparable differences in shape, height and tops are commonplace in other short rows and pairs in Britain, Ireland and Brittany it is a persuasive interpretation.

Burials and deposits were found against some stones, rarely on the eastern side, frequently on the west. (17) From the south end of the avenue where an unexplored field must cover other sarsens the thirteenth stone on the west had the bones of three individuals and a broken beaker beside it. Three stones to the north there was another burial and a complete grooved ware pot. Four stones further on was another burial. It is as though each new addition to the avenue received a deposit to consecrate it.

(18) Returning to Avebury it is safer to cross the lane again, go through the trees and walk past the Devil's Chair. Gates on the left, halfway along the busy road, allow entry to the south-west quadrant. Here the Outer Circle has a splendid run of impressive stones from the SSE entrance. The sixth covered a tragedy.

Before the Black Death of 1349 many of these heathen stones, especially the smaller, had been buried in deep pits, probably at the urging of the priest. (19) The hole for the sixth had not been big enough, leaving the slab leaning dangerously over it. An itinerant barber-surgeon with scissors, probe, silver pennies of 1307 and, no doubt, leeches, was persuaded to enlarge the cavity. The stone fell, killing him. 'No attempt seems to have been made to retrieve the body.' In 1938 his skeleton was sent to the Royal College of Surgeons, London, and was destroyed during the blitz in the Second World War.

Walk back towards Avebury's High Street where the excursion began. The Outer Circle degenerates into a run of obelisks until one comes to the final stone. (20) It epitomises of Avebury's fate. Bits of broken lumps, fragments, fractured blocks have been concreted and rodded together in a Picasso-like travesty of the grandiose sarsen it had been. Once it had stood majestically at the WSW entrance. Men had proudly raised it. Then greedy men smashed it. Today's ridiculous and shameful conglomeration embodies the story of Avebury.

'And this stupendous fabric', wrote Stukeley, 'which for some thousands of years, had brav'd the continual assaults of weather . . . [has] fallen a sacrifice to the wretched ignorance and avarice of a little village unluckily plac'd within it.'

Other things to see (21) The font inside the church has a carving of a bishop impaling a serpent, perhaps a representation of the triumph of Christianity over heathenism.

(22) In a field ³/₄ mile west of Avebury, SU 089 693, are two stones known as Adam and Eve or the Longstones. The eastern pillar, Eve, is the one remaining stone of the Beckhampton Avenue. The gross lozenge, Adam, like Eve surely wrongly sexed, was the eastern sideslab of a south-west facing Cove.

(23) Near Avebury Silbury Hill, SU 100 685, should be seen but not climbed. The great chambered barrow of West Kennet, SU 104 677, along a tediously uphill footpath, should be visited. The bare stones of the Devil's Den tomb, SU 152 696, will reward any zealot for megaliths. A few scattered stones of the Winterbourne Bassett stone circle, SU 094 755, are 3¹/₂ miles north of Avebury. (24) Most of all, go to Devizes Museum (closed Sundays, entrance fee). It is one of the finest museums of prehistory in western Europe.

W. Stukeley, *Abury, a Temple of the British Druids . . .*, London, 1743; I.F. Smith, *Windmill Hill and Avebury. Excavations by Alexander Keiller, 1925–39*, Oxford, 1965, *Plans*; Burl, 1979; Ucko et al, *Avebury Reconsidered. From the 1660s to the 1990s*, London, 1991, *Plans*; *Oxford Journal of Archaeology 12 (1)*, 1993, 29–53

83 THE SANCTUARY, Overton Hill (4, 2) [S5/2] Lat: 51°.4   SU 118 680 *4¹/₂ miles W of Marlborough, 1¹/₂ miles SE of Avebury. Layby on the S of the busy A4 at the top of Overton Hill. Site alongside. Easy. Map 3*
The site of the concentric Sanctuary stone circle on Overton Hill, formerly known as Seven Barrow Hill because of the Early Bronze Age round barrows on it, consists of six visually unexciting rings of low concrete pillars showing where posts had stood, and two equally

low rings of concrete slabs indicating the former positions of an inner and outer stone circle 46ft 8ins and 129ft 9ins (14.2, 39.6m) in diameters. They stood alongside the prehistoric Ridgeway.

The stone circles were destroyed in AD 1724. Around 2300 BC they had replaced circular timber structures, possibly roofed, whose sequence is unclear. They have been interpreted as a series of mortuary houses for the storage of corpses until desiccation was complete and the bones could be removed to nearby chambered tombs such as East and West Kennet and the Devil's Den.

The Sanctuary was once connected by the Kennet Avenue to Avebury (82). Excavation in 1930 recovered Neolithic sherds, flints and human bones. The skeleton of a young girl with a beaker and animal bones lay against the eastern stone of the inner stone circle, buried there before the stone was erected. Lying in line with the equinoctial sunrises hers may have been a sacrifice.

WAM 45, 1931, 300–31, *Plan*; Burl, 1979, 124–8, 193–8

84 STONEHENGE, Amesbury (3) [S5/1]
Lat: 51°.2   SU 123 422
9 miles N of Salisbury, 2 miles W of Amesbury. In State care, entrance fee. At present, car-park is off the A344. This may change. Administrative concerns about preservation have closed the interior of this ring to the public and one must, at the time of writing, view the stones from a distance of some 30 yards (27m). There are hopes that full access will be restored. Map 3
Standing on Salisbury Plain, the world's most famous circle is a skilful combination of engineering, astronomy and symbolism. The earliest earthwork contained alignments to the south and to the northernmost moonrise. The axis of the succeeding bluestone rings was directed towards the midsummer sunrise. The final sarsen ring, orientated on the midwinter sunset, was a marvel of woodworking techniques used on stone.

Stonehenge had four major phases:
I 3200 BC A spacious earthen ring or 'henge' with a central timber setting and an outlying stone.
II 2200 BC Two unfinished circles of Welsh bluestones replaced the posts. An earthen avenue was laid out.
III 2000 BC The two circles were removed and the well-known lintelled sarsen ring and internal horseshoe of five trilithons were constructed.
IV 1600 BC The bluestones were returned. Outlines of a bronze dagger, axes and a rectangular anthropomorph were carved on stones at cardinal points.

Each phase was a modified imitation of its predecessor.

The first Stonehenge was not monumental. Its circular chalk and earth bank and outer ditch enclosed a space 280ft (85.4m) across and surrounded either an open timber circle or a roofed wooden building, possibly a mortuary house whose framework of outer and inner rings of uprights topped by ring-beams would be reproduced by the concentric bluestone rings and by the later, uniquely-lintelled sarsen circle.

A narrow entrance through the bank lay at the south. At the north-east the lefthand side of a wider causeway stood in line with the most northerly rising of the midwinter full moon. Its position must have been determined by prolonged sightings through three lunar cycles of 18.61 years, two generations of observations as the moon slowly swung back and forth between its major (40°) and minor (60°) positions. Temporary posts across the causeway marked the changing risings. Their postholes can no longer be seen.

An association between the moon and death existed in the long barrows that were the burial-places of early Neolithic societies on Salisbury Plain. The similar lunar interest at Stonehenge suggests that the enclosure may have been a funerary centre in which corpses were left to decay before the final interment of their bones elsewhere. It also explains why, despite popular

Stonehenge, Wiltshire (84), the western trilithon, 57–8. To the right of the grooved bluestone is trilithon 53 with an inscription and carvings of a dagger and axes.

belief, the outlying Heel Stone beyond the north-east entrance was not orientated on the midsummer sunrise. Standing in line with the entrance's righthand side it had been erected midway between the northern moon's major and minor risings. When the rising moon reappeared to the left of the stone people knew that four years later it would be at its northernmost.

Stonehenge was briefly abandoned.

Then, around 2400 BC, fifty-six pits, the Aubrey Holes, named after John Aubrey who noticed some in 1666, the year of the Great Fire of London, were dug along the bank's inner edge. Backfilled and then redug to receive human cremations four pairs were neatly laid out to straddle each of the cardinal points. Twelve more pits occupied each of the intervening quadrants. Claims that the number fifty-six was specifically chosen as an abacus or computer for the prediction of eclipses are not supported by the differing numbers of 'Aubrey Holes' at several other comparable sites.

Excavations in the early twentieth century recovered evidence of burials, perhaps sacrifices, and other potent objects deposited in holes at significant places, at the entrances, at each end of the axis, with a child's cremation in line with the major southern moonrise where a lovely perforated stone macehead, perhaps from Brittany, was found by the excavator, Lt-Col. Hawley, in 1923. It is now in the evocative Salisbury Museum with its scholarly but imaginative displays of Stonehengiana. (Closed on Sundays except for July and August, entrance fee). All that can be seen today of the Aubrey Holes are markers of dull concrete discs.

Around 2200 BC there was further change. By widening the north-east entrance by 25ft (7.6m), backfilling the ditch, the users of beaker pottery that has been associated with a solar cult, shifted the axis of the monument 4° to the east causing the Heel Stone to stand almost in line with it and the midsummer sunrise. An earthen avenue, exactly straight for 1/4 mile, led up to the new entrance.

Inside the earthwork two incomplete rings, 86ft and 72ft (26.2, 22m) across, of Welsh bluestones were put up where posts had stood. Despite romantic myths of an heroic feat, men dragging and rafting the stones from the Preseli mountains 135 miles to the WSW, the blocks, of very varied and unselected quality, had more probably been shifted to within seven miles of Stonehenge by unheroic glaciation.

At the edges of the henge bank, four rough sarsens, the Four Stations, were set up around the rings at the corners of an astronomical rectangle, 263ft by 86ft (80.2 × 26.2m), its long SE-NW sides aligned on the major northern moonset, short SW-NE sides on the midsummer sunrise, and the ENE-WSW diagonal in line with the May Day

sunset. Two of these stones are lost but the south-east remains, prostrate, and the north-west survives, though only as a stump.

The bluestone rings were never finished. By 2000 BC they were uprooted and in their place gigantic sandstones or sarsens from the Marlborough Downs eighteen miles to the north were raised in a perfect circle 97ft (29.6m) across. These twenty- to fifty-ton monsters were brought by humans, probably employing oxen and portable trackways of timber.

The thirty uprights of the ring supported heavy lintels, replicas of the original wooden ring-beams. Inside, five huge trilithons, two pillars supporting a lintel, were erected in a horseshoe of archways that rose in height towards the south-west and the midwinter sunset.

It was an astonishing achievement. There was no good building stone near Stonehenge nor was there any megalithic tomb within seventeen miles. The natives of Salisbury Plain were woodworkers and they treated the sarsens as though they were timbers, making bevels, chamfers, pegs, mortise-and-tenon joints, tongues-and-grooves. The carpentry techniques can still be seen. Even the inner faces of the rock-hard sarsens were smoothed like planed wood. Some of the scoured and battered tennis-ball to football-sized stone mauls used for the tedious shaping can be seen in Salisbury Museum.

Close to 1800 BC two rings of pits, the Y and Z Holes, were dug around the sarsen ring to receive stones, perhaps the missing bluestones, but the project was never completed. Some two hundred years later the bluestones were brought back, the majority erected in a crude circle inside the sarsen ring, nineteen in a carefully designed horseshoe within the trilithons. A tall Welsh sandstone, the Altar Stone, was erected near the centre of the monument.

Outside the circle and nine feet (2.7m) apart, two pillars, the Slaughter Stone and a companion, the first now fallen, the other lost, were put up at the centre of the north-east causeway. They framed the midsummer sun as it rose above the horizon, its bright ray shining between the stones, into the circle and onto the Altar Stone.

Carvings of native Early Bronze Age axes and a bronze dagger on stones at the south and east were matched by rectangular figurines on sarsens at the west. They are still visible. Such representations are rare in Britain but numerous in the megalithic tombs of prehistoric Brittany where the axes, daggers and figurines were associated with a ghostly, weapon-bearing female guardian of the dead.

An extension to the avenue veering down to the River Avon, begun around 1100 BC was left unfinished and by the end of the Late Bronze Age Stonehenge was abandoned. Today only weather-ravaged stones remain, an impressive wreck from which many smaller bluestones have been stolen. But the curious visitor will notice the bank and ditch, make out the southern entrance, see the concrete markers for the Aubrey Holes, and looking around will recognise the low mounds of Bronze Age round barrow cemeteries outlined on the skyline. The builders of this wonders of the megalithic world are buried there.

W. Stukeley, *Stonehenge a Temple Restor'd to the British Druids*, 1740; R.J.C. Atkinson, *Stonehenge*, 1979, *Plans*; Burl, 1987; R. Castleden, *The Making of Stonehenge*, 1993; Cleal et al, *Stonehenge in its Landscape*, 1995.

YORKSHIRE
Mainly small embanked rings of the Bronze Age
85 BLAKEY TOPPING, Allerston (5)
Lat: 54°.3   SE 873 934

7¹/₂ miles NE of Pickering, 2³/₄ miles NE of Lockton. On a 'singular hill'. Driveable track from SE 853 938 for 1 mile ESE. Walk. Stones are ¹/₄ mile E of Newgate farm. Fair. Map 3
The site has been so pillaged that it cannot be claimed as a certain stone

circle. With a determined eye one can plot a ring about 51ft (15.6m) across with a 3ft 2ins (1m) high stone at the north, another 4ft 2ins (1.3m) at the south-east and the tallest, 5ft 7ins (1.7m) high, at the SSW. Between it and the north stone are three hollows on the west arc which may be the sockets of robbed stones.

65ft (19.8m) south of what can hardly be termed a setting, is a fourth stone 4ft 6ins (1.4m) high.

F. Elgee, *Early Man in N.E. Yorkshire*, 1930, 105. *No plan*

86 COMMONDALE MOOR (3)
Lat: 54°.5   NZ 637 108
3³/₄ miles WNW of Castleton, 1¹/₂ miles w of Commondale. From the unfenced road at NZ 640 100 the ring is 1100 yds (1000m) to NNE up a long hillside. Fair. Map 3
On a gentle slope from which the land falls steeply to the south some twenty small stones, none more than 1ft (30cm) high, stand and lie in a ring about 104ft NE-SW by 95ft (31.7 × 29m). The tallest stands 2ft (60cm) high at the ESE. This and its partner just to the SSE are the highest and are set radially to the circumference like portals. An untidy heap just north-east of the centre of the ring may be the result of recent digging when a few flints were found.

Another grass-covered mound on the western perimeter is probably a disused shooting-butt.

F. Elgee, *Early Man in N.E. Yorkshire*, 1930, 104–5, 145, 'Sleddale'; O.S. Southampton, *Plan*

87 DRUID'S ALTAR, Bordley (3)
Lat: 54°.1   SD 949 652
4¹/₂ miles NE of Kirkby Malham, 3¹/₂ miles WNW of Grassington, Walk. About 220 yds (200m) s of the lane from Threshfield to Bordley. Easy. Map 3
Called the Druid's Altar because by repute it had a trilithon on one of its sides this 'feature' has long since disappeared. The site is a 'Scottish' Four-Poster.

On a terrace falling to the south-west

a circular mound 41ft (12.5m) across
has three stones standing on it. Of local
limestone they form the corners of a
rectangle 11ft 6ins (3.5m) square from
which the south-western pillar is
missing. At its corner is 'a stump,
possibly the base of a prostrate stone'
which now lies, 5ft 10ins (1.8m) long,
near the centre. The 'square' in which
the stones were erected was, in fact, a
circle 16ft 3ins (5m) in diameter.

The tallest stone at the south-east is
3ft 7ins (1.1m) high. Between the
south-west and south-eastern stones is a
scatter of round cairnstones, perhaps
upheaval from a plundered central
burial.

H.A. Allcroft, *The Circle and the
Cross*, I, 1927, 225–6; Burl, 1988, 72–
3, *Plan*

2 miles north-east of Grassington are
two small embanked rings of tiny
stones, one about 30ft by 25ft (9.1 ×
7.6m), the other 28ft (8.5m) in
diameter.

YAJ 41, 1963–6, 324

88 HIGH BRIDESTONES, Grosmont (5)
Lat: 54°.4   NZ 850 046
*5 miles SW of Whitby, 1¼ miles ESE of
Grosmont, Walk. Just S of lane from
the village to the A169. Easy. Map 3*
On a bleak, often waterlogged,
limestone pavement the High
Bridestones have been all things to all
men. Even the name is deceptive. It has
nothing to do with nuptials, sex or
fertility symbolism. It relates to Brigid,
the goddess of the Brigantes, the Iron
Age tribe that inhabited this grim,
windblown region.

There have been varying
interpretations of the eleven stones of
which six stand. They have been called
the remains of two stone circles with
outliers to north and south; standing
stones among natural outcrops; and a
ruinous double row or avenue. They
may, instead, be the wreckage of two
Four-Posters.

A. At the north-west and at right-
angles to the line like a terminal stone
on Dartmoor there is a single stone 5ft
2ins (1.6m) high. To its south-east,

190ft (58m) away, are three stones at
the corner of a rectangle 25ft by 20ft
(7.6 × 6.1m) from which the north-east
stone is missing. The tallest pillar, 4ft
5ins (1.3m) high is at the south-east.
The setting resembles a 'christianised'
Four-Poster.

B. A further 76ft (23.2m) south-east
is a low, loose stump and 28ft (8.5m)
beyond it is a very questionable Four-
Poster in such a disastrous state that
little can be claimed for it. The biggest
stone, 7ft 6ins (2.3m) high, still stands
and around it in confusion lie three
slabs, 8ft 4ins, 10ft and 7ft 6ins (2.5,
3.1, 2.3m) long. When the heather is
full several outcrops around them can
be mistaken for even more stones.

If this megalithic disaster had been a
Four-Poster its rectangle would have
been about 15ft by 13ft (4.6 × 4m).
Like the more identifiable setting to the
north-west its sides would have been
roughly aligned on the cardinal points.

The circles on which these two sites
were laid out would have been
respectively 30ft 2ins and 19ft 6ins
(9.2, 6m) in diameter.

Burl, 1988, 74–5, *Plan*

89 TWELVE APOSTLES, Ilkley Moor (3)
Lat: 53°.9   SE 126 451
*2½ miles WSW of Burley-in-Wharfedale,
1½ miles SSE of Ilkley. Walk. From the
Cow and Calk Hotel, SE 134 466
follow footpath 1 mile SSW. Fairly easy.
Map 3*
This once neatly-embanked ring has
been sadly treated and its short stones
are nearly all down. The surviving
twelve slabs of local millstone grit used
to stand in a rubbly bank about 4ft
wide and 2ft high (1.2 × 0.6m). Their
circle was a good one, 52ft (15.9m) in
diameter.

Originally the ring would have had
between sixteen and twenty stones,
none of them big, the tallest now
standing at the ENE, 4ft (1.2m) high. At
the centre of the circle is a small
hummocky mound, probably the
disturbed remains of a burial-cairn.

Man 14, 1914, 163–4; *YAJ 29*,
1927–9, 357, *Plan*

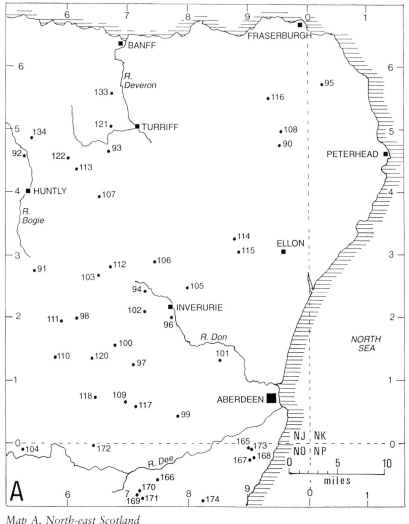

Map A, North-east Scotland

SCOTLAND

ABERDEENSHIRE
This county is notable for its great number of recumbent stone circles, probably of the very Late Neolithic and Early Bronze Age, c.2700–2000 BC

90 AIKEY BRAE, Old Deer (3)
Lat: 57°.5   NJ 959 471
10¼ miles N of Ellon, 1¼ WSW of Old Deer. Walk. On Parkhouse Hill. ¼ mile E of farm. Easy. Map A
On Parkhouse Hill, which the ring is sometimes called, and hidden behind a Christmas tree plantation, this is a fine recumbent stone circle, its graded stones in a good bank still 6ft wide and up to 3ft high (1.8 × 1m). Of an original ten stones plus the recumbent in a circle 47ft 2ins (14.4m), one pillar is missing at the northeast. The eastern slabs and the west flanker are fallen. Those standing range in height from 4ft 7ins up to 7ft 3ins (1.4–2.2m). The great recumbent, twenty-one tons in weight, is 14ft 9ins long and 4ft 3ins (4.5 × 1.3m) high. Although humped at its western end, it is mainly flat-topped.

Its base is naturally wedge-shaped and heavy chock-stones beneath the thinner end show how the slab was levered up and down until it was perfectly horizontal. It is quite well aligned on the major southern moonset.

Digging in the interior around 1875 'during a long summer day' to a depth of up to 8ft (2.4m) produced nothing but untidiness for today's visitor.
PSAS 19, 1884–5, 374–5; ibid 38, 1903–4, 266–70, Plan

91 ARDLAIR, Holywell (3, 4) [B1/18. Holywell] Lat: 57°.3   NJ 552 279
5 miles W of Insch, ¾ mile S of Kennethmont station. Walk. ¼ mile SW of farm. Easy. Map A
The recumbent, both flankers and a stone west of the west flanker remain standing in this ring, 37ft 7ins (11.5m) across. Like Easter Aquorthies (102), twelve miles to the ESE, two impressive

slabs, here 4ft 4ins (1.3m) long, jut at right-angles to the recumbent like supports. Near the centre of the ring the southern arc of a round cairn, about 16ft (5m) across, touches these props. The probable five other stones of the ring lie fallen and disturbed on the low hill. All of them are granite from the Correen Hills four miles away.

Lockyer suggested that the recumbent had been moved from the south-west where it had faced the May sunset and had been burned and cracked by 'solstitial priests'. This unlikely hypothesis brought a sarcastic response from Fred Coles.

An excavation of 1821 is rumoured to have unearthed an urn. Charles Dalrymple re-excavated the cairn in 1857 finding two sideslabs of a wrecked cist. Below it was a pit with cremated bone and charcoal.

The ring stands almost a mile NNE of the site of the Holywell recumbent stone circle (NJ 549 270) which was destroyed in the mid-nineteenth century when five hundred cartloads of small boulders were removed from its cairn.
PSAS 36, 1901–2, 557–9; Browne, 1921, 81–3; TTB, 182, Plan

92 ARNHILL, Ruthven (4)
Lat: 57°.5   NJ 531 456
3½ miles N of Huntly, 2 miles SE of Ruthven. Walk. 250 yds (230m) W of the B9022. Easy. Map A
Only the fine recumbent survives of a circle once about 60ft (18m) in diameter but the stone, lying at the SSW of the circumference, is worth a visit for its size, poise and art.

Weighing about sixteen tons, it is a block 11ft 9ins long, 5ft high and 2ft 6ins thick (3.6 × 1.5 × 0.8m). It is visibly balanced on small blocks. Near the centre of the inner face of the recumbent is a set of concentric semi-circles. Like the art in other recumbent stone circles they mark an astronomical position, here the major southern moonset. As if to emphasise this, the recumbent is not level-topped but sags naturally in the middle like a saddle between hills or an executioner's block,

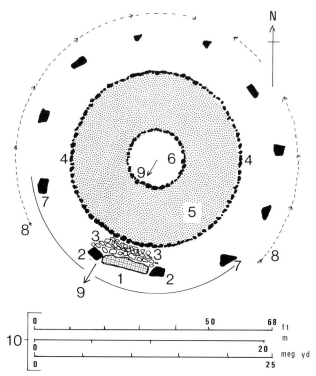

Architectural features of a Scottish recumbent stone circle. 1. recumbent stone; 2. flankers; 3. platform with scattered quartz; 4. kerbstones; 5. ring-cairn; 6. cremations; 7. arc of only stones with cupmarks; 8. stones decline in height; 9. alignment on the major southern moonset; 10. average diameter

markings.

PSAS 36, 1901–2, 571–4, *Plan*; *ibid 37*, 1902–3, 227

93 BACKHILL OF DRACHLAW (1) [B1/24. Blackhill] Lat: 57°.5   NJ 673 464
4 miles SW of Turriff, 2¼ miles ESE of Inverkeithny. Walk. 150yds (137m) N of track to Backhill of Drachlaw farm. Easy. Map A
A. Like South Ythsie the site is one of several in north-east Scotland in which a small ring is composed of large stones. Here, in an ellipse 27ft 9ins ENE-WSW by 24ft 2ins (8.5m × 7.4m), are five heavy stones from 3ft to 4ft 6ins (1–1.4m) high, the heaviest standing at either end of the long axis.

Unusually, their broad faces do not lie along the circumference. They are rugged dark, basaltic stones with veins and pebbles of quartz in them, the biggest with a projecting vein of white quartz around it 'like a rope of crystal'. A sixth massive block, 6ft 9ins long by 3ft wide (2.1 × 1m), lies at the north-west.

A similar ring just to the south-west was destroyed to make way for farm-buildings in the nineteenth century.
B. *Cairn Riv* 300 yards (275m) north-east is the enormous Carlin Stone (NJ 674 465), a corruption of *cailleach*, 'the witch's or hag's stone'. By the B9024, it is 8ft 6ins high and 26ft 10ins round at its waist (2.6 × 8.2m),

over fourteen tons of rock flanked by two much lower stones. Fred Coles believed 'this boulder, rugged, unshapely, and most unusual in height though it be, should be accepted as the Recumbent Stone of the Circle that certainly once existed here.'

There are nineteenth-century reports of a Bronze Age stone axe-hammer, bronze bracelets, flints and a jet button being found either in or very close to this wrecked circle.

PSAS 37, 1902–3, 118–24; TTB, 186, *Plan*

94 BALQUHAIN, Inverurie (3) [B1/11]
Lat: 57°.3   NJ 735 241
3 miles NW of Inverurie, 1 mile E of Chapel of Garioch. Walk. Across fields 1/4 mile W of A96 . Not easy. Walls and barbed-wire. Map A
Known variously as Balquhain, Chapel of Garioch and Inveramsay this sadly damaged ring is important both geologically and astronomically. Only three stones and the recumbent of an original twelve are unmoved in a circle about 68ft (20.7m) across. Others lie near them. They are a mixture of local red granite, quartzite and basalt but the imposing recumbent, weighing over ten tons, 12ft 6ins long and 5ft 11ins high (3.8 × 1.8m), is a white-grained granite brought from some distance away. A tall outlying pillar of quartz, over 10ft (3m) high stands 21ft (6.4m) to the south-east.

The fallen east flanker has several cupmarks on it. There may be another on the top of the recumbent. The upright stone west of the west flanker has two very clear sets of cupmarks on its outer side. As usual in such circles the art was astronomically situated.

From the centre of the ring the east flanker once stood in line with the most southerly rising of the moon. The western end of the recumbent marked its setting. The lavishly decorated circle-stone was more esoterically placed. Only after long observations were people able to determine where the minor moon set several degrees north of south-west. They aligned the stone

on it.

A limited excavation by Coles in 1900 uncovered 'a rough pavement of boulders', maybe the disturbed stones of an inner ring-cairn.

PSAS 35, 1900–1, 230–7; TTB, 172, *Plan*; Ruggles and Burl, S57

95 BERRYBRAE, Newark (2)
Lat: 57°.6   NK 028 572
6 1/2 miles SSE of Fraserburgh, 5 miles ENE of Strichen. Walk. Only a few paces SW of junction of lanes to the E. Easy. Map A
Excavated by the writer between 1975 and 1978 this recumbent stone circle had been vandalised in prehistory. In historic times treasure-seekers left three untidy pits inside it.

Because its people wished the ring to be close to a patch of well-drained fertile land it was built on a noteable slope down to the south. To overcome this the builders cut into the hillside, using the upcast to raise a level platform on which nine circle stones and the recumbent were erected in an ellipse 42ft 8ins SE-NW by 35ft (13 × 10.7m). The recumbent, with a central hump, lay at the south-west end of the shorter axis. In front of it was a cobbled platform strewn with fragments of white quartz.

In these rings recumbent stones were chosen with discrimination, often selected in preference to stones closer to the circle. They had to be heavy blocks, usually with a tapering base to facilitate the levelling of the stone. Ideally they were level-topped but a natural central dip or lump was accepted as it could be used as sighting-device. The recumbent had to be aligned on the southern moon.

At Berrybrae the 10ft 10ins (3.3m) long, nine tons of irregular basalt was dragged, levered and adjusted in its shallow pit until its hump pointed like a stubby thumb towards the moon's minor setting. At the centre of the ring was a kerbed ring-cairn in which token deposits of human cremated bone were buried.

The time when the circle was erected

Berrybrae, Aberdeenshire (95), from the north. The author's excavation of 1975–8.

Castle Fraser, Aberdeenshire (97), the recumbent and flankers from the ESE.

is unknown but around 1760 BC people came to the place and vandalised the ring, smashing the tops of the smaller stones, toppling others, ripping up the ring-cairn and using its cobbles to build a thick, rough wall around the ellipse, concealing the prostrate stones and stumps. Only the recumbent was undamaged, perhaps because it was too heavy and hard to move.

Then, as if fearful of angering the disturbed spirits, the intruders placed freshly-broken urn sherds in a niche in their wall, stood a malformed late beaker under a plank beside it and covered both offerings under the clay capping of the wall. Charcoal from the plank provided two C-14 determinations of 1500 ± 80 bc (HAR-1849) and 1360 ± 90 bc (HAR-1893), c.1760 BC. The beaker toppled, the wood rotted, Berrybrae was abandoned. For over three thousand years it was undisturbed until looters dug into it and, later, in the nineteenth century, a pseudo-druidical grove of trees was planted around it.

PSAS 38, 1903–4, 288–91; A. Burl, Rings of Stone, 1979, 25–31, 124–5, Plan

96 BROOMEND OF CRICHIE, Inverurie (4) [B2/12] Lat: 57°.3   NJ 779 196
On the s outskirts of Inverurie. Walk. In a field just E of the A96. Easy. Map A
This ruined circle-henge lies near the River Don. Today it consists of a small henge about 100ft (30m) across with entrances at the north and south. On the central plateau there was a circle, 38ft (11.6m) in diameter. Of its six stones two remain, misplaced, with a carved Pictish Stone introduced from 150ft (46m) to the north-east when it was threatened by the laying of a railway line.

Excavation by Dalrymple in 1855 discovered a central pit containing a cist with human bones in it. Two cists were found by the NNW stone with cremations, an urn and a sandstone battle-axe. Cremations in cordoned urns lay by the holes of missing stones.

A wide avenue of standing stones once led to the henge from the south. Two of the stones survive 276ft (84m) away. Four cists lay at the far end with inhumations and four beakers, one with a horn ladle in it. The beakers, three N2 and one N3, and the ladle are now in the Royal Museum of Scotland, Edinburgh (E.Q. 1, 2, 23, 24).

There is an eighteenth-century report of a second smaller avenue that led 150ft (46m) northwards to a probable recumbent stone circle. A road, railway, sand-quarrying and a housing estate all contributed to its disappearance.

PSAS 7, 1866–8, 110–15; ibid 18, 1884, 319–25; Clarke, II, 510; TTB, 182, 216, Plan

97 CASTLE FRASER, Kemnay (1) [B2/3. West Mains] Lat: 57°.2   NJ 715 125
6½ miles SSW of Inverurie, 2¼ miles SSW of Kemnay. Walk. Best approached from side-lane, NJ 715 124. In Rt field. Easy. Map A
Also known as Balgorkar this is one of the best recumbent stone circles. It stands on levelled ground at the edge of a south-west falling terrace.

Of its original ten stones six still stand on the circumference of a circle 66ft 10ins (20.4m) in diameter. They are well graded towards the recumbent which is flanked by tall pillars. The ring was aligned upon the major southern moonset.

Within the ring is a good ring-cairn. In the nineteenth century charcoal and cremated bone were discovered in its central space. Sherds of a 'thick and massive urn' were found by the fallen stone west of the west flanker.

727ft (222m) to the east is a fine pair of standing stones, 48ft (14.6m) apart, each 7ft (2.1m) high, one flat-topped, the other peaked.

A mile and a half to the NNE, at the junction of a road and a lane is the Lang Stone o'Craigearn, 11ft 6ins (3.5m) high, around which, it is rumoured, covens of witches would assemble, NJ 723 149.

PSAS 35, 1900–1, 197–201; PSAS 109, 1977–8, 269–77; TTB, 198, Plan

Cothiemuir Wood, Aberdeenshire (98), from the north.

98 COTHIEMUIR WOOD, Castle Forbes
(3) Lat: 57°.3   NJ 617 198
*5¼ miles ssw of Insch, ½ mile NE of
Keig. Walk. Best approached from the
lane to its s at the 2nd bend to E, NJ
618 198, Walk directly w for about
100 yards (90m) through the trees. In a
clearing. Easy for the calm-headed.
Map A*
This is a fine recumbent stone circle to
visit. Stones are missing on its east but
the ring is in good condition around its
recumbent which rests on a heavy 2ft
square (0.6m) granite block. The circle-
stones are granite, mostly red, one grey,
but the recumbent is a dark basalt.

At the ssw of a circle about 75ft
(23m) in diameter the great recumbent
is 13ft 8ins (4.2m) long and is flanked
by two elegantly tall pillars, 9ft 6ins,
east, and 9ft high, west, (2.9, 2.7m)
respectively. They are imposing stones
and fit snugly against the twenty tons
of the recumbent.

There are possible cupmarks, known
as the Devil's Hoofmarks, at the west
end of the recumbent's outer face. From
the centre of the ring the west flanker,
against which the markings lie, is neatly
aligned on the major southern moonset.

At the centre of the circle is a heavy,
squarish block of granite, some 3ft 4ins
by 4ft (1 × 1.2m), lying over a small
pit and it may have been Cothiemuir
Wood to which the Rev. James Garden
referred when writing to John Aubrey
in 1692. 'They did see ashes of some
burnt matter, digged out of the bottom
of a little circle (set about with stones
standing close together) [the kerbed
central space of a ring-cairn] in the
centre of one of those monuments
which is yet standing near the church of
Keig.' The old church near Castle
Forbes was much closer to Cothiemuir
Wood than to the better-known ring of
Old Keig 1½ miles to the west.

Aubrey, I, 186; *PSAS* 35, 1900–1,
214–17, *Plan*; Browne, 1921, 77–8

99 CULLERLIE, Echt (2) [B2/7]
Lat: 57°.1   NJ 785 043
*4¼ miles NW of Peterculter, 3 miles ESE
of Echt. Walk. In a tidy clearing close
to lane to its w. Easy. Map A*
This lovely ring was erected on a patch
of well-drained gravel in an area
surrounded by swamps. Eight tall
stones of coarse red granite formed a
circle 33ft 5ins (10.2m) in diameter.
They rise in height towards the north.

Their bases were shaped into points to give them greater stability in the loose gravel. Acidic peat rising around them in later prehistory ate into their sides, eroding the lower parts of the stones.

Excavation in 1934 found that the site had been levelled and a fire of willow ignited inside the ring. After it had died down seven small, neatly-kerbed open rings were piled up around a much larger one 11ft (3.4m) across. Cremated bones with charcoal of oak and hazel were deposited in the rings before their interiors were filled with cairn-stones.

PSAS 35, 1900–1, 187–9; *ibid 69*, 1934–5, 215–23, *Plan*

100 DEER PARK, Monymusk (3) [B2/10. Monymusk]
Lat: 57°.2   NJ 684 156
3 miles W of Kemnay, ½ mile N of Monymusk. 100 yds (90m) E of lane. Easy. Map A
The north-west stone is missing from this Four-Poster which stands on a terrace overlooking the River Don. The three surviving stones stand on the circumference of a ring 15ft 4ins (4.7m)

in diameter. They are thick and heavy blocks, the tallest at the south-east, 5ft 2ins (1.6m) high.

The ring is small even by Four-Poster standards but it is the only one to exist at the heart of the recumbent stone circle distribution. It is close to Castle Fraser (97), three miles to the south-east, Cothiemuir Wood (98), 4½ miles north-west, and Easter Aquorthies (102), 4½ miles north-east. The circle of Nether Coullie, of which only the 9ft (2.7m) high west flanker remains, was just two miles to the east.

PSAS 36, 1901–2, 201–3; Burl, 1988, 92–3, *Plan*

101 DYCE (1) [B2/1. Tyrebagger]
Lat: 57°.2   NJ 860 133
7¼ miles SE of Inverurie, 1¾ miles W of Dyce. Drive to Dyce farm, NJ 861 129. Ring is ¼ mile uphill to NW. By pylon. Easy. Map A
Also known as Tyrebagger, 'the land of acorns', this is a splendid recumbent stone circle on the shoulder of a hill with magnificent views to the lowlands, coast and sea.

Standing in a low, rubbly bank are

Cullerlie, Aberdeenshire (99), the circle and its internal cairns from the west.

99

ten very tall stones ranging in height
from 4ft 4ins (1.3m) at the north up to
superb flankers 9ft 6ins and 11ft (2.9,
3.4m) alongside a gigantic recumbent
slab, twenty-four tons in weight, 10ft
long but an astonishing 10ft 6ins high
(3.1, 3.2m). Its top is not flat but rises
to a central peak. It is the focal point of
a good circle 59ft 4ins (18.1m) in
diameter. The standing stones are local
red granite but the recumbent is a
darker granite. Inside the ring are signs
of a ring-cairn.

   *PSAS 34, 1899–1900, 188–91;
Browne, 1921, 89–90; TTB, 194, Plan*

**102 EASTER AQUORTHIES (1) [B1/6.
Aquorthies Manar]**
Lat: 57°.3   NJ 732 208
*2½ miles w of Inverurie. In State care,
no charge. At NJ 748 216 turn w. 1½
miles. Ring is just to s. Easy. Map A*
Standing on a gentle hillside and
unfortunately incarcerated in a modern
drystone wall, this is a beautiful site to
visit. Its prehistoric builders had
pleasing polychromatic tastes.

   Different-coloured stones have been
symmetrically placed in an embanked
ring. It is not quite circular, measuring
60ft 6ins (18.4m) WNW-ESE by 59ft 6ins
(18.1m). All its stones are of local
granite but whereas those on the east
are whiteish pink those opposite are
dark grey. The flankers, 7ft 6ins (2.5m)
high are light grey. The 12ft 6ins long,
4ft 6ins high (3.8 × 1.4m) level-topped
recumbent is a deep reddish granite
striated with flecks and lines of white
quartz. It is supported inside the ring
by two monstrous blocks at right-angles
to the stone.

   Like many recumbent stone circles
the stones appear to have been erected
in opposing pairs with a single, lowest
stone at the NNE. At the SSW the axis of
the ring is aligned on the southern
moonset.

   In the interior of the ring is a
conspicuous mound hollowed at its
centre. There is a report of cist covered
by a capstone and the mound may be
the vestigial remnants of a ring-cairn.

   PSAS 35, 1900–1, 225–9; Browne,

1921, 69–70; TTB, 196, *Plan*

103 HATTON OF ARDOYNE (3)
Lat: 57°.3   NJ 659 268
*2 miles SE of Insch, 1½ SE of Old
Rayne. Walk. From Hatton of Ardoyne
farm, ¼ mile E. Easy. Map A*
Despite its shabby condition this is an
interesting ring. Nine of an original
thirteen stones stand in a circle 84ft
(25.6m) in diameter. They are of local
metamorphic gneiss from 4ft to 6ft
(1.2, 1.8m) in height. The recumbent
and its flankers are of a different stone,
light grey granite from the Bennachies
across the valley. The west flanker has
fallen. The recumbent is flat-topped,
thin, 5ft 4ins high but only 8ft long
(1.6 × 2.4m). In front of it is a short,
stony platform.

   Inside the circle are the remains of an
unusual ring-cairn, 69ft (21m) across. It
is kerbed with stones up to 1ft 6ins
high and set 2ft into the ground (0.5 ×
0.6m). Inside it is a very wide, kerbed
central space 64ft (19.5m) across.
Before 1856 an excavation by
Dalrymple found a rectangular grave in
it, 5ft 6ins long, 1ft 9ins wide and 4ft
deep (1.7 × 0.5 × 1.2m). On its paving
of small stones were cremated bones
and sherds of an urn 'burnt very red'. A
similar grave lay by the northernmost
circle-stone. It also had burnt material,
charcoal and fire-marked stones. It is
probable that both these pits were
intrusions to an old stone circle.

   *PSAS 35, 1900–1, 241–6, Plan;
Browne, 1921, 85–8*

104 IMAGE WOOD, Aboyne (5)
Lat: 57°.1   NO 524 990
*4¼ miles SE of Tarland, ½ mile NW of
Aboyne. From A93 at NO 524 985
take lane to N across railway. ¼ mile.
Ring is just W of lane in trees. Easy.
Map A*
Like Backhill of Drachlaw (93) this is a
tiny ring of disproportionately big
stones. Here five fat blocks of an
original six or seven stand irregularly
spaced in a ellipse 12ft 9ins N-S by 11ft
6ins (3.9 × 3.5m). The obese, rugged
stones are between 2ft 6ins and 4ft 6ins

(0.8–1.4m) high. There are wide gaps at the north-west and south-east.

Before 1904 Lord Huntly had a trench dug across the ring but 'found only black earth and cinders'. It is possible that the site is a nineteenth-century 'druidical' folly in the grounds of Aboyne Castle.

PSAS 39, 1904–5, 206–8; Ogston, *Prehistoric Antiquities of the Howe of Cromar*, 1931, 87–8, *Plan*

105 KIRKTON OF BOURTIE, Old Meldrum (3) [B1/7]
Lat: 57°.3   NJ 801 250
2¼ *miles* NE *of Inverurie*, 1½ *miles* S *of Old Meldrum. 200 yds (180m)* N *of the lane. Easy. Map A*
At the edge of a hillside sloping down to the south this is a badly damaged recumbent stone circle of which only the east flanker, recumbent and two western stones remain *in situ*. All are of local grey granite. The ring may have had a diameter of 71ft (21.6m). The flanker is 9ft 10ins (3m) high. The recumbent is remarkable in being the longest of all such stones, 17ft (5.2m) in length, and must weigh almost thirty tons. The western stones are 6ft and 7ft 9ins (1.8, 2.4m) high. Inside the ring are scatters of cairn material. Some missing stones can be identified in the gateway and in the adjacent north-south wall.

With an estimated azimuth of around 194° the recumbent at the SSW would have been quite well aligned on the major southern moonset.

PSAS 36, 1901–2, 513–16; Browne, 1921, 72; TTB, 164, *Plan*

106 LOANHEAD OF DAVIOT (2) [B1/26]
Lat: 57°.4   NJ 747 288
5½ *miles* NNW *of Inverurie*, 4 *miles* W *of Old Meldrum. 600 yds (550m)* NW *of Loanhead of Daviot. Walk. 200 yds (180m)* E *of lane beyond trees. Easy. Map A*
Because of its excavation this is one of the most informative of recumbent stone circles. In State care, it stands on a gentle slope down to the north into which a shallow ledge was cut to provide the ring with a level platform.

Trees obscure the views to south and east.

Immediately to the east of the circle are the badly-damaged remains of an enclosed cremation cemetery in which Early to Middle Bronze Age food-vessel urns and human cremations were discovered.

In the circle eight stones, two flankers, and a frost-fractured recumbent stand in a ring 68ft (20.7m) in diameter. The circle is only crudely graded, its stones ranging in height from 4ft 6ins (1.4m) to the 7ft 6ins (2.3m) of the west flanker.

Inside is a kerbed ring-cairn 54ft 3ins (16.5m) across with a sub-circular open centre about 13ft 6ins (4.1m) from side to side. It is of mathematical interest that Alexander Thom noted that the diameter of the stone circle was twenty-five of his Megalithic Yards of 2.72ft (0.83m), and that the ring-cairn measured twenty Megalithic Yards. It is of interest because he was unaware of the central space whose diameter is five Megalithic Yards. It is possible, therefore, that Thom's Megalithic Yard was the local unit of measurement used by the builders of some Scottish recumbent stone circles.

Excavation in 1932 revealed that a fire of willow, probably a funeral pyre, had burned inside the ring before the ring-cairn was raised over it. There was much evidence of ritual and the careful deposition of objects. Each of the circle-stones stood in a little cairn beneath which there was a pit holding charcoal and sherds of nondescript, undateable flat-rimmed ware. More sherds, charcoal and human cremated bone, including fifty skull-fragments of children aged between two and four years old were found in the central space. Flint scrapers and knives also lay there. 'A stone ladle' is reputed to have come from inside the circle in the early nineteenth century. Finds that have survived are now in the Royal Museum of Scotland in Edinburgh, NMAS Catalogue, EP60-161.

The discovery of indigenous Lyles Hill ware and some early beaker sherds,

Loanhead of Daviot, Aberdeenshire (106), *from the south-west.*

AOC and probable N/NR among them, suggest that the circle may have belonged to a period in the Late Neolithic, in the centuries after 3000 BC. It is likely that the adjoining enclosed cremation cemetery was constructed when the circle was falling into disuse.

There is art. The stone east of the east flanker has twelve cupmarks on its inner face. Significantly, remembering the suspected astronomical significance of cupmarks, a line from the centre of the ring, brushing the lefthand side of the stone, has an azimuth of 139° and a declination of −23°.8, that of the midwinter sunrise, an unusual solar sightline in a recumbent stone circle.

James Ritchie, examining the ring for such art, recorded that 'In the wood, a short distance to the north-west of the circle, there are a number of rocks exposed. On the upper surface of one of these, two plain cups are to be seen; but though they are similar in size and appearance to those on the standing stone, they do not seem to be connected with the circle.'

In spite of the unexpected sunrise line at Loanhead of Daviot there was also a more customary lunar alignment. Sir Norman Lockyer, inexplicably

surveying not to the recumbent but across the ring from it determined an azimuth of 8° and a declination of 33°.23, which he suggested might have marked the rising of Arcturus in 660 BC or Capella in 1580 BC. Neither date nor stellar target is likely.

Instead, looking from the ring's centre to the end of the recumbent against the west flanker the declination is that of the major southern moonset.

New Craig recumbent stone circle is half a mile to the north, NJ 745 296, and the same distance SE a similar ring was destroyed around 1817 when a house was built near Daviot church.

PSAS 36, 1901–2, 517–19; *PSAS* 69, 1934–5, 168–222, *Plan*; Clarke, II, 511; Ruggles and Burl, S68, RSC 59

107 LOGIE NEWTON, Kirk Hill (3)
Lat: 57°.4   NJ 657 392
8 miles E of Huntly, 4¾ NW of Rothienorman. Drive from NJ 666 390 to farm at NJ 662 392. Walk. ½ mile WNW up gentle hill. Fair. Map A
Near the crest of a long, low hill these three tiny, battered, disturbed and robbed rings are also heavily overgrown. In an ENE-WSW line 140ft (43m) long, (a) the ENE circle of almost contiguous stones and crowded with

shattered rocks is only 18ft 6ins (5.6m) across. (b) The central is 22ft 9ins (6.9m) and (c) the wsw 21ft (6.4m). There is cairn material in all of them.

The justification for including these 'pretty ruinous' sites in the Guide is not that the wsw with its big stones is 'the most remarkable Druidical circle in the parish'. The reason is the quartz. The rings consist of brilliant white quartz blocks, jagged, unshaped and spectacular.

A stone from the western ring was taken to a nearby field to mark where 'an urn containing human bones was found'. It is still there. The urn was broken up 'and pieces were given away to curious friends'.

PSAS 37, 1902–3, 97–101, Plan

108 Loudon Wood, Pitfour (3)
Lat: 57°.5   NJ 962 497
2¼ miles wnw of Mintlaw, 2½ miles ne of Maud. Walk. From forest entrance at NJ 959 494 1 mile e along forest tracks. Be warned. As Fred Coles learned in 1903, 'The site is an extremely difficult one to find, and we *received scarcely any help towards its discovery in the dense woodlands from anyone on the policies.' The writer has endured the same experience. Frustrating. 1:25,000 map recommended. Map A*

In a maze of Forestry Commission tracks this recumbent stone circle is often waterlogged and muddy, spoiled by pony-trekkers plodding through it.

It is a true circle, 60ft 8ins (18.5m) in diameter, and characteristically stands at the edge of a south-facing terrace.

The north-eastern stones are missing, the east flanker is down and two other stones are prostrate. Against its west flanker, 6ft 5ins (2m) high the recumbent is a heavy, level-topped block 10ft 3ins long and 4ft wide and high (3.1 × 1.2m). Of local granite its base tapers to the west where its builders would have levered it until the top was horizontal. The stone is in line with the major southern moonset.

PSAS 19, 1884–5, 374–5, Plan: ibid 38, 1904–5, 270–2, Plan

Midmar Kirk, Aberdeenshire (109), from the south. Chockstones can be seen supporting the tapering but exactly horizontal recumbent stone.

109 Midmar Kirk, Echt (2) [B2/17. Midmar Church]
Lat: 57°.2   NJ 699 064
3¹/₄ miles SW of Dunecht, 2³/₄ miles WNW of Dunecht. In churchyard just N of Q974. Enter from lane to W. Easy. Map A

Like many recumbent stone circles in north-east Scotland this one has suffered interference. The 'new' Midmar church was built against it in 1797 and, ironically, a graveyard was laid out around it in 1914. It is claimed that the stones of the ring were not disturbed but the grossly uneven grading makes this unlikely. It is probable that some fallen stones were wrongly replaced.

Two fine pillars, each 8ft 3ins (2.5m) high, flank a huge, twenty-ton recumbent. It is 14ft 9ins (4.5m) long and provides clear evidence of the preparatory work when such circles were erected. Its base tapers to the west and levers held it steady until chockstones were wedged underneath to keep the recumbent's flat top horizontal. The flankers were shaped to fit better against the stone.

There is no trace of an inner ring-cairn. The entire central area, 56ft 10ins (17m) across, has been converted into a neat lawn.

The ring also offers an insight into astronomical problems. The recumbent, like its partner at Sunhoney (117) a mile to the east, faces not the major but the minor southern moonset, a lunar event much more difficult to detect. It was a target forced upon the builders because the major setting was never visible. Hardly a mile to the south the Hill of Fare rose so high on the skyline that it obscured any sighting of the southernmost moon either rising or setting. A similarly elevated horizon affected the alignment at Sunhoney.

In the small wood just north of the circle is the Balblair stone. It is 100 yards (90m) north of the circle and, from the lane, easily seen amongst the trees. It is about 8ft 6ins (2.6m) high but leans quite considerably towards the south. In 1864 it was claimed that it was the survivor of a stone circle. It is unusual to find two recumbent stone circles so close together and it may be that the stone is an outlier like another at Balquhain.

The circle inspired poetry. In his *Fane of the Druids: a Poem* the Rev. John Ogilvie, 1733–1813, incumbent of Midmar parish, wrote:

Time-hallow'd pile, by simple builders rear'd!
Mysterious round, through distant times rever'd!
Ordained with earth's revolving orb to last!
Thou bringst to sight the present and the past.
Rapt with her theme, bold Fancy wings her flight
To silent ages long involved in night
Bids clouded forms arise to sight display'd
And scatters light along th'oblivious shade.

Enjoy your Fancy in this transformed and Christianised ring.
PSAS 34, 1899–1900, 179–81, no. 17; *ibid* 53, 1918–19, 64–5; Browne, 1921, 63; Thom, 1967, 135, 142, *Plan*, 146

110 North Strone (2)
Lat: 57°.2   NJ 584 138
2 miles WNW of Kirkton, 1¹/₂ miles SSE of Alford. From Guise farm at NJ 588 132. Walk. ¹/₂ mile NW uphill. Quite easy. Map A

This is an almost elfin, 'singularly beautiful' ring, unique and frail as though youngsters, unable to lift heavy weights, and uncertain of the required number of stones, had fashioned their own version of a recumbent stone circle.

On a pronounced slope falling to the east a batch of little stones stands in a ring some 65ft NW-SE by 62ft 6ins (19.8m × 19.1m). The average height is only 2ft 9ins (84cm). The lowest stone, fallen, is opposite the recumbent, which is the smallest of all such 'blocks', a mere 4ft 9ins long, 1ft 6ins thick and once 2ft 7ins high (1.5, 46cm, 79cm). It has fallen inwards onto a stony platform leaving its chockstones exposed. Quite against the architectural canon the east flanker was no taller than the recumbent although its top may be broken. Behind it is a possible triangular tip, 4ft 7ins (1.4m) long. Its prostrate western counterpart, however, was little bigger.

The bank of small stones in which the circle-stones stand is low and about 5ft (1.5m) wide except behind the recumbent where it swells outwards in a kind of apse. The recumbent is well-aligned on the major southern moonset.

The ring is attractive because of its colours, ten stones of lucent white quartz-porphyries intermixed with four pink and two grey Bennachie granites. Alexander Keiller thought the quartz had been quarried and that this would account for the diminutive slabs.

Around 1897 five stones were re-erected when the ring was partly explored and restored. The interior of the circle was paved with rough stones. Under them were seven 'ancient graves', one with bits of bone, a tooth and two flints, another with bones and decorated urn-sherds suggesting that these may have been Bronze Age interments.

PSAS 36, 1901–2, 493–6, Plan

111 OLD KEIG (3)
Lat: 57°.3   NJ 597 194
2¹/₂ miles NNE of Alford, 1 mile W of Keig. Walk. Best approached from N at NJ 596 199. Gate. ¹/₄ mile S down through airy trees to a now-desolate circle. Easy. Map A
Stones lie where excavations have left them. The ring-cairn is overgrown. Despite the magnificence of its recumbent one of the greatest of these stone circles is now miserably neglected.

The chosen site was a typical terrace commanding spacious views over the Howe of Alford to the south-west. Once a majestic recumbent stone circle it has been ravaged by the removal of stones and the building of a wall to the west. Today only the recumbent, its flankers and a stone at the east remain of a circle 82ft 6ins (25.2m) in diameter. It stood in a bank, still in good condition, about 10ft (3m) wide.

The surviving stones are immense, the west flanker 8ft 10ins (2.7m) high, the east even taller, 9ft 6ins (2.9m), and the recumbent an awesome 16ft long block, rising 6ft 9ins above ground and 6ft thick (4.9 × 2.1 × 1.8m), over

forty tons, the heaviest recumbent of all.

Excavations first by Gordon Childe and then by Bill Varley showed that inside the stone circle the turf had been stripped and a pyre of hazel with some birch, willow, alder and oak ignited. When it cooled a kerbed ring-cairn, 61ft (18.6m) across was constructed, placed eccentrically inside the circle. Its kerbed open central space, 15ft (4.6m) across, contained a large pit dug through the fire-reddened area. In it were cremated bones, charcoal, and sherds of flat-rimmed ware and beaker, possibly N/NR in style. There were also flints and a small, broken lignite armlet. The finds are now in the Royal Museum of Scotland, Edinburgh, Catalogue EP 28–49.

Despite its ruinous state the circle rewards a visit. The recumbent is an astonishment. It is not local. Its tons of sillimanite gneiss were dragged up a steady hillside at a gradient of 1:14 from a source several miles to the south-east. A hundred or more labourers must have been demanded. Or reluctant oxen. It is the most monstrous of all these colossi. Below its tapering eastern end chock-stones can be seen propping it. The thicker, dog-legged western end was used as a fulcrum as the block was levered up and down until its long, flat top was exactly horizontal.

Astronomically it conformed to the norm. A sightline from the central space to the east flanker, a more usual target than the bland width of the recumbent itself, pointed to the major southern moonset.

Browne, 1921, 78–9; PSAS 67, 1932–3, 37–53, Plan; ibid 68, 1933–4, 372–93, Plans

112 OLD RAYNE, Candle Hill (4) [B1/13] Lat: 57°.3   NJ 679 280
7 miles NW of Inverurie, ¹/₂ mile ESE of Old Rayne. Often in crop, frustrating a close inspection. On lane from Old Rayne to Strathorn. Close and visible to N. Map A
Only its excavation justifies the inclusion in this Guide of such a

dreadfully ruined recumbent stone circle. In a ring once about 87ft (26.5m) in diameter only one stone at the south-east still stands of an original ten or so. The rest are megalithic dismay. Look but do not linger.

The site was excavated by Dalrymple in 1856. Under a central cairn a pit, 2ft 6ins (76cm) deep, held cremations, charcoal, coarse sherds and a broken archer's wristguard of pale green stone. Rectangular and with three perforations at either end, it is a type associated with W/MR beakers. The fragment, measuring 1⅛ by 1⅜ins (2.9 × 3.5cm), is now in the Royal Museum of Scotland, Edinburgh, Catalogue AT-5.

There is a report that the Bishop of Aberdeen held a court of justice here in 1349, the year of the Black Death in England.

Stuart, I, 1856, xxi; *PSAS 34*, 1901–2, 527–31; TTB, 176, *Plan*

113 RAICH, Glen Dronach (3)
Lat: 57°.5   NJ 618 436
6 miles ENE *of Huntly, 2¼* S *of Inverkeithny. From NJ 624 440 take lane* SW, *past distillery, for ½ mile. Ring is 100 yds (90m) in field to* S. *Easy. Map A*
On the northern periphery of recumbent stone circle distribution, this little ring stands on a east-facing terrace. It may be a transitional form of Four-Poster.

Its stones stand on a distinct mound over 3ft (1m) high. The site is conspicuous. Although virtually the entire western half is fallen and disturbed two much taller stones stand at the south-east, 4ft 8ins (1.4m) high, and NNW 4ft 4ins (1.3m) in a ring of much lower blocks. Assuming that two equally high had stood in the eastern quadrant they would have formed a Four-Poster 14ft 6ins (4.4m) square, the stones in a circle 21ft 3ins (6.5m) in diameter.

Both Fred Coles and Alexander Keiller noticed the likeness of Raich to others such as Shethin and South Ythsie (115).

PSAS 37, 1902–3, 126–7; Burl, 1988, 96–7, *Plan*

114 SHETHIN, Tarves (3) [B1/10. Fountain Hill] Lat: 57°.4   NJ 882 328
5 miles WNW *of Ellon, 1¼ miles* NE *of Tarves. Walk. From Shethin farm ¼ mile* W. *Easy. Map A*
This very small ring, possibly the smallest in Aberdeenshire, stands on Fountain Hill. The stones are a local mixture of basalt, quartz and granite. They are low, almost contiguous blocks like the kerbstones of a cairn.

Originally there may have been about twenty in a circle 16ft 10ins (5.1m) in diameter. Most of the eastern side has disappeared. Four, of which two are missing, may have been much taller than the others. One at the south is 4ft 6ins high and another at the WNW 5ft 4ins (1.4, 1.6m). It is possible that this ruined site is a combination of a cairn and an embryonic Four-Poster rectangle 12ft 6ins (3.8m) square, its pillars standing on the circumference of a circle 17ft 6ins (5.3m) across. If so, it has affinities with similar rings at Backhill of Drachlaw (93), Raich (113) and South Ythsie (115).

PSAS 36, 1901–2, 526–7; Burl, 1988, 98–9, *Plan*

115 SOUTH YTHSIE (1) [B1/9]
Lat: 57°.4   NJ 884 305
4½ miles W *of Ellon, ¾ mile* WSW *of Tarves. Walk. From lane just* S *of trees at NJ 883 305 ring is 250 yds (230m)* E. *Easy. Map A*
On a hillslope at the eastern edge of foothills north of the main concentration of recumbent stone circles this is a ring of six heavy stones. Before its removal they stood in a mound about 36ft across and 3ft high (11 × 1m). It had a central hollow, 6ft (1.8m) wide with a single kerbstone at the ENE.

The stones form an ellipse 28ft SSW-NNE by 24ft (8.5 × 7.3m). In 1900 Coles recorded their heights as: NE 5ft 6ins; E 4ft 4ins; SSE 2ft 8ins; SSW, which was split, 5ft 7ins; WSW, a huge block seamed with quartz, 4ft 3ins; and NNW 2ft 6ins (1.7, 1.3, 0.8; 1.7; 1.3; 0.8m).

Since his time the mound has been levelled leaving more of the stones exposed so that Thom recorded their present heights as: 5ft; 6ft; 5ft; 8ft; 8ft; and 5ft (1.5, 1.8, 1.5, 2.4, 2.4, and 1.5m). The fact that they stand in the old land surface proves that the mound was heaped up around them at some time after their erection.

The four tallest of the slabs form a rectangle 23ft 4ins SW-NE by 14ft (7.1 × 4.3m) and stand on the circumference of a circle just over 47ft (14.3m) in diameter. Their disposition suggests that the site is a transitional form of Four-Poster with the tallest, and by far the most bulky, rising at the south-west and WSW.

The ring is only 1½ miles south of another 'Four-Poster' at Shethin (114).

PSAS 36, 1901–2, 524–6; Burl, 1988, 100–1, *Plan*

116 STRICHEN (2) [B1/1. Strichen House] Lat: 57°.6　　　　　NJ 936 544
13 miles WSW of Peterhead, ¾ miles SW of Strichen. Approach from the ruined

Strichen Hall at NJ 938 540. Walk. ¼ mile N. Easy. Map A
Standing on a gentle hilltop some 300 yards (275m) north of Strichen House this recumbent stone circle must head any list of disrupted rings. Its name sounds appropriate. It was modified from timber to stone, robbed, gothicised, destroyed, misconstructed, destroyed yet again and finally re-erected. That it deserves visiting is a megalithic miracle.

Even in August 1773, when Samuel Johnson and James Boswell called on Mr Fraser, later Lord Lovat, it was no more than a skeleton. Mr Fraser, Johnson remembered, 'shewed us in his grounds some stones yet standing of a druidical circle, and what I began to think more worthy of notice, some forest trees of full growth.' Boswell was just as unimpressed 'for all that remains is two stones set on end, with a long one laid upon them . . . and one stone at a little distance from them.'

This is what Alexander Thom saw around 1960 and it may be that the ring had already suffered not only the

Strichen, Aberdeenshire (116), the reconstructed recumbent stone circle from the south. A crescent of white quartz fragments lies opposite the recumbent stone. Excavated by the author and colleagues, 1979–82.

removal of stones but a rearrangement. An archive of 1794 recorded that labourers were employed 'in hurling [hauling?] dung to [the] Druid's Temple', presumably as fertiliser for the planting of trees and shrubs. It suggests that the stones were being 'enhanced' to become a retreat for Gothic contemplation. The later discovery of broken port bottles inside the ring tends to confirm this romantic whim.

The sanctuary was short-lived. Around 1830 a tenant farmer removed the stones. Lord Lovat, who in 1821 built the now ruinous Strichen House, ordered them replaced. It may have been then that the stones were wrongly positioned.

Certainly by 1885 the Rev. J. Peter remarked on the recumbent stone lying at the north, rather than south, of a wide circular bank 62ft (18.9m) in diameter. Following a visit in 1897 the Buchan Field Club noted that although the recumbent and its flankers remained *in situ* there was 'a new circle made round a chestnut tree on the south of the rostrum'.

In 1903 the percipient Fred Coles observed that 'all the Stones are placed several feet within the compact and continuous earthen bank at this spot . . . utterly at variance with any of the arrangements hitherto observed in our surveys.' By 1960 Thom stated 'This circle has certainly been re-erected.' Finally, when this writer visited the site in 1972 there was nothing to be seen. The circle had been destroyed for a second time. During the course of tree-felling in 1965 all the stones were torn up and dumped in a nearby quarry.

Indignant protests from the inhabitants of Strichen caused the recumbent and its flankers to be replaced. Excavations by the writer in 1979 on the 'modern bank' finding broken willow-patterned cups and saucers, and then by Abramson and Hampsher-Monk in 1980–2 on the prehistoric site, revealed that the original situation of the circle had been to the north of the recumbent which had lain at the SSE of a ring about 48ft (14.6m) in diameter.

The stony bank in which the stones stood was liberally strewn with quartz. A natural boulder at the east stood among a scatter of quartz chippings

Sunhoney, Aberdeenshire (117), *the group of cupmarks, outlined in chalk, can be seen at the east end of the recumbent stone.*

indicating that this was where the quartz had been smashed into bits before its ritual deposition. The cremation of a female and an urn were discovered near the hole of a missing stone. A cupmarked stone in a stone-lined pit lay at the north of the ring.

Within the badly disturbed central ring-cairn with a damaged cist there appeared to be the holes of an earlier timber ring, an antecedent suspected in several recently excavated stone circles.

In 1981 and 1982 stones were recovered from the gully and, with considerable effort, re-erected in stoneholes located during the excavation, recreating the original grading up to the focus of the recumbent. The east flanker was 6ft high and the west 6ft 6ins (1.8, 2m). The thin recumbent, which had a dip at the centre of its upper surface, was 8ft 6ins long and 2ft 6ins high (2.6 × 0.8m). It lay nicely in line with the most southerly moonrise.

Even today there are puzzles. It is surprising that a detailed Estate Map of 1768, showing flower and nursery gardens, lawns, ponds, the old Mansion, even a quarry and dovecote, does not show the circle. Nor do maps of 1796 and 1847.

Radiocarbon assays offer 'dates' that are, in Stuart Piggott's famous phrase, 'archaeologically unacceptable'. Two of 200 ± 60 bc (BM-2315) and 100 ± 80 bc (BM-2317) probably come from a superimposed Iron Age hut-circle. A third, 1140 ± 60 bc (BM-2316), about 1425 BC, from a disturbed area in the ring with cremated bone and undistinguished sherds, is best interpreted as the time when a Late Bronze Age burial was interred in an abandoned ring. It may have been the first of a succession of violations.

PSAS 19, 1884–5, 372; *ibid 38*, 1903–4, 279–80, *Plan*; *Current Archaeology 84*, 1982, 16–19, *Plan*

117 SUNHONEY (1) [B2/2]
Lat: 57°.1   NJ 716 058
8¹/₂ miles WNW of Peterculter, 1¹/₂ miles W of Echt. Walk. From Sunhoney farm

¹/₄ *mile N and W. Easy. Map A*
This fine recumbent stone circle stands in a grove of trees on a shallow hill-shoulder. From the awkward relationship of the fallen recumbent and its flankers the ring has probably undergone some reconstruction. A large fragment lies in front of the recumbent.

The circle is 83ft 3ins (25.4m) in diameter. Between its east and west flankers, 7ft 6ins and 6ft 7ins (2.2, 2m) in height respectively, the recumbent, 14ft 9ins (4.5m) long is a thin slab of grey granite unlike the red granite and gneiss of the circle-stones. They stand in a low rubble bank.

Inside is an overgrown ring-cairn, 64ft across and 1ft high (19.5 × 0.3m). In 1865 Dalrymple dug in the kerbed central space, 8ft (2.4m) across, finding eight deposits of cremated bone and fire-marked stones. A cist with some plain sherds lay to the south.

The recumbent, which appears to have fallen inwards, is lavishly cupmarked, most of the thirty-one cups being on the eastern half of the slab. They are astronomically situated. Like Midmar a mile to the WNW the southern skyline was too high for the most southerly moon ever to appear. Instead, the axis of the ring is well-directed towards the saddle between Meikle Tap and Greymore, the place where the southern moon at its minor setting would descend.

Stuart, I, 1856, xxi; *PSAS 34*, 1899–1900, 181–7, 'Sean Hinny'; *ibid 52*, 1917–18, 88–9; Browne, 1921, 56–60; *TTB*, 196, *Plan*

118 TOMNAGORN, Bankhead (3)
[B2/16] Lat: 57°.2   NJ 651 077
6¹/₂ miles W of Dunecht, 4 miles NNE of Torphins. Walk. To S of lane at NJ 652 081, just E of wood, ring is 600yds (550m) S and W. Barbed wire. Fair. Map A
Tomnagorn, perhaps 'green hill', stands on a hillock in an inconspicuous position. It is in fair condition.

In a circle 73ft 4ins (22.4m) across the stones are well graded up to the recumbent whose west flanker is shattered. The recumbent and east flanker stand a full 5ft (1.5m) inside the circumference and are linked by the eastern sideslab of a platform to an internal ring-cairn 46ft 9ins (14.3m) in diameter. A fine run of its kerbs survive from south to west. It had a stone-lined central space about 12ft (3.7m) across.

PSAS 34, 1899–1900, 173–9; Browne, 1921, 73–6; TTB, 220, *Plan*

119 TOMNAVERIE (4) [B2/9]
Lat: 57°.1   NJ 486 034
4 miles NW *of Aboyne,* ¼ *mile* SE *of Tarland. Walk. Just* S *of B9044. Climb short knoll. Easy. Map 1*
Tomnaverie, 'the hill of worship', a once fine recumbent stone circle is a wreck. Described in 1845 as a 'distinguished Druidical temple' its stones are now a jumble, wrecked by a quarry that surrounds the ring immediately to south and west. Circle-stones can be seen lying in it.

Many have disappeared. Those that survive are a pale red granite. Not unexpectedly, the recumbent is different, a dark basalt. Before the damage there was the recumbent, now fallen inwards, its flankers, now fallen outwards, and perhaps nine stones in a circle about 61ft (18.6m) in diameter. Inside was a ring-cairn, 48ft (14.6m) across, many of whose outer kerbs can still be made out. Virtually nothing remains of its 22ft 3ins (6.8m) central space. In 1904, when Coles saw it a dozen kerbs were apparent but even then the quarry was 'close up to, within indeed 3 feet of, one of the few Standing Stones yet *in situ*.'

PSAS 39, 1904–5, 208–13; Sir A. Ogston, *Prehistoric Antiquities of the Howe of Cromar*, 1931, 93–5; TTB, 210, *Plan*

120 WHITEHILL (3) [B2/18. Tillyfourie Hill] Lat: 57°.2   NJ 643 135
4½ miles ESE *of Alford,* 2¾ WSW *of Monymusk. From lane at NJ 656 133 take forestry track* W *for a mile. Walk. Ring is* ¼ *mile* N *in trees. Fair. Map A*
Although in a wood this is not the Whitehill Wood ring (121) but a

recumbent stone circle twenty-two miles to the south. It is in quite good condition and its internal ring-cairn is considerable.

The well-graded stones appear to have been brought from the shoulder of a hill ¼ mile to the north-east to be erected on the chosen terrace. Of reddish quartz porphyry they differ from the recumbent which is a dark grey 'heathen' stone veined with quartz.

The circle is about 72ft (22m) across. The recumbent is at the SSW, seven tons in weight, with a tall west flanker and fallen east flanker. From here a pavement of rough stones extends to the great cairn, 55ft (16.8m) in diameter and up to 5ft (1.5m) high, surrounded by a 'veritable rampart' of kerbstones. At its centre is a wide open space, irregular in shape, some 16ft by 13ft (4.9 × 4m).

Although difficult to make out in the darkness of the wood and the undergrowth the ring is closely surrounded by small cairns and 'ancient field-walls'.

PSAS 35, 1900–1, 203–8; Browne, 1921, 84–5; TTB, 224, *Plan*

121 WHITEHILL WOOD (3) [B4/1. Carnousie House]
Lat: 57°.5   NJ 678 505
3½ miles ESE *of Aberchirder, 3 miles* W *of Turriff. At NJ 678 504, where lane turns* W *through trees. Walk.* ¼ *mile* N. *Easy. Map A*
A. In undergrowth and bracken *Whitehill Wood* is the smaller of two adjacent circles. It is very damaged. Only two stones remain standing of a ring some 27ft (8.2m) across. When erect the stones would have been disproportionately tall in such a diminutive ring. The biggest, about 6ft 3ins (1.9m) high, standing at the south suggests that the circle had once been graded.

B. 82ft (25m) to the south is a much larger ring, 78ft (23.8m) in diameter, known as *Cairn Ennit*. It also is ruinous. It once had an enormous boulder, 8ft high by 11ft broad (2.4 × 3.4m) on its southern arc. A similar site existed at the Carlin Stone (see: Backhill of Drachlaw, 93) 2½ miles to the south. There a massive southern block was flanked by two much smaller in a ring rather larger than Cairn Ennit.

The Carlin Stone may have been an aberrant form of recumbent stone. The same might have been true at Cairn Ennit. Existing as they do at the northern edge of the 'classical' recumbent stone circle territory in a peripheral area where there are other examples of idiosyncratic circle architecture this seems a sensible interpretation of the rings.

PSAS 37, 1902–3, 137–40; TTB, 234, *Plan*

122 YONDER BOGNIE WARDEND (3) [B1/ 23] Lat: 57°.5   NJ 601 458
5¾ miles NE of Huntly, 1¾ miles WSW of Inverkeithny. Walk. ¼ mile S of Yonder Bognie farm. Easy. Map A
The land on which this recumbent stone circle stands has been farmed by the Shand family for almost five hundred years. During that time they have looked after the ring well.

The stones were erected on a pronounced slope even though there was a level knoll just to the east. Two stones at the north-west and north-east are fallen but four stand on the circumference of a circle about 65ft (19.8m) in diameter. At the SSE, however, the recumbent and its flankers are a full 9ft (2.7m) inside the perimeter. The east flanker is prostrate, 7ft (2.1m) long, the west flanker stands 5ft 7ins (1.7m) high and between them the level-topped, regular block of the recumbent is 9ft 2ins long, 4ft thick and 4ft 6ins high (2.8 × 1.2 × 1.4m). Its weight has been estimated to be over ten tons.

There is little sign of any internal ring-cairn today but in September 1856, an excavation in its central space found a paved area beneath which was a deep layer of 'pulverised bones', burnt matter and broken urns. The sherds are now in the Royal Museum of Scotland, Catalogue EA 102, 103.

From the middle of the ring the recumbent lies in line with the smoothly rounded, wooded Colyne Hill three miles to the south. The alignment is also towards the major southern moonrise.

PSAS 4, 1860–2, 448; Stuart, II, 1867, xxii; *PSAS* 37, 1902–3, 127–31; TTB, 184, *Plan*

ANGUS
The rings, probably Bronze Age, are small, often ruinous. Western influences from Perthshire are apparent

123 BALKEMBACK (3)
Lat: 56°.5   NO 382 384
4½ miles N of Dundee, 2½ miles E of Kirkton of Auchterhouse. Walk. 200yds (180m) N of lane to Balkemback. Easy. Map B
This is a very irregular setting of four stones, two fallen, which may be the ruins of a Four-Poster.

On a south-facing terrace the stones form a trapezoid about 29ft SSW-NNE by 22ft (8.8 × 6.7m) but conform to a circle 36ft (11m) in diameter. The area enclosed, about 750 s.ft (70m²), is more than three times that of the average Four-Poster.

The tallest stone is at the south-east, 3ft 8ins (1.1m) high but the fallen south-west pillar is some 5ft (1.5m) long. Typical of these Four-Posters it is the south-east stone that bears art, some thirty-seven cups and cup-and-rings on its wider eastern and western faces. The west has only cups but the east has large guttered cup-and-rings intermixed with small cups. A winding groove runs up the slab's lefthand side.

JBAA 37, 1881, 260, 262; Burl, 1988, 102–3, *Plan*

ARGYLLSHIRE
The county is more notable for its standing stones, cairns and decorated outcrops. Stone circles are few but interesting

124 STRONTOILLER, Lorne (3) [A1/2. Loch Nell] Lat: 56°.4   NM 906 291
3 miles E of Oban, ½ miles N of N end

of Loch Nell. From NM 890 292 take farm lane E for 1 mile. Turn N towards Strontoiller farm. Ring is in field 200yds (180m) after the turn. Easy. Map 1

This is a pleasing complex of a stone circle, standing stone and a kerb-cairn. The circle, of local granite erratics, has thirty-one stones remaining of a ring about 65ft (19.8m). The north-west arc is good, the east less so and there is a wide gap at the south. The tallest stone, no more than 3ft (1m) high, is there.

600ft (183m) to the SSE is a tall standing stone, Clach na Carraig, 13ft 4ins (4.1m) high. Just to its south-east is the kerb-cairn known as Diarmid's Grave. Inside a heavily kerbed area, graded up to the south and 16ft (4.9m) across, was a central pit excavated in 1967. In it was human cremated bone and a scatter of quartz bits.

GAJ 2, 1971, 1–7; PSAS 106, 1974–5, 30–3; TTB, 140, Plan

125 TEMPLE WOOD, Ri Cruin, Kilmartin Valley (2) [A2/8]
Lat: 56°.1   NR 827 979
6½ miles NNW of Lochgilphead, ¾ mile SW of Kilmartin, Alongside the lane at Slockavullin. Easy. Map 1

Sometimes known as Half Moon Wood this is one of the most interesting settings in Scotland. Standing against a line of impressive cairns, one of them, Nether Largie South, a chambered tomb, another, Nether Largie North with a lavishly decorated cist-slab in its accessible interior, in sight of the lunar Kilmartin Stones, and in a region of elaborately carved rock surfaces, the area is a megalithic paradise (pagan).

A. Excavations, first in 1928–9 and then between 1974 and 1980, proved the existence of a small northern ring, 34ft 6ins N-S by 32ft 10ins (10.5 × 10m), that began as a timber setting of the early fourth millennium BC only to be transformed into a stone circle that was never completed. A C-14 assay of 3075 ± 190 bc (GU-1296), from oak in the hole of the ENE stone, even if the tree had been 300 years old when felled, would still make this one of the

earliest recorded circles in Britain, dated to around 3500 BC.

The assay, however, may date the earlier post setting which with a 'playing-card' recumbent slab aligned north-south at its centre, may not have been a timber ring. 'It could follow that the earliest northern structure was not a circle at all, but some form of observatory, in which timber posts played some part.'

B. Just to its south was the well-known stone 'circle', in fact an ellipse 43ft 7ins N-S by 39ft 8ins (13.3 × 12.1m). What was not well-known was its involved history. Starting as a free-standing ring two of its twenty stones of local schist were decorated. The outer face of the northern stone bore two spirals, one noticed by the writer, the eastern anti-clockwise, the western clockwise. A stone at the NNE had a rather rough motif of concentric circles. Suggestively, the stone at the north and one opposite at the south were chlorite schists, mineralogically different from other slabs in the ring. This emphasis on the north-south alignment was common to both rings.

The site was changed. Drystone walling was inserted between the stones with an entrance left at the east. Later, two short cists inside revetted cairns were constructed to the north-east and west of the modified ring. Both had contained inhumations. That in the north-eastern was no more than a phosphate stain but lay with a N3 beaker, three flint arrowheads and a scraper. Set at the centre of the ring a large cist, 4ft 7ins long and 2ft 7ins wide (1.4 × 0.8m), rifled before the excavations of 1928, provided evidence of a cremation, a form of burial common to this and all later burials. It was an indication of a functional change from ritual to burial.

It was not the end of alteration. The drystone walling was thrown down and in its place slabs on edge were erected between the stones and across the entrance. Kerb-cairns were added inside the circle and the whole setting surrounded by a heavy, wide bank. A

Temple Wood, Argyll (125), from the south.

series of six radiocarbon determinations ranging from 1090 ± 55 bc (GU-1297) down to 857 ± 50 bc (SRR-530) show the continuing use of the site in this phase as a hallowed cemetery from about 1350 BC to 1050 BC.

Today the reconstructed site shows it as it would have looked in this final phase.

PSAS 63, 1928–9, 189, 'Poltalloch'; ibid 64, 1929–30, 130–1; GAJ 15, 1988–9, 53–124, Plans

ARRAN

There is a fine variety of rings on the island, Four-Posters, cairn-circles, concentrics, small ovals. Mostly in good condition

126 AUCHAGALLON, Machrie Bay (3)

Lat: 55°.6   NR 893 346
4 miles N of Blackwaterfoot, overlooking Machrie Bay. Alongside the lane just E of the A841. No walk. Very easy. Map 1
On a steeply-sloping ridge overlooking the sea this is an intriguing mixture of cairn, stone circle and recumbent stone.

In an irregular circle about 47ft (14.3m) across fifteen stones of local red sandstone surround a stony interior, partly field-clearance, partly the remains of a cairn in which an undocumented nineteenth-century excavation uncovered a cist.

The ring is not complete. There is a gap at the north-east. The stones range in height from 3ft to 7ft 8ins (0.9, 3.2m). The latter is the thin flanker to a 'recumbent' slab at the west, 6ft high and 4ft 10ins long (1.8 × 1.5m). The stone to its east is 5ft 6ins (1.7m) high. In the arrangement of the three stones, the internal cairn and the orientation the setting could be a variant form of recumbent stone circle.

Bryce, 119–20, *Plan*

127 AUCHELEFFAN (1)

Lat: 55°.5   NR 978 251
5½ miles ESE of Blackwaterfoot, 1 mile SSW of Carn Ban chambered tomb.
From Torryline, NR 960 215, drive N 1 mile to edge of forest. Walk. Ring is 2½ miles uphill along track, NNE then NW. Hard going. Map 1
Unless very fit, with plenty of time and enthusiasm, do not attempt the walk to Carn Ban, NR 991 262. The tomb is

interesting but the approach is long, steep and demanding.

Aucheleffan is a perfect Four-Poster, beautifully preserved and once with a lovely view across the sea to Ailsa Craig at the south. Today the ring is engulfed in a coniferous Forestry plantation.

On a hill-shoulder four stones stand at the corners of a 16ft (4.9m) square, and on the circumference of a circle 23ft (7m) in diameter. They are almost exactly north-south, east-west of each other. Of local granite the heights are: NW, 3ft 7ins; NE, 3ft 3ins; SE, 2ft 6ins; SW, 3ft 10ins (1.1, 1, 0.8, 1.2m).

Excavation in 1910 found nothing. The name of the ring means 'halfpenny field', a record of its mediaeval rental value.

Bryce, 123–4; Burl, 1988, 110–11, *Plan*

128 LAMLASH (3)
Lat: 55°.5   NS 018 336
1½ miles S of Brodick, 1½ miles NNW of Lamlash. Immediately E of the A 841. Easy. Map 1
Near the east coast of Arran this damaged ring now consists of three large and one smaller boulder of local granite. Originally there may have been seven stones in a ring about 22ft (6.7m) across. Of those that remain the south-west is 4ft high, the WNW only 2ft 4ins, the NNW 3ft (1.2, 0.7, 1m). At the south-east is a massive fallen boulder, the largest of all. A possible outlier of conglomerate stands 4ft (1.2m) high 64ft (19.5m) to the south.

On 28 September 1861, having explored the circles on Machrie Moor, James Bryce excavated the centre of the ring discovering a small cist, only 2ft 2ins long and 10½ins deep (66, 27cm) roughly cut into the solid sandstone bedrock. In it were fragments of bone, black earth and flints. There was a violent storm. 'Exposed in this elevated spot to the full fury of the south wind and force of the pelting rain, our men could hardly keep their footing, yet did they work away bravely till I had fully explored the rude cist.' He also dug

around the outlier but found nothing.

PSAS 4, 1860–2, 513; *ibid 40*, 1905–6, 296–9, *Plan*

129 MACHRIE BURN (1)
Lat: 55°.6   NR 908 351
6¾ miles W of Brodick, 4½ miles N of Blackwaterfoot. Walk. From Auchagallon cross moor for 1 mile ENE. Fair. Map 1
This is a fine Four-Poster of low stones. None more than 2ft (60cm) high, they form a rectangle 11ft 2ins NNE-SSW by 8ft 9ins (3.4 × 2.7m), and a circle 13ft (4m) in diameter. An excavation in 1909 found nothing.

There are hut-circles 160 yards (146m) to the east, and 130ft (40m) to the NNE is an overgrown field-wall.

Bryce, 150; Burl, 1988, 118–19, *Plan* (the scale is wrong)

130 MACHRIE MOOR (3) [A8/6. Machrie Moor II]
Lat: 55°.5   NR 912 324
2¾ miles NNE of Blackwaterfoot. All these sites are in State care. They may be visited without charge. Cars must be left behind at the roadside gate NR 895 330. Walk. 1¼ miles. Track for 1 mile to open moorland. On a fine day it is a comfortable walk. The visitor will be rewarded with the sight of what may be the best group of architecturally varied stone circles in western Europe. Map 1
On Machrie Moor there is a splendid collection of prehistoric monuments, the ruins of chambered tombs, hut-circles and six megalithic rings. They stand on a low-lying triangle, five square miles of fertile soil as the name Machrie implies, 'machair', a stretch of flat sandy land.

There is such a variety of design among the rings, some plain, some with stones of alternating heights, one with an inner ring, that it is likely that they were put up over several centuries. Traces of hut-walls and enclosures to the west hint that they were erected in a 'sacred area' to the east where no settlements were allowed. Two were built of tall sandstone pillars, probably from the coastal cliffs a mile away.

Machrie Burn Four-Poster, Arran (129), *from the south.*

Others were made of rounded granite boulders plentiful on the moor itself. Excavations by James Bryce in 1861, by the writer in 1978–9, and by Alison Haggarty in 1985–6, have revealed something of the changing history of the rings.

A. From the sign-posted road to the west the first site to be seen is a complex ring-cairn known as *Circle X*, NR 900 327. Partial excavation by the writer in the wet autumn of 1979 showed that the cairn had been enclosed in an exact circle of thin sandstone slabs with a diameter of 71ft 6ins (21.8m). A bank of closely-packed fist-sized stones of local granite surrounded it. Inside was the doughnut-shaped cairn of heavy boulders. Once it had an open central space but this had been filled in with sand and scattered boulders. A mass of small red angular sandstones had capped the cairn. The famous Machrie Moor circles stand 1100 yards (1000m) to the ESE, for the most part along a good track.

B. The site of *Circle I*, NR 912 324, had been farmed by Early Neolithic communities before two concentric rings of posts were erected around a horsehoe-shaped timber setting open to the north-west. The outer ring was irregular, about 65ft 6ins (20m) across. It enclosed a better circle 47ft 7ins (14.5m) in diameter. Radiocarbon determinations ranging from 2520 ± 50 bc (GU-2316) to 2030 ± 180 bc (GU-2325) offer a median date for the rings of about 2900 BC. Earlier agriculturalists using round-bottomed Grimston/Lyles Hill pottery left debris that averaged about 3900 BC.

The rings were replaced by a stone circle, once of twelve but now eleven stones, in which grey granite boulders alternated with reddish sandstone pillars. Bryce dug into the oval 48ft SE-NW by 40ft (14.6 × 12.2m) but found nothing. Careful examination of the old land-surface in 1978 failed to detect either of the focal points that should have existed to lay out the hypothetically precise ellipse. Only some poor implements of Arran pitchstone were discovered. By the tumbled north-west boulder was a pile of stones, probably the result of field-clearances by later people.

C. 200ft (61m) to the WNW is *Circle II*, NR 911 324. Here only three tall

115

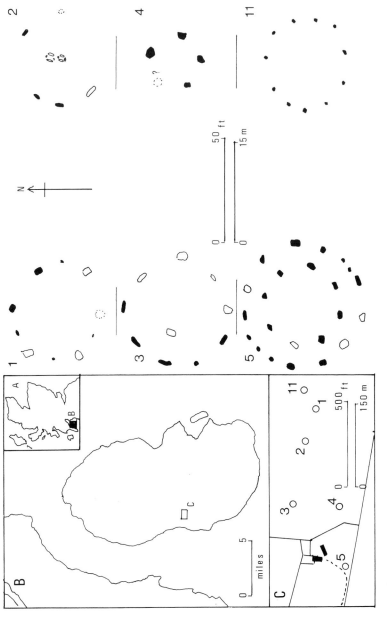

Machrie Moor, Arran (130)

Machrie Moor XI, Arran (130g), *from the south-west showing the newly-discovered circle. The author's excavation in the wet autumn of 1978.*

sandstones stand at the west to north-east of a circle 42ft (12.8m) in diameter. They are roughly dressed. The tallest is a towering 17ft 5ins (5.3m) high. It is likely that the stones had to be brought from Achanar a full two miles away.

Inside the ring Bryce found two short cists. The central contained an Early Bronze Age food-vessel, and four flints the nearest source of which was in Co. Antrim forty miles to the south-west across the North Channel. The second cist was empty. The finds are in the Royal Museum of Scotland, Edinburgh.

In modern times some stones were toppled to be shaped into millstones. Two lie inside the ring, one of them perforated.

D. *Circle III*, NR 910 325, is 400ft (122m) to the WNW. One tall pillar of sandstone stands, three stumps are visible and five lie buried, up to 14ft (4.3m) long. The ring was egg-shaped 53ft 7ins SSW-NNE by 50ft 5ins (16.3 × 15.4m). Bryce found two more short cists in the interior, the central having a sherd and flint arrowheads in it. To its south the second had two other

arrowheads and parts of the skeleton of a round-headed twenty-two-year old man.

E. *Circle IV*, NR 910 324, 250ft (76m) to the south, may be foreign in its architecture. Four low granite boulders lie at the corners of a poor trapezoid but a fifth stone could have stood at the north-west where an ancient track cuts through the western arc of a circle only 29ft 6ins (9m) across. With its lowest stone at the south-west the ring was possibly an Irish Five-Stone circle. A short cist at its centre, dug by Bryce in September 1861, held bone fragments, a small bronze awl, a food-vessel and three flint arrowheads.

F. *Circle V*, NR 909 324, 350ft (107m) to the west was a concentric ring with eight small boulders in its inner ring and fifteen smaller in the outer, an irregular circle 59ft 5ins (18.1m) in diameter. Its central cist had been wrecked.

The ring is known as Suidhe Choir Fhionn, 'Fingal's cauldron seat' and a block at its south-east has a natural ledge in which there is a weatherworn

117

hole. Fingal used it for tethering his dog, Bran.

G. The most exciting result of the 1978 excavations was the uncovering of a previously unsuspected circle that, following Bryce's numbering, became *Circle XI*, NR 913 324. Peat had almost entirely engulfed it and only the very tips of a few stones could be seen.

Like Circle I it had been preceded by an uncircular timber ring of ten posts. It was impossible to fit a circle to the shape which may have resulted from the conjunction of two semi-circles to form a ring 48ft 3ins by 42ft 4ins (14.7 × 12.9m). Excavations in 1985 and 1986 recovered sherds of grooved ware, impressed sherds and beaker.

The timber ring was replaced by an equally assymmetrical stone ring 44ft 7ins by 40ft (13.6 × 12.2m) to which it was impossible to fit a circle, oval, egg-shape or spiral. Of the ten, small standing stones nine were sandstones, and one at the north-east granite. Finds of waste flint flakes, and knives and scrapers of Arran pitchstone gave no indication of the age of Circle XI but, in 1985, an assay from material not directly associated with the ring, 1740 ± 50 bc (GU-2323) suggested that it had been standing before 2150 BC.

A detailed survey by John Barnatt in 1978 showed that the six rings, I, II, III, IV, V and XI, had been discriminatingly situated on Machrie Moor below a prominent notch on the high skyline to the north-east where Machrie Glen divides into two steep-sided valleys. Four of the rings 'are sited so that the notch is intersected exactly on midsummer morning.' The other two are only slightly misplaced. 'It explains why all six circles are located in only one restricted area of the three zones of high prominence on the moor' and that 'this midsummer orientation offers the most coherent explanation' for the situation of the rings.

H. Three-quarters of a mile east at NR 924 322 is a ruined Four-Poster at Ballymichael Bridge.

PSAS 4, 1860–2, 499–24; Trans

Glasgow A.S. 15 (2), 1963, 59–67; Arran Naturalist 4, 1980, 21–6, Plans; Scottish Arch. Review 2 (2), 1983, 101–16; PSAS 121, 1991, 51–94

BANFFSHIRE
The circles of Banffshire share architecture from the W with the Clava cairn tradition and from the S where there are recumbent stone circles and smaller rings

131 DOUNE OF DALMORE (5)
Lat: 57°.4   NJ 185 308
10¼ miles SW of Dufftown, 8 miles N of Tomintoul. Walk. From NJ 186 304. ¼ mile N to the E of the R. Spey. Fair. Map 1

This ring is in such a ruinous state that it is impossible to tell whether one is looking at a wrecked Clava ring-cairn or a devastated recumbent stone circle. The writer is inclined, with total uncertainty, to believe the former.

There are the remains of an outer stone circle possibly 52ft (15.9m) in diameter. Originally perhaps of ten local quartzites it seems to have been graded to the south-west. There are six prostrate stones confusedly lying around the circumference with three standing at the NNW, east and SSE. The shortest, 4ft 6ins (1.4m) long lies at the north but at the SSW is a slab 8ft (2.4m) long with another 7ft 6ins (2.3m) long just to the west.

There is a suspicion of the outer kerbs of a ring-cairn about 36ft (11m) across inside the circle. They are low and few. Within the 'setting' is a central space perhaps 20ft (6m) across in which there is a problematical rectangle 6ft 6ins by 3ft (2 × 1m) of four stones.

PSAS 41, 1906–7, 136–9, Plan; Henshall, II, 274, footnote

132 MARIONBURGH (3)
Lat: 57°.4   NJ 183 364
9 miles WSW of Dufftown, ¼ mile NE of Upper Lagmore. Walk. From the A95 at NJ 185 364, 300yds (275m) to the W. Easy. Map 1

Among trees this wrecked ring appears

to have Clava affinities. Five standing stones and four fallen form the circumference of a ring about 75ft (23m) across. They range from 2ft 3ins high at the south-west to 9ft high at the ssw (0.7–2.7m). Remains of a central cairn, up to 2ft (0.6m) high can be seen.

PSAS 41, 1906–7, 151–4; Henshall, I, 391, Plan

133 NORTH BURRELDALES (3) [B4/2. Burreldales] Lat: 57°.6   NJ 676 549 *4¹/₂ miles NW of Turriff, 3¹/₂ miles NE of Aberchirder. Walk. ¹/₄ mile W of the B921. Easy. Map A*
On Brownside Hill in a romanticised grove of trees are the disrupted grey granites of a small ring once about 21ft (6.4m) across. Two stand at the wsw and north-west, both about 3ft 4ins (1m) tall. There are four smaller fallen stones on the eastern side with a squarish slab about 3ft by 4ft (1 × 1.2m) at the south-east.

This may have been a Four-Poster with its largest stone at the south-east.

PSAS 40, 1905–6, 165–7; Burl, 1988, 123, Plan

134 ROTHIEMAY (3) [B4/4. Milltown] Lat: 57°.5   NJ 550 487 *5¹/₂ miles N of Huntly, ¹/₄ mile N of Milltown. Walk. In a field immediately s of the B9117. Easy. Map A*
A. Not a great deal survives of this recumbent stone circle. Despite this paucity the ring is of considerable interest.

In a circle once about 92ft (28m) across only the recumbent and four tall stones, each about 6ft (1.8m) high, survive of an original twelve. Others were taken away *circa* 1845 and two were dumped by the gateway to the field. In 1867 surveyors reported that 'when entire there was generally an outer and inner circle with a sort of intervening embankment carried round the circle to the east and north-east.' Nothing can be seen of it in the level field.

The huge recumbent must have lain near to 216° from the centre of the

ring. (The plan in Thom, Thom and Burl, 1980, 238, mistakenly shows True North 90° to the east). It is a tremendous block, flat-topped for two-thirds of its length, 14ft long, 4ft thick, 5ft high (4.3 × 1.2 × 1.5m), 20 tons of dark basalt. On its inner face is an astonishment of megalithic art, over a hundred cupmarks and several cup-and-ring marks, almost nothing at the stone's jagged east end, a wide NW-SE band down the centre with others low down at the western end.

The stone 27ft (8.2m) to the east of the recumbent is also cupmarked. 4ft 9ins high and 4ft wide (1.5 × 1.2m) it has seven cups on its outer face with others, half-concealed in the grass, near its base. With the known association of such art in recumbent stone circles it is unsurprising to find that the pillar stands in line with the major southern moonrise. There may be a rare solar alignment through the centre of the recumbent to the midwinter sunset.

PSAS 37, 1902–3, 133–7; ibid 40, 1905–6, 180–1; Browne, 1921, 83–4; PSAS 52, 1917–18, 104–8; TTB, 238, Plan
B. On Avochie Hill 1¹/₂ miles ssw of Rothiemay and near to NJ 541 470, is another heavily decorated stone. Of dark basalt and measuring 11ft long by 9ft thick by 2ft 3ins high (3.4 × 2.7 × 0.7m) it may have been the recumbent of a destroyed circle. At its north-west corner are twenty-nine cups and eight cup-and-rings, in the centre are twenty-nine cups and two cup-and-rings, and low down at the south-east are a further five cups and six cup-and-rings.

PSAS 40, 1905–6, 318–20; ibid 69, 1934–5, 224

135 UPPER LAGMORE, Bridge of Avon (3) Lat: 57°.4   NJ 176 358 *7 miles SW of Charlestown of Aberlour, ¹/₂ mile W of Bridge of Avon. Walk. From NJ 177 355, uphill ¹/₄ mile through a field. Easy. Map 1*
A. The circle is a ruinous Clava passage-tomb with a well-preserved entrance. Its surrounding circle was about 54ft (16.5m) in diameter. Of an

original nine stones five stand, the tallest, 7ft 3ins (2.2m) high, at the west, with a fallen stone at the south-east 12ft (3.7m) long. They are of local quartose schist.

Inside are the remains of a ring-cairn 42ft (12.8m) across. At its SSE is an entrance constructed of two stones 3ft high and 2ft apart (1 × 0.6m) with a displaced lintel leaning on them. The passage did not lead to the centre but to the south side of a central chamber about 11ft (3.4m) across. It may have been corbelled.

B. 300 yards (275m) to the east across the road are the remains of the Lower Lagmore circle, NJ 180 359, perhaps a second passage- tomb. Today three erect stones 3ft 10ins to 5ft 8ins (1.2, 1.7m) high and two prostrate are all that survive of a ring some 65ft (19.8m) in diameter. There are cupmarks on the north-east stone.

PSAS 41, 1906–7, 141–9; Henshall, I, 389–90, Plan

BERWICKSHIRE
There is one large, but probably late ring here

136 BORROWSTON RIGG, Dabshood (5) [G9/10] Lat: 55°.8   NT 560 521
4¾ miles WNW of Westruther, 3½ miles NNE of Lauder. Walk. From Burncastle farm, NT 538 514, ¼ mile downhill along track to the Earnscleugh Water. ¼ mile steep climb up the scarp then 1 mile ENE across the moor. Very demanding. Map 1
Standing at 1150ft (350m) O.D. this exceptionally large ring of small stones is an ellipse measuring 136ft 2ins ESE-WNW by 120ft (41.5 × 36.6m). Thom suggested that it was egg-shaped, its design based on the overlapping of a WNW ring, 84ft 4ins (25.7m) across, that coincided at its ESE with the centre of a larger ESE circle 136ft (41.5m) in diameter.

On the Ordnance Survey maps, however, the ring is marked as a cairn and its surviving thirty-two low stones, never more than 2ft (0.6m) high, may

be the kerbs of a levelled mound. Other damaged cairns lie 80ft (24.4m) to the north-west and 200ft (60m) to the south.

The site is seven miles due east of the ploughed-down Overhowden henge, 328ft (100m) across, with a single entrance at the north-west. The Leader Water separates the enclosures.

Borrowston Rigg is the only remaining stone circle in Berwickshire. Another at Kirktonhill was demolished around 1864.

RCAHM-Berwick, 1915, xxxi, no. 226; Thom, 1967, 69, Plan, 71

BUTE
The rings here are undistinguished. They are not in a good state

137 ETTRICK BAY (3) [A9/2]
Lat: 55°.9   NS 044 668
3¼ miles NW of Rothesay, 1½ miles WSW of Kaimes Bay. Walk. 150 yds (135m) S of the A844. Easy. Map 1
Sometimes known as the Kilmachalmaig circle, four tall stones, the biggest 7ft 3ins (2.2m) high at the north, and four broken stumps form an ellipse 50ft 4ins N-S by 39ft 6ins (15.3 × 12m). They are all of local slate. To the south a displaced stone is just outside the ring. There are two other stones to the ENE.

J.K. Hewison, *Bute in Olden Times, I*, 1893, 81–3, *Plan*

CAITHNESS
The few rings here tend to be large and open but ruinous. There are two, once three, megalithic horseshoes

138 ACHAVANICH, Loch Stemster (3)
Lat: 58°.4   ND 188 417
12 miles SW of Wick, ¾ mile SE of Achavanich on lane branching SE from the A895. Immediately E of the lane. Easy. Map 1
A. Just south of Loch Stemster in an area of heather and peat this almost unique site is not a megalithic ring but a megalithic horseshoe. The name,

sometimes quoted as Achinloch, means 'field of the stones'.

Originally there were fifty-four stones in a horseshoe 225 ft (68.6m) and with an open mouth at the SSE about 85ft (25.9m) across. Today there are thirty-four including two stumps and three prostrate slabs. The stones stand in an embankment, most obvious at the west by the road.

On the western side twenty-seven stones are erect, averaging 3ft 3ins (1m) in height, with a tall terminal 6ft 6ins (2m) high at the southern end.

The eastern side is more damaged. Fourteen stones remain but they average 4ft (1.2m) high, a third taller than their western counterparts, a 'high-and-low' trait known in northern Ireland and Brittany. Rather than set conventionally in line with the perimeter, all the slabs stand radially across it like the cogs of a wheel.

In common with the multiple rows that are widespread in the counties of Caithness and Sutherland there is a cist, 5ft long by 3ft 9ins across (1.5 × 1.1m), at the head of the horseshoe. Nothing is known of its contents.

With a long axis, 340°–160° the setting is well-aligned on the major southern rising of the moon.

Sir Henry Dryden in: J. Fergusson, *Rude Stone Monuments . . .* , 1872, 530–1; *RCAHM-Caithness*, 1911, 293, *Plan*; Burl, 1993, 117

B. At *Broubster*, ND 048 608, 14½ miles north-west of Achavanich, there is a comparable but very badly preserved monument. The surviving stones also stand radially in a setting 140ft NNE-SSW by 90ft (42.7 × 27.4m).

The approach is difficult, one mile east and NNE avoiding Lochan Ealach and bogs to the north. In compensation, there are standing stones on the way at ND 046 600 and ND 048 601/2.

RCAHM-Caithness, 1911, no. 163

139 GUIDEBEST (3) [N1/13. Latheron Wheel Burn] Lat: 58°.3   ND 181 351 *3½ miles NNE of Dunbeath, 1½ miles NW of Latheron. Walk. 300 yds (275m)*

W of the lane between Janetstown and Den Moss. Easy. Map 1

So close to a burn at its south-west that the water threatens to wear away the bank against the stones, this was one of the biggest stone circles in Scotland. Its situation is low-lying, in a hollow. The ring is 188ft (57.3m) in diameter. Possibly once of thirteen stones, seven still stand and one is prostrate. The entire eastern half has been removed. The tallest stone, 4ft 9ins (1.5m) high, stands at the west.

There is a cairn just to the south and another, small and overgrown, at the north-east.

RCAHM-Caithness, 1911, no. 279; TTB, 324, *Plan*

DUMFRIESSHIRE

A fine county for stone circles, the major influences coming from the S and the Lake District. Large ovals are frequent

140 GIRDLE STANES (3) [G7/5] Lat: 55°.2   NY 254 961 *11 miles NE of Lockerbie, 6 miles NE of Boreland. Just W of the B709 200 yds (180m) down slope to the R. White Esk. Easy. Map 1*

This naturally damaged ring stands on level ground by the River White Esk among high hills. The river has changed its course since the erection of the stones and a larger part of the west side of the ring has fallen into the water as the bank collapsed.

Of an original forty to forty-five stones twenty-six survive in a ring that was about 128ft (39m) in diameter. They stand in a substantial bank that is most obvious at the north and east. Their heights range from 2ft 6ins to 6ft (0.8–1.8m) at the north.

In this emphasis on a cardinal point the ring is similar to the rather smaller Swinside (26) in the Lake District and the resemblance becomes closer when there appears to be an entrance at the south-east where two stones, 4ft 4ins and 4ft 10ins (1.3, 1.5m) high frame an 11ft (3.4m) wide gap. Other prostrate

The Girdle Stanes, Dumfriesshire (140), from the east. The River White Esk is at the far side of the eroded ring.

The Loupin' Stanes, Dumfriesshire (142), from the east. The ring stands on a manmade platform.

stones outside them may have been portals.

From the centre of the ring to the northern stone of the entrance the azimuth is directed towards the towering hillside and the southernmost rising of the sun in early November, the festival of Samain, a solar alignment akin to Swinside's solstitial sightline.

Two fallen stones lie about 400ft (120m) to the north of the Girdle Stanes at the head of a slight ridge. They may be the remains of a row or avenue that led to the Loupin' Stanes (142) about 600 yards (550m) to the north.

PSAS 31, 1896–7, 281–9; J. and R. Hyslop, *Langholm As It Was*, 1912, 17–46; TTB, 298, *Plan*; Burl, 1993, 38–9, 231

141 LOCHMABEN STANE, Gretna Green (4) Lat: 55°.0   NY 312 659
7 miles E of Annan, ¼ mile SW of Gretna Green. Ask at Old Graitney farm, NY 312 666. Stone is 700 yds (640m) S. Easy. Map D
Also known as the Clochmabenstane this isolated and tumbled boulder would have no place in a Guide to stone circles were it not for the C-14 determination that dated it. This huge eighteen ton granite erratic, 9ft 6ins long and 18ft in circumference (2.9 × 5.5m), fell in February 1982. Charcoal of oak, willow and hazel from its shallow stonehole gave an assay of 2525 ± 85 bc (GU-1591), approximately 3275 BC, a very early date, but one in accord with the postulated age of the great Cumbrian rings across the Solway Firth.

It had been part of a large stone circle. In 1841 the Rev. James Roddick wrote that 'On the farm of Old Graitney . . . was seen not many years ago a number of white stones placed upright circling half an acre of ground in an oval form. One of them, the largest, is all that now remains, as some suppose, of a Druidical temple, the rest having been removed for the cultivation of the soil.'

The area and the shape offer clues

about the destroyed ring. Other large megalithic ellipses, the Twelve Apostles (143) and Whitcastle (144), are known in Dumfriess-shire, the ratio of their long and short diameters being about 6:5. If the country parson's estimate of half an acre was well-judged the Lochmaben Stone would be the survivor of an oval some 180 by 150 ft (55 × 46m) with an internal area of about 2360 s.yds (1970m²), or 0.49 acres. Standing at the northern end of the most useful ford across the Solway firth, the Sulwath or 'muddy ford', still negotiable today, the ring's hypothetical size and shape are explained by its proximity to the great Lake District circles.

'Lochmaben' may be derived from the Celtic deity, Mabon or Maponus, the 'great youth, Apollo', a whisper of tradition connecting the ring with rituals involving the sun. It was a place of sufficient importance for English and Scottish commissioners to meet there in 1398 to discuss the terms of a truce following a Scottish invasion and the Battle of Otterburn in 1388.

Old Statistical Account, Dumfriess, 1841, 266–7; *RCAHM-Dumfriess*, 1920, 92–3; *TDGNHAS 58*, 1983, 16–20, *Plan* of stone and hole

142 LOUPIN' STANES (1, 4) [G7/4] Lat: 55°.3   NY 257 966
11 miles NE of Lockerbie, 600 yards (550m) N of the Girdle Stanes. Walk is easy but can be waterlogged. Map 1
There is one good and two almost undetectable rings here on the holm, an area of flat land near the River White Esk.

A. The central ring, about 37ft 3ins N-S by 34ft 6ins (11.4 × 10.5m) is strange but well-preserved. It was erected on an artificial platform on ground falling to the south. On it twelve stones, ten between 1ft and 2ft (30–60cm) high, squat in contrast to two much higher, 8ft (2.4m) apart, at the west. The WSW, 5ft 4ins (1.6m) high, is a thinnish tapering pillar, unlike its heavier, flat-topped partner, also 5ft 4ins tall but 4ft (1.6 × 1.2m) wide.

The name, 'the leaping stones' comes from the habit young men had of jumping from the top of one tall pillar to the other. The sport was abandoned when one of them predictably broke his leg.

B. Just to its north-west are a few stones, almost hidden, that may have been part of a circle 44ft (13.4m) in diameter.

C. About 90ft (27m) east of the first site are some fallen stones of a probable oval, measuring some 75ft by 60ft (23 × 18m).

There is an interrupted, meandering line of fallen stones curving around a knoll from the rings towards the Girdle Stanes at the south.

J. and R. Hyslop, *Langholm As It Was*, 1912, 19–20, 41–2; *TDGNHAS 11*, 1923–4, 106; TTB, 296, *Plan*

143 TWELVE APOSTLES, Holywood (3) [G6/1] Lat: 55°.1   NX 947 794
3 miles wsw of Locharbriggs, 2½ miles NW of Dumfriess. Walk. 300yds (275m) SE of junction of B729 and lane to E. In field. Easy. Map 1
Divided by a hedge and on a slight slope down to the north this is a very large but much disturbed ring. It is probably an oval 284ft N-S by 260ft (86.6 × 79.3m), originally perhaps of eighteen stones spaced quite regularly 48ft (14.6m) apart. With an interior of almost 58,000ft^2 (5,390m^2) it is the seventh biggest ring in Britain.

One of the twelve stones had been removed before 1837. Only five of the remaining eleven stones stand. Others have been shifted. Unexpectedly, only four are local, the rest apparently having been transported by man-power from Irongrey Hill two miles away. A tall stone, 6ft 6ins (2m) stands at the north-east. Opposite is a vast fallen slab, a huge block 10ft 6ins long by 7ft 6ins by 4ft 10ins (3.2 × 2.3 × 1.5m). The south-westerly alignment is a good one towards the midwinter sunset.

Ploughing has turned up unusual amounts of white quartz. Aerial photography has revealed the presence of two nearby cursuses. Some 1500

yards (1370m) north-west of the circle is the squared end of one lying NNW-SSE. A second, a third of a mile from the ring, has a curved northern terminal. Arranged NNE-SSW it would, if extended, run directly towards the Twelve Apostles.

PSAL 10, 1883–5, 303–4; *PSAS 28*, 1893–4, 84–90; *RCAHM-Dumfriess*, 1920, no. 284; TTB 288, *Plan*

144 WHITCASTLES, Hartfell (4) [G7/6] Lat: 55°.2   NY 224 881
6¼ miles NE of Lockerbie, 4 miles SE of Boreland. Drive N from NY 233 858 for 1 mile to where farm lane veers W and S. Walk. Follow footpath ¾ mile NW. Ring is 150yds (140m) to N. Fair. Map 1
The ruins of this large ring lie on open moorland. Nine massive granites lie raggedly around the circumference of an oval about 180ft NE-SW by 148ft (55 × 45m), 2325 s.yds (1944m^2). The longest are at the north, 7ft 4ins long, and south, 7ft 1in (2.2, 2.2m). This interest in the cardinal points is a recurrent feature of the rings around the Solway Firth. The stones may have fallen because of their shallow and badly-prepared holes.

RCAHM-Dumfriess, 1920, no. 307; TTB, 300, *Plan*

**145 WHITEHOLM RIGG (3) [G7/2. Seven Brethren]
Lat: 55°.1   NY 217 827**
5 miles E of Lockerbie, 5 miles NNE of Ecclefechan. Walk. 150yds (135m) E of the A709. On moorland. Easy. Map 1
There may once have been twelve stones in this now dishevelled ring where seven or eight stones, 1ft 2ins to 2ft 4ins (37–75cm) high, form a circle about 65ft 6ins (20m) in diameter. The ring lies on level moorland to the south of the Water of Milk.

Despite the modest size of its stones the ring has affinities with the great circles of south-west Scotland and the Lake District. Exactly to the north at a distance of 28ft (8.5m) lies a slab some 3ft 5ins (1m) long, probably an outlier placed at a cardinal point.

Balbirnie, Fife (146), from the south.

RCAHM-Dumfriess, 1920, no. 603,
Plan; *TDGNHAS 11*, 1923–4, 106

FIFE
*There are three attractive and quite
dissimilar rings here, a multi-phase ring,
a possible Four-Poster and the
fragments of a great circle-henge*

146 BALBIRNIE (2)
Lat: 56°.2   NO 285 029
*6¹/₂ miles N of Kirkcaldy, ³/₄ mile NW of
Markinch. Immediately E of the A92 in
Balbirnie Park, Alongside the track
260 yds (240m) S of North Lodge. Easy.
Map B*
This excellent ring is not in its original
position. It has suffered both in
prehistory and in historic times. With
some stones removed in the eighteenth-
century, dug into in 1883 when bones
and sherds were found, damaged by
trees, it was finally excavated and
restored in 1970–1 when threatened by
the widening of the A92. It was re-
erected about 120 yards (110m) to the
south-east.

The site had three distinct prehistoric
phases. Known locally as the Druids

Circle ten stones had stood in an ellipse
49ft 3ins SW-NE by 45ft 10ins (15 ×
14m). Five were erect, there were three
stumps and two were missing. Spaced
14ft 5ins (4.4m) apart the tallest were
at the south, up to 6ft (1.8m) high.
Two at the NNE and north-east, 8ft
(2.4m) apart, were slightly angled
outwards from the circumference and it
is interesting that from the centre of the
ring an alignment to the northern side
of the north-east stone would have been
in line with the midsummer sunrise.

Cremated bone was discovered in
four stoneholes with minute bits in a
fifth. Grooved ware sherds lay in the
hole of the north-east stone.

At the open centre of the ring was a
slab-lined rectangle, 10ft 10ins N-S by
9ft 2ins (3.3 × 2.8m) which may have
been a form of mortuary enclosure.
Charcoal from the soil that had
accumulated above this feature gave a
date of 890 ± 80 bc (GaK-3426),
approximately 1100 BC, a time
probably relating to the third and final
phase.

The circle was transformed into a
cemetery. Four cists, and possibly a
fifth, were inserted in the space between

the stones and the rectangle. One at the east contained some cremated bone and a finely cup- and cup-and-ring marked sideslab. It is now represented by a concrete replica.

A very small cist in a pit at the north-east held the cremated bones of a female and child. With them was a bone bead. At the north-west corner of the rectangle a third cist of four big slabs had the cremations of another woman and child, a food-vessel and a flint knife. Just outside to its south was a carefully decorated slab bearing seventeen cupmarks with toolmarks visible on it. A fourth cist at the south-east corner of the rectangle survived only as a single slab. By it lay a v-perforated jet button.

Against a little clutter of stones near the rectangle's south-west corner lay an S4 beaker, flattened between two wooden planks whose charcoal provided an assay of 1330 ± 90 bc (GaK-3425), a time just before 1600 BC. Perhaps shortly later the cists were covered by a low cairn whose edges were supported by drystone walling between the circle-stones. The date, the walling, the planks and the beaker are remarkably like the finds made by the writer at Berrybrae in Aberdeenshire.

The third phase consisted of an intermittent series of cremations poked into the cairn accompanied by what seemed to be deliberately broken cordoned urns. On a similar sherd from the 1883 investigation were five imprints of naked barley.

This sherd and all the finds are in the Royal Museum of Scotland, Edinburgh.

RCAHM-Fife . . . , 1933, no. 418; *Arch J 131*, 1974, 1–32, *Plan*

147 BALFARG (2)
Lat: 56°.2   NO 281 032
3¼ miles SE of Falkland, 1¼ NW of Markinch. From the B969 turn SE at the roundabout (with a modern stone circle). Signpost. Easy. Map B
About 330 yards (300m) WNW of the Balbirnie circle, on the other side of the A92, this great circle-henge was excavated in 1977–8 in advance of housing development. The site had been so eroded by wind and weather that to have recovered so much information was a triumph of archaeological techniques.

A stone circle had been suspected for a long time from the evidence of two large stones standing WNW-ESE of each other, 44ft (13.4m) apart, 6ft 6ins and 5ft 3ins (2, 1.6m) high respectively. An aerial photograph of 1947 showed that they lined the north-west causeway of a huge horseshoe-shaped ditch and bank widely open to the WSW at the edge of a steep gully.

The central plateau of this henge was 213ft (64.9m) across. On it broken Neolithic pottery, burnt wood and bone had been thrown down before the erection of a ring of sixteen heavy posts in a circle 82ft (25m) in diameter. None of the débris lay in the ditch suggesting that the henge had been a later feature. The holes of fifteen of the posts were discovered, increasing in width and depth up the west where two even heavier posts had stood outside as impressive portals.

Grooved ware, charcoal and burnt bone had been deposited in the postholes and four C-14 assays ranging from 2085 ± 50 bc (GU-1161) to 2365 ± 60 bc (GU-1163) dated the setting to the years around 2900 BC.

Five slighter timber rings, very difficult to distinguish on the worn-down surface, had stood outside and inside the main circle and may have supported hurdling or a palisade to conceal the interior from the outside world.

In an undateable later episode the rings were replaced by two concentric stone circles, also graded to the west, the outer about 210ft (64m) across, the inner, which included the innermost of the two remaining pillars, some 165ft (50.3m) in diameter. It may have been after the erection of these circles that the ditch of the henge, 26ft wide and 8ft deep (7.9 × 2.4m), and with entrances at WNW and south, was quarried to provide material for an outer bank.

Around 1900 BC a pit was dug near the centre of the rings. In it the body of a young man was buried with a flint knife. Close to his hands was a handled beaker with a capacity of two pints which, in the excavator's sympathetic words, 'one hopes was intended to make this person's journey to the underworld a little less cold and cheerless.'

Balfarg has been partly reconstructed. Markers stand in the positions of the massive timber ring. The new town of Glenrothes was redesigned to leave the circle standing in an open space. To visit it and the nearby pleasure of Balbirnie (146) is a megalithic imperative.

PSAS 84, 1949–50, 58–9; ibid 111, 1980–1, 63–171 (Plans, 66ff)

148 LUNDIN LINKS (3)
Lat: 56°.2   NO 404 027
7¼ miles SSE of Cupar, 1¼ miles NE of Leven. 200 yds (180m) E of lane N to Thomsford. But on private golf-course. Ask. Map B
On the fairway of the Lundin Ladies Golf Club, hence the 'Links', three thin, contorted pillars of coarse red sandstone stand at the corners of a long rectangle 100ft SSE-NNW by 30ft (31 × 9.1m). The NNE stone is missing. As late as 1792 it lay by its stump, broken by treasure-hunters. The NNW stone is 16ft 8ins tall (5.1m), the SSW leans, 15ft (4.6m) high, but the lowest, the SSE, is also the biggest, only 13ft 8ins tall but 6ft 5ins (4.2 × 2m) broad.

An early eighteenth-century exploration found cists, bones and a round 'very curious' object, possibly a v-perforated jet button. It is lost.

Alexander Thom deduced two possible alignments, one SSW towards the distant Comrie Hill and the minor southern moonset, the second SSE to the minor southern moonrise behind the prominent Bass Rock. Both sightlines would have been very difficult for prehistoric observers to determine.

Lundin Links appears to be an exaggerated form of Four-Poster, a type of stone circle prevalent in Perthshire a few miles to the west.

PSAS 37, 1902–3, 212–15, Plan; A. Thom, Megalithic Lunar Observatories, 1971, 55–6, P4/1; Burl, 1988, 126–7, Plan

HEBRIDES, see OUTER HEBRIDES, also MULL, SKYE

INVERNESS-SHIRE
The Clava tradition is predominant here with both chambered tombs and ring-cairns with kerbs and stones graded to the SW

149 AVIEMORE (3) [B7/12]
Lat: 57°.2   NH 896 134
11½ miles NE of Kingussie, 4½ miles SW of Boat of Garten. Just E of the A9 the cairn is strangely situated in a housing estate at the N end of Aviemore. No walk. Map 1
This fine Clava ring-cairn stands on level ground in the Spey valley. In 1877 seven stones still stood in the stone circle, 76ft (23.2m) in diameter. It is graded to the south-west where the tallest stands 4ft 9ins (1.5m) high. Today only five remain, one of them fallen at the SSE.

Inside are the graded kerbstones of a ring-cairn 43ft (13.1m) across. Most of the cairn has gone and there is little sign of the 28ft (8.5m) wide central space, just three or four of the slabs that lined it.

PSAS 40, 1905–6, 249–52; Henshall, I, 360–1, Plan

150 BALNUARAN OF CLAVA (2, 3, 2) [B7/1] Lat: 57°.5   NH 757 444
5¼ miles E of Inverness, 1½ mile SE of Culloden battlefield, 1746. Carpark. No walk. Map 1
In a 340ft (104m) long NE-SW line there are two Clava passage-tombs with a ring-cairn between them. A small kerb-circle lies inconspicuously just to the east of the ring-cairn.

In a delightful leaflet (1983) Edward Meldrum wrote, 'A visit to the Clava cairns on a summer night of bright moonlight is one way to absorb the

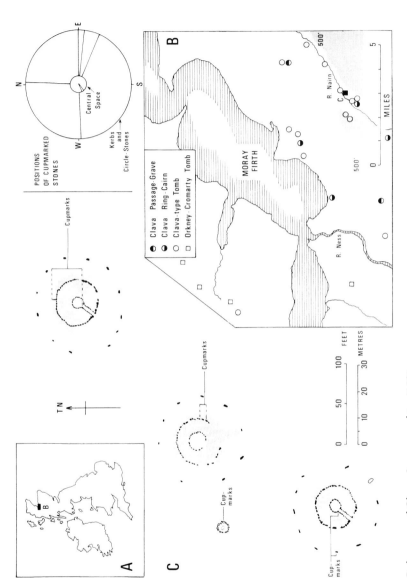

POSITIONS
OF CUPMARKED
STONES

N
E
W
S

Central
Space

Kerbs
and
Circle Stones

Cupmarks

TN

A

B

Clava   Passage Grave
Clava   Ring Cairn
Clava-type Tomb
Okney - Cromarty Tomb

MORAY
FIRTH

R Ness

R Nairn

C

500'

500'

MILES

0   5

C

Cupmarks

Cupmarks

Cup-
marks

Cup-
marks

FEET
METRES

0   50   100
0   10   20   30

Balnuaran of Clava, Inverness-shire (150)

Balnuaran of Clava north-east passage-tomb, Inverness-shire (150a), a cupmarked kerbstone.

eerie mystery and fascinating character of these long-deserted stone tombs standing in their leafy glade of old trees on the haugh of the River Nairn.' The present writer agrees. With their unique architecture and stone circles he believes them to be late in chambered tomb history, perhaps not much earlier than 3000 BC.

A. *The north-east passage-tomb*, NH 757 444, is surrounded by a graded stone circle, actually an ellipse 114ft 3ins NE-SW by 104ft 2ins (34.8 × 31.8m). Eleven of its twelve stones survive, some broken. The biggest is a great flat-topped slab 9ft (2.7m) high.

Inside, the passage-tomb, 55ft (16.8m) across, stands on a well-built bank of small and big stones. The bank is some 10ft (3m) wide and rises to a height of 1ft 6ins (45cm). It was possibly added later when kerbstones were being forced outwards by the weight of the 10ft (3m) high cairn in which there is a stone-lined, lintelled entrance at the south-west. Its 20ft (6m) long passage leads to a small

central chamber in which the lower courses of the former corbelled roof can still be seen. Excavation around 1854 found some bones in the chamber whose floor consisted of a thick layer of black earth resting on red sand.

There is a profusion of cupmarks on a kerbstone at the north. A western sideslab at the entrance to the chamber is also decorated.

The passage is well aligned on the midwinter sunset which was framed in a 'window', whose base was created by the distant skyline and top by the lintelled entrance.

B. Some 180ft (55m) to the south-west of the tomb, and somewhat off-line from the south-west passage-tomb, is *the central ring-cairn* which was restored *circa* 1881. Its outer circle, lacking stones at the north-east, is 103ft 7ins (31.6m) in diameter. The tallest stone at the WSW is 7ft 6ins (2.3m) high.

Within it the low cairn is oval, about 60ft by 52ft (18.3 × 15.9m). Its kerbs are graded, the biggest 4ft 3ins (1.3m)

129

Balnuaran of Clava ring-cairn, Inverness-shire (150b), *from the ssw.*

high being at the ssw. The cairn has a large central space which, in 1953, was found to be blackened by charcoal in which there was a scatter of cremated bone. There was a suspicion that there may once have been a cist there.

There may be a cupmark on the south-east circle stone and another on the westernmost. These may be no more than weathering but two adjacent kerbstones at the ese are less equivocal.

Three 6ft (2m) wide, kerbed stony 'causeways' extend from the cairn to the east, south-east and wnw. They are unexplained.

c. About 136ft (41.5m) ssw of the ring-cairn is *the south-western passage-tomb*, NH 756 443. It also stands inside a supporting bank about 10ft (3m) wide. Originally the tomb was encircled by a ring, 103ft 7ins (31.6m) across, of twelve stones of local sandstone graded to the south-west. One is now missing at the north-east. Six of the stones were re-erected *circa* 1876.

The tomb in its big cairn, has a south-west entrance and is 52ft 6ins (16m) across. It has kerbstones similarly graded to the south-west. The

central chamber had a clay floor. Excavation in 1828 or 1829 'exactly at the centre' of the chamber recovered two broken, coarse flat-bottomed 'vases', possibly flat-rimmed ware, and cremated bone.

There are cupmarks at the entrance to the chamber and on the western circle-stone. Like the other passage-tomb the entrance was aligned on the midwinter sunset.

D. Just over 50ft (16m) to the east of the ring-cairn are the fifteen heavy and contiguous boulders of a *kerb-circle* no more than 12ft (3.7m) in internal diameter. The stone at the ese carries cups and cup-and-ring markings.

Excavation in 1953 located a shallow grave in the interior but any inhumation had long since decomposed. Over it there had been a layer of white quartz pebbles.

In the garden wall of Balnuaran farm nearby is a profusely cupmarked stone, presumably from one of the cairns.

PSAS 18, 1883–4, 345–8; *Arch 73*, 1922–3, 217–22; *PSAS 88*, 1954–6, 188–90, 192; Henshall, I, 361–6, *Plan*

151 Bruiach (3)
Lat: 57°.4   NH 499 414
3½ miles SW of Beauly, ½ mile SE of
Culburnie ring-cairn. Walk. 200 yds
(180m) SW of junction of lanes from
Aultfearn to Culburnie and to Bruiach.
Easy. Map 1
Inside a fairly well-preserved stone
circle about 73ft (22.3m) in diameter
and with stones ranging from 1ft 3ins
to 4ft (0.4–1.2m) in height is a ring-
cairn, 47ft (14.3m) across with an
almost complete circuit of kerbstones.
Two, at the south and north-west, are
cupmarked.

Walling has been built between the
circle-stones at the west. The ring is not
concentrically placed around the cairn
suggesting that the two structures may
not be contemporary.

Henshall, I, 366–7, *Plan*

152 Corrimony, Glen Urquhart (2)
Lat: 57°.3   NH 383 303
13½ miles SW of Beauly, 3 miles ESE of
Cannich. At NH 394 302 take lane to S
(Lt). Tomb is ¾ mile. Immediately on
N. Easy. Map 1
Excavated in 1952 the Clava passage-
tomb is surrounded by an irregular
stone circle 70ft (21.3m) in diameter.
Of its eleven stones four are modern
additions. The original number is
unknown. Re-erected before 1874 two
stones west of the entrance are actually
composite settings of two and three
stones set back to back. Two stones
south of the entrance were set up after
1882. Others at the south-east also
have been reset. Unsurprisingly, neither
the shape of the ring nor its spacing is
symmetrical.

On a platform 62ft NE-SW by 57ft
(18.9 × 17.4m) the cairn, 8ft (2.4m)
high, also is oval, about 50ft by 45ft
(15.2 × 13.7m). Much broken quartz
had been strewn around the graded
kerbstones during the construction of
the tomb.

The stony south-west entrance opens
onto a passage leading to a now
unroofed but once corbelled chamber,
12ft (3.7m) across and originally 8ft
(2.4m) high. Its floor was composed of

waterworn boulders. Below it was a
layer of packed yellow sand with a
setting of flat slabs at its centre. There
was much charcoal. The stain of a
crouched inhumation was all that
survived of a burial. An eroded bone
pin was also found.

On the cairn lies a slab 8ft long and
5ft wide (2.4 × 1.5m). On it are
numerous cupmarks. It is unclear today
whether this was the capstone of the
chamber or an uprooted circle-stone.

PSAS 88, 1954–6, 174–84, 197–8,
200–7, *Plan*

153 Culburnie (3)
Lat: 57°.4   NH 491 418
3½ miles SW of Beauly, ½ mile NW of
Bruiach ring-cairn. From minor road N
at NH 492 415 go ¼ mile N. Cairn is in
W just beyond house. Easy. Map 1
There are eight stones of an original
nine in a ring 70ft (21.3m) in diameter
and graded in height from 2ft 9ins
(0.8m) at the NNE to a fine slab of mica
schist, 8ft high and 3ft wide (2.1 × 1m)
at the SSW. The missing north-east
pillar is said to have been removed in
the nineteenth-century by a mason who
'according to popular rumour, died a
sudden death in consequence of this
violation.'

The pillaged ring-cairn, still 5ft
(1.5m) high, is kerbed with closely-set
blocks up to 4ft (1.2m) high at the
south to south-west. There is a 17ft
(5.2m) wide central space.

Cupmarks may exist on a SSW kerb
and on NNW and south-west circle-
stones.

PSAS 16, 1881–2, 316–18; Henshall,
I, 370–1, *Plan*

154 Culdoich (3) [B7/2. Miltown of
Clava] Lat: 57°.5   NH 751 438
5½ miles ESE of Inverness, ¼ mile SW of
Balnuaran of Clava. ¼ mile W of
Ballagan farm in valley fields. Easy.
Map 1
This ring-cairn on a low hillside is 59ft
(18m) across. Its kerbstones are graded
to the south-west but a quarry has
removed the southern arc. At the centre
of the cairn is a semi-elliptical open

space, clay-floored, 22ft 7ins E-W by 19ft 9ins (6.9 × 6m). In 1953 an excavation found charcoal underneath an infill of stones. Mixed with it were the cremated bones of a middle-aged man and woman. The bones had been smashed into splinters after being extracted from the pyre.

27ft (8.2m) to the south-west is a cupmarked 12ft high 8ft wide (3.7 × 2.4m) 'playing-card' slab, its broad face facing the cairn. It has been assumed that this was the only survivor of a stone circle some 113ft (34.4m) across. When the slab fell in 1981, however, a resistivity survey all around the cairn found no buried stones or stoneholes. If this were a solitary outlier then with an azimuth of 228° and a declination near to −20° it did stand vaguely in line with the minor moonset. Its cupmarks intimate that this had been intended.

Nearby, postholes, ard marks, a cupmarked stone and an isolated sherd were evidence of earlier agricultural activity.

PSAS 18, 1883–4, 338–41; ibid 88, 1954–6, 190–2; Henshall, I, 371–2, Plan; Discovery and Excavation, Scotland, 1982, 14

155 DAVIOT (3) [B7/5]
Lat: 57°.5   NH 727 411
4½ miles SE of Inverness, 2¼ miles SW of Balnuaran of Clava. From B851 at NH 725 413. Walk. Through trees for 250 yds (230m) E. Easy. Map 1
At the northern end of a low, flat plateau this grey Clava ring-cairn remains in fair condition despite the loss of kerbs at the east and the collapse of others at the west. It is elliptical, 50ft 2ins E-W by 47ft 7ins (15.3 × 14.5m), surrounding a central space some 18ft (5.5m) across. Around 1820 a cist was found there containing a skull and 'other remains'.

The kerbing is graded with a heavy, flat-topped block at the south-west standing opposite a 9ft 6ins high (2.9m) triangular pillar of the outer stone circle. Only that stone and an upright lower slab to its east survive of a ring once about 90ft (27.4m) in diameter.

PSAS 18, 1883–4, 338–9; Henshall, I, 374, Plan

156 DELFOUR (3) [B7/10. Easter Delfour] Lat: 57°.2   NH 844 085
4 miles SW of Aviemore, 2 miles NNE of Kincraig. From A9 at NH 851 080 take lane NW through trees for ¼ mile. Turn SW at Easter Delfour. Cairn is alongside track. Easy. Map 1
This Clava ring-cairn is in good condition but, like Culdoich, presents an architectural problem.

In the ring-cairn, 60ft (18.3m) wide, the kerbs, as usual, are graded up to the south-west. So are the slabs lining the central space nearby 28ft (8.5m) across. Their little ring is broken at the south-west.

The problem is the surrounding stone circle. At the SSW, 22ft 6ins (6.9m) beyond the kerb, is a single pillar, in profile like a megalithic milk bottle, 9ft 6ins high, 1ft 6ins thick and 5ft 6ins broad (2.9 × 0.5 × 1.7m). Presumed to be the remaining stone of a circle 105ft (32m) in diameter, it may instead be an outlier like that suspected at Culdoich. This is made likely at Delfour because the stone stands at an azimuth of 219°. With the distant horizon rising 2° above the site the declination is that of the midwinter sunset.

Henshall, I, 374–5, *Plan*; Thom, 1967, 98, 143, *Plan*, 87

157 DRUIDTEMPLE (3) [B7/18. Druid Temple] Lat: 57°.5   NH 685 420
4¾ miles WSW of Balnuaran of Clava, 2¼ miles S of Inverness. Just behind Druidtemple farm. From Inverness take B861 for 1¼ miles to Balloan. Turn E (Lt). ¾ mile to Hilton. Turn SE for 1 mile. Take W lane to farm. Easy walk. Map 1
However mistaken the name Druidtemple may be it is certainly preferable to 'Leys' which this Clava passage-tomb on Leys Castle estate used to be called. The nineteenth-century antiquarians who believed the ring to be a druidical sanctuary were at least on feasible lines. Built, abandoned, re-used as a cemetery, then a hiding-

place, the site has been plundered in modern times.

It lies in ruin on a north-west facing ridge. Only five stones of its outer circle stand. Others lie displaced near them in a ring once about 74ft 4ins (22.7m) across. In 1824 fifteen were erect.

Inside is the less battered tomb, its kerbed cairn elliptical, 43ft 6ins SSE-NNW by 38ft (13.3 × 11.6m). The grading is imperfect. The tumbled stones of a passage, unusually aligned south-north, lead to an even more wrecked chamber. In it there may have been a cist. In 1882 David Cameron reported, 'I have seen a cist found a few yards beyond the outer circle of Leys. It contained no remains. Another cist was found recently in this circle.'

A proper excavation in 1952 showed that the turf had been stripped from the chamber and rounded white quartz pebbles laid down. A few scraps of cremated bone were all that remained of a single individual. Another discovery suggested that late in the Bronze Age a valuable part of a tinker's hoard had been concealed here and never reclaimed.

'A funicular rod or torc of gold was dug up within the great circle of Leys ... in 1824 ... It measured 22 inches [56cm] long and was hooked at both ends.' This lovely ornament, elegantly twisted and decorated, had been broken and subsequently straightened for remelting. Whoever left it had not returned. Similar misfortune befell whoever failed to collect the cache of two brilliant gold bracelets from the megalithic tomb of Rondossec near Carnac in Brittany.

Alexander Thom thought that the tallest pillar in the circle, 9ft 6ins (2.9m) high, standing just to the west of the entrance, had been erected to be in line with the midwinter sunset.

D. Wilson, *Prehistoric Annals of Scotland*, I, 1863, 163; *PSAS* 57, 1922–3, 163; Henshall, I, 375–6, *Plan*; Thom, 1967, 68, 95, 143, *Plan*, 69

158 GASK (3) [B7/15]
Lat: 57°.4   NH 679 358

5¼ miles S of Inverness, 3¼ SW of Daviot. Just E of the B861 ¼ mile N of Hillton. Easy. Map 1

This ring-cairn, the biggest in the Clava group, stands on a gentle hillside above the River Nairn. Its layout suggests that its stone circle and internal ring-cairn may not have been built at the same time.

Three stones still stand in a circle 119ft 10ins (36.5m) in diameter. Others lie quite regularly around the circumference of a damaged ring-cairn. From their heights and lengths the stones were well graded to the SSW where the tallest is 11ft high and 9ft 9ins wide (3.4 × 3m).

The kerbstones are also graded to the SSW. They surround a pillaged ring-cairn 82ft 10ins (25.3m) across. Examination of the plan shows that the centre of the cairn is a full 5ft 6ins (1.7m) north of the ring's centre. It is an indication that the ring-cairn may have been inserted inside an ancient sanctuary.

A fallen circle-stone lying on the kerbs at the north-east has three cupmarks on it.

Henshall, I, 378, *Plan*

159 KINCHYLE OF DORES (4) [B7/19. River Ness] Lat: 57°.4   NH 621 389
4¼ miles SW of Inverness, 9 miles WSW of Balnuaran of Clava. Immediately E of the A862, but in copse. Difficult of access. Map 1

Known also as Scaniport this denuded Clava passage-tomb is a visual disaster. Alongside the A892, the 'new' military road of General Wade, but cowering in a wilderness of gorse the stones are of historical rather than archaeological interest.

Five stones of the outer circle stand in a ring 69ft (21m) across. They are graded towards the south to the tallest, 6ft (1.8m) high. The entrance to the tomb was opposite it on the circumference of circular kerbing only 30ft (9.1m) in diameter. The cairn has gone. It is possible to make out the passage and collapsed chamber. An excavation in 1952 found a little bowl-shaped pit cut in the boulder clay. Near it were the cremated bones of one person.

In August 1773, Boswell and Johnson rode by the tomb. 'About three miles beyond Inverness', wrote Boswell, 'we saw, just by the road, a very complete specimen of what is called a Druids' Temple. There was a double circle, one of very large, the other of smaller stones. Dr Johnson justly observed that to go and see one druidical temple is only to see that it is nothing, for there is neither art nor power in it: and seeing one is quite enough.'

Readers of this Guide should disagree; but not for this site.

PSAS 88, 1954–6, 185; Henshall, I, 380–1, *Plan*, 381; Thom, 1967, 95; TTB, 272, *Plan*

160 NEWTON OF PETTY (3)
Lat: 57°.5   NH 734 485
4³/₄ miles ENE of Inverness, 2³/₄ miles NNW of Balnuaran of Clava. ¹/₄ mile N of A96. In fields. Fair. Map 1
Damaged at its north by the laying of the railway line it is unclear whether this is a Clava passage-tomb or ring-cairn. Four stones stand in the south-west quadrant of a circle once 92ft (28m) in diameter. The tallest, at the south, are 4ft 6ins and 5ft (1.4, 1.5m) high respectively. The ungraded kerbs of the inner cairn are almost complete and enclose an area 54ft (16.5m) across from which all the cairn material has gone.

PSAS 18, 1883–4, 359; Henshall, I, 383, *Plan*, 384

161 TORBRECK (5)
Lat: 57°.4   NH 644 404
3¹/₄ miles SSW of Inverness, ¹/₂ mile SW of Torbreck. Walk. From NH 646 409 at the E end of a wood go ¹/₂ mile SSW. Fair. Map 1
This ring has been misidentified as a robbed Clava cairn. It is more likely to be an free-standing stone circle with Clava affinities. Nine stones, the tallest 6ft 6ins (2m) at the south-west, form a ring only 17ft (5.2m) across. The northern stone is fallen but the circle is clearly graded. It has been suggested

that it was the central space of a ring-cairn from which the cairn, outer kerb and stone circle had been removed. As the stones are not contiguous but are evenly spaced 3ft (1m) apart this is improbable.

There is a local tradition that people would go there 'to pray to the stones'. The site is also known as Cullaird.

PSAS 18, 1883–4, 355–6, 361, *Plan* 355; Henshall, I, 385

162 TORDARROCH (3) [B7/16. Farr West] Lat: 57°.4   NH 679 334
7¹/₂ miles S of Inverness, 4¹/₂ miles SW of Daviot. Walk. 200yds (180m) E of side lane from Farr to Tordarroch. Easy. Map 1
Even in ruin this Clava ring-cairn is impressive. The big stone circle is in fair condition, 113ft (34.4m) in diameter with seven of perhaps eleven original stones standing, graded to the SSW.

Inside is a badly-ruined ring-cairn, a long arc of kerbstones fallen at the south and wide gaps at the east and north. It is uncircular, measuring about 67ft 4ins E-W by 61ft 3ins (20.5 × 18.7m). Little remains of the cairn itself or its central space.

A large kerbstone, fallen outwards against a 5ft (1.5m) standing kerb at the SSW has over thirty cupmarks on what would have been its inner face. Perhaps by coincidence, from the centre of the ring the tallest stone in the circle, over 9ft (2.7m) high and with a pointed top, is in line with the decorated slab and with the major southern moonset, possibly yet another lunar association with cupmarking.

PSAS 16, 1881–2, 324–5; Henshall, I, 385–6 *Plan*, 386

163 TULLOCHGORM (4) [B7/4. Boat of Garten] Lat: 57°.3   NH 965 215
3¹/₄ miles ESE of Carrbridge, 3¹/₄ miles SW of Dulnain Bridge. Walk. 100yds (90m) E of A95. Easy. Map 1
The remains, probably of a Clava ring-cairn, stand on a hillside two miles north-east of Boat of Garten. The outer kerbing, 47ft 7ins E-W by 43ft 7ins

(14.5 × 13.3m), is all that remains of a robbed cairn. Inside are the disturbed stones of the central space about 11ft (3.4m) across.

Some 10ft (3m) to the north-east of the kerbs is the stump of a stone. It, and a fallen one to the NNE, may be all that is left of a once substantial circle some 68ft (21m) in diameter.

This wrecked site is of historical interest. On 6 March 1693, the Rev. James Garden of Aberdeen wrote to John Aubrey. In Inverness-shire, he recorded, in the 'parish of Duthell [is] another of these Stone monuments consisting of two circles of stones, which is called chappell-Piklag, and Carrachan Piklag, from a Ladie of that name who used to repair to that Monument for the exercise of her devotion, before a church was built in that part of the country.' A nearby grove was considered so sacred 'that no body will cutt a branch out of it.'

Five hundred yards (450m) south-east of Tullochgorm are standing stones by the River Spey.

Aubrey, I, 211; Henshall, I, 386, *Plan*, 385

ISLAY
Apart from a ruinous Four-Poster at Ardilistry, NR 442 491, there is only Cultoon to see

164 CULTOON, Kelsay (4)
Lat: 55°.8   NR 195 569
3¼ miles NE of Portnahaven, ⅔ mile NE of Kelsay. Walk. 165 yds (150m) W of unfenced road. Easy. Map 1
Only two stones were standing when Alexander Thom surveyed this site in 1973 for the Islay Historic Works Group. Others were prone, half concealed or completely buried below peat. They lay in an ellipse 135ft NE-SW by 110ft (41.2 × 33.5m).

Excavations in 1974 and 1975 proved that many stones had never been erected. Some lay by holes that had not been occupied, others had no sockets at all. In one stone hole there

was a fine flint arrowhead. Charcoal from the overlying peat gave an assay of 765 ± 40 bc (SRR-500), showing that the work had been abandoned some time before 950 BC. The project is likely to have been planned many centuries before then.

The stones were all local, a mixture of Lewissean gneiss, schists and granites with the most massive block over 10ft long and 3ft 7ins (3.1 × 1.1m) at the north-east end of the long axis. Analysis of the alignment showed that to the south-west it pointed to Slieve Snaght mountain in Co. Donegal, fifty-five miles away across the Irish Sea. It was in line with the midwinter sunset around 1800 BC.

The project may simply have been given up. There were indications, however, that a more hostile reason was possible for the abandonment. 'That some kind of destruction may have been visited on the site was suggested by the fact that one of the uprights had been snapped off short and that no fallen fragments were found next to it.'

E.W. MacKie, *Science and Society in Prehistoric Britain*, 1977, 44–5, 92–5, *Plan*, 93; *RCAHM-Argyll V*, 1984, 66–7, no. 94, *Plan*

KINCARDINESHIRE
This county, to the S of Aberdeenshire and E of Perthshire, not unexpectedly contains circles that are variations of its neighbours: recumbent stone circles, Four-Posters and ring-cairns

165 AUCHQUHORTHIES (3) [B3/1. Aquorthies Kingausie]
Lat: 57°.1   NO 901 963
7 miles SSW of Aberdeen. 4¼ miles ESE of Peterculter. On W of A92. If coming S from Aberdeen take a lane to the E to underpass the main road. Walk. The circle is 200 yds (180m) N of Aquorthies farm at NO 901 962 on farm lane S from Auchlee. Easy. Map A. Old Bourtreebush is 300 yds (275m) SSE

There are two recumbent stone circles within 330 yards (300m) of each other, one in good condition, the other far from so. They are part of a remarkable complex, four rings in a buckled ssw-nne line 1¼ miles long, the two recumbents at the south, a Clava ring-cairn (167) to their north with a Four-Poster (168) beyond it.

All were dug into on the same day, 30 September 1858, when Alexander Thomson with Charles Dalrymple, four other gentlemen and 'two or three active labourers and the necessary tools' hacked into the middle of the rings. Auchquhorthies was the third to be explored.

Clearly visible on its ridge from the A92 half a mile to the east, Auchquhorthies is a fascinating circle. It stands on a south-falling slope on which an irregular stony platform about 130ft N-s by 75ft (40 × 23m) was raised to create a level site. In June 1692, James Garden informed John Aubrey that the well-preserved ring was '24 large paces across', a remarkably accurate measurement of the 75ft (22.9m) diameter of the true circle, Garden's pace being 3ft 1½ in (95cm).

Well-planned by James Logan in the early nineteenth-century, badly-planned by Fred Coles at the end of the century and best-planned by Alexander Thom in the mid-twentieth century the outer stone circle has ten standing and two fallen of an original twenty-eight stones, a number much greater than the average for such rings. The circle is well graded from a slight 2ft at the north to a tall 8ft (0.6–2.4m) pillar in 1899. It has since gone.

The recumbent is a thinnish flat-topped block, 9ft 9ins long and 5ft high (3 × 1.5m). The eastern flanker has disappeared. The west is 6ft (1.8m) high. Both it and the recumbent are of greyish granite streaked with quartz, but the majority of the circle-stones are reddish, another indication that, while they were probably found in the immediate vicinity, the heavier slabs had to be brought from a more distant source.

The ring is characteristic of the way that recumbents in Kincardineshire vary from 'classical' forms, with the recumbent itself lying to the east of south, 174°, and placed well inside the circumference of the circle. It is joined to the ring-cairn by a long slab, and from it the conspicuous kerbstones enclose an area about 50ft (15.2m) across. Most of the cairn material has been removed but there is a very obvious central space 11ft 6ins (3.5m) in diameter.

In 1792 a cist was 'accidentally uncovered by a countryman' at the east between the ring-cairn and the circle. It is variously described, in 1845 as 'containing neither urn nor bones', in 1856 as 'a cistvaen, about three feet long, and one and a half feet wide, [1 × 0.5m] containing some ashes' but in 1792 holding 'an urn and dust'. If so, the vessel is lost. In 1858 Thomson dug up the whole central space finding charcoal, cremated bone and small sherds.

Typical of so many recumbent stone circles, Auchquhorthies was erected against a patch of well-drained, fertile soil. This was remembered thousands of years later. James Garden was told that local people had 'a tradition that the Pagan priests of old dwelt in that place . . . [and] caused earth to be brought from other adjacent places upon peoples backs to Auchincorthie, for making the soile therof deeper, which is given for the reason why this parcell of Land (though surrounded with heath and moss on all sides) is better and more fertile than other places thereabout.'

The tradition did not deter a poor man from removing a slab from the ring for a hearth. He regretted it. He was continually 'troubled with a deal of noise and din about his house in the night time, until he carried back the stone to the place where he found it.' If only other stone circles had caused such nuisance.

The recumbent, looking towards a low southern skyline, is well aligned on the major moonrise.

See also Old Bourtreebush (173).

Aubrey, I, 183; Stuart, I, 1856, xxiii; PSAS 34, 1899–1900, 145–9; Thom, 1967, 147, *Plan*

166 CAIRNFAULD (4) [B2/11]
Lat: 57°.0   NO 754 941
9 miles NW of Stonehaven. ¹/₂ mile W of Balladrum. At NO 750939 on the A957 take lane E and in 250 yds (230m) go straight on on farm lane for 370 yds (340m). Walk. 200 yds (180m) to N. Easy. Map A
This ring near the south bank of the River Don may have been a recumbent stone circle. Four stones survive, one at the south-west having gone since Fred Coles's survey in 1899. They are graded, NNW, 3ft 10ins high; north-east, 5ft; south, 6ft 10ins, this stone and the former being incorporated in a wide NE-SW stony bank; and south-west, 4ft 9ins (1.2, 1.5, 2.1, 1.5m). They stand in the remnants of a ring 75ft ESE-WNW by 68ft (22.9 × 20.7m). The emphasis on the south and south-east is typical of the Kincardine rings.

In the nineteenth century human bones were dug up but there is no detailed report of the exploration.

A farmer removed some of the stones but almost immediately his cattle became diseased, some dying. The stones were replaced.

PSAS 14, 1879–80, 304; *ibid* 34, 1899–1900, 155–7; *ibid* 60, 1925–6, 306; TTB, 214, *Plan*

167 CAIRNWELL (4)
Lat: 57°.1   NO 907 974
6 miles S of Aberdeen. 4¹/₄ miles E of Peterculter. Walk. From NO 913 979 take lane S for ¹/₂ mile. Pass Craighead Four-Poster on way. Just S of burn go W ¹/₄ mile. Easy. Map A
Unobtrusive and on boggy land although this Clava ring-cairn is in poor condition it produced some interesting finds. Once of thirteen stones in a small ring 30ft (9.1m) across only three low ones remain in the south-east quadrant. The enclosed kerbed ring-cairn was 22ft (6.7m) in diameter with a largish central space

14ft 9ins (4.5m) in width.

For his second dig of the day Thomson plunged into the space disinterring fragments of bone, 'churchyard earth', charcoal and five coarse earthenware sherds arranged in a quincunx, four at the corners of a square, the fifth at its centre. Everything is lost.

PSAS 5, 1862–4, 131–3; *ibid 34*, 1899–1900, 149–52; Henshall, I, 400, *Plan*, 401

168 CRAIGHEAD BADENTOY (2?, 5)
Lat: 57°.1   NO 912 977
5 miles S of Aberdeen. 4³/₄ miles ESE of Peterculter. Walk. see Cairnwell (167). Map A
On top of a hill this ring has undergone constant change and is now difficult to interpret. On an artificial platform about 60ft across and 2ft 6ins high (18.3 × 0.8m) four stones of local gneiss and slate stand close to the cardinal points, the west, 5ft 3ins high; the north, 5ft 2ins; the east, 4ft; and the south, 7ft 5ins (1.6, 1.6, 1.2, 2.3m). Their rectangle measures about 28ft N-S by 24ft (8.5 × 7.3m) but as the stones do not stand on the circumference of a circle their identification as a Four-Poster must be questionable.

On agricultural land the ring seems to have been thrown down, 'cultivation has been the death of it', and then re-erected. In 1858 Thomson saw only three stones. By 1875 MacLagan noted that there were six with a wide gap in the south-east quadrant and with a central stone. In 1899 Coles was dubious about the site because the sides of the stones were scarred by wires supporting a central flagstaff whose erection may have required the rearrangement of the stones.

The ring was Thomson's first dig, but his party found only 'half-calcined bones and morsels of wood charcoal'. The site had been dug into previously. Thomson was disappointed. 'The results of our examinations are not very important.' He was uncertain whether the burnt bones were those of sacrifices, 'victims of a cruel superstition, or were great heroes in whose honour the stones were set up, we cannot tell.' The uncertainty continues.

PSAS 5, 1862–4, 130–1; ibid 34, 1899–1900, 152–3; Burl, 1988, 130–1, Plan

169 ESSLIE THE GREATER (SW) (3) [B2/4] Lat: 57°.0 NO 717 916
10 miles WNW of Stonehaven. 2¼ miles ESE of Strachan. Walk. 150 yds (140m) W of lane at NO 716 916. Easy. Map A
On the western slopes of Mulloch Hill there is a right-angled triangle of recumbent stone circles: Esslie the Lesser (170) at the north; Esslie the Greater ½ mile to its SSW; Garrol Wood (171), the best of them, ½ mile to the ESE of the Greater with Esslie the Lesser ¾ mile to the north. Landscape planning is unlikely.

Marked 'cairn' on the O.S. map, were it not so dishevelled in bracken and undergrowth Esslie the Greater would be a very pleasant recumbent stone circle. It stands on a slight platform. The flat-topped, drooping-shouldered recumbent is 9ft 6ins long, 6ft thick and 5ft high (2.9 × 1.8 × 1.5m). Its flankers, oddly, are little taller. The east is broad and detached from the recumbent. The west is thin, higher and nudging the block. A long slab at right-angles to the east flanker extends inwards towards the ring-cairn. Typical of the circles in this region the recumbent was set slightly to the east of south at 176°. It lies neatly in line with the major southern moonrise.

The stones of the 'circle' stand on the perimeter of an ellipse 87ft NNE-SSW by 76ft (26.5 × 23.2m). Inside is the south-western arc of a kerbed ring-cairn once 59ft (18m) in diameter with a well-defined central space 20ft 7ins (6.3m) across.

The ring was dug into in 1873. In the central space were three dark marks 'about the length of a not tall human being' with a fourth less well defined. They may have been the stains of secondary inhumations. Below them was a small cist containing bits of bone.

PSAS 14, 1879–80, 301–3; ibid 34,

1899–1900, 162–6; TTB, 200, *Plan*

170 ESSLIE THE LESSER (NE) (3) [B2/5] Lat: 57°.0 NO 722 921
10 miles NW of Stonehaven. ½ mile NE of Esslie the Greater. Walk. 200 yds (180m) E of unfenced road at NO 723 922. Easy. Map A
On a battered and grass-bristling platform just five stones and a slumped recumbent remain on the southern half of a stone circle once about 43ft 7ins (13.3m) in diameter. An even shorter southern arc survives of the kerbing of a ring-cairn some 32ft (9.8m) across originally.

The recumbent lies outside the circumference. It is 6ft (1.8m) long and its base is sharply keeled at the east end. It may have been dragged out of position. Its top appears to be overgrown and the angled bottom is farther away from the ring. The stone had lain at the precise south.

In 1873 the central space 'was opened to the depth of from 3 to 4 feet' (1–1.2m) and several flattish stones were encountered, probably the remnants of a disturbed cist.

PSAS 14, 1879–80, 303–4; ibid 34, 1899–1900, 66–7; TTB, 202, Plan

171 GARROL WOOD (3) [B2/6] Lat: 57°.0 NO 723 912
9½ miles WNW of Stonehaven. 3¼ miles SE of Banchory. ½ mile SE of Esslie the Greater. Walk. In trees. Along track 100 yds (90m) from NO 722 911. Easy. Map A
On the lower western slopes of Garrol Hill, shadowed in a conifer plantation and lurking in long grass this is a ring wondrous to behold. Also known as Nine Stones it is the most aberrant of the distinctive Kincardine recumbent stone circles, retaining all the 'classical' components of the Aberdeenshire recumbents but treating them parochially. It merits a visit to recognise the improvisations of a prehistoric community.

The outer stone 'circle', damaged at north-west and south-east, is an ellipse 63ft 6ins WSW-ENE by 51ft 2ins (19.4 ×

15.6m). The stones of reddish granite are not well-graded. Rough, tumbled walling links them.

The recumbent, perhaps of diorite, and its flankers are not on the circumference but some 6ft 6ins (2m) inside it. The recumbent, 7ft 6ins long, 5ft 4ins at its widest, and 3ft 9ins high (2.3 × 1.6 × 1.1m), has an azimuth farther to the east than any other, except perhaps for Old Bourtreebush (173), lying at 157°. Shallowly domed, it has a narrow saddle or dip midway along its top but if this was intended as a foresight towards the major southern moonrise it was carelessly placed. The east flanker, fallen since 1904 and now propped against the recumbent, was 5ft (1.5m) high. The west still stands 6ft 8ins (2m) high.

The ring-cairn is a travesty. It is a warped oval of indifferent kerbing, sharply dented at the south-east where a stony platform in front of the recumbent joins it. Yet there is an architectural surprise. Crudely 28ft by 24ft (8.5 × 7.3m), the badly-designed ring-cairn contains one of the most splendid of all central spaces. About 12ft 6ins (3.8m) across it was lined with six, once seven, tall, lean granite slabs on edge, finely graded to the south-east. It was well excavated by Fred Coles from 5 to 17 September 1904, a conscientious period of almost a fortnight very different from the diurnal rush of Alexander Thomson. Nor were any pickaxes used. 'The forester, Mr Crozier, and the three excellent workmen, William Maccullum, Alexander Marshall, and James Marshall, did all in their power to render the investigation complete and trustworthy.'

A pit was found at the middle of the central space. It was full of cremated bone and charcoal. 'In each case the individual had reached adult life'. Just to the north were coarse, undecorated urn sherds now in the Royal Museum of Scotland, Edinburgh, Catalogue EP 25.

PSAS 39, 1904–5, 190–203, *Plan*, 193

Glassel Four-Poster, Kincardineshire (172), from the south. The little outlier is in the foreground.

172 GLASSEL (1) [B3/6. Kynoch
Plantation] Lat: 57°.1   NO 649 997
*4 miles NW of Banchory, 2 miles SE of
Torphins. Walk. In wood just W of
lane. Difficult to find in the trees but
worth the effort. Map A*
This is a fine though diminutive Four-
Poster. Four of the five stones stand on
the circumference of a circle 12ft 6ins
(3.8m) in diameter. Clockwise from the
north-west their heights are: 2ft 10ins,
2ft 11ins, 3ft 3ins and 3ft 2ins (0.9,
0.9, 1, 1m). They stand in a rectangle
8ft 6ins WSW-ENE by 7ft 6ins (2.6 ×
2.3m). Near the northern stones is a
sandstone slab. To its north is a larger
of granite which may be the displaced
capstone of a cist.

Just to the south-east is a low outlier
only 2ft 9ins (0.9m) tall, 'playing-card'
in shape with its longer sides towards
the ring.

On 20 September 1904, Fred Coles
excavated the sand-covered central area
which had already been dug into *circa*
1879. His only finds were a small flint
flake and some charcoal.

PSAS 39, 1904–5, 203–5; Burl, 1988,
132, *Plan*

173 OLD BOURTREEBUSH (4) [B3/2.
Aquhorthies South]
Lat: 57°.1   NO 903 961
*4³/₄ miles SE of Peterculter. Walk.
300 yds (275m) SSE of Auchquhorthies.
Easy. Map A*
Standing on a wrecked manmade
mound 'much straightened by the
plough', the site is about a 'bowshot'
south-east of Auchquhorthies. Only half
a ring about 85ft (26m) survives, some
stones fallen, others gauntly rising from
4ft to 9ft 6ins high (1.2–2.9m). It had
been magnificent. One stone is 'actually
the broadest megalith in the district'
observed Alexander Keiller.

If this had been a recumbent stone
circle it was very unusual. The
presumed recumbent, 11ft 6ins (3.5m)
long, lies at the ESE at 106°, a bearing
of no astronomical significance. It is a
large stone and so are the others,
seemingly graded but, against the norm,
the tallest is at the west and the lowest

at the east, near the recumbent. In this
the layout conforms neither to the
recumbent stone circles of Scotland or
south-west Ireland.

This was Alexander Thomson's final
dig of the day. A thickish flat stone lay
at the centre. 'We turned it out, but
soon found it had been moved before,
probably more than once, and we
discovered nothing below it.'

It is probable that the ring has been
disrupted and rearranged.

Aubrey, I, 177–8; *PSAS 34*, 1899–
1900, 141–6; TTB 228, *Plan*

174 RAEDYKES (3) [B3/3, SE; B3/4, NW]
Lat: 57°.0   NO 832 906
*3¹/₂ miles NW of Stonehaven, ¹/₄ mile NW
of West Raedykes. From lane at NO
829 901 take farm lane NE for ¹/₂ mile.
Walk. From farm, ¹/₄ mile NW. Easy.
Map A*
On a south-facing hillside, just to the
west of a Roman marching-camp, four
ring-cairns lie in a bent line over a
distance of 102 yards (93m). Only the
outer cairns have stone circles.

A. *The north-west site*, Thom's B3/4,
has four or five tumbled stones of a
ravaged stone circle about 47ft (14.3m)
in diameter. The inner ring-cairn with
its kerbs graded to the south-west is
32ft 7ins across with a central space
12ft wide (9.9, 3.7m).

B. Sixty yards (55m) to the SSE is an
uncircled ring-cairn, 22ft (6.7m) across
and 17 yards (15.6m) to its east is
another, 28ft (8.5m) wide.

C. *The south-east ring-cairn*, Thom's
B3/3, 37 yards (34m) to the ESE, still
has eight stones of its circle standing in
a ring 57ft (17.4m) in diameter. There
are wide, robbed gaps at north-west
and south-east.

All that remains of its large ring-
cairn, once about 50ft (15m) in
diameter is a short arc of kerbstones at
the south-west. Partial excavation of it
in 1964 and 1965 yielded no finds.

PSAS 57, 1922–23, 20–8, *Plans 22,
24*; Henshall, I, 401–4; *D & E
Scotland*, 1965, 24; TTB, 230, *Plan*

KIRKCUDBRIGHTSHIRE

*The county is almost unique in having
several 'central pillar' rings of closely-
set stones. Eastern sites have affinities
with the Dumfriess-shire ovals although
in much smaller form*

175 CAULDSIDE BURN (3) [G4/14.
Cambret Moor East]
Lat: 54°.9   NX 529 571
*4¹/₂ miles W of Gatehouse of Fleet, 3¹/₂
miles ESE of Creetown. Walk. For the
energetic who have time and don't
mind hills and moorland this offers a
marvellous megalithic day. Starting at
the Cairnholy chambered tombs, NX
517 538, uphill from the A75, one can
walk 1¹/₄ miles north to the Claughreid
circle (176) with its centre stone, NX
517 560. From there a further 1¹/₂ miles
north-east will bring you to the
enticements of Cauldside Burn.
Glenquickan ring (179), NX 509 582,
with the best central stone in this Guide
is 1¹/₂ miles to the WNW. Unless you
have an amenable chauffeur (-euse)
who can read maps you are now just
over 3 miles N of your car in the
Cairnholy carpark. Map 1*
Just beyond a swampy stretch of
ground the Cauldside Burn ring, in a
saddle between the hills, is composed of
thin, family- sized slabs of local whin.
Perhaps as many as ten are missing
from a circle, 82ft (25m) across,
originally of twenty stones. They are
low, the tallest standing at the west, 4ft
(1.2m) high.

Immediately to the NNW is a large
cairn lumpily grey like an ageing
armadillo. A wrecked cist can be seen
at its top. Some 75 yards (70m) to the
NNW are two low stones, SSE-NNW of
each other and about 35ft (11m) apart,
maybe pointing a similar distance NNW
to an overgrown ring-cairn, NX 528
573, approximately 40ft (12m) in
diameter. From end to end the line,
exactly straight, measures 500ft
(152m).

There is even more. Across the burn
to the west, on the rock-strewn hillside,
there is a grey slab at NX 528 573. A
superbly symmetrical spiral has been
carved on it. Below are three much
fainter cup-and-ring marks. For the
fanatical there is comparable art ³/₄ mile
ESE on a schist outcrop, NX 541 567,
at the north-east of Cairnharrow hill. It
bears a cupmark surrounded by four
rings through which two grooves run.
There are also four smaller cup-and-
rings marks and nine cups. Best seen
after Claughreid and before Cauldside
Burn.

PSAS 29, 1894–5, 311–12; *RCAHM-
Kirkcubright*, 1914, nos. 16, 295; *TTB*,
286, *Plan*

176 CLAUGHREID (3)
Lat: 54°.9   NX 517 560
*5 miles W of Gatehouse of Fleet, 3 miles
E of Creetown. Walk. see: Cauldside
Burn (175). Map 1*
This is one several rings with centre
stones in south-west Scotland. Lying in
a saddle on the lower western slopes of
Cairnharrow Hill, nine little stones of
local granite, the tallest a mere 2ft 4ins
(0.7m) high, form a ring 34ft N-S by
30ft 6ins (10.4 × 9.3m). Within them
is a much longer pillar that has fallen
to the south. It measures 5ft 8ins in
length by 3ft 8ins and is 2ft thick (1.7
× 1.1 × 0.6m).

RCAHM-Kirkcudbright, 1914, no.
293, *Plan*

177 DRANNANDOW (3) [G4/3]
Lat: 55°.0   NX 401 711
*3¹/₂ miles N of Newton Stewart. Walk.
1¹/₂ miles. From NX 384 697 follow
track through wood to farm and then
NE. Fair. Map 1*
This ruinous ring is so inconspicuous
that the writer once stood at its centre
without noticing it. It lies, rather than
stands, at the edge of a low plateau
near the Strathannon Burn. Originally
there may have been thirteen stones but
today there are only six unimpressive
local boulders scattered around the
circumference of a ring about 89ft 4ins
(27.2m) across. The more imposing
Drumfern Cairn is just over the hilltop
but the sites are not intervisible.

RCAHM-Kirkcudbright, 1914, no.
366; *TTB*, 280, *Plan*

178 EASTHILL (3) [G5/9. Maxwell-town]
Lat: 55°.2   NX 919 739
3¹/₄ miles sw of Dumfriess. Walk.
600 yds (550m). A footpath at NX 922
743 leads sw through trees onto moor.
Circle is to s. Easy. Map 1
Eight stones stand on a prominent
knoll. There were probably nine
originally, but, inexplicably, the ring is
known as the 'Seven Gray Stanes'. All
are small.

Despite this the site has clear
affinities in its shape and orientation
with the vast ovals of Dumfriess-shire.
Only 3³/₄ miles ssw of the Twelve
Apostles (143) Easthill also is an ellipse
80ft n-s by 62ft (24.4 × 18.9m), but is
hardly one-fifteenth the area of its
larger and presumably earlier
counterpart. The ring stands on a
manmade mound.

On the eastern stone there may be
three cupmarks in a straight line about
10ins (25cm) long. They may be
natural. There is a possible outlier to
the north-east.

There are vague reports of an
unproductive excavation in the late
nineteenth century. Evidence survives in
the form of a hollow in the south-
eastern quadrant.

PSAS 29, 1894–5, 309–10, 'Hills,
Lochrutton'; *RCAHM-Kirkcudbright,*
1914, no. 332; TTB, 276, *Plan*

179 GLENQUICKAN (1) [G4/12. Cambret
Moor West]
Lat: 54°.9   NX 509 582
6 miles wnw of Gatehouse of Fleet, 2
miles e of Creetown. Drive e from
Creetown along Old Military Road for
2¹/₂ miles. Circle is visible 300 yds
(275m) to s in fenced fields. Fair. Map 1
This is the finest of all centre-stone
circles. Standing on level grassland it is
composed of twenty-nine very low,
closely-set stones in an ellipse 53ft e-w
by 49ft (16.2 × 14.9m). The three
tallest are at the sse, from 2ft to 2ft
10ins (0.6, 0.9m) high, but others are
much smaller and the apparent gap in
the ring at the south-west is filled by a
stone whose tip just shows above

ground. The interior of the ring is
tightly laid with small stones like
cobbling.

At the middle of the circle is an
immense upright pillar of grey granite
leaning to the south like the upturned
thumb of a giant. It is 6ft 2ins high, 3ft
3ins wide and 2ft 4ins thick (1.9 × 1 ×
0.7m). It weighs well over four tons
and would have needed a score of
labourers to erect it.

There is no sign of two ruinous
circles that were planned by Alexander
Thom in 1939. They were in such poor
condition in the late nineteenth century
that Fred Coles failed to find them.
They lay to the north-west of the circle
650ft and 1010ft (198, 308m) away,
the latter being destroyed when a drain
was trenched out.

Around 1809 when an adjacent cairn
was levelled, workmen discovered a cist
beneath it containing the skeleton of a
man 'of uncommon size'. One arm had
been almost severed by an axe of green
stone, 'a species of stone never found in
this part of Scotland', and perhaps from
a Land's End 'factory' in Cornwall or,
more probably, from the Scottish
Highlands. A fragment was embedded
in the bone.

*PSAS 29, 1894–5, 307–9; RCAHM-
Kirkcudbright, 1914, no. 292; Thom,
1967, 64, Plan; TTB, 282, Plan*

MORAY
*The few stone circles here seem
influenced by the recumbent and Four-
Poster traditions*

180 INNESMILL (5) [B5/1. Urquhart]
Lat: 57°.7   NJ 289 641
4³/₄ miles nw of Fochabers, 4¹/₄ miles
ene of Elgin. Walk. In field at the
junction of two lanes. Easy. Map 1
This is a tantalisingly spoiled ring.
Known variously as the De'il's Stanes,
the Nine Stanes and the Standing
Stones of Urquhart, today only five
stones still stand with two others
prostrate at the north near a fence.
They may be all that remain of a ring
of twelve stones, 110ft (33.5m) in

diameter. Most of its northern arc is gone and there is a wide gap at the south-west.

The obvious grading of the stones from a short 2ft 6ins at the NNE rising to a full 6ft at the south (76cm, 1.8m) and the reference in the nineteenth century to 'nine tall stones in a circle, two of them at the entrance to the altar' hint aggravatingly that this large ring may have been a recumbent stone circle from which the recumbent and its flankers have been taken. It is significant that the surviving western stone, 5ft (1.5m) high, has several cupmarks on it and occupies that restricted arc from south-east to WSW where decorated stones only occur in recumbent stone circles.

There were recumbent stone circles no more than sixteen miles to the south-east at Nether Dumeath, Aberdeenshire, and Gingomyres whose recumbent was blown up by apprentice masons around 1845.

Before 1870 there was an unproductive excavation at Innesmill but it is known that many flint arrowheads had been found both in and just outside the circle.

In the nineteenth century a stone was removed for a building half a mile to the north at Viewfield. 'Uncanny signs and omens began to manifest themselves' and it was decided to return the stone. Just before reaching the circle the carthorse could not surmount a steep bank. The fearful stone was carefully buried there out of sight.

It is said that to walk round the ring three times at midnight will raise the Devil. How this is known is not recorded.

PSAS 40, 1905–6, 198–201; TTB, 240, *Plan*

181 TEMPLESTONE (3)
Lat: 57°.6   NJ 068 568
10 miles WSW of Elgin, 2¼ miles SE of Forres. Walk. ¼ mile. A little farm lane at NJ 067 570 leads SE to the ring. Easy. Map 1
Almost overgrown by gorse bushes on its north side this is a small but good

Four-Poster. Four heavy blocks stand at the corners of a rectangle 7ft 2ins NE-SW by 6ft 4ins (2.2 × 1.9m). A circle 10ft (3m) across would pass through their centres. The tallest pillar, a sandstone, stands 4ft 7ins (1.4m) high at the south-west.

Kerbing slabs lie between the stones at the south-east and south-west and line a little cairn no more than 4ft 6ins (1.4m) across. It had been dug into at some unknown time.

Fred Coles, after his long years of fieldwork among the stone circles of central and north-eastern Scotland, was the first to recognise the identity of the site, 'because it is rather a square than a circle – one of those nearly rectangular arrangements, at any rate, which are more frequent in Perthshire than in the north-eastern areas in Scotland.' He was correct. The nearest certain Four-Poster to Templestone was the now-destroyed Hill of Bucharn 30 miles to the ESE near Huntly in Aberdeenshire.

PSAS 41, 1906–7, 167–9; Burl, 1988, 140, *Plan*

MULL, INNER HEBRIDES
The island has some intriguing stone rows but few circles

182 LOCH BUIE (1) [M2/14]
Lat: 56°.4   NM 618 251
13¾ miles ENE of Bunessan, 8¾ miles SW of Lochdonhead. Walk. ½ mile. From Lochbuie village a side-road winds NE and NW onto open land. Easy. Map 1
In 1848 it was reported that the circle was situated in a field called the 'Field of the Druids'. Few rings could be more evocative. Erected in a small area of level ground, the only one for miles, the circle is in wonderful condition, its stones tall, its circle perfect, 43ft 9ins (13.3m) in diameter.

Except for one low modern replacement at the exact north these are ancient, lovely stones, man-sized, shapely, the tallest, a broad slab, 6ft 3ins high (1.9m) at the WSW.

Loch Buie circle, Mull (182), from the south. The slender outlier is on the right.

Ring of Brodgar, Orkney (183), from the south. The outlying Comet Stone is in the left foreground.

There is a low outlier to the south-east and two much finer, one 9ft 4ins (2.8m) high, to the south-west. To the NNW, 394 yards (360m) away, is a fourth outlier, a ragged block 6ft 6ins (2m) high. It stands like a signpost towards Gleinn a Chaiginn Mhoir, the only pass through the mountains to the north.

A much-damaged kerb-circle, about 22ft (6.7m) across, lies some 270 yards (250m) north-west of the stone circle. It has a 'false entrance' at its south-east like other small rings in western Scotland such as Temple Wood (125) and Kintraw.

RCAHM-Argyll, III, 1980, 69–70, no. 110; TTB, 318, 320, *Plan*

ORKNEY

The Orkneys are megalithic oddities. Here are two huge rings but no small ones. There is also a paucity of stone rows

183 RING OF BRODGAR (1) [O1/1. Ring of Brogar] Lat: 59°.0   HY 294 133 *10 miles* WNW *of Kirkwall, 3³/₄ miles* NE *of Stromness. Immediately* W *of the B9055. In State care. No charge. Map 1* This magnificent circle-henge stands on a low-lying neck of land between the lochs of Harray and Stenness. The ring of Stenness (184) is nearly a mile to the south-east, the Ring of Bookan about the same distance north-west. Maes Howe chambered tomb is 1¹/₂ miles to the ESE.

Among these splendours Brodgar is one of the most famous of all megalithic rings, deservedly so. But any description must epitomise the frustration of those who study stone circles. As Shelley wrote of other marvels,

> Look on my works, ye Mighty, and despair!
> Nothing beside remains. Round the decay
> Of that colossal wreck . . .
> *Ozymandias*

Despairingly, little has been learned about the age and purpose of the ring since 1694 when James Garden wrote to John Aubrey about 'two rounds sett about with high smooth stones or flags about twenty foot above ground, 6 foot broad and a foot or two thick, and ditched about: whereof the largest [Brodgar] is 110 paces [3ft 1¹/₂ inch, 95cm. see also Site 165] diameter, and reputed to be high places of worship and sacrifice in Pagan times . . . the ancient Temples of the Gods.'

Once known as the Temple of the Sun, Stenness being the Moon, the circle stands on a plateau, 370 ft (113m) across, sloping down to the east and surrounded by a rock-cut ditch up to 30ft wide and 10ft deep (9 × 3m). There are wide causeways at the north-west and south-east but no trace of an outer bank estimated to have been as high as 9ft (3m). Its absence is attributed to natural erosion and a human desire for easily-obtained broken stones for the walled fields of neighbouring farms. The dark heather inside the ring contrasts with the greenness of the grass on cultivated land outside it.

Close to the inner edge of the ditch people erected a well laid-out circle 340ft (103.6m) across. Now of twenty-nine but once of sixty stones the ring is vast. With an area of 90,790 square feet (8,435m²) it ranks third after the Outer Circle at Avebury (82) and the Great Circle at Stanton Drew (75). Its stones are fittingly big, 7ft (2.1m) high on average but with soaring pillars at two cardinal points, a 12ft 6ins (3.8m) tall stone at the south, an even greater and heavier at the west, fully 15ft 3ins (4.7m) in height. In shape the stones vary between wide-waisted triangular-topped lozenges and straight-sided inverted guillotine-blades, but there is no systematic pairing.

The circle lacks any central feature, but on a low circular platform 450ft (137m) to the south-east is the bulky Comet Stone, 5ft 9ins (1.8m) high rising out of waves of curling grass. The stumps of two others, SW-NE of each other, lie at right-angles to it. The setting is an enigma and has been interpreted variously as an unusual Four-Poster or an even more unusual

Cove, perhaps akin to that inside the nearby ring of Stenness (184).

The source of the circle-stones is debateable. Of laminated Orcadian sandstone that splits regularly into 'playing-card' slabs they may have come from a source near the Ring of Bookan. Very similar blocks have been noticed at Vestra Fiold six miles to the NNW where there are several cairns.

Little has been found to date the ring which is encircled by round cairns, presumably of the Bronze Age. A stone axe, a quartzite hammer-stone and a reddish leaf-shaped flint arrowhead have been unearthed inside it. Excavations in 1973 at the north, north-east and south established the width and depth of the ditch and the effort that was demanded to quarry into solid rock with only stone tools and human muscle-power but nothing to demonstrate when the work was done. A runic inscription on a stone a little to the east of south was carved in Christian times.

The Thoms put forward three tentative phases for when alignments to the moon might have been laid out:

1750–1650 BC, 1500–1480 BC, or preferably 1600–1400 BC. This is the uncalibrated equivalent of 1300 to 1100 bc and exceptionally late in the Bronze Age. A date for Brodgar around 2700 BC is more feasible.

Nor are the alignments persuasive. It was suggested that the site had been selected because of the natural foresights it and its cairns offered, the cairns providing 'a perfect platform along which the observer could move as he watched the setting moon'. From the centre of the circle one sightline towards the cliffs of Hellia on Hoy eight miles to the south-west seemed to define the minor southern setting of the moon. A second to a notch on Mid Hill, four miles to the south-east, could have been directed to the minor southern moonrise. Yet with no alignment to the more obvious, calendrically more important and more easily determined major risings and settings of the moon, and with a medley of cairns of all sizes and conditions, the astronomy is inconclusive, conjectural rather than cogent.

The Stones of Stenness, Orkney (184), from the south. The strange Cove is in the centre background.

Following the excavations of 1973 it was computed that 12,000 tons of rock had been quarried, prised and hoisted from the ditch, 80,000 hours of labour. How many people were involved demands even more conjecture.

Brodgar could comfortably have accommodated 3000 men, women and children. Even if this number is halved to allow space for the ceremonies, this still permits an assembly of 1500. This is not unlikely. With known settlements such as Skara Brae only five miles away, with Rinyo village on Rousay, the Knap of Howar homesteads on Papa Westray, with the cluster of houses at Barnhouse hardly a mile to the south-east of Brodgar, and with other hamlets and farms as yet undiscovered, a population of two or three thousand on Orkney and its outlying islands is not an improbability.

Of the hypothetical 1500, some would be too old or too young or too disabled, maybe of the wrong sex or the wrong status, to be part of a work-gang but if a mere fifth were suitable this would still provide a force of 300 labourers. Fifty men could have raised the heaviest stone. Gangs of ten could have hacked out the ditch, heaped up the bank. Working an unlikely unionised eight-hour day with no breaks for weekends, hauliers could have dragged the stones to the site, put them up, dug the ditch, built the the bank and returned to domestic drudgery within a month.

Mathematically, the computation is immaculate. In terms of prehistoric life, it may be no more than fantasy. And what happened inside the completed arena may rest forever unknown.

RCAHM-Orkney, II, 1946, 299–302, no. 875, *Plan*, 300; Renfrew, *Investigations in Orkney*, 1979, 39–43, 212; Thom and Thom, 1978, 122–37

184 STANDING STONES OF STENNESS (3)
Lat: 59°.0　　　　　　　HY 306 125
9 miles W of Kirkwall, 4 miles NE of Stromness. Immediately E of the B9055. In State care. No charge. Map 1
Astonishing even in its present

devastated state this Late Neolithic circle-henge may once have been even more impressive than the Ring of Brodgar (183) whose stones are visible to the north.

Partly ruined in the early nineteenth-century, some buried or fallen stones were re-erected and set in concrete in 1906 and 1907. Excavations in 1973–4 located where other stones had been removed, explored the ditch and reconstructed the Cove that stood inside the circle.

The rock-cut ditch was some 19ft (5.8m) wide and up to 6ft 6ins (2m) deep. Outside it had been a bank, now denuded, but originally about 21ft (6.4m) in width. In height it may have risen 6ft (1.8m) above ground. In the ditch was a grooved ware bowl and the débris of thistles, weeds, buttercups, nettles, twigs and bones including those of a wolf or dog, ox, and sheep. Charcoal from the lowest level gave a date of 2356 ± 65 bc (SRR-350), about 3050 BC.

The ditch enclosed an irregular central area 148ft (45m) across, with one wide entrance at the north. On the plateau had been a ring of towering sandstone slabs of which four remained erect, one a stump. Calculations have suggested that the stones stood in an ellipse 106ft N-S by 98ft (32.3 × 29.9m) but the writer prefers to believe in a reasonably good circle 104ft (31.7m) in diameter. The tallest and most elegant of these 'playing-card' slabs stands at the south 18ft 9ins high, 4ft 7ins wide but only 10ins thick (5.7 × 1.4 × 0.3m). It weighs about six tons.

Its partners to the west are 17ft 4ins and 15ft 9ins high (5.3, 4.8m). There is a tall stump at the north 6ft 6ins (2m) in height. They are the survivors of an original eleven or twelve, the doubt arising from the absence of any stone having stood in a small hollow at the south-east, a position, perhaps significantly, in line with the midwinter sunrise.

The circle may have been set up on the site of an earlier Skara Brae type of house for its centre coincided with a rectangle of flat slabs very similar to the hearths in such homesteads. Charcoal from it was dated to 2238 ± 70 bc (SRR-351), c.2900 BC. A timber structure was associated with it in line with the henge's entrance. Between it and the entrance was a 'dolmen' whose capstone had been thrown over in 1972. It was this vandalism that led to the excavations.

The 'capstone' was bogus, introduced in the nineteenth century by James Cursitor, 'an enthusiastic but misguided Victorian antiquarian' who believed that there had been a small megalithic burial chamber here composed of three upright slabs upon which a missing stone had rested. He was mistaken.

The setting had consisted of the three erect stones, two in line side by side, N-S, separated by a narrow gap behind which the third stood like the backstone of a chamber. It is a form of Cove.

There are impressive standing stones near Stenness. 765 yards (700m) south-east is the tall, wide Barnhouse Stone. 130 yards (119m) to the north-east of Stenness is the 18ft 6ins (5.6m) high Watch Stone, perhaps once one of a row or avenue of similar stones leading to the circle-henge.

Regrettably, what may have been the most interesting of these menhirs, the holed Stone of Odin, about 150 yards (135m) north of Stenness, was destroyed in 1814. Once known as the Stone of Sacrifice because it was believed that druids had pinioned their human victims to the pillar, young couples, more innocently, would plight their troth by clasping hands through the stone.

An older story told of a Viking. 'For nine moons, at midnight, when the moon was full, he went nine times on his bare knees around the Odin Stone of Stainness. And for nine months, at full moon, he looked through the hole in the Odin Stone', hoping for a vision of the future. Nine years was the time it takes the moon to complete its cycle from major to minimum rising and

setting, a journey known and perhaps imitated in prehistoric dance or procession around the stone.

It is likely that Stenness was a place of assembly. Standing where the land contracts between two lochs, it may have been at the edge of a territory where natives and strangers met in safety for trade and ceremony, at times determined by the sun and the moon.

RCAHM-Orkney, II, 1946, 302–4, no. 876; PSAS 107, 1975–6 (1978), 1–60, *Plan 8*

OUTER HEBRIDES, LEWIS
There is a considerable difference in size between the large rings of the Uists and the small ovals on Lewis

185 CALLANISH (1) [H1/1. Tursachan Callanish] Lat: 58°.2   NB 213 330
13 miles W of Stornoway, 1½ miles S of Breasclete. In State care. No charge, but this is likely to change with the opening of the exhibition centre. At the S end of the village. Easy. Map 1
This site, important for its grandeur, its design and its astronomy, is a complex, like a buckled Celtic cross, of a diminutive stone circle, a central stone, an avenue, three rows and a chambered tomb.

Almost certainly the monument was of several phases. The writer favours a sequence of a standing stone followed by a stone circle to which the avenue and rows were added. Because it is known to have been built on material upcast from the circle's stoneholes, the chambered tomb has been proved to be the final addition several centuries later. It is noteworthy that there is hardly any native architecture in either the circle or the tomb. Outside influences are probable.

The circle stands conspicuously on a ridge overlooking the waters of Loch Roag. It was erected on land that had been farmed by earlier agriculturalists. Three-quarters of a mile ESE are two other circles, 'Loch Roag' and Cnoc Fillibhir. Two miles to the south is a

Callanish, Lewis, Hebrides (185), *from the south.*

third, Ceann Hulavig, near Garynahine. The marked individuality of their architecture has been obscured by attempts to rename them Callanish II, III and IV after the so-called 'main' ring, Callanish itself, H1/1. In passing, 'Loch Roag' is too general a term to be applied to one unobtrusive ring. East and West Loch Roags cover miles of water. The ring stands on Cnoc Ceann a'Gharaidh and this name, suggested by the Pontins but here shortened to Cnoc Ceann, has been substituted.

Callanish and its 'central' stone are uneasy partners. The pillar is almost 3ft (0.8m) west of the true centre. It is 'playing-card' in shape, 15ft 9ins high, 5ft wide and about 1ft thick (4.8 × 1.5 × 0.3m). Its long faces are aligned almost perfectly N-S. Shaped like the rudder of a ship it weighs about seven tons and could comfortably have been set upright by a gang of thirty workers. The ring, which has been casually described as a circle 37ft 4ins (11.4m) in diameter, has also been analysed as a Type A Thom ring flattened on its east, 43ft 10ins N-S by 39ft 3ins (13.4 × 12m). Its long axis conforms approximately to sixteen of Thom's

Megalithic Yards. As no attempt had been made to level the site such niceties of mensuration are unlikely. An accurate plan was made by the Department of Geography, Glasgow University in 1974.

It is probable that the ring is an ellipse like the three others in the locality and like the larger ones on North Uist. It measures 43ft 10ins SSW-NNE by 38ft 9ins (13.4 × 11.8m). With thirteen stones averaging 10ft (3m) in height it is an imposing spectacle. It was less impressive until 1857 when an excavation removed 5ft (1.5m) of Iron Age peat from the bottom of the pillars.

Imposing though it may be, it is also cramped. With an internal area of only 1334 s.ft. (124m²) it is the third smallest of its group, only the distant Ceann Hulavig being less. Cnoc Ceann is two-and-a-half times its size. The gigantic ellipses on North Uist exceed them all. With an average area of 11,624 s.ft. (1080m²) they are over six times as spacious as those around Loch Roag.

Leading to the circle from the NNE the avenue, 273ft (83.2m) long, is an imposing structure of thin, graceful stones, once thirty-nine in number but now nineteen, nine on the east side, ten on the west where, at the far end, it culminates in a tall pillar, 11ft 7ins (3.5m) high. Both terminals are high and heavy and set at right-angles to their rows like blocking-stones. The avenue is not parallel but fanlike, contracting from 22ft (6.7m) wide at the NNE to 19ft 7ins (6m) against the ring. Its stones of Lewissean gneiss may have come from a cliff at Na Dromannan a mile away. With an azimuth of 190° the central line of the avenue was well aligned on the major setting of the southern moon.

It may originally have been a short avenue. From the circle the avenue stones steadily decrease in height but halfway along they begin to rise, climbing like an addition to the tall terminals, the western having its broken tip replaced in 1978.

The avenue also possesses an architectural trait, known elsewhere only in northern Ireland and Brittany, of having one side higher than the other, the eastern being no more than three-quarters the height of the western. There is a legend that the stones of Callanish were brought in ships under the leadership of a High Priest and erected by 'black men'. Although the stones are local it is a possibility that the avenue at least may have been planned and constructed by dark-haired Irishmen from the south.

The discovery on Lewis and North Uist of porcellanite axes from Co. Antrim shows that early links between the north of Ireland and the Outer Hebrides did exist. Shale from Skye also points to contacts with mainland Scotland.

Callanish has not only an avenue to the NNE but three short rows to the ENE, south and WSW. They are astronomically significant. The ENE, now of five stones after its buried terminal was re-erected in 1982, is 76ft (23.2m) long. It has been thought to be aligned on the lovely cluster of stars, the Pleiades.

The southern row, with an almost unbelievably precise N-S orientation, has five stones in a line 89ft 3ins (27.2m) long. The western row is shorter, only 42ft 7ins (13m) long and of four stones. With an uneven western skyline the row is neatly directed towards the equinoctial sunsets which occur not at the west but the WSW.

Diodorus Siculus, the first-century BC Greek historian, may have referred to these rows. Mentioning a 'spherical temple', thought to be his vague idea of a stone circle, he wrote that in it '[The moon] dances continuously the night through from the vernal equinox until the rising of the Pleiades . . .' This temple has often been interpreted as Stonehenge but that is an astronomical impossibility. The Wiltshire ring is 500 miles too far south of the correct lunar latitude.

If the 'spherical temple' was not Callanish it is a remarkable concidence that it was only the moon, the equinox and the Pleiades that Diodorus mentioned. Callanish seems associated with all of them. The avenue was directed towards the southern moonset; the western row was oriented on the equinoctial sunset. Although other stars are feasible targets the eastern row could have been aligned on the Pleiades around 1550 BC, the third of the heavenly bodies named by Diodorus.

It may be that the rows were the initial sides of intended short avenues. It is noticeable that not one is aligned on the centre of the ellipse. The east, with the tallest stones, points 6ft (2m) to its south, and the south and west are 3ft (1m) to its west and south respectively. Callanish may be yet another example of an abandoned prehistoric project, perhaps interrupted by the intrusion of the chambered tomb builders.

Excavations in 1980 and 1981, recovering local Hebridean pottery, AOC and N4 beakers and grooved ware sherds, suggest that the circle was erected in the Early Bronze Age around 2200 BC. The avenue may have been an addition, the three rows perhaps even later.

The puzzle is the tiny chambered tomb, only 21ft (6.4m) across, that was squashed in between the eastern stones and the central pillar. In it cremated bone and late beaker sherds may have belonged to the centuries around 1700 BC. The tomb was desecrated by later farmers, then partly rebuilt before its final abandonment as peat began to form over the countryside early in the first millennium BC. What is puzzling is that the tomb has no resemblance either to local forms or to others in western and south-western Scotland. The nearest in likeness are two similarly small tombs, Nev Hill, 35ft (10.7m) across, and Hoxa Hill, 'The Wart', 32ft (9.8m), 150 distant miles by sea to the ENE, on South Ronaldsay in the Orkneys.

There are legends that the stones are giants petrified for refusing to embrace christianity and that the ring has powers of fecundity. As late as the nineteenth century natives would go there because 'it would not do to neglect the stones'. With the advent of an Exhibition Centre they will be less neglected still.

Arch 73, 1923, Plan, 203; RCAHM-Outer Hebrides, 1928, 24–7, no. 89 Plan; G. and M. Ponting, New Light on the Stones of Callanish, 1984

186 CEANN HULAVIG (3) [H1/4. Callanish IV] Lat: 58°.2   NB 230 304
12¼ miles W of Stornoway, 2 miles SSE of Callanish. Walk. 200 yds (180m) W of unfenced B8011. Easy. Map 1
Ceann Hulavig is one of six sites near Garynahine hamlet and is the most isolated of the four rings near Loch Roag. It is also the smallest. Like the others it stands conspicuously on a ridge. It was cleared of peat in 1857–8.

It is yet another ellipse 43ft 7ins SSE-NNW by 31ft (13.3 × 9.5m), the tallest of its five upright stones, 8ft 7ins (2.6m) standing predictably at the end of the long axis, here at the SSE.

The western side of the ring is a disaster but just possibly the ellipse once consisted of thirteen stones irregularly spaced about 9ft (2.7m)

apart on the 118ft (36m) long circumference.

Just to the north-west of the centre is a 2ft (0.6m) erect slab which is not quite aligned on the long axis of the ellipse. It stands in a dilapidated cairn some 6ft (1.8m) across.

RCAHM-Outer Hebrides, 1928, 28, no. 93, Plan

187 CNOC CEANN A'GHARAIDH (3) [H1/2. Callanish II]
Lat: 58°.2   NB 222 326
12½ miles W of Stornoway, ⅝ mile ESE of Callanish. Walk. 600 yds (550m) SW of unfenced A858. Easy. Map 1
Formerly called Loch Roag because it is only 100 yards (90m) from the water, this is probably a site of three distinct phases. Like Cnoc Fillibhir (188) its architecture has little in common with Callanish (185) which can just be seen to the WNW across an inlet. And like Cnoc Fillibhir it was placed on a ridge to be conspicuous.

When 3ft (1m) of peat was removed in 1848 four holes, one 1ft by 1ft 8ins (31 × 51cm), across, were noticed, three grouped in an arc at the north-west, a fourth at the south-west. Wood charcoal found in them suggests that they are the remains of the first monument here, a timber circle about 32ft (9.8m) in diameter.

This was replaced by a larger stone circle of tall stones in an ellipse 71ft N-S by 62ft (21.6 × 18.9m). The highest, 10ft 9ins (3.3m) in height, stands at the north-east. A pronounced stretch of banking can be seen around the ring at the south.

A cairn, 28ft (8.5m) across, was added just east of the middle of the ring. Its scattered stones contain a cavity 6ft (1.8m) wide 'shaped like a large round-bodied bottle with a short neck'.

Near the cairn lay a stone, 7ft long by 3ft thick (2.1 × 1m), with some incised markings more likely to be natural than manmade. The stone has gone, reputedly taken to Lews Castle, Stornoway.

PSAS 3, 1857–60, 116; RCHAHM-Outer Hebrides, 1928, 27, no. 90, Plan

188 Cnoc Fillibhir (3) [H1/3.
Callanish III] Lat: 58°.2   NB 225 325
*12½ miles w of Stornoway, ¾ mile ESE
of Callanish. Walk. ¼ mile w of the
unfenced A858. Easy. Map 1*
Conspicuous on its ridge when
approached from the north-west, this
ring, like Cnoc Ceann (187), is
architecturally different from Callanish
(185). It consists of concentric ellipses,
the outer irregular but about 45ft SSE-
NNW by 43ft (13.7 × 13.1m). Eight tall
stones still stand and five have fallen,
their sum of thirteen being a preferred
number amongst the rings around Loch
Roag. The stones are jagged and rough
as though broken from the living rock.
'This outer ring has a rather scattered
appearance'.

Inside is a more pronounced oval on
the same axis, 34ft 6ins by 21ft 7ins
(10.5 × 6.6m), now of only four stones
but even taller. The highest, 7ft (2.1m)
stands at the NNW of the longer axis.
There is no sign of a central mound or
cairn.

The site was cleared of peat in 1858.
Cnoc Ceann is very visible 300 yards
(275m) to the WNW across flat ground.

PSAS 38, 1903–4, 189; *RCAHM-
Outer Hebrides*, 1928, 27–8, no. 91,
Plan

NORTH UIST

189 Loch a Phobuill (4) [H3/18.
Sornach Coir Fhinn]
Lat: 57°.6   NF 829 630
*6½ miles sw of Lochmaddy, 1 mile SE
of Clachan. From E end of tiny Oban
na Curra loch, on unfenced B894.
Walk. 550 yds (500m) sw. Easy. Map 1*
Difficult to make out when the heather
is high this is an embanked ring whose
site appears to have been cut into the
hillside at the east and banked up into
a level platform at the west. Like other
Outer Hebridean rings it is an ellipse,
about 130ft SE-NW by 115ft (39.6 ×
35.1m). Once of a possible fifty low
stones, sixteen of local granite stand
and lie in the western half. The eastern
is virtually denuded.

Just inside the ring at the ENE and
south-east are two 'playing-card' slabs
on edge, each arranged SE-NW. Thom,
who mistakenly called the ring Sornach
Coir Fhinn, suggested that one was
aligned on the Neolithic chambered
tomb of Unival, NF 800 669, on a
steep south-western hillside three miles
to the north-west. He calculated that
the midsummer sun would set behind
the cairn which is also known as
Leachach an Tigh Cloiche, 'the stony
house on the hill'.

RCAHM-Outer Hebrides, 1928, 83,
no. 249; TTB, 312, *Plan*

190 Pobull Fhinn (1) [H3/17]
Lat: 57°.6   NF 844 650
*5 miles wsw of Lochmaddy, ½ mile SE
of Barpa Langass. At NF 833 657 a
farm-track leads ¾ mile SE. Walk.
250 yds (230m) E. Easy. Map 1*
The writer is biassed. Having seen this
ring on a fresh, sunlit day he remains
convinced that it has one of the
loveliest settings of any stone circle. It
is strangely beautiful on its hillside of
bracken and heather overlooking
Langass Loch and distances of tiny
lochs, machair bright with water lilies,
marsh marigolds and orchids,
overflown by lapwings, thinly whistling
dunlins and oystercatchers. Beyond
them is North Ford and, beyond its
waters, Benbecula four miles in the
distance.

The 'white or holy people' is a
splendid ring on a south-facing hillside
into which people cut a shelf at the
north and piled the earth up at the
south to fashion a level platform on
which to erect the stones of a flattened
ellipse 124ft ESE-WNW by 92ft (37.8 ×
28m). A wide bank was heaped up. The
northern stones are inside it, the
southern outside.

The stones range from turf-level to
6ft 6in (2m) in height. What
distinguishes the ring architecturally is
that it has portalled entrances at either
end of its long axis. That at the west,
some 9ft (2.7m) wide, has a 5ft long
fallen pillar and 3ft 6ins high stone
(1.5, 1.1m) outside the gap in the bank.

Pobull Fhinn, North Uist, Hebrides (190), *from the north-east. Loch Langass is in the background.*

At the ESE two circle stones 4ft and 6ft 6ins high respectively (1.2, 2m) stand 15ft apart (4.6m) with two low portals outside them.

Half a mile to the north-west is the Neolithic chambered tomb of Barpa Langass, NF 837 657. This fine circular cairn, 79ft across and still 13ft high (24 × 4m) has an eastern entrance from which a well-preserved passage leads to a polygonal chamber. Perfection.

RCAHM-Outer Hebrides, 1928, 83, no. 250; TTB, 310, Plan

PEEBLES-SHIRE
A county lacking great stone circles

191 HARESTANES, Kirkud (3)
Lat: 55°.7   NT 124 443
7¹/₂ miles WNW of Peebles, ³/₄ mile s of Blyth Bridge. In the garden of Old Toll Cottage. Ask. Map 1
Five disproportionately large boulders lie on the circumference of a ring about

10ft (3m) across. The biggest, 4ft 7ins high and about 4ft square (1.4, 1.2 × 1.2m) is at the south-east. Outside to the north-east was a thin slab, perhaps sandstone, no more than 1ft 10ins (56cm) high. In 1900 it stood 'in the manner of a modern headstone'. It has since fallen.

PSAS 37, 1902–3, 199–201; RCAHM-Peebles, 1967, 63–4, no. 107, Plan

PERTHSHIRE
The county is noteable not only for being the heartland of Four-Posters but also contains some larger ovals. For good measure, there are some variant recumbent stone circles

192 AIRLICH (3) [P1/16. Mickle Findowie] Lat: 56°.5   NN 959 386.
4³/₄ miles WSW of Dunkeld. Walk. 1¹/₂ miles. From NN 938 386 a footpath leads SE. crossing the River Braan. ¹/₂

153

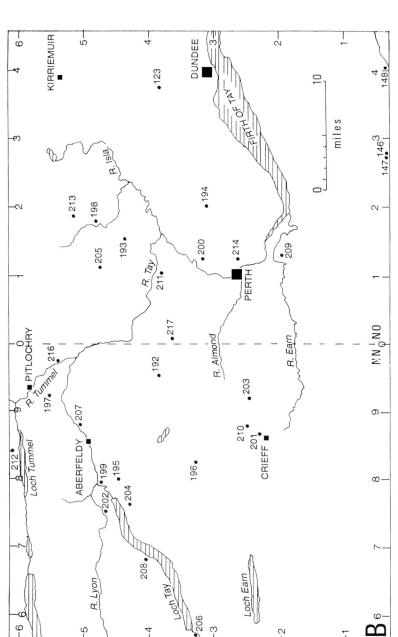

Map B, Perthshire

mile turn NE to cross moor. Circle is 1
mile but visitors have to cross the
Corrody Burn. Difficult. Map B
On the north-west slope of a hill near
the River Braan stand and lie the stones
of an ellipse 25ft 10ins SE-NW by 22ft
(7.9 × 6.7m). The northern half is in
fairly good condition. The low stones,
up to 3ft 6ins (1m) high stand in a
wide rubble bank. Much larger stones
up to 7ft (2.1m) long lie on it at the
south, south-west and west suggesting
that the ring was once graded in height
towards the south-west like so many in
central and north-east Scotland.

In 1909 an inner kerbed cairn was
visible, about 12ft 6ins (3.8m) across
and also graded to the south-west. Its
stones have gone.

PSAS 44, 1909–10, 159–63; TTB,
344, Plan

193 ARDBLAIR (1, 4) [P2/1. Leys of
Marlee] Lat: 56°.6   NO 160 439
4¹/₂ miles NW of Coupar Angus, 1¹/₂ mile
SW of Blairgowrie. The circle straddles
the B947. No walk. Alert eyes and ears
are essential. Map B
This disrupted ring, which looks in
good condition, was already ruinous
when the B947 road was laid through it
around 1856. Take care when visiting.
The road is straight and the traffic fast.

Like many circles in this part of
Scotland it consisted of six stones
which now stand on the circumference
of a circle 48ft 6ins (14.8m) across.
They are big. The ring is graded to the
south-west where the tallest and
heaviest, 5ft 11ins (1.8m) high, stands.

The western stone is 7ft (2.1m) inside
the ring. Both it and one at the north-
east stand radially to the perimeter and
were moved to make room for the
road. At that time the northern stone
was prostrate. The smallest stone at the
south was broken during the
alterations. It was iron-banded and set
up in concrete.

The ring's alternative name, the Leys
of Marlee, is interesting. It has nothing
to do with landscaped lines. 'Ley' is an
anglicisation of the Gaelic, *lia*, 'a stone'.
Coles suggested that Marlee was a

corruption of *mor liae*, 'the great
stones'. The title is fitting. 'In the whole
of the Stormont [region] there is no
group of Standing Stones greater than
those of this Circle.'

PSAS 43, 1908–9, 115–20; TTB,
330, Plan

194 BANDIRRAN (3)
Lat: 56°.5   NO 207 310
5¹/₂ miles S of Coupar Angus, 3¹/₄ miles
W of Abernyte. Walk. 1 mile N of the
B953 just before trees to E. Fair. Map B
Green with moss and in the shadows of
an overgrown copse there are now
seven stones, several of them fallen, in
an ellipse once of nine stones, 27ft
10ins NE-SW by 25ft 4ins (8.5 × 7.7m).
The tallest is at the south-west. A
hundred yards (90m) to the east is a
pair of stones 6ft (1.8m) apart. The
eastern is a rectangular block. The
west, prostrate, is a thinner, taller
peaked pillar.

On a wooded terrace the circle is so
little known that, even though it is very
close to the farm, the farmer did not
know of its existence. There is no
published plan.

PSAS 98, 1964–6, 142–3. No known
plan

195 CARSE FARM NORTH (2) [P1/4.
Weem] Lat: 56°.6   NN 802 488
3¹/₄ miles W of Aberfeldy, 2³/₄ miles NE
of Loch Tay. Immediately S of the
B846. Easy. But often in crop. Map B
On the carse or low-lying land by a
river, here the Tay, this Four-Poster
was excavated in 1964. In 1907 only
three stones were erect with the south-
west lying between the northern slabs.
The north-east stone is 4ft tall, the
south-east 5ft and the north-west 4ft
(1.2, 1.5, 1.4m). There are cupmarks
on both the north-east and south-east
stones.

The excavation discovered the south-
west stonehole and the fallen stone, 5ft
10ins (1.8m) long, was erected in it. The
four stones now stand at the corners of
a rectangle 12ft ENE-WSW by 8ft (3.7 ×
2.4m) and on the circumference of a
ring 14ft 5ins (4.4m) across.

Inside the ring by the north-east stone was a pit filled with cremated bone and sticky black earth. At the bottom was a collared urn with a decorated rim. Other pits inside the circle were thought to have 'been used for stabilising props during the erection of the stones.' As the heaviest stone, that at the north-west, weighed about six tons it would have taken about thirty people to pull it upright. Sturdy timbers would have made the work safer.

Two hundred yards (180m) to the south are the remains of a second Four-Poster of which only one stone is upright.

Burl, 1988, 148–9, *Plan*

196 CLACH NA TIOMPAN (2)
Lat: 56°.5   NN 831 329
10 miles s of Aberfeldy, 3¾ miles wnw of Newton Bridge. Walk. Four miles from Newton, NN 886 317. Long stroll by the river. Map B

On a terrace in the narrow, mountain-shadowed glen of the River Almond this spoiled Four-Poster, 'the stone of the rounded, or drum-like knoll', was excavated in 1954. To its north-west is an enormous chambered tomb.

In 1910 only one stone could be seen of the ring, standing at the western edge of a low cairn. Excavation proved the cairn to be lined with boulders. At the centre were bits of wood and charcoal and patches of burning. More than a hundred quartz pebbles were discovered.

Two stoneholes at north and south and the stump of a stone at the east showed that this had been a Four-Poster, the stones at the corners of an irregular quadrilateral, three sides measuring 10ft 3ins with a shorter, 8ft 2ins long (3.1, 2.5m) at the north-west. The stones had stood on the circumference of a circle 13ft 6ins (4.1m) in diameter. The stones had occupied cardinal positions.

A prostrate slab lay 6ft (1.8m) to the south.

PSAS 88, 1954–6, 122–4; Burl, 1988, 152–3, Plan

197 CLACHAN AN DIRIDH (3) [P1/18]
Lat: 56°.7   NN 924 558
4½ miles s of Killiecrankie, 3 miles w of Pitlochry. Walk. 1½ miles From Port na Craig, NN 940 575, lane and then track into wood ssw for 1 mile. w for ¼ mile. Circle is at w edge of wood in front of Loch na Moine Moire. Beautiful site. Map B

Standing at the edge of a mountain terrace 1150ft (350m) above sea-level this damaged Four-Poster, sometimes known as Fonab Moor, commands a marvellous view. 'Amid this wild Highland landscape the huge standing stones, grey with the moss of ages, produce a grand and imposing effect; and from the idea of lofty height the distant mountains suggest, they convey a stronger impression of gigantic proportions than is produced even by the first sight of the giant monoliths of Salisbury Plain.'

Even when Daniel Wilson, the Scottish antiquarian, wrote those words in the mid-nineteenth-century the NNW stone was missing. The remaining three, of local sandstone, are 'playing-cards', their long faces on a NNE-SSW axis. The NNE is 3ft 3ins high, the SSE, 5ft 10ins, and the south-west, 6ft (1, 1.8, 1.8m). At the corners of a rectangle 14ft 6ins SSW-NNE by 13ft 7ins (4.4 × 4.1m) they also stand on the circumference of a true circle 20ft (6.1m) in diameter.

The name which means 'stones of the ascent or brae' reflects the steepness of the slope above which the Four-Poster stands. There is no sign or record of an excavation.

Local tradition claims 'that the stones marked the scene of some periodical religious meeting or ceremonial of which nothing is now known'. Local tradition is almost correct.

Burl, 1988, 154–5, *Plan*

198 CRAIGHALL MILL (4) [P2/4.
Courthill] Lat: 56°.6   NO 185 481
4 miles w of Alyth, 2 miles n of Blairgowrie. Immediately e of lane. Easy. Map B

Sometimes mistakenly called Glenballoch this is a somewhat untidy

Craighall Mill, Perthshire (198), the ruined Four-Poster from the south-east.

Four-Poster. Another possible Four-Poster, near NO 182 482 at Glenballoch Farm, was destroyed before 1870. From it came a magnificent cordoned urn which is now in the Royal Museum of Scotland, Edinburgh.

At Craighall Mill are four stones, so low and rugged that it is difficult to tell whether they stand or lie. They form an approximate 16ft (4.9m) rectangle. Close to the cardinal points they are also on a circle about 22ft 6ins (6.9m) in diameter.

To the north, about 220 yards (200m) away, is a fallen stone some 10ft (3m) long. On its south-east face are thirteen cupmarks and a long vertical groove.

Burl, 1988, 158–9, *Plan*

199 Croft Moraig (1) [P1/19. Croftmoraig] Lat: 56°.6   NN 797 472 *4 miles wsw of Aberfeldy, 2 miles NE of Kenmore. Immediately s of the main road. In State care, no charge. Map B* Because it is so close to the Aberfeldy-Kenmore road noted Fred Coles in 1910, 'the most unobservant pedestrian

or rider – always excepting the begoggled motorist – cannot but see the green mound bristling with great grey Stones.' Coach drivers would slow down, calling out, 'Yon's the Druid Stones'. This charming ring has lost nothing of its attraction.

It stands at the north-east of Loch Tay on low ground below steep mountainsides. Its stones of local schist, almost luminescent in their greys and fawns, stand on an artificial platform. There is a pair of tall pillars just to the east. Excavation in 1965 proved the monument to have a complex history.

Its first phase, in the Late Neolithic around 3000 BC, consisted of some fourteen heavy timber posts arranged in a horseshoe pattern open to the SSW and measuring 26ft NNE-SSW by 23ft (7.9 × 7m). A boulder lay at the centre with a scatter of burnt bone near it. There was a constricted entrance, no more than 3ft (1m) wide, at the east composed of two pairs of wooden uprights. Outside this setting was a surrounding ditch.

The narrow mouth of the horseshoe, only 11ft (3.4m) across, had a post

157

Croft Moraig, Perthshire (199), from the south-west. The cupmarked prostrate slab is in the right foreground.

standing just inside it. With a high skyline beyond the post was well aligned on the major southern moonset.

At some indeterminate time the posts were replaced by eight stones graded in height from 2ft 6ins to 4ft 6ins (0.8–1.4m) towards the ssw. Their horseshoe was similar in size to their predecessor, about 26ft by 21ft (7.9 × 6.4m) with an open mouth 13ft 6ins (4.1m) wide. A small stone stood outside it. Local Neolithic ware and some coarse, flat-based vessels were associated with this phase.

A kerbed rubble bank, 60ft (18m) across, enclosed the stones. On it, at the ssw, lay a 6ft 6ins (2m) long dark-grey, mottled stone with twenty-three cupmarks carved on it. As in the previous phase, the decorated slab was in line with the southern moonset. Another cupmarked stone at the north-east of the horseshoe stood close to where the midsummer sun would rise above the mountains.

Finally, a circle, about 40ft (12m) in diameter, of twelve big stones, about 5ft 6ins (1.7m) in average height, was

erected around the horseshoe. To the ESE, some 18ft (5.5m) outside the ring two stones 8ft 6ins (2.6m) apart formed a wide entrance. The northern stood close to the equinoctial sunrise.

At a later date graves may have been dug outside these stones. At the foot of the 6ft (1.8m) high northern stone a pit was just big enough to accommodate the curled-up and barefooted body of a young woman. The 'grave' by the 7ft (2.1m) tall southern pillar accepted a substantial male student volunteer with ease.

The platform, the grading, the supine cupmarked stone, the southern moon, all link Croft Moraig in its later phases with the recumbent stone circles of north-eastern Scotland.

Except for the first timber structure, everything else, apart from the students, can be seen here.

PPS 37, 1971, 1–15, Plans

200 DRUID'S SEAT (3) [P2/3. Blindwells]
Lat: 56°.5   NO 123 313
5½ miles N of Perth, 1½ miles SW of Stanley. Walk. Less than ¾ mile. From

NO 133 312 go ¹/₂ mile NW through wood, turn SW towards Blindwells farm. Ring is 330 yds (300m) S of track in trees. Map B

In a wood about a mile east of the River Tay this ruined ring once consisted of twelve stones in a circle 28ft (8.5m) in diameter. Today the eastern half is in collapse. The largest stone stands at the SSW.

Colen stone circle is about a mile to the WSW and Blackfaulds is 1¹/₄ to the ENE. From that ring it is just over a mile ESE to the ring at St Martins. Such regular spacing is probably an indication of farming territories, family holdings that the small size of the circles hints at.

TTB, 354, *Plan*

201 FERNTOWER (5)
Lat: 56°.4   NN 874 226
³/₄ mile NE of Crieff, just W of the A85. Walk. 200 yds (180m) but on a private golf-course. Map B

This possible Four-Poster and two stones to its east have been subjected to unrecorded disturbance because they were on the line of an intended fairway. It cannot be certain that what one sees today is what was laid out in the Bronze Age.

Four very low stones form an irregular trapezoid but lie on the circumference of a circle about 25ft 4ins (7.7m) in diameter. The tallest, only 2ft 4ins (71cm) high, is at the SSW. There was an intention to blast the south-east stone and a drill-hole can be seen. By an unhappy coincidence there is a cupmark alongside it.

26ft (7.9m) to the east are two stones on a NW-SE axis. As is customary in Perthshire pairs it is the western that is taller, 7ft 9ins (2.4m) high, thick and flat-topped. Its fallen partner is shorter, 6ft (1.8m) long, and would have stood no more than 5ft (1.5m) high. It would have risen to a peak.

Burl, 1988, 164–5, *Plan*

FONAB MOOR see Clachan an Diridh

202 FORTINGALL NE, SW, S (3, 4)

[P1/6] Lat: 56°.7   NN 747 470
7 miles WSW of Aberfeldy, ¹/₄ mile E of Fortingall. By lane. Map B

On a low-lying terrace just to the west of the River Lyon are the savaged remains of three stone circles, two Four-Posters and an almost obliterated recumbent stone circle. All were excavated in 1970 by a team from Leicester University that included the writer.

A. *Fortingall North-East* Before excavation only three stones were visible here. At the south-east was a thick block 5ft 5ins (1.7m) high; the south-west 5ft 11ins and the north-west 6ft 1in (1.8, 1.9m). Five others had been pushed over in the nineteenth century and buried. The 'missing' north-west stone was 7ft 2ins (2.2m) long and would have stood about 5ft 3ins (1.6m) high. Between these four tall stones were four much lower ones.

The original setting had been a rectangle 20ft 9ins NE-SW by 16ft 5ins (6.3 × 5m) with the four large blocks standing on the circumference of a circle 27ft 8ins (8.2m) in diameter. At the centre was a burnt patch with charcoal, sooty earth and burnt bone.

B. *Fortingall South-West* This also had been a Four-Poster with a smaller stone at the middle of each of its sides. Like its partner 82ft (25m) away only three stones were apparent before 1970. Their rectangle was 25ft 1in SSE-NNW by 19ft 3ins (7.7 × 5.9m), and their circle 32ft (9.8m) across. The five lost stones had been buried in a sandy pit 2ft 6ins (0.8m) deep, toppled into prepared pits. The three standing stones, when exposed down to the old land surface, were 6ft 9ins high, NNE; 5ft 10ins, SSE; and 6ft 8ins, SSW (2.1, 1.8, 2m).

There was the faintest evidence of a flooring of tiny pebbles. Part of an Iron Age jet ring was found at the south-west and several quartz stones lay near the SSW stone.

C. *Fortingall South* 136ft (42m) south-east of the Four-Poster was a peculiar setting of three stones, almost in line, in a 20ft (6m) long SE-NW row.

The two outer stones, each about 5ft (1.5m) high, were set SE-NW at right-angles to the lower SE-NW boulder between them.

The arrangement was reminiscent of the flankers and recumbent of circles in Aberdeenshire and a limited excavation discovered the hole of a missing stone 15ft (4.6m) to the north-west of the western 'flanker'. If projected the diameter of this hypothetical ring would have been about 48ft (14.6m). The putative recumbent stone, 4ft 6ins (1.4m) long, lay at the SSW with a midpoint at about 205°. If the suggested recumbent stone circle association is correct, it is not surprising that the stone lies well in line with the major southern moonset. Because the three known stones stand on an arc, a recent suggestion that the setting had been a variant Four-Poster like those to its north is unpersuasive.

Without further excavation the interpretation of a vandalised recumbent stone circle must remain unproven, but there is indirect support for it. The variant recumbent stone circle of Croft Moraig (199) is only 2¼ miles to the east and another possible recumbent at Coilleachur is a further three miles in the same direction.

It is said that Pontius Pilate was born at Fortingall, son of a Roman legionary and a Scottish mother. As Pilate died no later than AD 40 and as the Roman army under Agricola did not reach central Scotland until AD 80 the chronology, if not the gestation, seems to be premature. It is more conceivable that the Four-Posters were already some 2000 years old.

Burl, 1988, 167–75, *Plans*

203 Fowlis Wester, E, W (4) [P1/10]
Lat: 56°.4   NN 923 249
6½ miles W of Methven, 4½ miles NE of Crieff. Walk ½ mile. Easy. Map B
There is little here to excite the megalithic heart. On the dreariness of the Moor of Ardoch, on the highest, windiest point of a ridge, stones lie equally drearily in a collapsed stone circle and a smaller, disturbed ring to

its east. There are two outlying stones. One has fallen.

A. *The eastern ring*, once of twelve stones of which three are missing, is about 26ft 10ins (8.2m) across with stones graded to the south-west. Inside it is a kerb-cairn, 17ft 9ins (5.4m) across, also graded. Excavation in 1939 found that the kerbs rested on scatters of quartz. Inside was a clay floor reddened by fire. Burnt bone fragments lay at the centre under an untidy pile of four thin slabs.

There are three cupmarks on the SSW kerb. 37ft (11.3m) to the north-east is a 6ft (1.8m) high 'playing-card' outlier standing on a SW-NE axis. A line from the cupmarked kerbstone, through the circle to the outlier is well oriented on the major northern moonrise.

B. *The western circle*, roughly 22ft (6.7m) in diameter and open, is 61ft (18.6m) to the WNW of its partner. Just to its east is a prostrate large slab, 9ft long and 7ft 6ins wide (2.7 × 2.3m). The stones of the ring had been set up in holes so shallow that the pillars soon fell leaving their bedding of tiny white pebbles exposed. Inside the interior fires had burnt and there were deposits of charcoal and cremated bone.

Planning of the stoneholes of the rings during the excavation proved that both the eastern and western were true circles. Thom's supposition that the WNW site was an ellipse with a long axis aligned on the major northern moonset was based on the present positions of the tumbled blocks explaining why 'no foresight now appears on the horizon'.

PSAS 77, 1942–4, 174–84, *Plan*; Thom, *Megalithic Lunar Observatories*, 1971, 53–5

204 Greenland (3)
Lat: 56°.6   NN 767 427
6¼ miles SE of Aberfeldy, 1½ miles S of Kenmore. Walk 2¼ miles along track then mountainside. Steep. Map B
This 'lonely and elevated spot', at 1240ft (378m) O.D. in a fir plantation, commands widespread and fine views of a loch and mountains. Once of nine

stones in a circle 27ft 9ins (8.5m) in
diameter, today four stand and two lie,
the northern pair separated from the
others by a low stone wall. They are
graded in height from north to south:
NNW, 1ft 7ins; NNE, 4ft; east, 4ft 3ins;
south-west, 5ft 8ins (0.5, 1.2, 1.3,
1.7m). Near the south is a prone slab
7ft 8ins (2.3m) long, and at the west is
another, 6ft 9ins (2.1m) in length.

A dig in 1924 at the centre found a
shallow deposit of dark earth
intermixed 'with a white limy substance
consisting of calcined bones' and
charcoal. Around it the soil was red
where a probable pyre had burned.

A local name for the ring is
auchlaicha, 'the field of stones'.

PSAS 43, 1908–9, 271–4, Plan; ibid
59, 1924–5, 77–8

205 KINLOCH (3)
Lat: 56°.6 NO 117 475
6¾ miles NE of Dunkeld, 4½ miles NW
of Blairgowrie. Walk 1¼ miles from
Middleton. Keep dykes to S. Fair.
Map B
This is a Four-Poster whose stones
stand in a vague rectangle 11ft 6ins
SSE-NNW by 9ft 10ins (3.5 × 3m). The
site is a circle 15ft 9ins (4.8m) in
diameter. All the stones lean and are
stumps, the tallest at the south, 2ft 7ins
(0.8m) high.

There are hut-circles and cairns 200
to 300 yards (180–275m) to the south.
Burl, 1988, 178–9, *Plan*

206 KINNELL (1) [P1/3. Killin]
Lat: 56°.5 NN 576 327
½ mile E of Killin, by Kinnell Farm. ½
mile SW of the end of Loch Tay. Walk.
½ mile NE along farm track. Easy. Map
B
Six stones of dark grey schist stand
impressively on the circumference of an
ellipse 32ft 7ins SW-NE by 27ft 5ins (9.9
× 8.4m). They are graded in height
from 4ft to 6ft 6ins (1.2–2m) at the
SSW. The south-west stone leans and
has possibly been re-erected. The others
are erect. Such six-stone rings are
common in central Scotland.
TTB 330–1, *Plan*

207 LUNDIN FARM SE, NW (1, 4) [P1/7.
Aberfeldy] Lat: 56°.6 NN 882 505
1¾ miles NE of Aberfeldy. Walk. ¼ mile
SE along track from A827. Easy. Map B
A. This fine Four-Poster, on a gentle
slope down to the south, commands a
magnificent view towards Ben Lawers
on the west. On its high mound it is
reminiscent of Château-Bû (374) in
Brittany. The tall, grey stones of local
quartziferous schist form a rectangle
13ft E-W by 11ft (4 × 3.4m) and stand
on the perimeter of a circle 19ft (5.8m)
across. The highest, 7ft 3ins (2.2m) is
at the north-east. The north-west is the
smallest. The south-east is 'playing-
card' in shape and is whitened with
quartz.

The ring was erected on a natural
mound of moraine gravel about 30ft
across and 5ft high (9 × 1.5m).
Excavation in 1962 showed that a V-
shaped ditch had been dug around its
base. Then the hummock had been
deturfed and, alongside a burnt patch,
organic material, cremated bone and
sherds were placed in a hollow at its
summit. After the pit was filled in the

Lundin Farm SE Four-Poster, Perthshire
(207), from the south-west.

four stones were erected around the deposit. The ditch was back-filled.

The sherds came from a collared urn with plaited-cord decoration around its rim; from coarse undecorated ware; and from an AOC beaker. The finds, of the Early Bronze Age, are now in the Royal Museum of Scotland, Edinburgh.

At the south-eastern base of the mound is a prostrate slab with forty-three cupmarks. With an azimuth of about 140°, had the stone been erect, it would have stood in line with the midwinter sunrise.

PSAS 98, 1964–6, 126–49, *Plan*; Burl, 1988, 182–5

B. Eighty yards (73m) to the north is the ruin of *Lundin Farm NW*, NN 882 506. Two standing stones, 3ft 8ins high at the north-west, 2ft high at the south-east (1.1, 0.6m) are all that remain of a second Four-Poster. Between them is a prostrate cupmarked slab which is probably one of the two missing stones.

Burl, 1988, 180–1, *Plan*

208 MACHUINN (3)
Lat: 56°.5   NN 682 401.
8¼ miles NE of Killin, ½ mile NE of Lawers. Immediately W of the A 827. Walk. ¼ mile from field to N. Easy. Map B
On a long natural mound overlooking Loch Tay four massive stones from 3ft 7ins to 4ft 10ins in height (1.1–1.5m) stand on the western arc of an overgrown ellipse 22ft WSW-ENE by 19ft (6.7 × 5.8m). A fifth, 4ft 5ins (1.4m) high stands at the south-east. Two others lie at the north-east and there is an enormous slab, 6ft 5ins by 5ft (2 × 1.5m) lying at the south. The ring is very neglected.

PSAS 44, 1908–9, 126–30, *Plan*

209 MONCREIFFE (2) [P1/20]
Lat: 56°.4   Originally NO 132 193
2½ miles SSE of Perth. ¼ mile N of the River Earn. Walk. 200 yards (180m). Easy. In private grounds of Moncreiffe House. Ask permission. Map B
This stone circle has been moved to NO 136 193 because of road-widening

during the construction of the M90. It stood at the foot of Moncreiffe Hill with long views to east and west along the valley of the River Earn. The site had a complex history.

Before its excavation in 1974 it had already been disturbed. A barrow had stood at its centre and around 1830 it was reported that a decorated stone, lying just outside the ring, had 'been removed from the centre of the circle about forty years ago.' During the same century a box with parts of a man's skeleton was buried in the upcast thrown over the ring when the drive to Moncreiffe House was widened.

The first prehistoric structure was a henge with an outer hurdle-lined bank, about 37ft N-S by 34ft (11.3 × 10.4m) across. There was an entrance at the north-east. Inside, nine pits formed a circle about 21ft 5ins (6.5m) across. A small and undiagnostic beaker sherd was found in the backfill of the ditch. Just outside the entrance a tenth pit, containing cremated bone and a child's tooth in an inverted cordoned urn, lay on the major axis but, with an azimuth of 17°, the alignment was of no astronomical significance.

Whether the pits had held posts was unclear, but in the site's second phase a ring of eight heavy stones of local granite was set up in a circle some 29ft (8.8m) across. It was not concentric with the henge. Inside, a small kerbed ring-cairn was built. Plain, flat-rimmed ware and 2 cwt of deliberately smashed quartz lay in it but there was no trace of any cremation.

Later still the ring-cairn was dismantled and a larger one put up, layered with quartz. It was surrounded by a type of recumbent stone circle, 'beautifully graded in height', 30ft (9m) in diameter. It also consisted of eight stones. Between four of them in the south-west quadrant were low prostrate stones like uneasy versions of the recumbent stones of Aberdeenshire. A slab with nineteen cupmarks, perhaps an outlier, may have belonged to this phase.

The ring-cairn was finally demolished

Monzie kerb-circle, Perthshire (210), *from the south-west. The decorated outlying boulder and distant ring.*

by Late Bronze Age metal-workers who set up a turf windbreak at the south-east and then cleared away the cairn, dumping its stones at the north-east of the ring. Clay-walled pits and stakeholes marked their working-area and, when they abandoned the site, they left the rubbish of lead-bronze castings, a chisel, crucibles and slag of smelted iron behind them. 'These people destroyed and desecrated, and seemed to have taken a particular pleasure in smashing burial urns and obliterating a memory.' Similar vandalism affected the recumbent stone circle of Berrybrae (95) 150 miles to the north-east.

PSAS 115, 1985, 125–50, Plans, 130, 136

210 MONZIE (1) [P1/13]
Lat: 56°.4   NN 882 243
2 miles NE of Crieff, ³/₄ mile SE of Monzie. Walk. Short, just W of Gilmerton-Monzie lane. Easy. Map B
Below the heights of mountains to its north, this tiny kerb-circle stands in a wide pasture field. Its hollowed centre

and surrounding upcast are the results of excavation in 1938.

Ten low granite boulders lie contiguously in a circle 16ft 5ins (5m) across. The three heaviest stones are at the west arranged like a recumbent block and its flankers. There is a gap at the south-east and originally there may have been fifteen stones here. The south-east stone is cupmarked.

Just to the south-west is a large prostrate slab of metamorphosed grit, its upper surface profusely carved with cups and cup-and-ring markings. It was linked to the circle by a rough causeway, 11ft long and 3ft wide (3.4, 1m), of cobbles like the 'spokes' from the Balnuaran of Clava Centre ring-cairn (150b), Inverness.

The interior of the ring had been deeply burnt by a hazelwood fire. Near the centre in a crude cist were the cremated bones of an adult and a six-year-old child. Two rim-sherds of flat-rimmed ware were found in an upper layer. Pieces of white quartz had been scattered around the kerbs.

PSAS 73, 1938–9, 62–70, Plan, 67

211 MURTHLY (5)
Lat: 56°.5   NO 103 386
5¹/₂ miles south-east of Dunkeld, 3¹/₄
miles N of Stanley. Walk. In Murthly
hospital grounds, 300 yards (275m) NE
of gate. Easy. Map B
This damaged ring stood in a wide,
open field until the site was landscaped
in 1863–4 during the building of
Murthly Hospital. Oaks were planted
and an earthen bank was raised around
the stones.

There are gaps at north and south-
west of the ring which now retains five
of a probable eight stones in a circle
about 32ft 6ins (9.9m) in diameter.
They are graded from 3ft 5ins up to 8ft
(1–2.4m) at the south-west. Four are
jagged lozenges but the tallest is a
straight-sided pillar. Cinerary urns were
found in the nineteenth century close to
but not inside the ring.

PSAS 42, 1907–8, 158–61, Plan

212 NA CARRAIGEAN, EDINTIAN (1)
Lat: 56°.7   NN 839 620
4³/₄ miles W of Killiecrankie, 3 miles SW
of Blair Atholl. Walk. 2³/₄ miles
through Allean Forest from NN 863
600. In 1³/₄ miles bear WNW. Steep. Map
B
This is a fine Four-Poster in a
magnificent position. 'Here site,
scenery, megalithic remains, and
surroundings all combine to render the
investigation of this group memorable
and specially interesting', wrote Fred
Coles, and with the beautiful mountain
of Schiehallion on the skyline far to the
WSW only the unimaginative would
disagree.

Coles believed it an ideal setting for a
'Star-and-Hill worshipper' and thought
it strange that its builders erected 'only
four great unshapely, somewhat squat,
and very rough boulders'.

The stones were set up on a low,
kerbed circular mound 55ft (16.8m)
across. They form the corners of a 10ft
(3m) square and are graded to the
south-west where the tallest is 3ft 10ins
(1.2m) high. This comparative lowness
is compensated by the thick bulk of the
boulders. The north-eastern block leans.

The circle on which they were laid out
is some 14ft 2ins (4.3m) in diameter.

There is a hollow in the middle but
there is no record of any excavation in
this site which is also known as *Na
Clachan-Aoraidh*, 'the stones of
worship'.

*PSAS 42, 1907–8, 105–8, Burl,
1988, 186–7, Plan*

213 PARKNEUK (1)
Lat: 56°.7   NO 195 515
4 miles N of Blairgowrie, 3¹/₂ miles NW
of Alyth. Walk. ¹/₄ mile N of lane to
Heatheryhaugh. Fair. Map B
A. On high ground with good views all
round this lovely Four-Poster is in fine
condition. The NNE stone has fallen
inwards but the others stand in a
rectangle 14ft 10ins SSW-NNE by 12ft
6ins (4.5 × 3.8m). Coles noted that this
was 'a truly circular group having a
diameter of 19ft' (5.8m). The ring is
graded to the SSW where the tallest,
leaning a little, stands 4ft (1.2m) high
opposite the lower, fin-like stone at the
NNE.

B. On the Hill of Drimmie 600 yards
(550m) to the SSW is the Four-Poster of
Woodside. At NO 196 511 300 yards
(275m) SSE of Parkneuk is a large
glacial boulder with ten cupmarks on it.

Burl, 1988, 188–9, *Plan*

C. 'If you pace from Stone A [the
SSW] in a south-westerly direction for
ninety yards, you reach Stone D [the
north] in the ground-plan of the second
group of now mostly fallen Stones near
Parkneuk.' This is the ruined site of
Tullymurdoch, NO 194 514, with one
stone erect and five fallen in a ring once
about 45ft (13.7m) across.

PSAS 43, 1908–9, 97

**214 SANDY ROAD WEST, Scone (2) [P2/
11. Scone]**
Lat: 56°.4   NO 132 265
*2 miles NNE of Perth, ¹/₂ mile W of New
Scone. In Greystanes Close. Walk.
None. Map B*
This is the ideal site for the slothful.
Except when thick with heather it can
be seen from one's car. Now in a post-
war housing estate there were once two

adjacent rings here in an attractive wood but the eastern has been destroyed. It was almost tangential to its partner which was excavated in 1961 in advance of house building. Slender silver birches rise around it.

The low stones are graded to the south-west where the tallest, flat-topped and rectangular, is 2ft 6ins (0.8m) high. Seven of an original nine survive in a circle 21ft 3ins (6.5m) in diameter. Thom thought it might be an ellipse 9 N-S by 7½ of his Megalithic Yards [24ft 6ins by 20ft 3ins; 7.5 × 6.2m].

Just north of the centre was a pit containing a large but broken flat-rimmed bucket urn, 1ft (31cm) high, holding what was no more than a token offering of cremated bone. Charcoal, probably alder, inside the pot gave a date of 1200 ± 150 bc (GaK-787), *circa* 1500 BC, one of the latest dates yet obtained from a stone circle. The eccentric position of the pit, however, warns that it could have been a secondary intrusion.

Paired rings are not uncommon in Perthshire. Other sites include Blackfaulds, the very ruinous Shian Bank, and Tullybeagles (217).

TPPSNH 11, 1966, 7–23, Plan, 18

215 SPITTAL OF GLENSHEE (1) [2/14]
Lat: 56°.8   NO 117 702
13½ miles NE of Pitlochry, 6¾ miles NNE of Kirkmichael. Walk. ½ mile E up steepish hillside. Fair. Map B
This neat Four-Poster stands on a large knoll of glacial moraine. Also known as Diarmid's Grave, the Gaelic hero who was killed in a boar-hunt, it was dug into in August 1894.

The four low stones stand at the corners of a SSW-NNE rectangle about 12ft (3.7m) square and on the circumference of a circle 17ft (5.2m) across. Both the north-east and south-west stones are 2ft 3ins (69cm) high but the south-west is bigger and broader.

The excavation proved the mound on which the stones stand to be natural – but only after digging a determined pit 22ft (6.7m) deep.

'Spittal' is a contracted Scottish form of 'hospital', often associated with a leper-house standing in a remote area.
PSAS 29, 1894–5, 96–8; Burl, 1988, 190–1, Plan

**216 TIGH-NA-RUAICH, Ballinluig (1)
[P2/2. Ballinluig]**
Lat: 56°.7   NN 975 535
3¾ miles SSE of Pitlochry, ½ mile N of Ballinluig. In garden alongside the road. No walking needed. Map B
Sometimes corrupted as *Tynrich*, this well-preserved ring, 'the house of the heather', was invisible in gorse and bramble until the ground was cleared for a garden in 1855, the year of the Crimean War when Sebastapol was captured. It was also the year when Charlotte Brontë died. She was thirty-seven.

A characteristic six-stone ring of central Scotland the great stones of Tigh-na-Ruaich, all from the neighbouring hillsides, are graded to the SSW where a slab fully 6ft 6ins high and 7ft wide (2 × 2.1m) leans inwards. The stones form an ellipse 25ft 9ins N-S by 21ft (7.9 × 6.4m). They appear to have been erected with their pointed ends used as bases.

Following the removal of the undergrowth a calamitous 'excavation' with workmen trenching with picks and spades unearthed four vast clay-coloured urns with blackened interiors and filled with burnt bones. Each was about 2ft (60cm) high. One was intact. All were smashed or crumbled on being lifted. There are vague reports of flat slabs being dug up which may have been the sides of unrecognised cists. The soil inside the ring was a dark-brown 'as if saturated with blood' and was strewn with charcoal, cinders and mixed with burnt bones.
PSAS 42, 1907–8, 116–21; TTB, 352, Plan (but North is shown at the east. Turn one-quarter anti-clockwise)

217 TULLYBEAGLES, E, W (4) [P1/14]
Lat: 56°.5   NO 013 362
4¼ miles S of Dunkeld, 3½ miles W of Bankfoot. Walk. 1 mile along softly

rising track from Glack, NO 023 358. Pleasant. Map B

On a high and exposed site two ruinous circles slump close to each other, almost exactly east-west. In both the long, flat stones lie close together more like kerbs than the upright stones of a circle but they are fallen and their appearance is deceptive.

A. The *western* ring is the more badly damaged. One stone stands in a circle about 31ft 5ins (9.6m) across. Originally of about ten stones it was graded to the south.

B. Twenty-seven ft (8.2m) away the *eastern* ring is a circle about 23ft (7m) in diameter. Three of its former twelve or thirteen stones still stand at the south. They are the biggest.

PSAS 45, 1910–11, 102–3; TTB, 342, *Plan*

ROSS AND CROMARTY
Strongly influenced by the Clava tradition

218 CARN URNAN (3)
Lat: 57°.5   NH 566 523
7¹/₂ miles NW of Inverness, 3¹/₂ miles SE of Conon Bridge. Walk. 200 yards (180m) from lane along farm track. Very easy. Map 1

Just behind the farm is a Clava passage-tomb in fairly good condition. Four stones are erect and three are fallen in its surrounding stone circle which is about 72ft (22m) in diameter. It is graded to the ssw where the tallest, 5ft 10ins (1.8m), stands.

Inside, concentrically placed, is a ring-cairn, 41ft (12.5m) from kerb to kerb. A entrance at the ssw leads onto a 16ft (5m) passage. At its end at the centre of the now emptied cairn is a chamber 14ft by 11ft (4.3 × 3.4m). There are no known excavations.

Henshall, I, 343, *Plan 341*

ROXBURGHSHIRE
Mainly ovals varying in size, perhaps late versions of the great rings to the west

219 BURGH HILL (3) [G9/15. Allan Water] Lat: 55°.3   NT 470 062
6 miles ssw of Hawick. Between Allan Water and Dod Burn. Walk. Only 220 yards (200m) from lane to east, but steep. Map 1

Called Allan Water by Alexander Thom, visitors may wish that the ring actually was near the stream rather than on top of Burgh Hill. They face a climb of 1:3. As the sign for the Cuween chambered tomb on Orkney used to warn, 'Not for the aged or obese'.

On the northernmost of the hill's two summits, close to an outcrop, this site provides magnificent views. It has been termed the finest stone circle in the county.

The ring is an ellipse 53ft 2ins SW-NE by 42ft 10ins (16.2 × 13.1m). Of its twenty-five little slabs thirteen still stand. The majority are very small, from turf level to 1ft 2ins (0–35cm) high, but there is an exceptionally long one, 5ft (1.5m) in length, lying close to the south-west end of the longer axis. At the north-east end is a slab 2ft 8ins (0.8m) high.

With an azimuth of 43° to that stone and with lower land to the north-east the axis has a declination of 23°.6, that of midsummer sunrise. The use of a longer axis and taller stones for an astronomical sightline might explain the elliptical design.

Before 1873 the ring was 'well explored but yielded nothing of a sepulchral nature'.

RCAHM-Roxburgh, II, 1956, 446, no. 1011; TTB, 308, *Plan*

220 FIVE STANES (3) [G8/7. Dere Street III] Lat: 55°.4   NT 752 168
10³/₄ miles s of Kelso, 6³/₄ miles ESE of Jedburgh. Walk. 1¹/₂ miles s from lane, uphill then down. Fair. Map 1

A. The remains of this small ring are on a ridge immediately to the east of Dere

Street, the Roman road that led northwards from Corbridge to Melrose.

Perhaps once of eight stones three stand and two others lie near their stoneholes. Three more are prostrate 50ft (15m) to the east. No stone was more than 3ft (1m) high. Like other rings in the county this was an ellipse in miniature, about 20ft N-S by 19ft (6.1 × 5.8m).

There is a confusing reference of 1845 to a 'druidical circle' that was 'pretty entire' and about 48ft (14.6m) in diameter. To add perplexity to confusion, in 1885 Dr Hardy of the Berwick Naturalists' Club spoke of concentric rings of which the outer had all but disappeared and only four, widely spaced, survived of the inner.

B. Half a mile to the south, NT 751 161, is *Trestle Cairn*, Thom's Dere Street II, G8/6. It is not a circle. It is a wrecked cairn within which was a ring, about 39ft (12m) across. Two stand, the other fifteen have been thrown down, some being broken.

RCAHM-Roxburgh, I, 1956, 181, no. 349; TTB, 302, *Plans*

221 NINESTANE RIGG (3) [G8/2]
Lat: 55°.3   NY 518 973
10¾ miles S of Hawick, 1½ miles NE of Hermitage Castle. Walk. 1 mile. Very steep, almost precipitous first 220 yards (200m), use fence for support. Then open moorland. Map 1
This unusual ring of one prostrate and eight upright stones stands in a forest clearing. It is an ellipse 23ft 5ins SW-NE by 19ft 8ins (7.1 × 6m). Most of the stones are small, perhaps stumps, but there are two contrastingly tall, 4ft 4ins high at the south and 5ft 8ins at the WSW (1.3, 1.7m). There is a small stone between them. Its azimuth of 211° is in line with the major southern moonset.

Legend has it that in the early thirteenth century the wicked Lord Soulis of Hermitage Castle, for his witchcraft and kidnapping, was put to death inside the circle.

On a circle of stones they placed the pot,
On a circle of stones but barely nine;
They heated it red and fiery hot,

And the burnished brass did glimmer and shine.
They rolled him up in a sheet of lead –
A sheet of lead for a funeral pall,
They plunged him into the cauldron red,
And melted him body, lead and all.

As the cauldron was only 20ins (51cm) in diameter and as it was left behind when the Jacobite army camped at Ninestane Rigg in 1715 there seem to be serious anatomical and historical problems about this report.

TTB, 294, *Plan*

SHETLAND
Very unusual stone circles if that is what they are

222 HALTADANS, Fetlar island (5)
Lat: 60°.6   HU 622 923
2¾ miles E of Ugasta pier, 1 mile N of Houbie. Walk. From North Dale, HU 605 920, 1 mile to the ENE. Easy. Map 1
An easy walk if one can find this controversial site. It must be bewitched. The writer has been offered three different grid references by colleagues: 618 928; 622 923; 623 924. He is also informed that the site is on a Bird Reserve. Visitors should consult the warden.

An inhabitant of Fetlar states that the ring is 60 yards (55m) east of Skules Water at HU 626 918. 'Several circles or cairns are marked [on the Ordnance Survey map] to the North of Skules Water. But Haltadance is east of the loch and half way its length'. If the ring is not at the official grid reference, try this one. It is 700 yards (640m) south-east of the first.

Haltadans is a 37ft (11.3m) wide ring of twenty-two large blocks on edge, 'rough serpentine boulders'. Inside there is an earthen circle about 26ft (7.9m) across with a 5ft (1.5m) wide entrance at the south-west. Two tall stones stand erect at its centre. Whether the site can be classified as a stone circle is questionable.

Known locally as the Fairy Ring, Haltadans, 'the limping dance' is pleasantly said to be a group of girls turned into stone for dancing on the Sabbath. Less pleasantly, the stones are grotesquely ugly and surly trolls who danced there by moonlight until the sunlight of dawn petrified them. The two central stones are the fiddler and his wife.

550 yards (500m) NNW, HU 618 927, are three cairns with heavy kerbs. They are known as the Fiddler's Crus or enclosures.

Feachem, 85–6; Grinsell, 183

223 LOCH OF STROM (3) [Z3/3]
Lat: 60°.2   HU 403 501
7 miles NNW of Lerwick, 1¹/₄ miles N of Haggeston. Walk. Only just west of the road where it becomes open. Easy. Map 1
This little ring stands at the head of a narrow inlet near the north of Loch Strom. It is an ellipse 16ft 4ins SSW-NNE by 13ft 7ins (5 × 4.1m). Of its eight upright stones seven are low and the eighth, 4ft (1.2m) high, stands at the southern end of the long axis. There are three fallen boulders.
JHA 9, 1978, 60; TTB, 368, Plan

224 WESTINGS HILL, Tingwall (3)
Lat: 60°.2   HU 406 460
5¹/₄ miles NW of Lerwick. Walk. Just below the road before it reaches the top of the hill on the W side of the Tingwall valley. Easy. Map 1
This ring must be very similar to the Loch of Strom. It consists of an untidy oval of pointed blocks, most of them low and fallen. None is more than 3ft (1m) high. The ring is often concealed in heather.
Fojut, *Guide to Prehistoric Shetland*, 56

SKYE, Inner Hebrides
Several stone rows but few rings, all small

225 NA CLACHAN BHREIGE (5) [H7/9.
Strathaird] Lat: 57°.2   NG 543 176
7¹/₂ miles SW of Broadford, ¹/₂ mile W of Kirkibost. Walk. ¹/₄ mile W along track, turn N before trees. ¹/₄ mile across burns. Fair. Map 1

On an open, heather-thick moor and close to a tiny loch these are 'the false stones', men turned to stone for deserting their wives. Two standing stones on North Uist at NF 770 703 are called *Fir Bhreige* but supposedly this is because in outline they look like men.

Only three stones stand at Na Clachan Bhreige at the corners of an incomplete quadrilateral 12ft 3ins ENE-N by 10ft 4ins N-WNW (3.7 × 3.2m). It is just possible that they are the remains of a Four-Poster. If so, the diameter of their circle would be about 22ft (6.7m).

The stones are a whitish quartzose sandstone, the WNW 5ft high, the north, which leans, 6ft 6ins and the ENE 6ft (1.5, 2, 1.8m). At the south there is a great prostrate pillar, 11ft 6ins (3.5m) long. It is a reddish grit.

Casual digging around 1860 found a black polished stone 'somewhat resembling a small pestle', 1¹/₂ins (4cm) long.

Thom claimed that probing had detected five more stones buried under the peat. In 1863 it was reported that this druidical temple 'had originally consisted of large upright stones, very few of which now remain.'

RCAHM-Outer Hebrides, 1928, 214, no. 667, *Plan*

SUTHERLAND
Small and presumably late rings. A local feature is that many stones are set radially to the circumference

226 ABERSCROSS (3) [N2/2. The Mound]
Lat: 58°.0   NH 770 991
6 miles NNW of Dornoch, 3³/₄ miles WSW of Golspie. Walk. 30 yards (27m) up steep slope just E of the A 839. Easy. Map 1
On a natural platform at the foot of Craigmore Hill the name Thom gave to this ring, The Mound, is better than Aberscross which is ³/₄ mile to the north-west.

In bushes and trees below a rock-scattered hillside three stones stand and two lie on the circumference of a circle about 25ft (7.6m) across. The tallest, a broad and thin slab, is 6ft 6ins high and 6ft broad (2 × 1.8m). It is at the SSE and the ring may originally have been graded towards the south. The NNE stone is 3ft 6ins high and the WNW, 4ft 6ins (1.1, 1.4m).

A trench dug E-W across the site in May 1867, discovered the capstone and a oval cist 2ft (0.6m) deep at the middle of the ring. It was empty save for ¹/₂in (13mm) of acidic rainwater. Above it, however, 'in the circle centre exactly', were the eroded radius and humerus of an adult cremation.

Digging around two of the circle-stones produced nothing but many flint flakes lay on the circle's hillside platform.

PSAS 7, 1866–8, 473–5; RCAHM-Sutherland, 1911, 99, no. 291, Plan

227 ACHANY (4)

Lat: 58°.0   NC 560 029
2³/₄ miles SSW of Lairg, 1¹/₂ miles S of S end of Loch Shin. In Gruids Wood. Walk. From road at NC 561 036 take forest track S for ¹/₂ mile. At sharp bend to W (Rt) circle is ¹/₄ mile in trees. Difficult. Map 1
Also known as *Druim Baile fiur*, 'the farm on the ridge', the stones of this ring are deep in peat. There were about ten originally, spaced irregularly about 28ft (8.5m) apart in a probable oval 95ft SSW-NNE by 82ft (29 × 25m). All the stones on the east have fallen. On the west the uprights range from 2ft 9ins to the highest, 3ft 9ins (0.8–1.1m) at the north-west.

RCAHM-Sutherland, 1911, 158–9, 461, Plan

228 CNOC AN LIATH-BHAID (3)

Lat: 58°.1   NC 728 102
12 miles WNW of Brora, ¹/₂ mile NE of Braegrudie. Walk. From NC 755 090 follow steep track 1¹/₄ miles NW to Loch Grudaidh. Circle is ³/₄ mile to W. Alternative: at NC 744 075 a better track 2¹/₄ miles NW to ford over R. Brora. Ring is ¹/₂ mile NE up a steep slope. Both walks hard. Circle is worth it. Map 1

Below a hillside wrinkled like chilled skin and above the smooth curves of the River Brora this is an attractive, though disturbed, ring on open moorland. Five rewarding stones still stand on the perimeter of an oval 31ft 2ins ENE-WSW by 23ft 3ins (9.5 × 7.1m). Three others are fallen and out of position. The tallest stone, a gaunt grey column, is 6ft 6ins high (2m) at the WSW. Others range from 2ft to 3ft (0.6, 0.9m) in height. Just off the centre is an overgrown and disrupted cairn.

Like some other Sunderland rings the stones do not lie along the circumference but are set radially to it. The same is true of the megalithic horseshoe at Achavanich (138) in Caithness.

Making the long visit even more enjoyable and worthwhile, there are cairns and hut-circles extending south-eastwards from ¹/₄ to ³/₄ mile from the ring.

RCAHM-Sutherland, 1911, 181, no. 518; Caithness F.C. Bull 2.2, 1977, 71–2, Plan

229 LEARABLE HILL, NNE, SSW (4, 3)

Lat: 58°.2   NC 895 241, 893 235
10 miles NW of Helmsdale, 5 miles SSW of Kinbrace. Walk. Take the bridge, if safe, at Suisgill Lodge, across River Helmsdale. Cross railway line. 1 mile up steepish hill. Worth the effort. Map 1

This is a semi-megalithic treasure. On Learable Hill is an unacclaimed complex of a standing stone, multiple rows, cairns, clearance cairns and two stone circles. Farther away there are hut-circles.

The focus is the 5ft 2ins (1.6m) high stone, 'playing-card' in shape, 2ft 8ins wide but only 9ins thick (80 × 23cm), arranged N-S with a Christian cross carved on its wide west face. To its north and south are irregular lines of stones. The stone circles are farther away as though later additions to the group. Being almost half a mile apart and not inter-visible they cannot be considered a pair like those in Perthshire or even Shin River (230)

Torhousekie, Wigtownshire (233), from the south-east.

only twenty eight miles to the wsw of Learable Hill.

115ft (35m) south of the standing stone is a splayed fan of ten rows. At its head are large, probably burial, cairns. Smaller ones near them are likely to be the results of land clearance for cattle.

125ft (38m) north of the stone are five parallel rows aligned ESE-WNW with large cairns at their western end. A further 65ft (20m) to the north is a ragged double row, SW-NE, perhaps orientated on the May sunrise. Beyond it is the northern circle.

A. (4) On a slight rise are three fallen stones, 5ft 6ins to 8ft (1.7–2.4m) long, all that remain of a ring about 56ft (17m) in diameter. The northernmost pillar has several cupmarks on it.

B. (3) Some 90 yards (80m) WNW of the standing stone, down the slope, is the second ring, actually a tumbled oval 55ft SE-NW by 47ft (16.8 × 14.3m). Five low stones still stand in it, two are fallen and two more almost lost in the turf. Near the centre of the ring is an overgrown low mound.

RCAHM-Sutherland, 1911, 130–3, nos. 374–81; Burl, 1993, 129–31, *Plan*

230 SHIN RIVER, NW, SE, Lairg. (3, 4). [N2/3] Lat: 58°.0   NC 582 049 *1 mile s of Lairg. Walk. 200 yards (180m) s of junction of A839 and lane*

alongside the river. In field on E (Lt). Very easy. Map 1

On a low knoll between two streams and within 20ft (6m) of the river these two ruinous rings stand within 120ft (37m) of each other.

A. (3) *The north-west* is the better preserved with four low stones, the tallest only 2ft 3ins (0.7m) high, on the northern arc of a little circle once about 13ft 6ins (4m) in diameter.

B. (4) In worse condition *the south-east ring* is bigger. It was some 20ft 6ins (6.3m) across. Only three low stones stand, two at the south-west and one at the ENE.

RCAHM-Sutherland, 1911, 159–60, no. 462; TTB, 326, *Plan*

TIREE, INNER HEBRIDES
Characteristically of islands, very few circles

231 HOUGH, NE, SW (4)
Lat: 56°.5   NL 959 451, 958 451
6¾ miles W of Scarinish, ½ mile SE of Hough. Walk. From Hough take lane s towards Cuigeas. Circles are 220 yards (200m) to W (Rt) of road. Easy. Map 1
South-west of Coll on Tiree, *tir-lodh*, 'the land of corn', the windblown island so flat that it is known as, 'a kingdom whose heights are lower than the waves', are two diminished rings.

A. (3) *The north-east* is a large oval about 130ft NW-SE by 108ft (39.6 × 32.9m). Of its ten stones one stands at the NNE nearly 6ft (1.8m) high. There are five stumps, four are fallen and two have been taken away. Inside the ring is a low central mound

B. (4) 100 yards (90m) to the *south-west* is a tumbled and half-buried circle, perhaps 130ft (40m) across. Of its twelve stones eleven are prostrate and one is a stump.

RCAHM-Argyll, III, 1980, 68, no. 107, *Plan*, 69

WIGTOWNSHIRE

A mixture of influences, mainly from central and north-eastern Scotland

232 GLENTIRROW (1)

Lat: 54°.9   NX 146 625

5¹/₂ miles ENE of Stranraer, 2¹/₄ miles SW of New Luce. Walk. 250 yards (230m) W of road from New Luce, NX 147 624 where it bends to the W. Easy. Map 1

This is a daintily perfect Four-Poster whose stones, although low and half-obscured in the reedy grass, for the aficionado are a delight to see. Typically they are on a terrace.

They stand at the corners of a rectangle 9ft ENE-WSW by 8ft (2.7 × 2.4m) and on the circumference of a circle 12ft (3.7m) in diameter. The tallest stone is at the south-east, 2ft 3ins (0.7m) high, but the south-west block is bulkier.

Forty feet (12m) to the north-east is an outlying stone no bigger than those of the ring. Because of it the Royal Commissioner surveyors of 1912 thought the site was the remains of a concentric circle.

There are many round cairns in the vicinity in a 'truly singular line', nine within a mile, suggesting a large Bronze Age population.

Burl, 1988, 201, *Plan*

233 TORHOUSEKIE (1) [G3/7. Torhouse]

Lat: 54°.9   NX 383 565

6 miles SSW of Newton Stewart, 3¹/₂ miles W of Wigtown. Alongside B733 from Wigtown to Kirkcowan. No walk. In State care, no charge. Map 1

The stone circle of Torhousekie on the sandy and fertile machair near Wigtown is almost certainly a variant form of recumbent stone circle. It lies midway between the concentrations of such rings in north-east Scotland and south-west Ireland.

Its nineteen stones are graded in height though here, unlike the Aberdeen rings, they rise towards the south-east, ranging in height from a mere 1ft 10ins (56cm) at the north-west to 4ft 4ins (1.3m). They are all of local granite.

The ring is a spacious oval 70ft 3ins SW-NE by 65ft 6ins (21.4 × 20m). On a natural terrace a levelled platform of earth and small stones was raised to receive the ring. Within the ellipse is a unique central setting of three contiguous rounded boulders in a SW-NE line 18ft (5.5m) long. The two outer boulders, up to 3ft 9ins (1.1m) high, stand on either side of a much lower in an arrangement reminiscent of a recumbent stone and its tall flankers. Extending north-westwards from the setting is a broad D-shaped rubble bank enclosing an open space some 27ft long and 21ft deep (8.2 × 6.4m). It may be a variation of a ring-cairn.

415ft (127m) to the east at the head of a slight rise (NX 384 565) is a Three-Stone row on a NE-SW axis, graded in height to the south-west. With an azimuth of 224° the row is well aligned on the midwinter sunset.

In the drystone wall 20 yards (18m) east of the stone circle is a boulder with a deep oval hollow carved in it.

TDGNHAS 49, 1974, 24–34, *Plan*

WALES

CLWYD (Flintshire)
One uncertain site only

234 PENBEDW PARK, Cilcain (6) [W4/1. Penbedw Hall] Lat: 53°.2   SJ 171 679
5 miles NW of Mold, 7 miles E of Denbigh. By private drive at junction of A541 and lane SW to Llandyrnog. Walk. 300 yds (275m). Easy, but private land. Map 3
The ring, a true circle, was said to have a diameter of 87ft (26.5m), but Alexander Thom's survey amended this to 98ft (29.9m). It has been suggested that there were once eleven stones, 3ft to 5ft (1–1.6m) high, in the ring. Reputedly, six at the west and north were taken for farm buildings. Trees now attractively mark their former positions. Because there was no mention of this very noticeable site before the eighteenth century it has been suspected of being a folly, especially as it is in the grounds of a stately home. It is certainly very visible from the Hall, unusually situated on a slope, and two south-western stones are set radially to the circumference, all good reasons for mild scepticism about its authenticity.

On the other hand, it also stands on an important prehistoric route from the Graig Lwyd axe-factory on Penmaenmawr, Gwynedd, to the Peak District in central England. Judgement must be reserved.

There is a bulky outlier 5ft 4ins (1.6m) high 237 yards (217m) to the WSW and a round barrow 250 yards (230m) to the north. An excavation in 1860 uncovered large stones and urn sherds. The diggers were warned that they would be haunted by the spirits of the dead.

Grimes, 1963, 118–19; TTB, 374, *Plan*

DYFED (Cardigan, Carmarthen, Pembrokeshire)
A mixture of rings, mostly Bronze Age, of varied architecture. No apparent local styles

235 DYFFRYN, SYFYNWY, Pembrokeshire (3) Lat: 51°.9   SN 059 285
8 miles SE of Fishguard. ¹/₂ mile S of the Syfynwy Falls. Take track to Dyffryn Farm. Walk. Go sharply W 250 yds (230m). Easy. Map 3
Also known as Henry's Moat this is an oval, 72ft by 62ft (22 × 19m), with a long SSW-NNE axis. Originally it had eighteen stones from 3ft to 6ft 6ins (1–2m) high. Inside is a cairn, 3ft high and from 42ft to 62ft across (1 × 13 × 19m). The entire site is ruinous. The cairn has been robbed. Some circle-stones lie on it.

RCAHM-Pembrokeshire, 1925, no. 313, *Plan*

236 GORS FAWR, Mynachlog-ddu, Pembrokeshire (1) [W9/2]
Lat: 51°.9   SN 134 294
18 miles WNW of Carmarthen. Between the Afon Wern and the Eastern Cleddau. On a heath alongside the lane between Plasymeibion and Mynachlog ddu. Easy. Map 3
At Gors Fawr, 'the great marsh', is a fine stone circle, 73ft (22.3m) in diameter of sixteen local stones. They rise slightly in height towards the south. Such grading to a cardinal point has affinities with Dartmoor stone circles such as Fernworthy (44) and Brisworthy (38).

The Preseli mountains, some of whose bluestones were sludged by glaciation towards Salisbury Plain and Stonehenge (84), were until recently thought to have been a magical landmark for Beaker seafarers bringing copper from Ireland. They rest a few miles away on the northern skyline like a crumpled crown. Magical or not, only one of their doleritic or bluestone – pillars was chosen by their Bronze Age builders among the fifteen other glacial erratic boulders of the circle, suggesting that bluestones were not deemed to

Gors Fawr, Dyfed (236), from the south. The Preselis are to the far right.

possess otherworldly properties.

440ft (134m) to the north-east of the ring is a pair of standing stones, 48ft (14.6m) apart on a NE-SW axis. They are similar in height, that at the south-west being a little the taller, 6ft 2 (1.9m) high against the 5ft 7ins (1.7m) of its partner. Their north-eastern alignment looks towards the midsummer sunrise.

Grimes, 1963, 145–6 *Plan*; TTB, 386–7, *Plan*

237 MEINI-GWYR, Llandyssilio East, Carmarthen (3) Lat: 51°.9 SN 142 267 *17 miles WNW of Carmarthen, 1¹/₂ miles E of Llangolman, alongside a lane opposite the inn on the A478. Easy. Map 3*
Also known as *Buarth Arthur*, 'Arthur's enclosure', Meini-gwyr, 'the leaning stones', an important but despoiled embanked stone circle, was excavated in 1938. Detailed records of the investigation were destroyed during the war.

Within a rubbly bank 120ft (37m) across stood a ring, about 60ft (18m) in diameter, originally of seventeen stones, Edward Lhuyd claiming as many as twenty-three, of which only two survive. At the west was a long, stone-lined entrance some 6ft (2m) wide. At its front a pit filled with clay and fine charcoal was discovered. The site may have been desecrated in prehistory. In one stonehole there was a hearth and some Bronze Age food-vessel sherds.

In Camden's *Britannia* (1695, 628) there is a report that 'at the distance of about 200 paces [from Meini-gwyr], there stand on end three other large, rude stones'. Two are still erect, the third prostrate, at SN 139 266. Known as Yr Allor, 'the altar', they may be the remains of a Cove similar to others at Avebury (82) and Stanton Drew (75).

Grimes, 1963, 141–3, *Plan*; *Archaeology in Wales 31*, 1991, 27–8

238 YSBYTY CYNFYN, Ponterwyd, Cardigan (5) Lat: 52°.4   SN 752 791 *10¹/₂ miles E of Aberystwyth, 1¹/₄ miles S of Ponterwyd. By the A4120. In churchyard. Easy. Map 3*
Around the churchyard of Ysybyty Cynfyn, 'Cynfan's hospital' is a roughly circular earthwork. Standing on its bank, but not certainly with bases down to the old ground level, are five stones of which only the one at the north, 11ft high, 4ft wide and 2ft thick

(3.4 × 1.2 × 0.6m), is known to be in its original position. Of four others at the east two now act as gateposts.

There is no hint of a stone circle in records of 1755 or 1796 and Malkin who described the churchyard in 1804 mentioned only 'a large, upright stone'. But in his second edition three years later he wrote of 'a large druidical circle or temple. Many of the large stones forming the circle still remain . . .' As repairs and alterations to the church and its cemetery had taken place in the early nineteenth century a likely explanation is that some 'druidical' stones were imaginatively added to the site to enhance the churchyard and entice a growing number of profitable tourists.

It may be no more than coincidence that the church is only 1½ miles north of the Devil's Bridge over the River Mynach where the Devil was tricked by an old woman who saved her soul by sending her little dog to cross the bridge before her.

S. Briggs, *Arch Camb 128*, 1979, 138–46, *Plan*

GLAMORGAN
One embanked ring only

239 MYNYDD Y GELLI, Gelli (1)
Lat: 51°.6   SS 975 942
1 mile N of Tonypandy, ½ mile S of Gelli. Walk. At the E end of the village take Bwllfa farm track SW. In 270 yards (247m) take Lt fork to a footpath. The ring is just E of the head of a steep slope to the N. Fair. Map 3
This is a well-preserved embanked small circle about 33ft 6ins by 30ft (10.2 × 9m) in diameter, with a long ENE-WSW axis and a possible entrance at the south-east. Once there may have been fifteen stones in the ring. Although they are no more than 1ft to 2ft 3ins (30–70cm) high the minilithic oval of Mynydd y gelli, 'the wooded mountain', has been optimistically entitled 'The Welsh Stonehenge'.

Excavations between 1903 and 1905 discovered a rifled cist 6ft (2m) from the bank at the south-west. Charcoal, burnt stones, stone tools and the wreckage of three more dubious cists lay nearby.

About 60ft (18m) to the south is a low standing stone of local grit.

Arch Camb, 1906, 286–92; *Archaeology in Wales* 6, 1966, 30

GWENT (Monmouthshire)
One questionable site only

240 GREY HILL, Caerwent (5) [W13/1]
Lat: 51°.6   ST 438 935
6 miles SE of Usk and 6 miles W of Chepstow. Walk. ½ mile uphill along lane and footpath immediately to the E of the junction of lanes just N of Wentwood reservoir. Fair. Map 3
Rather than a stone circle this may have been a kerbed round cairn with an internal cist. It is in a sadly ruinous state today but the panoramic view is splendid overlooking the plain and the Severn estuary. The stones stand on Mynydd Llwyd, 'Grey Hill'.

If this had been a stone circle it was a very small one only 32ft (9.8m) across. Some thirteen stones remain, none more than 2ft (0.6m) high, set on edge and almost contiguous, much more akin to kerbstones than to a free-standing stone circle. If they had surrounded a cairn the mound was probably demolished for material to build the field wall to the east.

In the nineteenth century two stones stood inside at the south-east, the larger 6ft 6ins (2m) high, possibly the survivors of a large cist or even a megalithic chamber. Today both are fallen and have been moved.

There is an outlying stone 8ft (2.4m) to the south-east, 5ft 9ins (1.8m) high. To the north-west, 180ft (55m) from the ring but clearly visible from it is another standing stone which now leans to the east. It is 7ft 6ins (2.3m) high and tapers almost to a point.

Uphill from the ring there are other stones in the gorse. There are many cairns on the hillside.

Rev. W. and M.E. Bagnall-Oakley,

*An Account of the Rude Stone
Monuments and Ancient Burial
Mounds in Monmouthshire, 1889*
16–17; *TTB, 398, Plan*
8½ miles to the NNE at Trellech is
the famous Three-Stone row known as
Harold's Stones, SO 498 052.
  Burl, 1993, 159–60

GWYNEDD (Caernarfon,
Merioneth)
*Embanked rings, Five-stone circles,
ovals*

241 BRYN CADER FANER, Llandecwyn,
Merioneth (3) Lat: 52°.9   SH 648 353
*5 miles NE of Harlech, 5½ miles ESE of
Portmadoc. Walk. 4 miles of lane and
mountain track from Eisingrug (SH 615
345), a mile S of Talsarnau on the
A496. Avoid swampy area a mile E of
Eisingrug then turn NE. Demanding.
Map 3*
This is one the minor wonders of
prehistoric Wales and well worth the
steep 2½ mile climb by lane to Moel-y-
glo then by soggy, boggy track to this
cairn-circle.
  Spectacularly visible from the track a
low, vaguely-kerbed cairn, 28ft (8.5m)
wide, has been ravaged by nineteenth-
century treasure-seekers, who left a
large hole at its centre exposing the
remains of a cist.
  The attraction of the site is the fifteen
tall stones leaning out of the body of
the cairn like a crown of thorns
silhouetted against the mountain sky.
Originally there may have been about
thirty pillars, each some 6ft (2m) long,
but damage by the army during the
Second World War has reduced both
the number and the heights.
  See also Llyn Eiddew Bach (247)
  Bowen and Gresham, 87–8, *Plan*

242 CEFN COCH, Dolbenmaen,
Caernarfon (4) Lat: 53°.0   SH 548 427
*2½ miles NNW of Portmadoc, 4¼ miles
SSW of Beddgelert. Close to Afon
Dwyfor. Walk. From Golan. SH
52.52., take road ESE. In ¾ mile turn N.
In a mile take track on E. 'Standing*

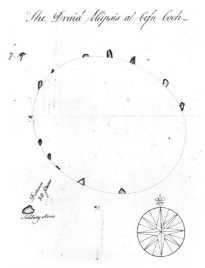

Cefn Coch, Gwynedd (242), *the 1762
plan by Farringdon showing the ring's
elliptical shape and ESE-WNW axis.*

*stones' are 200 yds (180m) to the S.
Quite hard going. Map 3*
On a smooth-topped ridge this
inconspicuous ring, 'the red ridge', once
about 76ft by 62ft (23 × 19m) is now
virtually destroyed. It is included here
because when Farringdon, the Welsh
antiquarian, recorded it in 1769 he
called it 'an ellipsis' arranged ESE-WNW
of fourteen stones, twelve of them
standing, measuring 44 × 36 of
William Stukeley's druids' cubits of
20.8 inches. The dimensions may have
been incorrect but there was no reason
for Farringdon to invent either the
ellipse, a shape typical of many stone
rings in North Wales, nor the long ESE-
WNW axis, a direction favoured by the
builders of rings in the same region. It
seems to mark the night of Beltane, the
May Day festival of fire.
  Farringdon added that there was a
tall outlying pillar eighty paces to the
south-west. There was a second circle a
mile away at Cwm Mawr, SH 553 414.
It is said to have been blown up.
  Grimes, 1963, 113–14, *Plan; CBA
Report 35*, 1985, 80–1

243 CERRIG ARTHUR, Sylfaen farm,
Merioneth (3) Lat: 52°.7   SH 631 188
*2 miles NE of Barmouth on W side of
valley. Take minor road from Cultiau,
SH 635 188 to Sylfaen Farm, Walk.
The ring is ¹/₄ mile uphill to the NW.
Fair. Map 3*
Possibly embanked this is an oval, 52ft
by 42ft (15.9 × 12.8m), with a longer
SE-NW axis. A dozen or so stones are
just visible. Three at the south-east are
taller, 3ft 6ins and 4ft (1, 1.2m) high.
The builders took care to establish a
level site, cutting a shelf into the
hillside, removing 3ft (1m) of rubble
from the upper side to raise a 3ft high
platform at the lower end.

Bowen and Gresham, 38–9, *Plan*

244 CERRIG PRYFAID, Caerhun,
Caernarfon (1) Lat: 53°.2   SH 724 713
*5 miles SSW of Conway on the N side of
the Afon Tafolog valley. From Tal-y-
Bont (SH 76.68.) take the NW lane for 3
miles through Llanbedr and Hafoty
gwyn. At T-junction turn W. In just over
¹/₂ mile ring is over the wall to the S.
Easy. Map 3*
This well-preserved ellipse, 'the stone of
the flies', of eleven or twelve low

stones, lies opposite an outcrop on the
other side of the track. About 56ft by
51ft (17 × 15.6m) its long axis is from
ESE to WNW like that of Cefn Coch
(242) and the Druids' Circle (245). It is
in line with a 3ft (1m) high outlier 77ft
(23.5m) away.

Grimes, 1963, 115, *Plan*

245 DRUIDS' CIRCLE, Penmaenmawr,
Caernarfon (1) [W2/1a]
Lat: 53°.3   SH 723 746
*On Penmaenmawr headland, 1312ft
(400m) O.D. 4 miles WSW of Conway.
In Penmaenmawr at the pedestrian
traffic lights turn S into Fernbrook
Road. Take 2nd Rt, Merton Park. At T-
junction turn Lt. Shortly turn then Rt
into narrow Mountain Lane. ³/₄ mile at
two pillars leave car. Walk. 30 minutes
SE up broken metalled track. Four sites,
¹/₂ to 1¹/₄ miles. Fair.*
A. *Red Farm* SH 732 750 In ¹/₂ mile on
the left, near the top of the track, is an
arc of four surviving low stones of a
circle. The ring, probably an oval about
81ft by 69ft (25 × 21m), had a long
WNW-ESE axis. There is a huge 'playing-
card' stone in the next field to the
south-west. The Druids' Circle is a

*Druids' Circle, Gwynedd (245). 1. Red Farm; 2. Circle 275; 3. Druids' Circle; 4.
Circle 278; 5. To major southern moonset; 6. Cists*

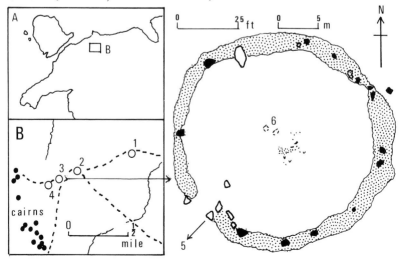

Circle 275, Penmaenmawr, Gwynedd (245b), an 'Irish' Five-Stone ring from the north-east. The stones of the Druids' Circle stand on the skyline.

further half-mile to the wsw.

Grimes, 1963, 118. No plan.

B. *Circle 275*, Penmaenmawr (1) [W2/1b]   SH 725 747
275 yards (250m) ENE *of the Druids' Circle*
This little ring is a Five-Stone circle about 13ft (4m) in diameter. It was excavated in 1959. In a central pit there was a dense mass of broken quartz fragments. With its low south-west boulder like a squat recumbent stone and its deposit of quartz it is probably an outlier of the Five-Stone rings that are numerous in south-west Ireland, its builders perhaps connected with the trade in copper from that region. The Druids' Circle is visible to the west.

PPS 36, 1960, 317–18, *Plan*

C. *Druids' Circle* (1) [W2/1a]
                                            SH 722 746
There has been uncertainty over whether this ring was the temple of one or of several druids but the plural appears to be correct. Their famous ring, *y meini hirion*, 'the tall stones', on Penmaenmawr, 'the great stone headland' stands alongside an old trackway ¼ mile south-east of the

Graig Lwyd Group VII Neolithic axe-factory, SH 717 760, whose products were densely distributed in north Wales, and also in northern and southern England.

The oval setting, 85ft ESE-WNW by 80ft (25.9 × 24.4m), was erected in an inconspicuous position, only readily noticeable from the trackway which may explain its situation. About thirty stones of local granite, unevenly spaced, stand in a low rubble bank with a collapsed portalled entrance of four stones, 8ft (2.4m) wide, at the wsw.

Like other portalled rings such as Swinside (26) and Long Meg and Her Daughters (25) in the Lake District the entrance appears to indicate a celestial event. From the centre of the circle the two southern portals stood in line with the major southern moonset. Like several rings in the region the long axis was from ESE-WNW. Thom's plan shows an azimuth of 296°, an alignment on the May Day or Beltane sunset.

An excavation in 1958 uncovered scatters of 'foreign' quartz chippings and a central concentration of local stones covering two cremations, one in

Druids' Circle, Penmaenmawr, Gwynedd (245c), From the east.

a small cist of a child under an enlarged Early Bronze Age food-vessel, the other also of a child. A second food-vessel, a small bronze knife and three sandstone whetstones for sharpening metal implements were discovered.

With its portals and its proximity to Graig Lwyd, the ring has affinities with Late Neolithic circles and may have been erected as early as 3000 BC. The burials, perhaps sacrifices, were possibly secondary deposits inside an ancient sanctuary.

As its name implies there are legends about the Druids' Circle. North of the entrance is the Stone of Sacrifice with a natural ledge on it. Folklore claims that this was 'the "altar" on which the slain bodies of infants were placed during sacrificial ceremonies.' On the other side of the ring is the Deity Stone, a heavy block that would strike anyone who swore near it. It is said that a disbeliever went to the ring at night to jeer and blaspheme. His corpse was discovered next day at the foot of the stone. If this is not sufficient deterrent, then sceptics should be aware that a coven of witches, holding an orgy inside the circle, were so frightened by threats suddenly booming from the stones that two of them went mad. Be circumspect.

PPS 36, 1960, 305–17, 322–39, *Plan* 307; *CBA Report* 35, 1985, 79.

D. *Circle 278* (1)   SH 722 746
160 yds (146m) W *of the Druids' Circle*
This ring-cairn, 40ft by 35ft (12.2 × 10.7m) was excavated in 1959. A low, stony bank, more prominent than that around the Druids' Circle, up to 8ft (2.4m) thick, surrounded an open central space. This was lined with contiguous standing stones, one fallen at the south-west being 4ft (1.2m) long. Kerbs edged the exterior of the cairn at the north-east.

An urn with a cremation lay against the inner wall at the north-west. Exactly opposite was a long stone by a scatter of cremated bones, probably of a woman. Charcoal from the excavation provided assays of 1405 ± 155 bc (NPL-10) and 1520 ± 145 bc (NPL-11), approximate equivalents of 1780 BC, late in the Early Bronze Age.

It is possible that the line to the south-east was orientated on the major southern moonrise.

PPS 36, 1960, 318–22, 327–9, *Plan,* 319.

246 FFRIDD NEWYDD, Llanaber,
Merioneth (4) Lat: 520.8   SH 616 213
*3¹/₂ miles N of Barmouth, 4 miles SW of
Llanbedr. Walk. For the dedicated only.
1¹/₂ mile walk uphill from Gors-y-gedol
at SH 600 230 with little to see at the
end. But notice the ruined megalithic
cairn and vast toppled capstone, Coetan
Arthur. SH 603 228. Map 3*
The former and the modern names for
the two rings explain their history:
carneddau hengwm, 'cairns in the old
valley', became *ffridd newydd*, 'the new
pasture' and they are now difficult to
make out.

They were ditched and banked stone
circles, the northern 108ft (33m) across,
the southern larger, about 166ft (51m)
in diameter and once with some forty-
five stones. Excavated in 1919 a pit
near the centre of the north ring
contained ashes and rusticated beaker
sherds.

At SH 614 205 are two long cairns,
both badly damaged but both with
megalithic chambers.
Arch Camb, 1920, 99–133; Grimes,
1963, 119–20, *Plan*

247 LLYN EIDDEW BACH III, Llandecwyn,
Merioneth (3)
Lat: 52°.9   SH 642 346
*4 miles ENE of Harlech. A visit can be
combined with that to Bryn Cader
Faner. Just over ¹/₂ mile SW of that ring
take the sidetrack leading NE. The site is
200 yds (180m) on the S side. Map 3*
The 'little ivy lake' is an incomplete
ring of seven stones, one fallen, with a
diameter of 42ft (12.8m). Originally
there were thirteen or fourteen stones,
the tallest about 2ft 6ins (75cm) high.

No publication

248 MOEL TY UCHAF, Llandrillo,
Merioneth (1) [W5/1]
Lat: 52°.9   SJ 057 371
*4 miles SSW of Corwen. From the B440
1 and ¹/₂ mile N of Llandrillo take the
first of two lanes to the E. Walk. The
circle is 3/5 of a mile uphill and 200 yds
(180m) NE of the summit. Fair. Map 3*
Not quite at the top of a steep-sided
hill at an altitude of 1375ft (419m) is

the almost perfect cairn-circle of Moel
ty Uchaf, 'the high bare hill'. About
39ft (11.9m) across and slightly
flattened at the north it was perhaps
meant to be seen from the valley below.
It consists of forty-one stones, all about
1ft 6ins (0.5m) tall. There is a probable
entrance at the SSW. A finely-preserved
cist can be seen at its centre. 'That its
purpose was sepulchral there can be
little doubt.'

There is an outlying stone to the NNE.
Eighty yards (73m) to the south and
50ft (15.2m) lower down the slope are
the remains of a cairn from which
much white quartz was recovered. The
ring of Tyfos can be seen in the valley
bottom opposite at a height of 550ft
(168m).
Bowen and Gresham, 80–2, *Plan*;
TTB, 376, *Plan*

249 TYFOS, Llandrillo, Merioneth (1)
[W5/2] Lat: 52°.9   SJ 028 388
*4¹/₂ miles SW of Corwen, 1¹/₄ miles NNW
of Llandrillo and immediately to the W
of the lane near the Nant Llyn
Mynyllod stream. Easy. Map 3*
Tyfos-uchaf, 'the high, ditched house',
is a site probably of two distinct
phases. It stands in a gently sloping
field overlooking the River Dee. The
site has been interpreted as a denuded
ring-cairn but it is possible that
originally there was a free-standing
stone circle here with over twenty
stones enclosing an area about 55ft
(16.8m) across.

To this a cairn may have been added
much as happened at Bryn Cader
Faner. It is still 3ft (1m) high.
Bowen and Gresham, 78–9; Grimes,
1963, 95, note 4; TTB, 378, *Plan*

POWYS (Brecknockshire, Montgomery,
Radnorshire).
*Open rings, a Four-Poster, ovals and
paired circles. All probably Bronze Age*

250 BANC DU, Llanbadarn Fynydd,
Radnor (3) Lat: 52°.4   SO 042 792
*9 miles SSW of Newtown, 6¹/₄ miles ESE
of Llanidloes. Walk. From David's*

Well, SO 060 786, take track NW for 1¹/₄ miles. At its junction turn S for a quarter of a mile. Fair. Map 3
On the western slopes of Banc Du mountain is a cairn and a 3ft 6ins (1m) high stone known as Fowler's Arm Chair. Hypothetically, it is the centre stone of a ruinous circle once about 60ft (18m) across. The same distance separates the 'ring' from the cairn. Some 250 yards (230m) to the south-east at SO 043 789 is Fowler's Horse Block, a natural outcrop 5ft (1.5m) high.
Grimes, 1963, 128–30 *Plan*

251 CERRIG DUON, Brecks (1) [W11/3. Maen Mawr] Lat: 51°.9   SN 851 206
14 miles E of Llandeilo, 9 miles SE of Llandovery. Going N from Tafern-y-Garreg inn on the A4067 take the first lane to the W. The ring is 2¹/₂ miles to the N close and visible from the country road. The shallow River Tawe must be crossed. Easy. Map 3
Standing on a knoll above the narrow valley of the River Tawe with steep mountainsides immediately to east and west is a complex of a stone circle, avenue and aberrant Three-Stone row. The 'circle' known as Cerrig Duon, 'black rock', is actually ovoid, 67ft by 60ft (20.4 × 18.3m), its longer axis ESE-WNW. The stones of local sandstone are small, the tallest no more than 2ft (60cm) high.
Thirty feet (9m) to the NNE is a massive block, Maen Mawr, 'the huge stone', 6ft 6ins (2m) high, thickset, broad, weighing about nine tons. The longer sides of this monstrous pillar point towards the ring. Eleven feet (3.4m) to its NNE and in line with it are two tiny stones 2ft (0.6m) apart. Similar untypical Three-Stone settings with one huge and two small stones, occur at the circles of Nant Tarw (257) four miles to the NNW and at Nisabost, Harris, 400 miles north where a standing stone 10ft 6ins (3.2m) high, 'Clach Mhic Leoid', *McLeod's stone*, has two low slabs 8ft 6ins (2.6m) to its west.
'Playing-card' standing stones across

the valley SO 854 208, 854 214 may have been set up as 'signposts', their long sides directed towards the ring.
At Cerrig Duon a splayed avenue of minute stones 47ft (14.3m) east of the ring ascends the knoll from the river to its north-east. At the lower north-east they are 21ft (6.4m) apart but they are not parallel and at the south-west they have contracted to only 16ft 6ins (5m). The east row is about 81ft (24.7m) long while the west is a line 148ft (45m) in length. If extended, the avenue would pass well to the east of the circle, missing it by 25ft (7.6m), suggesting that the two lines were additions to an older monument.
Grimes, 1963, 138–9, *Plan*; Burl, 1993, 160

252 CERRIG GAERAU, Llanbrynmair, Montgomery (3) Lat: 52°.6 SH 903 005
On Newydd Fynyddog mountain 1¹/₂ miles SSE of Llanbrynmair. Walk. ³/₄ mile. Opposite a lane S to Bryn-bach farm a track and footpath, SH 900 999, lead N up a steepish slope to the summit of Newydd Fynyddog. Demands good breathing. Map 3
Two stone circles stand within 120 yards (110m) of each other. At the WSW Cerrig Gaerau consists today of eight fallen stones in a ring about 69ft (21m) across. The stones tend to be longer than the average for a Welsh upland ring, their mean being about 5ft (1.5m) in length.
See also Lled-croen-yr-ych (256).
Grimes, 1963, 122–3, *Plan*

253 FOUR STONES, Walton, Radnor (1) [W8/3] Lat: 52°.2   SO 245 607
4 miles SW of Presteigne, 2³/₄ miles E of New Radnor. Immediately W of the Kinnerton-Knapp farm lane in the corner of a field. Easy. Map 3
Interpreted variously – and wrongly – as the remains of a chambered tomb, and of a partly ruined stone circle, one of its uncarveable boulders supposedly shaped into a font for Old Radnor church during the reign of King John (1199–1216), the Four Stones are

Cerrig Duon, Powys (251), from the NNE. *The massive block of Maen Mawr is in the foreground with the low stones of the ring beyond it.*

Four Stones Four-Poster, Powys (253), from the east.

exactly what their name implies, a fine example of a 'Scottish' Four-Poster ring. The boulders are believed to be erratics from the volcanic rocks of Hanter Hill two miles to the south.

Like other Four-Posters the stones are not at the corners of a perfect rectangle but stand on the perimeter of a circle 17ft 3ins (5.3m) in diameter. Clockwise from the north-west their heights are 6ft, 4ft 6ins, 5ft 6ins and 5ft (1.8, 1.4, 1.7, 1.5m). The heaviest weighs some six tons and would have required thirty labourers to haul it upright. The interior of the ring, however, would be cramped for even two people so that whatever rites were performed here must have been watched by a congregation outside the circle.

On the top of the south-west block are three possible cupmarks, a common form of megalithic art in this type of ring in Scotland but very rare in Wales. At Llanerch Farm, SO 1575 5868, 5½ miles WSW of the Four Stones, however, is a boulder , with thirty-two cupmarks on it. Not far away at SO 156 568 Alfred Watkins believed there was a second Four-Poster. 'Pedwar Maen' is, in fact, a Four-Stone row.

The stones reputedly mark the graves of four kings killed in a nearby battle. When they hear the church-bells they go down to Hindwell Pool, ½ mile to the east, to drink.

Burl, 1988, 202–3, *Plan*; A. Watkins, *Early British Trackways*, 1922, 18

254 GELLI HILL, Bettws Diserth, Radnor (3)
Lat: 52°.2   SO 095 583
For the determined. 3 miles SE of Llandrindod Wells. From the A481 take the lane at SO 136 570 NW then W for 1½ miles. At SO 119 576 turn NW to Bylchau farm. Walk. In 200 yds (180m) take the footpath to the W. The circle is 1½ miles in a saddle of Gilwern Hill at a height of 1300ft (396m) O.D. Fair. Map 3
This is a ruinous oval with a maximum diameter of 70ft (21m). Of the fourteen low stones, up to 2ft (60cm). only half stand. There may be a long, fallen

outlier 130 yards (120m) to the west.
Grimes, 1963, 130–1 *Plan*.

255 KERRY HILL, Montgomery (5) [W6/1 Kerry Pole]
Lat: 52°.5   SO 158 860
8 miles SSW of Montgomery, 4½ miles SE of Newtown. From the B4368, halfway between two woods, Walk. At SO 154 860 climb the easy slope to the N. 300 yds (275m). Easy. Map 3
At the north-eastern end of a gentle escarpment nine low and dark sandstones stand in a ring some 87ft by 81ft (26.5 × 24.7m). The plan is strangely-shaped, narrowing from a broad base like the magnified top of a human skull. Some stones are thin slabs, others chubby boulders. Near the centre lies a pillar 4ft (1.2m) long.

The long axis is almost exactly east-west, with two stones set closely one behind the other at the east. Perhaps significantly, one is flat-topped, the other pointed like many pairs of standing stones in Ireland, Scotland and Wales that have been interpreted as male and female symbols.

Alexander Thom suggested that the ring had a complex geometrical design based on two circles with diameters of thirty-two and sixteen of his Megalithic Yards of 2.72ft, the equivalents of 87ft and 43ft 6ins (26.5, 13.3m), with a perimeter of 97.38 M.Y., 264ft 10ins (80.7m).

The ring lies a short way south of an important prehistoric trackway from western Wales to the River Severn near Bewdley.
Grimes, 1963, 123–4; see also 171–92; Thom, 1967, 87–8, *Plan* 88.

256 LLED-CROEN-YR-YCH, Llanbrynmair, Montgomery (3)
Lat: 52°.6   SH 904 005
120 yds (115m) ENE of Cerrig Gaerau stone circle. Easy. Map 3
The stones here are smaller than those at Cerrig Gaerau (252) but some in the southern arc give signs of having their bases 'keeled' like a beak to facilitate their erection. The ring is rather irregular, between 75ft and 81ft (22.9,

24.7m) in diameter. A low outlying stone stands some 30 yards (27m) to the south-east.

The name of the ring, 'the width of the ox-hide', derives from a belief that this was the burial-place of a bereaved ox. At his death his hide was stretched out and surrounded by standing stones. A similar story is told of the Maiden Bower Neolithic causewayed enclosure and Iron Age hillfort in Bedfordshire.

Grimes, 1963, 122–3, *Plan*; Grinsell, 1976, 264

257 NANT TARW, Brecks (1) [W11/4. Usk Water] Lat: 51°.9   SN 820 258 *6 miles sw of Llandovery. Walk. 1¹/₂ miles.From Blaenau-isaf at SN 846 258 follow lane and forest track to NW. At the W end of the path the rings are ³/₄ mile to the W across the brook. Fair. Map 3*

A. There are two stone circles at Nant Tarw, 'the bull brook'. *The ESE ring is* 68ft (20.7m) across. Three hundred and sixty-six feet (112m) to its WNW is the *second circle*, 63ft (19.2m) in diameter. The stones of both are small.

B. Just to the east of the ESE ring is a fallen stone 8ft (2.4m) long, and 300ft (91m) west of the circle is a prostrate pillar 10ft (3m) long. Twenty-eight feet (8.5m) west of the second ring is a Three-Stone setting reminiscent of that at Cerrig Duon. A large prostrate stone, 10ft (3m) long, is the first of a short row of a tall and two small stones in a WSW-ENE line 10ft (3m) long.

Grimes, 1963, 136–7, *Plan*; TTB, 394. *Plan*

258 RHOS Y BEDDAU, Llangynog, Montgomery (1) [W6/2] Lat: 52°.9   SJ 058 302 *9 miles ESE of Bala, 4³/₄ miles SSE of Llandrillo. From Llanrhaedr-ym-Mochnant, (SJ 12.26.) take the NW road for 4 miles to Tan-y-pistyll. Walk. 1 mile W uphill. Demanding. Map 3* After a steep climb above the spectacular Pistyll Rhaiddar waterfall this remote ring, marked as a 'cairn' on the O.S. map, stands at the head of a long and steep-sided valley. Much of

the ground around it is boggy and many of the stones are difficult to distinguish. The name means 'the moor of graves'.

The stone circle, about 42ft (12.8m) across, although of small stones, is in good condition except that at its middle is 'a deep hollow, the site, no doubt, of the sepulchral chamber'. To the ENE of the ring are the remains of an avenue. It ends 25ft (7.6m) from the perimeter of the ring, pointing tangentially to the south side of the circle.

On its northern side there are fifteen stones, five of them fallen, and on the south there are twenty-four stones, two prostrate. The avenue is about 162ft (49.4m) long and between 8ft to 12ft (2.4–3.6m) wide. It is not quite straight and may be composed of two successive elements. Like many 'high-and-low' Irish avenues the stones on one side are taller than their counterparts.

There is a possible stone circle (5) 440 yards (400m) to the north at SJ 059 305. It is egg-shaped, 38 by 35ft (11.6 × 10.7m). Its low stones are loose and questionable.

There is an unquestionable café at the foot of the falls.

Grimes, 1963, 120–2, *Plan*; Burl, 1993, 77–8

259 SIX STONES, Bryngwyn, Radnor (3) Lat: 52°.2   SO 163 516 *7¹/₂ miles E of Builth Wells. For the dedicated. From Glasnant take the sw road (SO 184 911) for ¹/₂ mile. Walk. Join the track to the w. In a mile turn N across the hill for ¹/₂ mile, keeping Mawn Pools to the w. The site is close to the Glasnant stream. Fair. Map 3* The stones of this 80ft (24.4m) diameter circle are very low and difficult to detect in the knee-high heather. Winter or Spring visits are best rewarded. Unusually, many of the thin slabs of purplish sandstones are set on their sides. Even more unusually, there are fourteen or more stones at the Six Stones.

Grimes, 1963, 133–4

260 TRECASTLE MOUNTAIN, Brecks (3)
[W11/2. Y Pigwyn]
Lat: 52°.0   SN 833 310
*4¹/₂ miles SE of Llandovery. At Trecastle
take the Cwmswygsg lane to the WSW.
After 600 yds (550m) follow the Roman
road to the W. Walk. In 1³/₄ miles the
track continues NW. In one mile the
rings are 300 yds (275m) to the N. Fair.
Map 3*
Two stone circles lie just over 300
yards (275m) ESE of two early
rectangular Roman marching-camps,
one inside the other at Y Pigwm, 'the
beacon'. The outermost camp is the
earlier.

A. The pair of stone circles stand NE-
SW of each other on Trecastle
Mountain. *The ENE ring is the larger,
some 76ft (23.2m) across. A mound
near its centre may cover a burial.*

B. *The smaller circle is 94ft (28.7m)
to the WSW, 24ft (7.3m) across. Its
stones, however, are much larger. 54ft
(16.5m) to the south-west is an
overgrown SW-NE row of four tiny
stones. It is about 60ft (18m) long and
like the avenue at Rhos y Beddau
points tangentially to the south sector
of the small circle.*

There is a prostrate pillar to the
south-east of the circles.

Grimes, 1963, 135–6, *Plan*; TTB,
390, *Plan*

261 YNYS-HIR, Brecks (1) [W11/5]
Lat: 52°.0   SN 921 383
*11 miles SW of Builth Wells, 9¹/₂ miles
NW of Brecon. Alongside a track but on
a Ministry of Defence firing range.
Dangerous and inaccessible without
written permission from the
Sennybridge Training Area, near
Brecon, Powys LD3 8PN. Map 3*
At Ynys Hir, 'the long island', is a
fine stone circle 59ft (18m) across.
Similar to Gors-fawr (236) 50 miles to
the west its local stones are graded
from tiny at the north up to 2ft (60cm)
high and heavy at the S-SSW. No
artefacts were discovered in the 1940
excavation. A pit near the centre may
have been modern. At the SSE a
posthole was found 5ft (1.5m) inside

the ring. It had no astronomical
significance.

A small cairn 122ft (37m) to the
south-west contained cremations with
Bronze Age pottery, anthracite beads
and a small pygmy cup.

Arch Camb 97, 1943, 169–94;
Grimes, 1963, 134–5

YNYS MONA (Anglesey)

262 BRYN CELLI DDU, Llanddaniel-fab
(4) Lat: 53°.2   SH 508 702
*3 miles SW of the Menai Bridge, 1 mile
ESE of Llanddaniel-fab. Signposted.
Visible from lane. Leave car. Walk.
Half a mile along farm road. Easy.
Map 3*
Although it was destroyed by Late
Neolithic passage-tomb builders over
4000 years ago the former circle-henge
here is so informative about prehistoric
practices and conflicts that it cannot be
omitted from a guidebook about stone
circles. Discovered in 1777, the
megalithic passage and chamber were
first excavated in 1865 and
subsequently more thoroughly in
1927–8.

Today the site is occupied by the
restored passage-tomb, 85ft in diameter
and about 12ft high (26 × 3.7m). The
kerbed mound partly covers a well-
preserved ditch, 17ft wide and 6ft deep
(5.2 × 1.8m).

A stone-lined passage leads to a
chamber where skeletons were found.
To the right is a free-standing stone
akin to others in Brittany believed to be
embodiments of a female guardian of
the dead. Head-high on the chamber's
lefthand sideslab is a faint and
wretched spiral carving, so badly-
executed that it may be a modern
graffito. Outside the tomb's entrance
the burial of a young ox was
discovered.

Before the construction of the tomb a
circle-henge had stood there, a ring of
standing stones inside a circular
earthwork whose external bank was
later levelled to provide material for the

Bryn Celli Ddu, Ynys Mona (262), *the passage-tomb from the east.*

mound. The ditch had surrounded an oval of upright stones, the number usually cited as fourteen but more probably sixteen, two being taken for the entrance to the tomb. Measuring 63ft (SW-NE) by 57ft (19.2 × 17.4m), the ellipse was wrecked by the tomb-builders. Five stones were removed, one buried, others toppled and smashed with heavy blocks.

The location of deposits show that the ring had been a ritual enclosure. The two largest stones had stood at the south and north. By the south stone, 7ft (2.1m) long, were fragments of quartz. By the north pillar, 8ft (2.4m) in length, was the cremation of an eight-to-ten-year-old girl. The partial cremation of a second girl lay by the west stone. Emphasis upon cardinal points is common in early stone circles.

The stones were not evenly spaced around the ring but erected in opposing pairs whose diagonals passed over a central pit. It may have held a post, perhaps carved or painted, but the hole was recut by the tomb-builders who placed a fragment of human earbone

there before covering it with a slab and setting up a pillar decorated with chevron patterns similar to others in the tomb of Barclodiad-y-Gawres, 'the apronful of the Goddess', eleven miles to the west, SH 328 708.

In 1908 the astronomer, Sir Norman Lockyer, visited Bryn Celli Ddu while the site was still in a 'state of dilapidation'. His survey showed that the passage of the tomb was in line with the midsummer sunrise but in this the builders had done no more than respect the long SW-NE axis of the oval of stones. Preference for a sightline to the east was usual in a chambered tomb but the majority of stone ovals in northern Wales have alignments towards the west: the Druid's Circle (245c); Cefn Coch (242); Cerrig Pryfaid (244); even Gamelands (78) in Westmorland. It is possible that if an astronomical line existed in the Bryn Celli Ddu ring it was towards the south-west and the midwinter sunset. Such an heretical direction may have been anathema to the tomb-builders who demolished the ring.

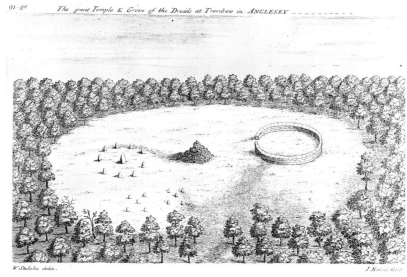

Tre'r Dryw, Ynys Mona (263), the imaginary sketch of a druidical grove by Henry Rowlands in 1723, copied by William Stukeley.

Ghosts are said to inhabit the chamber in which the central stone has alarmingly been mistaken for a 'figure in white'. At Bryn Celli Ddu, 'the hill in the dark grove', the spirits may have been those of the 'last Druids, who died cruelly at the hands of the Romans'.

Arch 80, 1930, 179–214, *Plan*, 185; F. Lynch, *Prehistoric Anglesey*, 1991, 91–101; Grinsell, 1976, 256; *CBA Report 35*, 1985, 80

263 BRYN GWYN STONES, Llanidan (5)
Lat: 53°.2   SH 462 669
6 miles SW of the Menai Bridge, 1¹/₄ miles SE of Llangaffno. Walk. By a field-hedge 200yds (180m) N of the A4080. Easy. Map 3
Some 440 yards (400m) WSW of Castell Bryn-Gwyn, 'white hill castle', a circular Neolithic enclosure or henge that was later transformed into a defensive site, is a pair of gigantic stones, 10ft and 13ft (3, 4m) high. They are two of the biggest standing stones in Wales. By repute they are the survivors of a stone circle some 40ft (12m) in diameter that was once surrounded by a wide bank. In 1766 the Rev. Henry

Rowlands reported three stones there with the stump of a fourth and 'one may easily calculate their number and order to have been eight or nine great pillar-stones, pitched in a circle about an included area of about twelve or fourteen yards diameter.' Doubts have been expressed because of Rowlands's ability to imagine druidical remains in other parts of Anglesey such Tre'r Dryw Bach half a mile north-east of Bryn Gwyn where, he claimed, had been the 'remains of a ring or coronet of very large erected columns or stone-pillars' Nothing survives of it.

This does not disprove Bryn-gwyn. Seventy years earlier John Davies, rector of Newborough, said that two miles from his parish at Bryn-gwyn were 'stones pitch'd on end, about twelve in number, whereof three are very considerable, the largest of them being twelve foot high . . .' It seems to confirm that a circle did stand there at the end of the seventeenth century only for the smaller stones to be removed before Rowland's visit.

F. Lynch, *Prehistoric Anglesey*, 1991, 151

United Kingdom

Channel Islands, Isle of Man, Northern Ireland

CHANNEL ISLANDS

As with most islands stone circles are scarce. They are absent from Guernsey. On Jersey rings known as 'cists-in-circles' seem related to the recumbent stone circles of south-western Ireland

JERSEY

264 HOUGUE DES PLATONS, La, Trinity (3) Lat: 49°.3   656 556
At the N of the island, 550yds (500m) NW of Les Camps du Chenin. Walk. Follow a footpath at 653 554 NE for 220yds (200m). Easy but this 'cist-in-circle' is overgrown and hard to find. Base Map
Excavated in 1914 and 1936, the oval ring 30ft N-S by 27ft (9 × 8.2) enclosed an off-centre cist in which the cremated bones of an adult and child were found. Some of the slabs came from Mont Mado 1¼ miles to the west. The cist is in La Hougue Bie museum.

I. Kinnes and J. Hibbs. *The Dolmens of Jersey*, 1988, 74–5; Johnston, 90–1, *Plan*

265 VILLE-ÈS-NOUAUX, St Helier (1) Lat: 49°.2   635 499
On Mont Cochon Hill, St Aubins Bay. 1½ miles WNW of St Helier. In First Tower public park. Walk. 200yds (180m). Easy. Base Map
Just inside the park are two adjacent monuments, an allée-couverte and a 'cist-in-circle'. The 'cist-in-circle' is an 'Irish' recumbent stone circle

with a boulder-burial.

It is a distorted oval 21ft N-S by 19ft (6.4 × 5.8m) of some sixteen largish stones with smaller ones interspersed between them. At the WSW is a 6ft long, 3ft high (1.8 × 1m) recumbent slab lying between two low flankers. Almost opposite at the east is the tallest stone in the ring, 6ft 6ins (2m) high like one of the portals in a typical Irish recumbent stone circle.

Inside the ring is a boulder-burial whose large capstone covers a rectangular cist. Originally it lay under the heavy dome of a clay mound. Excavation in 1883 found nothing.

The allée-couverte is 19ft (5.8m) to the south. In it were nine beakers, more sherds, six fine 'Jersey Bowls' and a schist wristguard.

Bulletin Annuel de la Société Jersiaise I, 1884, 422–35; Johnston, 75–7, *Plan*

ISLE OF MAN

Like other islands it lacks any 'classical' stone circle

266 MEAYLL HILL, Cregneish (5) Lat: 54°.1   SC 189 677
12½ miles WSW of Douglas, ¾ miles SW of Port Erin, Walk. 100yds (90m) E of lane between Port Erin and Cregneish. Easy. Map 3
Except for the Western Isles of Scotland and the Orkneys stone circles are almost non-existent on any island. The

Isle of Man is no exception. Despite occasional misinterpretations Meayll, or Mull, Hill is not a stone circle. Its similarity, however, and its unusual architecture merit its inclusion here.

The ring stands on a slight slope just below a hill summit. It is an intriguing monument. In plan it is as though a novice had decorated an iced cake by clumsily pressing tiny T-shaped blocks around its edge, three on the right, three on the left with wide spaces at the top and bottom. The blocks were both badly-cut and badly spaced but there is a crude symmetry to the design.

The setting was first recognised as an antiquity in 1863 and was excavated in 1893, then in 1911 and 1971. Built of local slate it is a ring 53ft 3ins N-S by 51ft (16.2 × 15.6m) with an open interior about 44ft (13.4m) across.

The circumference is composed of six long, rectangular chambers in pairs, three on the east with short gaps between them at north-east and south-east, three on the west similarly separated. There are wider spaces at NNW, 16ft, and SSE, 17ft (4.9, 5.2m) and these have been interpreted as entrances.

Access to each pair of chambers was by a narrow intervening passage, its end jutting beyond the perimeter like a cogged wheel. Across the passage lie slabs on edge, flanked by pillars like the septals and jambs of Irish Neolithic chambered tombs.

Some western stones at Meayll Hill stand over 3ft (1m) high giving the site a superficial resemblance to a stone circle. From the south-west these uprights are so conspicuous that 'fishermen take its prominent stones in line with the Calf [Sound] for one of their fishing grounds.'

Cremated bone lay in the chambers intermixed with Lyles Hill sherds, one with grain impressions. There were also jet beads, flint arrowheads, knives, a scraper and white quartz pebbles.

The interior of the site was filled with rubble beneath which was a central structure, a cist or a chamber. The site had been so ransacked 'for building and repairing fences', every capstone of the chambers having been stolen, that it was impossible to tell what this feature had been.

It is probable that Meayll Hill was a two-phase monument, a primary cairn with a central burial having the chambers and passages added around its circumference, they in turn being covered by a large kerbed cairn some 80ft (24.4m) in diameter.

The chambers are like others such as Five Wells in the Peak District and the Water of Deugh in south-west Scotland, all of them perhaps of Irish inspiration. The Isle of Man has long been recognised as a staging-post between Ireland and the British mainland, susceptible to traditions from west and east but transmuting them into idiosyncratic insular monuments. This was realised as long ago as 1893 by the excavators who observed that each of the strange T-settings 'is in fact the *model* of a passage-grave'.

Meayll Hill may be a rare site in which both the burial-place and the settlement of its people are known. Not far away are lines of hut-circles and from the circle's south entrance 'a level track, like a road way' curved 'down the slope of the hill to the hut village'.

A touch of romance spices architectural knowledge. On occasion a ghostly army of horsemen has been glimpsed riding by the ring.

There is an interesting village folk museum in Cregneish.

P.M.C. Kermode and W. Herdman, *Manks Antiquities*, Liverpool, 1914, 40–53, *Plan* 42; S. Piggott, *Neolithic Cultures of the British Isles*, Cambridge, 1954, 160, 161 etc (Mull Hill)

Ville-ès-Nouaux, Jersey (265), the 'Irish' recumbent stone circle from the north with a 'Breton' allée-couverte in the background.

Meayll Hill 'stone circle', Isle of Man (266).

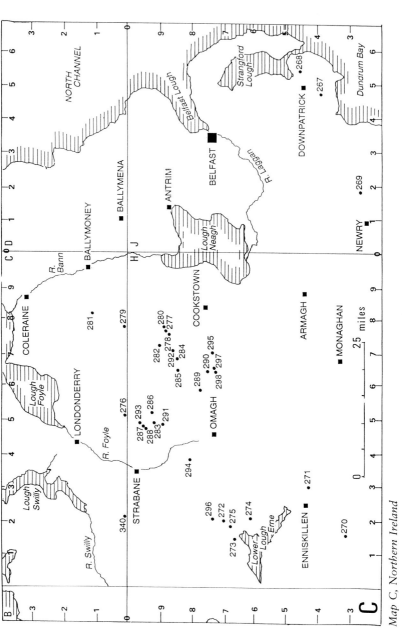

Map C, Northern Ireland

NORTHERN IRELAND

Co. DOWN
The few coastal rings here are separated by miles from the circles in the hills of other counties in Northern Ireland. Lying near the Irish Sea they appear to have much in common with prototypes overseas

267 BALLYNOE (1)
Lat: 54°.3   J 481 404
4¹/₂ miles E of Clough, 2¹/₂ miles S of Downpatrick. Walk. Signposted. At J 485 402 in Ballynoe a footpath leads W for ¹/₄ mile to the ring. Easy. In State care, no charge. Map C
At Ballynoe, 'new town', is one of the great rings of western Europe. Enclosing an area of some 8737 s.ft (812m²) it could comfortably have accommodated a hundred and fifty participants. In its spaciousness, its closely-set stones, its portalled entrance and its cardinal and calendrical alignments it has close affinities with the fine, open circles of Cumbria. Standing less than five miles from Dundrum Bay and the Irish Sea it is arguable that this was a 'foreign' ring erected by Neolithic incomers engaged in the exchange of stone axes from the Lake District. A date around 3000 BC would be feasible.

On land sloping to the west, people basketed earth and cobbles to make a level platform for a megalithic ellipse 108ft NE-SW by 103ft (32.9 × 31.4m). There is a plundered arc at the NNW but originally some sixty-five to seventy local stones of Ordovician grit and granite stood almost shoulder to shoulder, heavy boulders 3ft to 7ft (1–2.1m) high. Notably big ones were erected at north and south.

In the ring there is a 7ft (2.1m) wide gap just south of west. Outside this entrance are two portals very like the arrangement at Swinside (26) in the

English Lake District, one hundred miles of sea to the east, with the Isle of Man as a convenient staging-post halfway between.

Fourteen miles to the south-west two of the Mourne mountains jut sharply like twin pyramids against the skyline. It has been calculated that it was behind one, Slieve Donard, 2700ft (823m) higher than Ballynoe, that the midwinter sun would set. This might explain the location of the ring. It does explain the WSW entrance. With a skyline much higher to the south-west than to north-west the midpoint between the midwinter and midsummer sunsets would be not at true west but at the WSW, the direction that the entrance and its portals do face.

27ft and 120ft (8.2, 36.6m) to the NNE of the circle are two tall outlying pillars. Two more are 27ft and 150ft (8.2, 45.7m) to the SSW. Neither pair is in line from the centre of the ring or with each other but their alignments are of no astronomical significance. Other stones lying in the field may be no more than glacial erratics.

Ballynoe suffered interference. Whether of one or several phases a long mound, ENE-WSW, was constructed in the eastern part of the ring. Excavations of 1937 and 1938 have never been fully published, mainly because the fieldnotes for 1938 were incomplete. Compounding uncertainty the WSW end of the tumulus lay in upheaval, an untidiness of stones, slabs and cobbles that has led to varied interpretations of the mound as a wrecked court-cairn, a despoiled passage-tomb or a ravaged multiple-cist cairn.

What may have been a complete oval of low slabs 59ft ENE-WSW by 46ft (18 × 14m) today is a horseshoe widely open to the WSW. Damage rather than design is likely. Inside this setting a long oval cairn, later covered with soil and rubble, was built, 43ft long, 30ft wide and 3ft 6ins high (13 × 9 × 1m). From it came a single decorated Carrowkeel rimsherd. At the eastern end of the cairn was a large, well-made rectangular tripartite cist – or

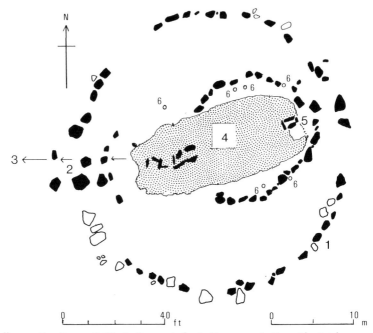

Ballynoe, Co. Down (267). 1. Stone circle; 2. Entrance; 3. To midpoint between the midwinter and midsummer sunsets; 4. Cairn; 5. Cist; 6. Baetyls

segmented chamber – containing the cremated bones of young adults. What may have been a comparable cist at the western end lay in upheaval. Beyond it, at the entrance to the stone circle, stood a shallow crescent of six stones.

In the narrow space between the mound-covered cairn and the ring of slabs several *baetyls*, literally 'sacred meteoric stones', were found, upright in the ground, smooth egg-shaped stones that have been likened to 'the ovoid, cylindrical or conical dressed stones . . . found in the southern Spanish passage-grave culture named after [the cemetery of] Los Millares.' Similar stones were placed outside the Knowth passage-tomb. A connection with death is unequivocal, an association with fertility less sure. But the phallic Turoe Stone in Co. Galway, M 030 223, has also been termed a baetyl.

At the multiple-cist cairn of Millin Bay, J 628 495, eleven miles north-east

of Ballynoe, excavation in 1953 uncovered cists, inhumations, cremations, standing stones, decorated slabs and rows of baetyls. The site was re-covered. All that can now be seen are a few large stones and a low oval mound.

There is dispute over the sequence of events at Ballynoe but if the circle was, as the writer believes, based on English models its builders would not have set it up around anything. Such rings were open and uncluttered. It is more probable that the cairn and cists were intrusive. There are parallels. A passage-tomb was put up inside Callanish (185) in the Hebrides. A stone circle was actually destroyed to make way for a passage-tomb at Bryn Celli Ddu (262) on Anglesey, one hundred miles to the sse of Ballynoe. One must be thankful that Ballynoe itself did not suffer the same fate.

Palaeohistoria 18, 1976, 73–104, *Plan*, 82

Ballynoe, Co. Down (267).

268 CASTLE MAHON (3)
Lat: 54°.3   J 552 470
*4¹/₄ miles ENE of Downpatrick, 2³/₄
miles SW of Strangford. Walk. At the
end of the farm road, J 546 469.
700 yds (640m) NE. Fair. Map C*
Lying on a terrace of Castle Mahon
mountain this is a large but
inconspicuous ring once of six standing
stones. Today three are erect, all low,
in an ellipse 70ft SW-NE by 65ft (21.3 ×
19.8m). The tallest, just over 3ft (1m)
high, stands at the north-east end of the
long axis. Some stones are missing.

Excavation in 1953 discovered a
small pit by the broken WNW stone. It
held oak charcoal, flints and sherds of
carinated Neolithic bowls. Near the
centre of the ring was a larger pit in
which a great fire of hazel had burned.
Alongside it was a small cist with the
cremated bones of a child and a plano-
convex flint knife.

In its design and contents the ring
has similarities to others in north-

western England.
UJA 19, 1956, 1–10, Plan

269 MULLAGHMORE (1)
Lat: 54°.2   J 191 272
*6¹/₂ miles E of Newry, 4 miles S of
Rathfriland. Walk. Just S of the main
street in Mullaghmore. Easy. Map C*
The site is best-known for its two ring-
barrows side by side on the crest of a
hill. Excavations in 1947 and 1948
discovered that the larger at the north,
70ft (21.3m) across, surrounded a
central cairn, beneath which a boulder-
covered pit contained the cremated
bones of four people and a blue faience
bead. Some 300 coarse Bronze Age
sherds were scattered in the cairn.

The smaller ring, only 27ft (8.2m)
across, was barren.

Unappreciated at the time was a tiny
Four-Poster circle just to the south-east
of the barrows. Four small stones stand
at the corners of a rectangle 12ft 2ins
N-S by 9ft 2ins (3.7 × 2.8m), and on

Castle Mahon, Co. Down (268). The 1953 excavation from the south.

the circumference of a circle 15ft 5ins (4.7m) in diameter. A pit at the precise centre of the ring and under a patch of burning held cremated bone and sherds of a Knockadoon-type bucket-shaped pot.

Just west of the site is a prostrate outlier.

The situation of this tiny Four-Poster, almost exactly halfway between the Four-Posters of central Scotland to the NNE and those of Cork and Kerry 450 miles to their ssw, may be an indication of a movement of people in the middle centuries of the second millennium.

Burl, 1988, 76–7, *Plan*

Co. FERMANAGH

A characteristic of many of these small rings between Upper and Lower Lough Erne is their association with tangential alignments of standing stones

270 AGHTIROURKE (5)
Lat: 54°.3   H 169 320
9 miles sw of Enniskillen, 6³/4 miles se of Belcoo. Walk. 600 yds (550m) downhill from road at H 172 322. Easy. Map C
Down the slope from a sub-circular rath about 40ft (12m) across are five large and rough stones in an untidy banked ring approximately 8ft (2.4m)

across. They are from 1ft 6ins to 2ft (45–60cm) high but thick and heavy. Comparisons have been made with a somewhat similar site at Kiltierney (274), H 216 625, twenty miles to the NNE. A closer likeness might be with the Five-Stone ring of Circle 275 (245b) in North Wales and with the Five-Stone circles of Cork and Kerry.

Chart, 177, *no plan*

271 CAVANCARRAGH (4)

Lat: 54°.3   H 299 449
4¹/₂ miles E of Enniskillen, 1¹/₂ miles N of Lisbellaw. Walk. 100 yds (90m) W of lane at H 306 435. Easy. Map C
The removal of up to 12ft (3.7m) of peat in the early nineteenth century uncovered two cairns surrounded by a series of small cists. The cairns were empty but the cists are said to have contained a Bronze Age food-vessel and cremations. One cairn was floored a foot deep (30cm) with cream-coloured sand that had 'been brought from a considerable distance'.

Just to the west were four long, straight rows of low standing stones of local sandstone. One line has gone. To the west is a shorter row which led

tangentially to a shy stone circle, about 20ft (6m) across and originally of about twelve stones. It is destroyed.

The excavator thought the circle and its adjacent rows stood in the sort of position 'a small army acting on the defensive would seek to occupy. It is defended upon one side by a deep ravine and upon the other by steep declivities.' The site certainly commands extensive views.

JRSAI 14, 1876–8, 499–510, *Plan, 501*

272 DRUMSKINNY (1)

Lat: 54°.6   H 201 707
15¹/₂ miles W of Omagh, 6 miles ENE of Pettigoe. In State care, no charge. Walk. Immediately E of the road from Letterkeen to Drumskinny. Easy. Map C
Excavated in 1962 this is the northernmost of several rings near Montiaghroe a mile to the south. Standing in the shadow of Rotten Mountain, Drumskinny is an irregular ellipse 45ft 9ins ESE-WNW by 42ft 6ins (14 × 13m). Typical of many rings in Northern Ireland, its stones are closely set together, only 1ft to 2ft (0.3–0.6m)

Drumskinny, Co. Fermanagh (272), from the west.

apart but, untypically, some of them
are tall, ranging from 1ft 3ins up to 5ft
10ins (38cm–1.8m) in height. There is a
wide gap at the wnw.

A yard or so (1m) outside this
possible entrance is a kerbed cairn 13ft
(4m) across. Tangential to the ring's
western side, but leading directly to the
cairn, is a 49ft (14.9m) long row,
aligned n-s, of characteristically little
stones.

The only finds were a single Neolithic
sherd on the old land surface near a
circle-stone and some flints.

UJA 27, 1964, 30–32, *Plan*, 24

273 Formil (4) Lat: 54°.6   H 159 676
*3¹/₄ miles ENE of Pettigoe, 2³/₄ miles
NNW of Kesh. Walk. From H 162 674
on the Clonelly – Drummoney Bridge
road, ¹/₄ mile NW. Fair. Map C*
The attraction here is not the megalithic
ring, which is now a wrecked semi-
circle of small stones, but the splayed
avenue tangential to it, narrowing from
10ft (3m) to 4ft (1.2m) at its west
against the circle. This is one of the
typical northern Irish 'high-and-low'
avenues. Its south side consists of eight
large stones, several fallen but once
from 5ft to 8ft (1.5–2.4m) high. In
contrast the northern line has nineteen
stones, all of them low.

The deliberately chosen difference in
heights is an architectural trait that may
have originated in Brittany.

Burl, 1993, 232

274 Kiltierney (Destroyed)
Lat: 54°.5   H 218 625
*3 miles NNW of Irvinestown, 1¹/₂ miles S
of Ederny. In Castle Archdale deer
park. No walk. The circle has gone.
Map C*
This is one of the tragedies of stone
circle archaeology. The ring that stood
here was intriguing because of the
possibility that it was a variation of the
recumbent stone circles of north-eastern
Scotland. It was destroyed in 1974
during the course of farm
'improvements'. It is included in this
guide because of its architectural
importance.

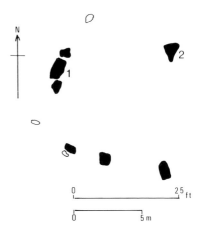

Kiltierney, Co. Fermanagh (274).
1. *Possible recumbent stone;*
2. *Cupmarked stone*

It was one of a group of monuments
that underwent change from the early
Neolithic into the Iron Age on land
which became the site of a medieval
grange belonging to the Cistercian
abbey of Assaroe.

At the north was the ransacked
remains of a passage-tomb, 65ft across
and 7ft high (19.8 × 2.1m), the
decorated slabs of its chamber being
dumped on the mound. Around it,
discovered during excavations in 1983–
4, a rock-cut ditch was dug in the early
Iron Age, and outside it nineteen small
cairns were raised to receive cremations
with artefacts, some of them
ornamented in La Tène style. A
previous excavation of 1969 had found
a small Carrowkeel sherd in the
passage-tomb.

The stone circle had stood 250 yards
(229m) to the south-east. On the slope
people raised a level platform to receive
as many as fifteen stones of an ellipse
some 36ft 6ins ESE-WNW by 33ft 4ins
(11.1 × 10.2m). The stones were not
graded in height, all save one being
about 5ft (1.5m) high. The biggest at
the north-east had an oval cupmark
carved in a natural hollow near its top.
The pillar was of red sandstone 'which

must have been brought from a distance'.

On the WNW arc of the ring were two upright stones, each 5ft (1.5m) high flanking a lower and longer one, 5ft 10ins long but only 3ft high (1.8 × 0.9m). Such an arrangement is very reminiscent of the Scottish flankers and recumbent, although the WNW alignment is unknown among them. Outside the 'recumbent' was a crescent of low stones, similar to settings known in Scottish rings such as Strichen (116).

Interference followed. In the Early Bronze Age the ring was converted into a cremation cemetery in a manner not unlike that at Berrybrae, Aberdeenshire (95). By the stones five burials were accompanied by an inverted cordoned urn, three sherds patterned in beaker forms, stone beads and pendants. Near the middle of the ring a spread of cremated bone with some Carrowkeel sherds overlay a miniature cist with more burnt bone and stone and amber beads.

There was a standing stone 40ft (12m) further down the slope.

Like Mullaghmore, Co. Down (269), Circle 275 in Gwynedd (245b), and Torhousekie, Wigtownshire (233), sites such as Kiltierney with apparent recumbent stone circle affinities seem geographical intermediaries between north-east Scotland and south-western Ireland. It is an archaeological tragedy that such a vital ring should be destroyed.

UJA 40, 1977, 32–41, *Plans*, 36, 37

275 MONTIAGHROE, SW, CENTRE, SE (4, 3, 4) Lat: 54°.6
       H 191 692, 194 693, 197 691
5¹/₂ miles WNW of Pettigoe, 1 mile S of Drumskinny. Walk. Alongside and 100 yds (90m) E of road. Easy. Map C
A. *South-east*, (4) Only three stones remain of a circle here. They are 5ft 10ins, 5ft 7ins and 4ft (1.8, 1.7, 1.2m) high and are 3ft and 2ft 7ins (0.9, 0.8m) apart.
B. *Centre*, (3) In a ring some 50ft (15m) in diameter twenty-four low stones still remain, half-hidden in the reedy grass. To their north-east are the remnants of two tangential rows. An outlying pillar, 2ft (0.7m) high, stands 100ft (30m) to the south-east.
c. *South-west*, (4) Four low stones survive in this ring. 60ft (18m) to the north is an impressive Three-Stone row with heights of 5ft 9ins, 4ft 10ins and 3ft 9ins (1.8, 1.5, 1.1m).
Chart, 144. *No plan*

Co. LONDONDERRY

The rings here, probably Bronze Age, are small, averaging 35ft (10.7m), and are usually of numerous closely-set, low stones like kerbs. A quarter are concentric, some have internal chamber-tombs, or cairns or cists suggesting that they may owe their origins to the Carrowmore passage-tomb cemetery (364) seventy miles to the south-west where stone circles of almost contiguous stones surround central chambered tombs or free-standing dolmens. It is a theory made more feasible by the presence of an analogous, though larger, ring about halfway between at Beltany, Co. Donegal (340).

276 ALTAGHONEY (3)
Lat: 54°.9   C 515 013
11¹/₄ miles SE of Londonderry, 4¹/₄ miles SSW of Claudy. Walk. From the junction of lanes at C 517 011, 500 yds (460m) W. Fair. Map C
This ruinous and inconspicuous ring is an irregular ellipse, 54ft 6ins N-S by 53ft 2ins (16.6 × 16.2m). Of its forty-two stones the tallest stands only 3ft (0.9m) high at the south-east. The average is 5ins (13cm). All are local, one of them being quartz. In the middle are two low stones, perhaps all that is left of a central cist.

A parallel avenue, ESE-WNW, 110ft (33.5m) long, reaches the southern arc of the ring from the east. It is predictably 'high-and- low'. The northern line of twenty-six almost buried stones is 24ft (7.3m) away from the twenty-five blocks of its higher partner.

200 yards (180m) north of the ring is Cashelbane wedge-tomb, the 'White Fort'. It stands well inside a circular ditch suggesting that it may have been built inside an earlier ring-barrow.

McConkey, 53, *Plan*, fig. 45

277 BALLYBRIEST NNE (3)
Lat: 54°.7   H 765 887
3¹/₄ miles s of Draperstown, 1100 yds (1000m) SSE of Black Water Bridge. Walk. Immediately to E of unfenced road. Easy. Map C
There is a dual-court cairn at Carnanbane, H762 886. Excavated in 1937 its northern half was removed during land-clearance. 150 yards (137m) to the south-west is a small wedge-tomb which was uncovered from bog in the early 20th century.

The circle is 600 yards (550m) ENE of Carnanbane. It is a tiny ring, only 19ft (5.8m) with six remaining stones, all of them low.

Chart, 212; Evans, 149. *No plan*

278 BALLYBRIEST SSW (3)
Lat: 54°.7   H760 880
4¹/₂ miles s of Draperstown, 1 mile s of Black Water Bridge. Walk. To the E of the B162 and w of unfenced lane from Ballybriest to Black Water Bridge. 500 yds (460m) w of lane, uphill. Fair. Map C
There are eight visible stones, all of them low, the tallest no more than 1ft 6ins (0.5m) high, on the circumference of a ring about 21ft (6.4m) across.

There are the faintest indications of a possible central cairn.

Chart, 212. *No plan*

279 COOLNASILLAGH (5)
Lat: 54°.8   C 785 003
4 miles w of Maghera, 3¹/₂ miles NW of Tobermore. Walk. From farm lane at C 787 000 ring is ¹/₄ mile NNW on the lower eastern slopes of Coolnasillagh mountain. Easy. Map C
This 'stone circle' may be the remains of a cairn. It is concentric, 42ft (12.8m) in diameter for its outer ring and no more than 10ft (3m) for its not quite central inner circle which contains an eccentrically-placed cist which is now only visible as a pit.

There is a collapsed Three-Stone row just to the north-east with one erect stone, 4ft 6ins (1.4m) high, and two fallen, 9ft 6ins and 6ft 3ins (2.9, 1.9m) long respectively.

900ft (275m) to the north-west is a ruinous single row, NE-SW, just over 50ft (15m) long.

Chart, 208, *no plan*

280 CORICK (4) Lat: 54°.8   H 779 896
6³/₄ miles N of Cookstown, 2¹/₂ miles s of Draperstown. Walk. About ³/₄ mile. Just SW of White Water Bridge a track at H 788 891 goes NW for 600 yds (550m). At end turn w for same distance up steepish slope. Rather demanding. Map C
This is a little-known but important group. By the east bank of a stream in the shadow of Slieve Gullion mountain with a passage-tomb high on its summit, the circle and rows at Corick are intriguing. Revealed by nineteenth-century peat-cutting, at a height almost 800ft (244m) above sea-level, there were four inconspicuous stone circles of which only part of one with a central pillar survives. It, an overgrown chambered tomb and six tallish stone rows lie on a bare, boringly flat moor within a few strides of each other.

The remaining ring, cut by a track, is little more than an arc of a circle once about 22ft (6.7m) in diameter. Near the centre is a standing stone 4ft 7ins (1.4m) high. A cluster of stones adjacent to it may be the remains of a chambered tomb or a very large cist.

The rows are more impressive. Although of rough, stubby boulders they are quite conspicuous on the open moorland. A little distance south-west of the centre-stone ring were three other stone circles. The west had an attached row. The middle and eastern had long s-n tangential rows nudging their east arcs. To the north a shorter line is arranged SE-NW with no ring, tomb or standing stone as its focus. A longer line, running N-S, is also unattached. By its southern end another row leads ESE-WNW almost at right-angles to the end of the attached row, but with no obvious target of its own. It is a combination of lines that, in their disposition, are reminiscent of the rows at angles to each other in western Brittany. The collection of rows at Corick also indicates the manner in which the multiple rows of Brittany and northern Scotland may have developed.

Burl, 1993, 102; McConkey, 53, *Plan*, fig. 18

281 CUILBANE (2)
Lat: 55°.0   C 830 122
9 miles ENE of Dungiven, 2¹/₂ miles SSW of Garvagh. NW of Magheramore hill. Walk. From lane at C 828 120¹/₄ mile NE. Easy. Map C
There may have been a central structure in this restored ring. If so, it is now only a jumble of stones.

The ring was wrecked during land clearance in 1984. It was re-erected in 1985. Of its original sixteen stones, averaging 1ft 3ins (38cm) in height, thirteen remain in an oval about 43ft SSE-NNW by 39ft (13 × 12m). There is a much taller stone at the ESE 4ft (1.2m) high.

A cache of well-made flints was discovered in the packing of a stone at the south-west. Containing scrapers, points, knives and some waste the collection seems to have been brought as nodules either from Co. Antrim or from the Slieve Gullion area fifteen miles to the south. The closest correlation to the cache is with others in Neolithic contexts such as two court-cairns. The report stressed that the flints had been found during restoration work rather than in a controlled excavation and that, therefore, its context was not entirely secure. Nevertheless, it is possible that Cuilbane is one of the earliest stone circles in northern Ireland.

UJA 48, 1985, 41–50, Plans 42, 43

282 OWENREAGH (4, 5)
Lat: 54°.8   H 742 903
9 miles NW of Cookstown, 3³/₄ miles SW of Draperstown. Walk. Either from footpath at H 756 912 SW for ¹/₂ mile to cairn then a further 700 yds (640m) across moor to circle. Easy. Or from H 734 906 at Old Church Bridge ¹/₂ mile SE up steep slope. Hard. Map C
Although damaged this is an interesting complex.

A. At the *south-east* are the remains of a circle now of nine stones, the north side missing, about 30ft (9m) across. Inside, south-east of the centre, three stones may be a ruined cist or chamber.

To the north-east of the ring is a standing stone 5ft (1.5m) high. Just outside the circle to its SSE are two more stones.

B. To the *north-west* are two contiguous rings. The south-western, 39ft (11.8m) in diameter, and with a track passing through it, is composed of low stones, most no more than 8ins (0.2m) high.

C. Touching the ring at its north-east are twelve low stones of *an oval* some 31ft E-W by 28ft (9.5 × 8.5m). Although they average no more than 1ft (0.3m) in height one is five times taller.

Inside the ring are eight more stones, four at the east resembling a ravaged chamber. It has been suggested that the 'ring' is all that is left of a megalithic tomb.

700 yards (640m) to the north-east is a large cairn.

Chart, 210–11. *No plan*

CO. TYRONE

The county contains almost half the known rings in Northern Ireland. They are small, averaging no more than 38ft (11.6m) in diameter, but they are often in groups such as Beaghmore, Castledamph and Moymore. Internal features, pits, cists and cairns, are common. So are tangential alignments both long and short. Excavations, of which there have been several, have consistently discovered Bronze Age material

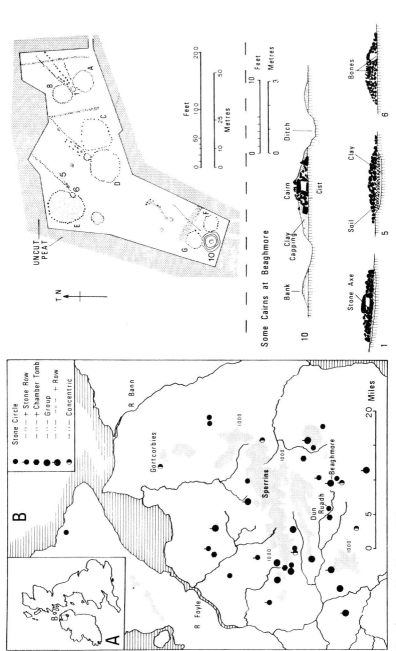

Beaghmore, Co. Tyrone (284).

283 AGHALANE (3)
Lat: 54°.8   H 495 925
1¼ miles NE of Plumbridge. At H 495
914 a mountain road goes N for ½
mile. Walk. From its end 350 yds
(320m) N up hillside. Easy. Map C
As late as 1936 there were three circles
visible here, half-concealed in peat. One
contained a cist that was disturbed
when the peat was cut. A second had
one abnormally big stone. Only the
third has survived.

This is a very large oval, 115ft by
94ft (35.1 × 28.7m), unusually
spacious for this part of Ireland and
perhaps early in the series. Around its
circumference are some forty-six stones
about 10ins (25cm) high but with taller
ones at the south-west end of the longer
axis and at the NNW, 2ft and 1ft 7ins
(0.6, 0.5m) high respectively. Just off
centre is a leaning block. It is a feature
better-known in south-west Scotland
than in Ulster.

An outlying stone, 3ft 9ins (1.1m)
high, stands 35ft (10.7m) to the ENE
and 130ft (40m) away in the same
direction is a Three-Stone row, NW-SE,
14ft (4.3m) long, with stones 2ft 9ins,
1ft 6ins and 4ins (0.8, 0.5, 0.1m) high.

There is another standing stone ¾
mile to the north-east. The
Castledamph (286) stone circles are 1¾
miles to the east.

Davies, 11, no. 52; Chart, 218. *No*
plan

284 BEAGHMORE A, B; C, D; E; F, G (2)
Lat: 54°.7   H 685 842
8½ miles WNW of Cookstown, 7½ miles
N of Pomeroy. Walk. Alongside a
minor road from Dunnamore to
Broughderg Bridge. Easy, In State care,
no charge. Map C
The circles, rows and cairns at
Beaghmore were discovered during
peat-cutting in the early 1940s and an
area was excavated in 1945–9. There is
more to be exposed. Vandalised in
1981 the toppled stones have been
delicately replaced.

A palynological investigation
provided material for C-14 'dates' of
1605 ± 45 BC (UB-23), 1535 ± 55 BC

(UB-11), and 775 ± 55 BC (UB-163),
indicating that the stones had been
erected at some time between 2000 and
950 BC. A 'true' date of about 1600 BC
during the Early Bronze Age is
plausible. A much earlier assay of 2185
± 80 BC (UB-608), c.2800 BC, from
charcoal in a hearth near one of the
cairns probably relates to previous
Neolithic settlement on the site.

Six of the seven rings are in pairs.
The circles of many little, closely-set
stones, are not examples of impressive
megalithic architecture. Of their
hundreds of stones only about 125 are
above 1ft 6ins (46cm) high. All the
rings are associated with small cairns
that already existed on the site.

Usually a short row of tall pillars and
a longer, rather sinuous line of lower
stones lead towards the cairn, the
stones rising in height as they approach
it. As well as the rings and the 'high-
and- low' rows there are at least six
independent cairns and it is arguable
that the misshapen circles were
additions to a Bronze Age cemetery.

The complex lies on a sandy terrace
overlooking a river valley to the north-
west that had been occupied in
Neolithic times. The worndown N-S line
of a field-wall underlies two of the four
rows connected to the first pair of
rings, the north-eastern A and B.

A. *Rings A, B* Ring A is buckled, 35ft
(10.7m) in diameter, B to the north-
west a more symmetrical 39ft (11.9m).
The stones are crowded together, fifty-
four in A, forty-four in B, nudging and
jostling their neighbours, more like
kerbs than the standing stones of most
circles. Conversely they are very like
their possible progenitors in the
Carrowmore cemetery of Co. Sligo
(364).

Two long splayed rows, 40ft and
78ft (12.2, 23.8m) long, are tangential
to the inner sides of the circles. Inside
them two more rows, 24ft, 72ft (7.3,
22m) of much taller stones, converge
on a low cairn lying between the rings.
It contained a polished porcellanite axe,
conceivably from the axe-factory of
Tievebulliagh, Co. Antrim, over 70

miles to the north.

B. *Rings C, D* Two more field-walls stretch N-S between A, B and the next pair, C, D, 46ft (14m) to the south-west. Of those grossly irregular rings. C is a horrible 60ft (18.3m) distortion of a circle, D a better 50ft (15.2m) across. Between the 'circles' two rows, one 60ft (18.3m) long of tall stones, its partner 70ft (21.3m) of lower, lead to a cairn touching the northern arc of D. Inside it a cist was empty but in ring C was evidence of pits, charcoal, hearths, flints and shouldered Neolithic bowls, a collection very similar to ritual centres such as Goodland, Co. Antrim, where offerings of fertile soil and broken artefacts had been deposited as offerings.

C. *Ring E* To the WNW, 70ft (21m) away, is a well-planned oval, Ring E, 68ft SSW-NNE by 55ft (20.7 × 16.8m), shaped like an inverted egg and studded with a wilderness of small sharp stones like a fakir's bed. Engulfed inside its eastern arc is a cairn which must be earlier. A low row, 100ft (31m) long, wanders to it. Under the cairn a cist held a cremation, fungus, moss, twigs. On a covering stone were human skull fragments. To the east three tall stones in a row 20ft (6m) long lead north-eastwards to a second cairn. To the south of Ring E is a cairn with a pit in which oak wood had been placed.

Circle E is similar to the platform cairns of the Carrowmore barrow cemetery in Co. Sligo, and to the cairns in the Brenig cemetery of Denbighshire, Clwyd. Radiocarbon assays from the latter ranged from 1680 ± 100 BC (HAR-501) to 1120 ± 90 BC (HAR-536), c.2050 to 1400 BC.

D. *Rings F, G* This final pair of rings, both about 30ft (9m) across, lie some 190ft (58m) to the south. A 68ft (21m) long row of low stones passes between them to an embanked and ditched cairn which covered an empty cist. The entrance of two tall and heavy stones 4ft (1.2m) apart on the south-eastern side of Circle G is comparable to others at the nearby Clogherny Butterlope (287) and Broughderg (285) rings and

may be an indication that Circle G was one of the first at Beaghmore.

Astronomically Beaghmore's long rows are a challenge. Although they do 'run tangentially from the circles in a north-easterly direction', they actually flow in the opposite direction like nearly every row in Britain, Ireland and Brittany, not down and away from but up a slope towards a cairn. Every long row has a cairn. It also has a solar alignment. With the exception of the ENE-WSW line tangential to Circle A five of the six long rows at Beaghmore are aligned NE-SW within a few degrees of 222°.

Dr Archie Thom found the astronomy towards the north-eastern horizon coarse and inconclusive. 'Were the erectors beginners and learning about the moon's movement or were the rows put there for other reasons?' The explanation is different.

The open countryside of today is misleading. Pollen analysis suggests a darkly-wooded prehistoric landscape. Given the slope of the ground at Beaghmore and the nearby south-western skyline low-growing hazels a hundred yards (90m) away would have raised the horizon to an elevation of 3°. A stand of mature oaks half a mile distant would have produced a skyline of similar height. The discovery of an oak branch, 'part of a tree of considerable size' in one cairn and birch twigs in another show that higher trees did grow nearby. With such an elevated horizon four of the rows have declinations between −23°.3 and −24°.9, clumsily directed towards the midwinter sunset. Archaeologically, south-west was correct, uphill and to a cairn.

Like the Three-Stone row at Ballochroy, Argyllshire, the lines were not only roughly aligned on the midwinter solstice but also related to death. The cremated bones, the partly-preserved pieces of human skull, spine and limbs in the cairn of Circle E and fragments of bone elsewhere prove that the cairns were burial-places. Such links between death and the sun or moon are commonplace in the megalithic monuments of western Europe.

Two of the long rows had declinations of −22°.7 and −21°.6. They are subtle. Declinations near −22° indicate sunset in early December and would warn observers that the winter solstice was close. It is possible, therefore, that the mixed long and short rows at Beaghmore were put up around 1600 BC, during the long transitional period between rows as processional ways and shorter lines of tall stones as calendrical indicators. The cairns are probably earlier.

The excavation of Bradley's Cairn, H 684 841, in 1979, 227 yards (208m) SSW of the complex, yielded only some scraps of burnt bone but it did produce an indirect date. Of five standing stones against it Thom concluded that the alignment of two 'could have been used to observe the upper limb of the rising moon about 1640 BC ± 200 years.'

May, *JRSAI 83*, 1953, 174–97, *Plans*; A.S. Thom, *UJA 43*, 1980, 15–19, *Plans*

285 BROUGHDERG, NE, SOUTH, SW (3, 4)
Lat: 54°.7   centred on H 653 843
14¹/₂ miles NE of Omagh, 10¹/₂ miles SW of Draperstown. Walk. Immediately by lane from Evishessan Bridge to Crocknaboley. Easy. Map C
This is an interesting group of inconspicuous rings with indications of how avenues developed from simple entrances.

A. *North-east ring* H 661 873 Very closely-set stones, averaging no more than a foot high (0.3m), form a vague ellipse 46ft by 40ft (14 × 12.2m). From the west a 'high-and-low' avenue leads to the ring, the northern side 50ft long of stones about 1ft 6ins high (15.2, 0.5m), the southern almost hidden in the turf. A quartz block lies near its middle. The site has many similarities to the Castledamph 'avenue'-circle (286) nine miles to the north-west.

B. *South ring* H 653 843 There are the remains of two contiguous rings here, the northern of ten low stones in an oval 29ft 6ins by 25ft 7ins (9 ×

7.8m). The tallest is 2ft 3ins (0.7m) high.

The southern ring is also oval, 29ft 6ins by 26ft 3ins (9 × 8m). Among its fourteen stones there is a wider gap at the west which may be an original entrance.

Between the rings is a standing stone 4ft 6ins (1.4m) high.

c. *South-west ring* H 650 861 Thirty-seven stones no more than 1ft 6ins (0.5m) apart form a slight ellipse, 51ft 2ins by 49ft 7ins (15.6 × 15.1m). On average they are 1ft (0.3m) high.

At the east, however, are two much taller stones, both about 2ft 8ins (0.8m) high. Standing 6ft 6ins (2m) apart, their difference in height and spacing make it probable that they form a genuine entrance.

D. To the *south* is the turf-banked ruin of another ring of very low stones surrounding a cairn in equally bad condition. Against the ring is a row of seven stones, two of which, nearly 3ft (1m) high, may once have been the entrance to a third, destroyed ring.

McConkey, 60–1; Burl, 1993, 57, 78, 227, 231. *No plans*

286 CASTLEDAMPH, N, S, E (3)
Lat: 54°.8   H 522 923
4¹/₂ miles NNE of Gortin, 2¹/₂ miles ENE of Plumbridge. Walk. ¹/₄ mile NW of the junction of the Castledamph farm lane and the lesser lane N to Glensass. Distance not far, hill-slope steep. Fair. Map C
The rings here lie on a spur of the Sperrin mountains overlooking the Glenelly valley. Until the nineteenth century the sites were buried under 6ft (1.8m) of peat which had preserved them from destruction. They are now in a dilapidated state.

A. *North rings* These are the remains of two contiguous circles, the western of seventeen stones, tall for northern Ireland, in a ring 42ft 8ins (13m) in diameter. The tallest stands at the WSW.

Alongside it the eastern ring is an oval 38ft by 36ft 9ins (11.6 × 11.2m) of twenty-seven stones. Like the conjoined circle and horseshoe at Er-

Lannic (379) in southern Brittany the three highest stones stand at the point where the circles touch.

B. *South ring* 100 yards (90m) south of site A. Excavated in June 1937, this is a concentric ring of very low stones, its decayed appearance worsened by an old field-wall that passes through its southern half. The outer ring is some 65ft (19.8m) across, the inner rather less than half that diameter and consisting now of only its northern semi-circle. Between the rings was a rough paving.

A ditched and unkerbed cairn, 12ft across and 2ft high (3.7 × 0.6m), lies at the centre of the inner ring. It covered a small cist in which was charcoal and the cremated bones of an eighteen-year-old youth. There was a suspicion of a posthole in the cairn. A loose cupmarked slab by the cairn may have been the capstone of the cist.

A 'high-and-low' avenue, aligned almost precisely N-S, led not quite tangentially to the outer circle from the south. Its eastern side, 75ft (22.9m) long was composed of sixteen stones up to 3ft (1m) high. In contrast, the row to its west had no stone more than 8ins (0.2m) in height. It stopped about 32ft (9.8m) from the ring.

Outside and halfway along the east row was a small, empty cairn. Just west of the avenue were three deepish pits which the excavator believed might have held upright posts.

c. *East ring* In dreadful condition there are the hardly recognisable stones of a concentric circle 150ft (46m) east of site A. Its more computable inner ring had a diameter of 18ft (5.5m).

JRSAI 68, 1938, 106–12, Plan

287 CLOGHERNY BUTTERLOPE (4)
Lat: 54°.8   H 493 947
2¹/₄ miles N of Plumbridge. In Butterlope glen W of lane from Eden to Butterlope. Walk. 300yds (275m) up short, steep slope. Fair. Map C
Until this century there was a complex of five stone circles here with approximate diameters of 19ft, 25ft, 25ft, 48ft and 51ft (5.8, 7.6, 7.6, 14.6,

15.6m). Only the fragments of two remain.

A. Excavated in the second week of June 1937, immediately following the excavation of Clogherny Meeneriggal (288). Fifteen stones stand on a level patch of ground in an oval 47ft by 38ft (14.3 × 11.6m). Averaging 1ft 4ins (0.4m) in height, the tallest, 2ft 8ins (0.8m) high, stands at the WNW.

No burials were discovered in the interior. There was a possible posthole just west of the centre, and some pits containing hazel charcoal with a small amount of oak and willow. A scatter of white pebbles lay near them.

The wreckage of a Four-Stone row lies to the east. A long prostrate stone to the east may have been an outlier.

B. Ten stones form a circle whose western half still lies under the peat. It is a small ring, 26ft 3ins (8m) across, of low stones. A taller triangular slab about 1ft 3ins (0.4m) stands at the SSE and a flat-topped block of similar height stands at the north-east. They are too far apart to have formed an entrance.

There is a low standing stone to the east.

UJA 2, 1939, 40–43, Plan 41

288 CLOGHERNY MEENERIGGAL (3)
Lat: 54°.8   H 488 945
500yds (460m) SW of Clogherny Butterlope. Walk. ¹/₂ mile W of the Butterlope Glen lane. Fair. Map C
Excavated in the first week of June 1937, this site consists of a well-preserved wedge-tomb inside a stone circle. The tomb was surrounded by a low cairn, 35ft (10.7m) across, which concealed a ring of heavy slabs on edge.

The south-west facing tomb was roofless and little was found in its two segmented chambers except material removed from a pyre: hazel charcoal, cremated bone, burnt flint and a broken barbed-and-tanged flint arrowhead, 'much glazed as if exposed to fire'.

Crudely-laid cobbling lay between the cairn and the stone circle which was about 60ft (18.2m) in diameter. Untypically, its seventeen 3ft (1m) high stones were well-spaced, about 5ft (1.5m) apart.

The excavator, Oliver Davies, was not impressed with the quality of these megalithic structures, remarking on 'the general inability of the prehistoric inhabitants of Co. Derry [sic] to build megaliths. In other parts of Ulster men had a developed sense of form and plan; north of the Sperrins they threw their megaliths together anyhow.' He suspected Scottish influences.

UJA 2, 1939, 37–40, Plan, 38

289 COPNEY (3, 4)

Lat: 54°.7   H 599 782

9¹/₂ miles ENE of Omagh, 3 miles S of Greencastle. Walk. ¹/₄ mile S of A505 Omagh-Cookstown road. On N slopes of Copney Hill. Fair. Map C

Perhaps akin to the great Beaghmore (284) complex the nine or more rings below a terrace on Copney Hill are still half-smothered in peat and it was only local knowledge that led archaeologists to them. Any subtleties of design or contents await discovery.

The three groups of rings extend on a WSW-ENE axis for almost 600ft (180m). A tall 'playing-card' stone on a ENE-WSW axis, 6ft high, 4ft 3ins wide but only 2ft 3ins thick (1.8 × 1.3 × 0.7m) 'dominates the group' from higher ground to the south. It is 49ft (15m) from Circle B.

A. *Western group* The westernmost ring, A, is a large circle, 51ft (15.6m) in diameter of thirty-six visible stones averaging a foot (0.3m) in height. Thirteen more were located by probing. There may be a central cairn but peat conceals it.

Circle B is even larger, 56ft (17m) across. Its thirty-nine apparent stones are just over a foot high (33cm). Probing detected twenty-three more.

From the ring a row of ten squarish blocks, unlike the smaller, rougher stones of the circles, extends ESE for 53ft (16m).

Ring C is flattened at its north-west as though to stop short of the row. Seventy-one stones can be seen, about 1ft 6ins (0.5m) high, of an oval 78ft

9ins NE-SW by 72ft (24 × 22m).

There is a 82ft (25m) long gap before the central sites.

B. *Central group* This consists of a heather-covered cairn (D) about 25ft across and 3ft high (7.6 × 1m). Alongside it is the smallish Circle E, seemingly egg-shaped with a longer SSW-NNE axis, 33ft by 26ft 3ins (10 × 8m). Its eleven obvious stones are no more than 4ins (0.1m) high. A central 'feature' may be a cairn or peat-cutting.

There is a 70ft (21m) gap before the eastern group.

C. *Eastern group.* Circles F and G are contiguous

Circle F at the north is small, about 30ft (9m) in diameter with ten very low stones. Circle G is the same size with twenty-two visible low stones and a further fifteen discovered by probing.

D. *Circles H, I and J* are all partly or almost wholly covered by deep peat and their dimensions are unclear. H is about 31ft (9.5m) across of nineteen known stones. I is even more deeply covered. Its twelve little stones form a ring about the same size as H. 'Circle' J is no more than a tenuous arc.

McConkey, 62–3. *UJA 46, 1983, 146–8, Plans*

290 CREGGANCONROE (3, 4)

Lat: 54°.6   H 648 752

12 miles ENE of Omagh, 3 miles NE of Carrickmore. Walk. Just W of the lane between Tremoge and Creggan. Easy. Map C

This pair of rings, and perhaps others, are being exposed by the extension of peat-cutting.

A. At the *north-east* is a good oval, 37ft by 31ft 2ins (11.3 × 9.5m). Its twenty-six stones are from 1ft to 1ft 6ins (0.3–0.5m) high.

B. Thirty feet (9m) to *the south-west* is a badly-damaged ring of which only nine low stones in an arc 25ft 3ins (7.7m) across remain. Most are no more than 8ins (0.2m) high, but one at the southeast stands nearly 2ft (0.6m) tall.

To the west is a possible long row, nw-se, tangential to the north-east ring. There is also what is either a second row or the remains of a third circle with five low stones in a line about 12ft (3.7m) long. A good circle alongside a court-cairn on Cregganconroe mountain to the east, H 663 758, has been destroyed.

McConkey, 66. *No plan*

291 CULVACULLION (3)
Lat: 54°.8   H 495 889
2 miles N of Gortin, 1¹/₂ miles of Plumbridge. Walk. A footpath at H 491 886 leads steeply uphill for ¹/₄ mile. Fair. Map C
This is a widely-spread group of four stone circles.

A. *Southern group* This appears to be the remains of four concentric rings, the outermost, 61ft (18.6m) in diameter, the tiny innermost no more than 4ft (1.2m) across. Alongside the ring an almost tangential row of twenty-seven stones runs E-W for 118ft (36m). 66ft (20m) north of the ring is:

B. *Central group* Here there are two small contiguous rings N-S of each other. The southern is about 34ft (10.1m) in diameter, its partner rather less, about 31ft (9.5m). All the stones are low. In the distance, 400 yds (36.5m) up the hillside is:

C. *Northern group* This is an eighteen-stone ring with an adjacent Three-Stone row. The ring is unusual. It is oval and markedly graded, measuring 33ft by 32ft 2ins (10.1 × 9.8m). The stones of its northern side are very low, almost hidden in the grass, but the four tallest in the southern arc are up to 2ft 8ins (0.8m) high.

A yard (1m) to the south-east is the row, NW-SE, 28ft 6ins (8.7m) long. Two stones still stand 2ft and 1ft 4ins (0.6, 0.4m) high. The third is prostrate and obscure in the grass.

In the Culvacullion complex are the ruins of a chambered tomb.

Chart, 224; McConkey, 58. *No plan*

292 DAVAGH LOWER (5, 4)
Lat: 54°.7   H 706 867
6³/₄ miles SW of Draperstown. In Davagh Forest Park. Walk. From lane at H 703 868 follow forest footpath SE

and E for ¹/₄ mile. Site is just N of path by Davagh Water. In trees. Fair. Map C
The major site here may be a despoiled ring-cairn rather than a true stone circle.

A. It is *an oval ring* 53ft (16.2m) across, but with its almost contiguous stones, 1ft 6ins to 2ft 6ins (0.5–0.8m) high, encircling what may have been a 6ft (2m) wide bank lined with inner slabs. There are many slabs missing at the north and east.

On its north side is a short tangential avenue, ENE-WSW, the south side of six stones in a 30ft (9m) long line, the west a meandering 44ft (13.4m) of ten stones.

B. 75ft (23m) to the north is *a ruined oval* about 33ft by 30ft (10 × 9m) which now appears to be a horseshoe open to the east. Alongside it is a collapsed Three-Stone row.

C. 40ft (12m) north-west of the possible ring-cairn is a collapsed *chambered tomb* with a 5ft (1.5m) square capstone. It stood in a circular cairn 20ft (6m) across.

Davies, 1939, 8, no. 21, *Plan*, 9

293 DOORAT (3) Lat: 54°.8   H 493 968
3¹/₂ miles N of Plumbridge. Walk. 200 yds (180m) W of the B48. Easy. Map C
There are two inconspicuous ovals here. At the east one about 39ft 4ins by 36ft (12 × 11m) consists of low rounded boulders about 6ins (15cm) high with one 1ft 2ins (36cm) tall at the east. The interior of the ring is slightly domed.

Beyond a possible cairn the second ring is 75ft (23m) to the west. Its twelve low stones surround an oval 31ft by 24ft 3ins (9.5 × 7.4m). Most of its stones are no more than 8ins (20cm) high but there is one twice that height at the NNW. A 26ft (7.9m) long Four-Stone row is tangential to the ring. To its west is a short pair of stones.

A quarter of a mile to the north-east, H 495 966, are the twenty-five stones of a 150ft (45.7m) long single row. A small cairn lies to its east. Nearby is a 4ft (1.2m) high standing stone.

Chart, 216; McConkey, 56. *No plan*

294 GLASSMULLAGH (3, 4)
Lat: 54°.7   H 387 804
*8¹⁄4 miles ESE of Castlederg, 5 miles NE
of Drumquin, 2³⁄4 miles W of a bend in
the River Strule. Walk. Follow a
footpath at H 387 798 N for ¹⁄4 mile.
Uphill but not over-steep. Fair. Map C*
Almost lost in the heather there are
four low circles of stones on edge and
two alignments here. The rings have
very similar diameters of about 26ft
(7.9m).

A. At the south are *two contiguous
ovals*, the west of ten 9ins (23cm) high
stones in a ring 25ft 7ins by 24ft 3ins
(7.8 × 7.4m). To the east its partner,
equally low, has fourteen stones, the
tallest at the south-west, in an irregular
ellipse 25ft by 24ft 8ins (7.6 × 7.5m).

B. Four feet (1.2m) to the NNE is the
central ring of thirty-one very closely-
set stones. It has the remains of a 26ft
(7.9m) long tangential row.

C. A further 15ft (4.6m) to the NNW
are twenty-one little stones in *an oval*
30ft NW-SE by 24ft 3ins (9.1 × 7.4m).

It contains two taller stones, each about
1ft 8ins (51cm) high, at the ESE and
NNE.

A pair of standing stones to the north
are 2ft 6ins (76cm) high.

Near the rings is the ruined
chambered tomb of Dermot and
Grania's Bed. It was excavated around
1900 by Lady Alexandra Hamilton
with no known results.

Some 300 yards (275m) west of the
rings was a fifth stone circle at H 386
805. It has been almost destroyed.

Chart, 231; McConkey, 61. *No plan*

295 MOYMORE (3, 4)
Lat: 54°.6   H 711 745
*6¹⁄2 miles WSW of Cookstown, 2 miles
NE of Pomeroy. To the W of Garagrim
mountain a farm lane runs NW . It
bends sharply to the E (Rt) at H 712
745. Walk. The circles are 200yds
(180m) to the W. Fair. Map C*
Astonishing. On the lower south-
western slopes of Garagrim mountain
this is an incredible example of
minilithic togetherness. 'Seven circles',

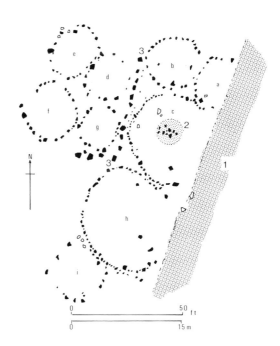

*Moymore, Co. Tyrone
(295) a-i. Rings; 1. Field
bank; 2. Cairn; 3. Stone
row*

0   50 ft
0   15 m

wrote Oliver Davies, 'six with tangential alignments, intertwined in such a way that it is difficult to sort them out accurately.' Huddled together like doughnuts on a tray, three of the nine circles, not seven, have been cut by a heavy field-bank that stretches SSW-NNE at the east of the group. The six rings to the west are intact.

A. At the north-east of the gaggle only the western half of a ring survives against the bank, a semi-circle of thirteen low, nudging stones with a diameter of 22ft 4ins (6.8m).

B. Touching it at the west is a complete oval, as buckled as anything at Beaghmore, 23ft 3ins E-W by 20ft (7.1 × 6.1m). Like all the other rings its stones are very low.

C. Abutting both A and B to its north is a large ellipse 38ft SE-NW by 35ft 9ins (11.6 × 10.9m). It has fifty-two almost contiguous stones about 10ins (25cm) high. At the centre are the disturbed stones of a small cairn. Immediately to the west of the circle and running from the western edge of A is a 44ft (13.4m) long row, NNE-SSW, of ten stones. Against it, to the west, is an unsymmetrical quadrilateral of four small rings.

D. The north-eastern of these is south-west of B and WNW of C. It is a good circle of sixteen stones, 19ft 8ins (6m) across. Fourteen of the stones are low but two stand 2ft (0.6m) high at the SSE and north-west.

E. Against D and to its north-east twenty-two low-set stones form an ellipse 22ft SW-NE by 18ft 9ins (6.7 × 5.7m). Two blocks, 1ft 6ins (0.5m) high stand well apart at the NNE and north-east.

F. To the south of this ring and against it twenty-six little stones form an uneasy oval 24ft 7ins SSW-NNE by 22ft 4ins (7.5 × 6.8m). The tallest stones are at the SSW.

G. To the east of F and between it and C is an oval 17ft SSW-NNE by 16ft (5.2 × 4.9m). It is constructed of nineteen low stones about 1ft 3ins (38cm) apart with the tallest, 1ft 10ins (56cm) high at the SSE. Below this ring

and tangential to it is a short Three-Stone row.

H. To the south of C is the biggest ring of all, its eastern arc wrecked by the bank. It was quite an elegant ellipse or egg-shape 46ft SSE-NNW by 40ft 7ins (14 × 12.4m). Of its fifty-three visible stones the tallest, 1ft 6ins (0.5m) high, stands at the southern end of the long axis. There are vague signs of a central cairn. The SSW end of the long single row ends against the north-western arc of this ring.

I. Finally, against the south-west arc of H is a strangely-shaped ring like a horseshoe open to the north-west but with a straight line of stones across its mouth. It measures 24ft SE-NW by 21ft 4ins (7.3 × 6.5m). As if this were not enough, several stones to the south-west of H may be all that is left of a tenth ring.

It must be assumed that the complex is the result of ring being added to ring over the decades and the way in which the long row, perhaps originally a tangential line to H, is now squashed between B and D and G and C lends credence to this belief. The Moymore rings may have been accretions to a simple ring with an internal cairn.

But certainly, as Davies observed of Clogherny Meenerrigal (288), there are no niceties of design in these casual rings. Even if they were set out by eye, it was on the morning after the night before.

Chart, 238; McConkey, 64, *Plan*, fig. 9

296 SCRAGHY (3)

Lat: 54°.6   H 208 743
7¹/₂ miles SSW of Castlederg, 7¹/₂ miles W of Drumquin. Walk. A footpath at 209 741 leads NNW for 170yds (156m). Very easy. Map C

The 'Druid's Circle' is a popular site. Its low, grey stones are very obvious alongside the footpath. They are heavy boulders, well spaced, about 2ft (0.6m) high, in a ring 60ft (18.2m) across. The tallest, 2ft 8ins high and over 3ft wide (0.8 × 1m) stands at the ESE. A drain passes through the circle.

To the south of the ring, in a field, are some stones which may be the remnants of a concentric stone circle. Chart, 234; McConkey, 63. *No plan*

297 TREMOGE NE (3)

Lat: 54°.6   H 657 736
10½ miles wsw of Cookstown, 2½ miles ene of Carrickmore. Walk. Just n of a lane to the n of Crocknakesha. e of an old cottage. Easy. Map C
There are the disturbed stones of two circles, both about 30ft (9m) in diameter. The east has nine stones and a stump, the west ten stones.

250ft (76m) to the north-west is a fallen row of seven stones, SSE-NNW. Four smaller stones lie by it.

A ruinous egg-shaped ring, 28ft 10ins ESE-WNW by 24ft 3ins (8.8 × 7.4m) of twenty-two low stones is close to the rings. By its south-east is a low Four-Stone row, SE-NW, 11ft (3.4m) long. Parallel to it, 1ft 6ins (46cm) to the west, is a 36ft (11m) long line of seven taller stones. There may be an overgrown cairn to its NNW.
Chart, 238; McConkey, 65, *Plan*, fig. 47

298 TREMOGE SW (3)

Lat: 54°.6   H 654 733
480 yds (440m) sw of Tremoge ne. Walk. Drive w from Tremoge ne for 500 yds (450m). Turn s (Lt) down farm track. 300 yds (275m) ring is 200 yds (180m) to the e. Easy. Map C
There are two adjacent rings here.

A. *The eastern* consists of twenty-seven stones, most about 10ins (25cm) high but with one 1ft 3ins (38cm) tall at the WNW. The diameter of the uneven circle is 34ft 6ins (10.5m).

A double 'high-and-low' row extends brokenly to the north side of the ring. One side is a Three-Stone row with stones 3ft, 1ft 9ins and 8ins (91, 53, 20cm) high. The row is 11ft 2ins (3.4m) long.

Parallel to it is a longer line, 40ft (12.2m) in length, whose stones are no more than 6ins (15cm) high.

B. Sixteen feet (4.9m) north-west of the eastern ring is *a broken western arc* of a ring about 15ft (4.6m) across.

C. At H 664 736 is *a spacious ring* of twenty-two stones, many known only by probing, in an ellipse 60ft by 36ft (18.3 × 11m). There is a wide gap at its south.
Davies, 8, Fig. 4; Chart, 239; McConkey, 65, *Plan*, fig. 46

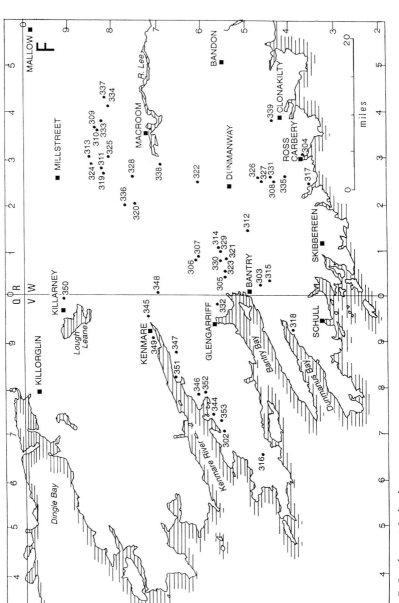

Map F, South-west Ireland

Republic of Ireland

Co. CAVAN

Around Killycluggin and in the adjacent townlands of Kilnavert and Lissanover, a triangle of hardly 600 acres just w of the River Woodford, are many circles, mostly small, of boulders on the tops of low hills. Some surround burial chambers. Tradition claims that it was in Co. Cavan that the stone circle, Crom Cruaich, was thrown down by St Patrick

299 CROM CRUAICH (destroyed)
Lat: c. 54°.1
Perhaps centred on H 25. 15. Map 2
On Magh Sleacht, 'the plain of tombs'– hence Moylett or Moylat near Bailieborough – by repute this was a centre of heathenism. 'It is generally supposed to have been the plain round about Kilnavert ['the church of graves'] and Killycluggin.'

Crom Cruaich or Crom Dubh was a circle of twelve stones with a much taller central pillar 'clad in gold and silver'. It was associated with the festival of Lughnasa, the harvest celebration in early August.

On the approach of St Patrick to this pagan place the decorated stone, Crom Cruaich, fell down, and the circle-stones sank into the ground up to their necks. Their collapse did not satisfy the saint. Destruction was demanded. 'He plied upon Crom a sledge[-hammer], from top to toe; with no paltry prowess he ousted the strengthless goblin that stood there.'

From the account John Aubrey deduced that the circle, and others, must have been pre-Christian. 'We may

from hence infer, that this Circle of Stones . . . was before the planting of Christianity in this Country a place of Idolatrous worship.'

Aubrey, I, 123; A. Ross, *The Pagan Celts*, 1986, 118

300 KILLYCLUGGIN (3)
Lat: 54°.1   H 239 160
8 miles w of Belturbet, 2¾ miles sw of Ballyconnell. Walk. 220 yds (200m) E of Killycluggin. Easy. Map 2
On the summit of a rounded hillock seven of the fifteen stones in this ring are prostrate. Those that stand are on the perimeter of a good circle, 75ft 6ins (23m) in diameter. Previous computations of 100ft and 60ft × 40ft (31, 18.2 × 12.2m) are mistaken.

Two great slabs lying at the north-east, their pointed bases just inside the circumference, may have formed an impressive entrance. This neglected site is further spoiled by the ditch-and-bank field boundary that passes through its western sector.

The site is important because of its association with a decorated Iron Age stele – a column, frequently carved with motifs – like others known in Ireland at Castlestrange, Co. Roscommon; Derrykeighan, Co. Antrim; Mullaghmast, Co. Kildare; and Turoe, Co. Galway.

In the early 1920s at Killycluggin part of the stele's engraved base was found carefully buried 30ft (9m) downslope, south-east of the ring. In the 1950s another piece, probably the domed top, was discovered a little way away. Both had been smashed 'by deliberate and systematic hammering'. They did not fit together but their respective lengths meant that the pillar must have been at least 6ft (1.8m) long exceeding the 5ft 6ins (1.7m) of the Turoe Stone.

Such decorated pillars have been likened to the stelae of Brittany such as the Kermaria Stone, Pont l'Abbé, Finistère, but the comparison is not close and it is more feasible that the stones in Ireland are native in origin of the first centuries BC and AD.

Excavation at Killycluggin in 1974 and the removal of the stele's fragments to the National Museum of Ireland, Dublin, elicted the observation that such heavy, cumbersome blocks were unlikely to have been moved far and surely not uphill. It is tempting, therefore, to think that the beautifully-carved stone with its swirling lines and spirals may have been dragged from the circle a few yards away.

Tradition claimed that it had been broken up by local farmers in the early twentieth century. There is another explanation. 'It may not impossibly have been', wrote Macalister, 'the work of people who lived so early that Iron Age paganism was not yet forgotten, and when it would seem both desirable and laudable to destroy pagan monuments.'

An ancient Irish poem mentions the stone circle of Crom Cruaich.

> Till Patrick came, they served a stone,
> And worshipped it within that space.
> . . . With heavy maul
> He smashed the paltry gods each one,
> With valorous blows destroyed them all,
> Nor left a fragment 'neath the sun.

Sir Thomas Browne in *Hydriotaphia* philosophised that 'What Song the *Sirens* sang, or what name *Achilles* assumed when he hid himself among women, though puzzling Questions, are not beyond all conjecture.' Despite his optimism the identification of Killycluggin as Crom Cruaich, if not beyond conjecture, is certainly beyond proof.

JRSAI 52, 1922, 113–16; ibid 82, 1954, 68; UJA 41, 1978, 49–54, Plan

301 KILNAVERT (5)

Lat: 54°.1   H 235 152

8½ miles W of Belturbet, 3½ miles SW of Ballyconnell. Walk. 200 yds (180m) W of minor lane from Killycluggin to Toberlyan. Fair. Map 2

The status of this ruinous site is questionable. On a ridge above peaty ground there is a low round cairn with stretches of kerbing at its south-east and west. It is 27ft (8.2m) across and surrounded by a rock-cut ditch with an outer bank. Close to it is a plain, open ring of almost contiguous stones. It is 41ft (12.5m) in diameter. It could be the remains of a second but denuded cairn.

Oliver Davies visited the site. Debating the origins of stone circles he wrote, 'I have seen at Kilnavert a circular cairn with ditch and marked kerb close to a stone circle. Transitional forms may be discovered in this or another district outside the Six Counties of Northern Ireland.'

JRSAI 68, 1938, 112, Plan

Co. CORK

There is a wealth of circles in this county. They range from large coastal rings with recumbent stones to smaller rings of five stones, also with recumbents, inland in the hills. Amongst them are a few Four-Posters similar to those in north-eastern Scotland. Some rings have radial cairns or tangential rows by them, and some enclose boulder-burials

302 ARDGROOM SW, NE (3)

Lat: 51°.8   V 707 553

5 miles SW of Lauragh, 1¼ miles ENE of Ardgroom. Ignore misleading signposts. From Ardgroom take lane east from Holly Tree pub and in a mile take first track to the S (Rt). Leave car just along track. Walk to gate, about ¼ mile, turn SE across reedy ground. Fair. Map F

A. Also known as Canfea, this is a fine though aberrant recumbent stone circle, its rather idiosyncratic design perhaps deriving from its position forty miles west of the fine group around Ross

Carbery (304, 317, 326, 327, 331, 335).

The thin grey stones are very tall, from 4ft 6ins up to 6ft 6ins (1.4–2m) high at the NNE portals. Nine still stand and two are fallen in a ring about 23ft 9ins (7.2m) in diameter. Gaps at the west and south-east may be the outcome of pillars being removed for gateposts.

The stones are well graded down to the SSW recumbent but this is a perplexing choice for what is normally a flat-topped slab. At Ardgroom it is tall, 4ft (1.2m) high, thin and sharply peaked, almost a lozenge in shape.

Some 20ft (6m) to the east is a 'playing-card' outlier, 8ft 3ins high, 6ft wide but only 1ft 4ins thick (2.5, 1.8, 0.4m), its long sides aligned on the south arc of the ring.

B. *Ardgroom NE*, V 728 563, is a ruined recumbent stone circle.

O'Nuallain, 1984a, 18, no. 21, *Plan 60*

303 BAURGORM NE, SW (3)
Lat: 51°.7   W 023 469
2 miles SE of Bantry. On the road SE

from Bantry to Cullomane cross-roads, at W 021 471 take side-lane SW for ½ mile. Ring is 200yds (180m) W of lane. Fair. Map F

A. This Five-Stone ring stands on a patch of level ground. In a circle about 8ft 3ins (2.5m) across the north-east stone has fallen. The portals are nearly 5ft (1.5m) apart. The western is split. The stones are graded down to the recumbent at the south-west.

About 14ft (4.3m) to the south is a pair of tall stones. One is prostrate. The other is 5ft 6ins (1.7m) high.

B. *Baurgorm SW*, at W 014 460, is another Five-Stone ring.

O'Nuallain, 1984a, 42–3, no. 85, *Plan, 67*

304 BOHONAGH (3)
Lat: 51°.6   W 308 368
1½ miles E of Ross Carbery. At Temple Bridge on the L42, H 302 364, turn N on lane to Quakers Cross Roads. In 300yds (275m) there is a garden centre on the east. Walk. Up the field to the south, Not the north, of the centre. Uphill 150yds (137m). Easy. Map F
Pronounced 'beau-nag' the name may

Bohonagh, Co. Cork (304), from the south-west.

mean 'place abundant in cattle' or 'yellow stream'. Bohonagh is one of the most impressive of all the Cork-Kerry recumbent stone circles. It stands on level ground with long views to the south and the sea and also to the north. The ring was excavated in 1959.

On a site stripped of its turf thirteen stones were erected in a ring 32ft 4ins (9.9m) across. Today nine remain, high and heavy blocks, dark grey and speckled with quartz inclusions.

Near the east two tall portals, about 8ft (2.4m) high, stand radially to the circumference. Opposite them the recumbent is a squat, chubby, flat-topped boulder like an old white loaf thick with currants. No hole was quarried into the bedrock for it. Instead it was laid on the ground with some chock-stones to hold it steady. Nearly 4ft 6ins (1.4m) high, it is flanked by a very low stone to its north but a very high one to the south whose top, like an inverted guillotine blade, slopes not down but up to the recumbent.

A stone at the north is supported by a large quartz fragment. A stonehole opposite at the south contains more quartz. A huge, pear-shaped boulder lies 20ft (6m) to the south-east of the ring, 15ft (4.6m) long and with a bulbous base 7ft 6ins (2.3m) wide. It is cupmarked.

Astronomical analyses have suggested that the E-W axis from the portals to the recumbent is in line with the equinoctial sunsets but the orientation is not very accurate and there is no feature on the western skyline to confirm this theory.

Excavation of a disturbed mound at the centre of the ring discovered an irregular and shallow pit in which only charcoal, some cremated bone and pebbles remained.

Nine yards (8.2m) to the south of the circle were twenty-one postholes of a rectangular hut 23ft by 10ft (7 × 3.1m). To the east is a boulder-burial with an enormous capstone weighing almost 20 tons. On its upper surface can be detected seven faint cupmarks.

JCHAS 66, 1961, 93–104, *Plan*, 93

305 BREENY MORE (4)

Lat: 51°.8   W 050 552

11 miles WNW of Dunmanway, 5 miles NNE of Bantry. Walk. 200 yds (180m) W of lane from Kealkil to Ardrah. Easy. On private land. Ask. Map F

This wrecked ring was set up on level ground from which the land falls steeply to west and north-west. It provides a splendid view of Bantry Bay. The ring has been devastated. Even the sign pronouncing that it is in State care has been uprooted.

The stone circle would have been about 46ft (14m) in diameter. Various stones lie in disorder around it, their sides striated as though scratched by some gigantic fork. Only three are erect. Two portals stand at the NNE, 6ft (1.8m) apart, the west 6ft high, its partner 6ft 6ins (1.8, 2m). Both have sloping tops that descend towards each other.

Opposite them is the recumbent, leaning inwards and almost prostrate. It is flat-topped, 5ft 3ins long and just over 3ft high (1.6, 1m).

Inside the ring, astride the axis but not centrally placed is a rectangle of four boulder-burials.

To the north-east, about a quarter of a mile away, is the neat Five-Stone circle of Kealkil (323).

O'Nuallain, 1984a, 19, no. 24, *Plan,* 57

306 CAPPABOY BEG NW (3)

Lat: 51°.8   W 082 612

10½ miles NW of Dunmanway, 4 miles NNE of Kealkil. At W 072 600 a lane climbs NE for a mile. Walk. Circle is at end on W. Easy. Map F

This is a diminutive but pleasantly constructed Five-Stone ring, its stones graded in height from heavy portals at the north-east to the rectangular, flat-topped recumbent at the south-west. The ring is slightly flattened, 7ft 6ins NE-SW by 5ft 10ins (2.3 × 1.8m), its stones ranging in height from 2ft to 3ft (0.6–0.9m).

There is a long view down the valley beyond it. Cappaboy Beg SE is a mile to the ESE.

O'Nuallain, 1984a, 39, no. 77, *Plan*, 66

307 CAPPABOY BEG SE (3)
Lat: 51°.8   W 097 604
10 miles NW of Dunmanway, 4 miles NE of Kealkil. Walk. From the T64, about 275 yds (250m) SW of Cappaboy school a lane and track on the W leads windingly N, W, N uphill for ¼ mile. Turn E through gate for ¼ mile. Climb low wall. Ring is in rough moorland. Hard going in hot weather. Map F
This an attractive complex of a weird Four-Poster, a radial-cairn, and a pair of standing stones.

The Four-Poster lies at the edge of a terrace falling to the east. There is high ground to west and north. The 'ring' is an irregular trapezoid about 14ft 9ins by 7ft 10ins (4.5 × 2.4m) with a towering block 9ft 2ins (2.8m) high at the north-east. There is a 4ft 3ins (1.3m) high stone at the south-west and two lower, each about 3ft (1m) high, at the other corners. A 4ft (1.2m) high, rectangular and flat-topped outlier stands 75ft (23m) to the south-east.

Across the waving matting of grass and rushes a radial-cairn and an outlier can be found 200 yards (180m) to the north-east and there is a pair of standing stones 110 yards (100m) to the south-west.

O'Nuallain, 1984b, 69, no. 1, *Plan*, 68

308 CARRIGAGRENANE (Unseeable)
Lat: 51°.6   W 254 432
6 miles SSE of Dunmanway. Map F
Despite its fame this fine recumbent stone circle, 'the rock of the house of the sun', about 31ft (9.5m) in diameter and with detached radial portals, is now completely overgrown in thick undergrowth and a visit is unmerited unless for authorised clearance.
JRSAI 35, 1930, 81–3, Plan

309 CARRIGAGULLA NE (3)
Lat: 52°.0   W 371 838
7½ miles SE of Millstreet, 7 miles NNE of Macroom. From Macroom take N road
for 6 miles to Ballynagree. In 1 mile take lane on W (Lt) going NNW for ½ mile. Park near gate overshadowed by trees. Walk 300 yds (275m) further N along lane. Forestry track on E (Rt) leads ¼ mile into plantation. Ring is 100 yds (90m) NE from SW corner of plantation. Into new growth marred by deep forestry ditches. Quite difficult. Map F
This is a fine Five-Stone ring, its low stones almost lost in the long, reedy grass. About 10ft (3m) across it has radial portals at the north-east 3ft 9ins and 4ft (1.1, 1.2m) high. They are thin slabs that loom over the small recumbent, almost flat-topped, but crumpled like a half-deflated football. The ring stands near the edge of a terrace with the land falling to the north-east.

O'Nuallain, 1984a, 32–3, no. 56, *Plan*, 66

310 CARRIGAGULLA SW (1)
Lat: 52°.0   W 370 834
As for Carrigagulla NE. Walk. At overshadowed gate walk into field to the E. 220 yds (200m) ENE. Easy. Map F
On the gentle lower slope of the field this is one of many megalithic delights in south-western Ireland. It is a lovely recumbent stone circle. 'The circle is the largest and best-preserved that I have yet seen', wrote Condon in 1917. It is true.

The stones are low, the recumbent long, and the ring is almost perfect, fifteen of an original seventeen stones still standing in a circle about 30ft (9m) across. The portals, each about 2ft 10ins (0.9m) high, stand radially 'like the entrance, the side-posts of a doorway'. From them the stones are nicely graded down to the recumbent a level-topped slab 1ft 4ins high but 5ft 6ins (0.4, 1.7m) long.

A 'central' block, 1ft 4ins (0.4m) high lies on the NE-SW axis, a little nearer to the recumbent than to the portals.

O'Nuallain, 1984a, 12, no. 4, *Plan*, 55

Carrigagulla sw, Co. Cork (310), from the south.

311 CARRIGANIMMY (1)
Lat: 52°.0   W 293 827
6¼ miles NNW of Macroom, 5 miles SSE
of Millstreet, 1 mile N of Carriganimmy
village on the W slope of Musherabeg
mountain. In Carriganimmy take the
lane immediately E of the Creamery. It
winds NNE for ½ mile. Take new
Forestry road NE at fork. In ½ mile
leave car. Walk. Nearly ½ mile uphill
along NE track with walled fields to the
W. At end of fields turn NW for ½ mile.
Still uphill. Hard going but worth it.
Map F
This beautiful Five-Stone ring stands at
the edge of a terrace falling steeply to
the south with fine views along the
valley. It is a typical example of the
little circles in the hills of northern
Cork. Only 10ft 10ins (3.3m) across its
stones are markedly graded in height.
Two thin, flat-topped portals, each
about 4ft (1.2m) high, face the long,
low, thicker recumbent at the south-
west with a azimuth of 217° and a
possibly lunar declination of -29°.5.
Nineteen feet (5.8m) to the south-east
of the ring is a flat-topped 3ft 7ins
(1.1m) high outlier.
   In late summer the site is a mass of
cotton flowers, pink heather and small
yellow blooms like tiny celandines.
Attractive.
   O'Nuallain, 1984a, 32, no. 55, *Plan,*
67

312 CLODAGH (3)
Lat: 51°.7   W 152 499
5 miles WSW of Dunmanway, 3 miles NE
of Drimoleague. On the E of the lane at
the junction of roads from Dunmanway
to Castle Donovan, W, and
Shroneacarton crossroads, S. Walk. In a
large field on the low hill 400yds
(365m) S of the junction. Fair. Map F
Sometimes known as Pookeen, 'the
place of fairies or witches', this is a
good Five-Stone ring with an
outlying pair of stones. Although field-
stones have been dumped inside it the
site is in good condition. With an 8ft
(2.4m) long axis two flat-topped
portals, 4ft 3ins (1.3m) high, and two
circle-stones slope down to the level
recumbent at the south-west. The pair
of stones extend to the south-west
beyond it. A second pair is nearer to
the junction.
   O'Nuallain, 1984a, 43, no. 88, *Plan,*
18

313 CLOGHBOOLA BEG (3)
Lat: 52°.0   W 305 853
8 miles N of Macroom, 3½ miles SSE of
Millstreet. At W 285 855 on lane SSE
from Millstreet turn E downhill on new
road ¾ mile to cattlesheds. Walk. S for
300 yds (275m). Easy. Map F
At the edge of a terrace falling to the
south-west is a damaged Five-Stone
ring. It is elliptical, 12ft 9ins NNE-SSW
by 9ft 2ins (3.9 × 2.8m). It has
radially-set portals and, opposite them,
a paradoxically taller recumbent with a
peaked top. The north-west stone is
now lying between the portals and the
stone at the south-east.
    23ft (7m) to the south is a radial-
cairn, 22ft (6.7m) across, of low but
conspicuous kerbs. About 12ft (3.7m)
to the north-east is a low outlier. Other
large stones prostrate near the cairn
may be the remains of a fallen row.
    O'Nuallain, 1984a, 31, no. 53, *Plan*,
70

314 COUSANE (3)
Lat: 51°.8   W 113 568
7½ miles WNW of Dunmanway, 6½
miles N of Drimoleague. Walk. ¼ mile.
On L40 at W 101 562 take track going
NE immediately before house to W. Skirt
fields to W. Onto moor. Easy. Map F
On a low hillock this is a well-
preserved Five-Stone ring. Its grading is
poor and it is difficult to distinguish the
recumbent from the other stones. It
squats at the western end of the long
axis, 10ft 6ins (E-W) by 7ft 10ins (3.2
× 2.4m). The stone opposite is
exceptionally flat-topped.
    In the field to the south-west is a
standing stone.
    O'Nuallain, 1984a, 40, no. 79, *Plan*,
66

315 CULLOMANE E (3)
Lat: 51°.7   W 035 455
13 miles WSW of Dunmanway, 3½ miles
SE of Bantry. At W 024 449 on the T65
take the lane to the S. In ½ mile it
swings to the E. An old lane W of the
farm peters out in 200 yds (180m) in a
field. Walk. Ring is at the W end. Easy.
Map F

This is a well-preserved Five-Stone ring
but its east portal and the next stone
are embedded in a bushy field-bank.
The ring measures 12ft 9ins NE-SW by
11ft 2ins (3.9 × 3.4m). Its stones are
from 3ft to 4ft (1–1.2m) high.
    On a knoll 110 yards (100m) to the
north-east is a 3ft (0.9m) high standing
stone curiously shaped like an
inquisitive walrus.
    In a triangular field to the west is a
standing stone, a cairn and a boulder-
burial.
    The name of Cullomane derives from
St Colman and until late in the
nineteenth century pilgrimages were
made in early May, the pagan festival
of Beltane, to his well in the west field.
The 'well' is now no more than a dry
hollow.
    O'Nuallain, 1984a, 42, no. 84, *Plan*,
66

316 DERREENATAGGART (3)
Lat: 51°.7   V 665 465
5½ miles SSW of Ardgroom, 1 mile NW
of Castletown Bearhaven. From there,
at V 672 458 take lane NW for ¾ mile.
Walk. Just past side-lane to W circle is
in a field 200 yds (180m) from lane.
Easy. Map F
This is almost a classic recumbent stone
circle. Only its orientation is unusual.
    Of a probable fifteen original
standing stones, light-grey mottled thin
slabs, nine are erect, three are down at
the west and three are missing. The
ring, a true circle, has a diameter of
27ft 10ins (8.5m).
    One of the portals is broken and no
more than a stump but the other is a
full 7ft 9ins (2.4m) high. The ring is
graded and the stones flanking the
recumbent have tops sloping down to
it.
    The recumbent is slightly domed, 4ft
3ins high and a wide 7ft 3ins (1.3 ×
2.2m) in length. It lies almost due west,
273°, but the hills behind it are high
and the declination is an un-equinoctial
5°.
    In the next field, which is difficult to
enter, there is a *fulacht fiadh* or ancient
cooking-place.

O'Nuallain, 1984a, 20, no. 26, *Plan*, 53

317 DROMBEG (1)
Lat: 51°.6   W 247 352
10 miles wsw of Clonakilty, 3 miles w of Ross Carbery, 1½ miles E of Glandore. On Ross Carbery-Glandore road at W 249 357 turn S. Take lane for ¾ mile. Parking. In State care, no charge. Short walk. Map F

Drombeg, 'the small ridge', also known as the Druid's Altar, is the best-known of the Irish recumbent stone circles and is one of the most interesting to visit because of the excavations of 1957 and 1958. It occupies the edge of a terrace from which the land falls to the south and west. There is a beautiful view to the sea a mile away.

Turf had been stripped and the site had been levelled, natural hollows being filled in with small stones and a shelf raised at the west, to create a horizontal platform. On this seventeen pillars of smooth-sided local sandstone were erected in a good circle 31ft (9.5m) in diameter. Their stoneholes were carefully dug to ensure the correct grading of the stones down from the entrance at the north-east. There, the portals, the western flat-topped and thick, the eastern more slender and with a pointed top, each stood 6ft 7ins (2m) high.

In sunlight the honey-coloured stones glow warmly in contrast to the grey recumbent which is darkly sombre, as though aware of its grim reputation as a sacrificial altar.

The angled tops of the circle-stones were shaped to point up to that block at the south-west. Like Bohonagh it had no prepared pit. Instead, it rested on the ground, held firm by underlying stones. It is not massive, 3ft high and 7ft long (1, 2.1m), but tapering away to the north. It has a very flat upper surface on which there is a cupmark inside what may be an axe-carving. A second cupmark is close to it. As usual with such art in stone circles the midpoint of the recumbent was set in line with a celestial event. As long ago

as 1908 Boyle Somerville calculated that with a south-western skyline nearly 3° high 'the winter solstitial sunset is . . . observable from the recumbent stone in a very conspicuous notch in the hills distant about a mile'. The alignment is good but not precise.

Most of the circle-stones were tall, sloping-topped rectangles, averaging 5ft 9ins (1.8m) in height. Because of this the excavator believed that the smallest stone, a pillar at the north, only 3ft 7ins high and 10ins wide (1.1m, 25cm), entirely different from the others, was a phallic symbol. It stood erect alongside a high 'female' lozenge at the NNW, 4ft 9ins high and 5ft 3ins wide (1.5, 1.6m) across its waist.

About 44 yards (40m) to the west of the circle, sheltered by higher ground, are the untended remains of two stone-built prehistoric huts joined by a common doorway. The eastern, nearer the ring, which had been preceded by a timber shelter, had a rectangular oven. The western, 15ft (4.6m) across, was linked by a paved way to a *fulacht fiadh*, a few paces to its south, a rectangular, flagged cooking-trough with an adjacent hearth for heating stones. There was a drain and a well to provide the water. Experiments demonstrated that by leaving stones in the fire until they were red-hot and then gradually adding them to seventy or more gallons of water a boiling temperature could be reached in eighteen minutes and sustained for almost three hours. More recent tests elsewhere confirmed this. After two hours in the water joints of lamb and venison were tenderly delicious.

At the recumbent stone circle the discovery of internal pits, broken pottery and cremated human bone makes it possible to imagine – but not prove – the initial ceremonies at Drombeg.

Nearby there had been a pyre on which the body of an adolescent had been consumed. The cremated bones had been raked up and placed in an already broken pot, its base missing, wrapped round with thick cloth. This

Drombeg, Co. Cork (317), from the north-west. The recumbent is the low, flat-topped slab at the right of the ring.

dedicatory offering, perhaps a sacrifice, was taken to a shallow pit near the middle of the ring where it was buried with eighty other deliberately smashed, poorly-fired sherds, four bits of shale, a collection of sweepings from the pyre recalling similar deposits at the recumbent stone circle of Loanhead of Daviot (106) in Aberdeenshire. A smaller pit to the north held dark soil.

Needing fertile soil and good harvests the people of Drombeg turned to the forces of nature, supplicating them in a ring with its symbolism of fecundity. They offered human remains, rich dark soil, and they covered the offerings under a 4ins (10cm) thick layer of gravel. The compacted earth and trodden pebbles at the entrance showed how for generations descendants had returned at midwinter to reaffirm their need for protection.

Dates from Drombeg have been consistently misleading. Charcoal dated to 13 ± 140 bc (TCD-38) was unhelpfully recalculated to AD 600 ± 120 (D-62). A more recent C-14 assay of 790 ± 80 bc (OxA-2683) agrees 'well with other radiocarbon dates obtained from undecorated, coarse LBA pottery'. Concomitant dates from Reanascreena (335) and Cashelkeelty (344) indicate that the ring is much later than previously believed.

In September, 1935, Boyle Somerville returned to Drombeg with a psychic, Miss Geraldine Cummings. She did not like the place. She felt it was a centre of nature and sun worship conjoined with the moon, a place where animals, if not small children, were sacrificed at each winter solstice. She 'saw' a priest in blue and saffron robes standing at the altar of the recumbent about to kill his human offering.

There were weekly ceremonies but 'the great Day of the Blood Sacrifice was near the end of December. Then horrible things were practised in the twilight. There were strange dances in which men and women stabbed each other in a frenzy. There was an abandonment in action and behaviour which I may not describe.' Drombeg was cursed. It was 'guarded by the spirits of darkness'.

Bring garlic, a cross and lots of friends.

JCHAS 64, 1959, 1–27, *Plans* 2,4; *ibid* 65, 1960, 1–17, *Plan* 4; *The Ley Hunter* 90, 1981, 10–11

318 DUNBEACON (3)
Lat: 51°.6   V 927 392
7½ miles sw of Bantry, 4¾ miles N of Schull. From L56 just sw of Blair's Cove a track at V939 404 runs s, soon turns w then sse for about ½ mile. To E a fine pair of standing stones. Circle is on w of track, 6 fields, ¼ mile. Fair. Map F
On a terrace of Mount Corin on the south side of Dunmanus Bay this recumbent stone circle is the only one on a peninsula that is dominated by the prehistoric copper mine of Mount Gabriel. The ring stands in fields on a bare hillside.

It is ruinous. Of its eleven tall stones only six still stand on the circumference of a ring about 26ft (8m) in diameter. The flankers are down and there is a small recumbent. The impressive uprights, grey, wrinkled slabs, are between 5ft 3ins and 6ft 3ins (1.6–1.9m) high. Near the centre of the ring is a squarish slab leaning badly.

The pair of standing stones at Coolcoulaghta to the left of the church, 380 yards (348m) east of the ring, 5ft 7ins (1.7m) high, were pulled down but re-erected after a public outcry. They stand NE-SW.

O'Nuallain, 1984a, 22, no. 32, *Plan*, 52

319 GLANTANE SW (3)
Lat: 52°.0   W 280 833
19 miles sw of Mallow, 4½ miles s of Millstreet. From Carriganimmy take L41 w and in ½ mile turn N onto lane. Ignore 1st E (Rt) but ¾ mile later turn NE for 300yds (275m). Walk. Along drive to w for 100yds (75m). Easy. Map F
Almost absorbed in the verdant undergrowth like Marvell's 'green thought in a green shade', this recumbent stone circle is half-camouflaged in the thick, lush grass of a walled and tree-planted enclosure. Its stones are green with moss, declining in

height from its heavy but low portals at the north down to the lowest of all, the recumbent whose surface has been manually shaped into a dome. The ring is small, hardly 16ft (5m) across and the stones are equally small, from 2ft to 3ft (0.6–0.9m) high.

The remains of the nearby Glantane NE wedge-tomb and a ditched recumbent stone circle at W 281 839 have been destroyed.

O'Nuallain. 1984a, 12, no. 3, *Plan*, 52

320 GORTANIMILL (1)
Lat: 51°.9   W 208 741
11 miles ssw of Millstreet, 8 miles w of Macroom. From Ballymakeery, w 21.61., take the T29 E. In 1 mile turn s and take the w fork for 1½ miles. Leave car at fork. Walk. Circle is 150yds (137m) se at foot of slope in rough ground. Fair. Map F
Immediately and oddly to the north of a 12ft (3.7m) high ridge Gortanimill is like a recumbent stone circle that has forgotten its ancestry. The portals of this very neat ring differ in width more than they do in height and, opposite them, the recumbent is almost lost in the swirling, draping grass. There is a vividly white stone inside the ring.

The circle is about 25ft (7.6m) across. The western portal stands 2ft 6ins tall and is 2ft wide (0.8 × 0.6m). The eastern is 2ft 2ins high but is 3ft 3ins wide (0.7 × 1m). On the far side of the ring, at the ssw, the 3ft 3ins (1m) long recumbent is hardly 7ins (18cm) high. As usual, the quartz 'centre' slab, no more than 8ins (20cm) high, lies on the axis but a little to the ssw of the middle of the ring. A piece, perhaps broken from it, lies nearby.

With the rising ground so close behind it the recumbent lies well in line with the midwinter sunset and this may explain the uncommon choice of situation.

O'Nuallain, 1984a, 14, no. 10, *Plan*, 55

321 GORTNACOWLY (3)
Lat: 51°.8   W 088 543

Gortanimill, Co. Cork (320), from the south-west. The long but very low recumbent is concealed by reedy grass in the gap between the two little stones at the front of the ring. Notice the tiny centre stone.

9 miles w of Dunmanway, 7 miles NE of Bantry. 1 mile E of Ardrah school in field just N of the lane. Easy. Map F
At the edge of land falling to the north-west in a pasture field were 'Four standing stones of Druidical Antiquity'. This Four-Poster has now been 'christianised' by the removal of its south-eastern stone.

It is an outstanding site. The WSW pillar is massive, 10ft high, 5ft wide and 2ft 7ins thick (3.1, 1.5, 0.8m). The other stones also are tall, the north-east 7ft 6ins, the south 6ft 6ins (2.3, 2m). In plan they form a trapezoid some 12ft 6ins by 9ft 2ins (3.8 × 2.8m).

O'Nuallain, 1984b, 69, no. 2, *Plan*, 70

stones, none of them high, form a ring 28ft (8.5m) in diameter. They are crudely graded up to the south, from 6ins up to 1ft 6ins (15, 46cm), all of them flat-topped except the two at the south which are peaked, the SSE 3ft 3ins in height (1m), the SSW the same but leaning inwards.

Inside the circle is a very visible ditch. There are three modern, untidy pits on the central plateau.

Just outside the ring to the south-west is a 6ft (1.8m) long prostrate slab of quartz. When erect it would have stood in line with a distinct saddle in the distant hills.

O'Nuallain, 1984a, 17, no. 18, *Plan*, 60

322 GORTROE (3)
Lat: 51°.8   W 259 605
5½ miles NNE of Dunmanway. 200 yds (180m) w of the L58. Easy. Map F
This is a strange ring that does not conform to the norm of stone circle architecture in south-western Ireland. Against barbed-wire and in rough country among the hills, up to ten grey

323 KEALKIL (1)
Lat: 51°.8   W 055 555
11 miles w of Dunmanway, 6 miles NNE of Bantry. Signposted. ¾ mile ESE of Kealkil. Take lane to E up steep hill. Near top two weathered stone gateposts stand on the N (Lt). Walk through. 200 yds (180m) across rough ground. Easy. Map F

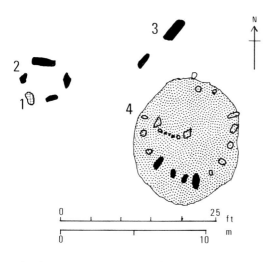

Kealkil, Co. Cork (323). 1. recumbent stone; 2. 5-Stone circle; 3. pair of standing stones; 4. radial-cairn

This famous Five-Stone ring, 'the narrow wood', stands on the shoulder of Maughanclea Hill. It is one of many similar rings built near patches of thin light soil suitable for cultivation, but it is one of only three sites, Knocknakilla (324) and Knockraheen (325) being the others, where a Five-Stone ring is associated both with a pair of standing stones and a radially-kerbed cairn.

It was believed that the recumbent slab lay atypically at the north but, as is customary, the sometimes leprously white, sometimes pinkish stones decline in height towards the true recumbent that O'Nuallain recognised to be the low slab at the south-west.

The ring is 9ft 3ins NE-SW by 7ft 10ins (2.8 × 2.4m). The portals, like those at Gortanimill, differ greatly in width, the western 4ft (1.2m) across, the eastern a mere 1ft 6ins (0.5m). Both stand 4ft (1.2m) high. The recumbent is an unimposing, domed pillar about 2ft 6ins (76cm) high. All the stones were set erect in very shallow sockets.

The circle was excavated over four weeks in Spring 1938. Nothing had survived in the acidic soil but two shallow ditches crossed at right-angles near the centre and it was surmised that they had supported a central post like a totem pole. Such a wooden feature,

unlike centre stones, would be unique in stone circle architecture.

Beyond the ring, 16ft (5m) to the north-east, two high pillars in a 13ft (4m) long line stand on a NNE-SSW axis that passes between the circle and a pillaged ring-cairn to the east. The stones are dissimilar. The north-eastern is the taller, more slender, flat-topped, 16ft (4.9m) high. Originally it was higher. It had fallen and broken and it was re-erected in 1938 'with much difficulty', its 3ft 5ins (1m) long stump was not combined with it.

The difficulty was unsurprising. There was no ramp to facilitate the lifting and even though the pillar weighed less than four tons it was awkwardly long. In prehistoric times a work-force would probably have been twenty labourers strong. The excavator had seven or eight men and his success was a tribute to determination and skill.

To the south-west the second slab of the pair is lower, broader and with an angled top. It stands 7ft 8ins (2.3m) high.

Six feet (2m) to the south-east of the stones is a cairn 25ft (7.6m) in diameter, with eighteen upright, sharp-pointed radially-set kerbs standing in a 21ft (6.4m) ring just within the

Knocknakilla Five-Stone ring, Co. Cork (324), from the south. The circle is beyond the pair of stones in the foreground. The radial-cairn is to the right of the ring.

circumference. It was noted that the ring did not lie concentrically with the cairn which has a 9ft (2.7m) wide central space, very like the ring-cairns of north-eastern Scotland. Excavation of the cairn produced nothing but three fragments of scallop shell.

On a clear day there are splendid views from Kealkil, and the stones of Breeny More (305) can be seen to the south-west.

JCHAS 44, 1939, 46–9; O'Nuallain, 1984a, 41–2, no. 81, *Plan*, 71

324 KNOCKNAKILLA (3)
Lat: 52°.0   W 297 841
8 miles NNW of Macroom, 3½ miles SSE of Millstreet. Signposted. Walk, 150 yds (137m) S of lane up sight rise. Easy. In State care, no charge. Map F
On the lower northern slopes of Musherabeg this little ring known variously as Muisire Beg and Cnoc na Cille, 'the stone of the church', was excavated in July 1930. It is a Five-Stone ring and, like Kealkil (323) and Knockraheen (325), is part of a complex of a pair of standing stones and a radial cairn.

Two fine, smooth schist-like portals

stand dominantly 4ft 4ins and 4ft 8ins (1.3, 1.4m) high at the north-west of a disrupted ring no more than 9ft (2.7m) across. Opposite them the recumbent stood 3ft 9ins high and 3ft wide (1.1 × 1m) 'very like a rough tombstone'. It is now prostrate. Nothing came from the interior of the ring but the excavator noticed cobbling around the outside and through the portals where there was a mass of white quartz fragments.

Twelve feet (3.7m) to the south-west, beyond the recumbent, lies a great slab 14ft long and 3ft wide (4.3 × 1m). A further 11ft 8ins (3.6m) away is a 12ft 7ins (3.8m) high stone leaning to the north.

The radial-cairn 23ft (7m) east of the circle lay unknown until uncovered during peat-cutting in 1970. Its messy kerbs form a circle 11ft 6ins (3.5m) across with an open centre.

JCHAS 36, 1931, 9–19; O'Nuallain, 1984a, 32, no. 54, *Plan*, 70

325 KNOCKRAHEEN (1)
Lat: 52°.0   W 303 802.
6½ miles SSE of Millstreet, 5 miles NNW of Macroom. 2½ miles SSE of the Knocknakilla circle. Just E of lane from

Lettergorman Four-Poster, Co. Cork (326), from the north-east.

Carriganimmy to Cackanode. Walk, From unfenced lane 50 yds (46m). Very easy. Map F
Here, in waving grass, is a pair of standing stones, a Five-Stone ring and various cairns, one of them ditched. Well worth seeing.

25 yards (23m) from the lane are two quartz stones, the south-west bulkier, both about 3ft 7ins (1.1m) high. A similar distance to the north-east is the Five-Stone circle, 13ft 6ins by 11ft 10ins (4.1 × 3.6m). Its stones are graded from 3ft down to 2ft (0.9–0.6m) at the level-topped recumbent. In the next field, 120 yards (110m) to the NNE, is a cairn with two stones standing to its NNW. There are traces of other cairns nearby.

From the ring the next field 60 yards (55m) to the SSE contains a ditched radial-cairn, some 25ft wide and 3ft high (7.6 × 1m), in which six upright kerbs can be seen. There is a slight outer bank.

O'Nuallain, 1984a, 34–5, no. 62, *Plans*, 69, 72

326 LETTERGORMAN NE (3)
Lat: 51°.7   W 267 473

7 miles N of Ross Carberry, 4 miles SE of Dunmanway. From Ballingurteen W 29. 47. take the L50 W for 1¼ miles. Where it bends to the N go straight on on lane to farm in 300 yds (275m). Ask, Through gate to S, 220 yds (200m) uphill. Easy. Map F
'This site is not a circle. It consists of three large stones with a distant outlier and a fourth stone, fallen, nearby. It is included here [in John Barber's dissertation of 1972] because of the possibility that it is a "Four Poster", a type of monument recently recognised in Britain and said to be derived from the recumbent stone circles of Aberdeenshire.' It was John Barber who was the first to recognise a Four-Poster in south-west Ireland.

On the flat top of a ridge the three stones stand at the corners of a rectangle 17ft 8ins SSW-NNE by 7ft 6ins (5.4 × 2.3m). The tallest at the SSW is a towering angle-headed pillar 9ft 3ins (2.8m) high. The south-east stone, flat-topped, is the lowest, 6ft (1.8m) high and the NNE, also flat-topped, is about 6ft 6ins (2m) in height. The easternmost stone may be the block, 5ft 3ins (1.6m) long, that lies by a track

60ft (18m) to the east. If so, the ring may have been 'christianised' like several other Four-Posters in Ireland. They tend to be much more oblong in plan than their rather squarer counterparts in Scotland.

A flat-topped outlier, 6ft 3ins (1.9m) high, stands 150ft (46m) to the west.

O'Nuallain, 1984b, 70, no. 4, *Plan*, 70; Barber, 39

327 LETTERGORMAN SW (3)

Lat: 51°.7   W 262 456

6 miles NNW of Ross Carberry, 5 miles SSE of Dunmanway, ¹/₂ mile NE of Kippagh Bridge. Walk. 120 yds (100m) E of Ross Carberry-Dunmanway road. Easy. Map F

Known also as Knockawaddra this is a ruined Five-Stone ring 10ft 2ins by 9ft 2ins (3.1 × 2.8m). It stands at the edge of a terrace from which the land falls steeply to the SSE.

Of the thin circle-stones the northern portal, 5ft 3ins (1.6m) long, is prostrate and hidden in a bush. The very level-topped recumbent is a much thicker stone, 2ft wide, 3ft 3ins high and 4ft 6ins long (0.6 × 1 × 1.4m).

A brilliantly white quartz block lies between the recumbent and the southern circle-stone. Its association, if any, with the circle is unknown. Stones cleared from the field have been dumped inside the ring.

The NE-SW axis of the ring towards the recumbent is in line with a marked saddle in the distant hills.

O'Nuallain, 1984a, 44, no. 89, *Plan*, 68

328 LISSACRESIG (3)

Lat: 51°.9   W 269 753

9 miles of Millstreet, 4¹/₂ miles WNW of Macroom. From Macroom take the T29 W for 3 miles. At Carrigaphooca Bridge take lane to the NW. In 1³/₄ miles at the T-junction leave car. Walk. Straight ahead along track. ¹/₂ mile. Fair. In State care, no charge. Map F

This is a large Five-Stone ring, 11ft 10ins by 10ft (3.6 × 3m). It stands at the edge of land falling to the south.

The portals and the two circle-stones

are much of a height. The recumbent, at the WNW is the bulkiest of all. The south-east portal, tapering to a point, is the tallest. The north-eastern has fallen.

O'Nuallain, 1984a, 37, no. 68, *Plan*, 67

329 MAUGHANACLEA ENE (3)

Lat: 51°.8   W 104 565

8¹/₂ miles NE of Bantry, 8 miles WNW of Dunmanway. Walk. On the L40 1¹/₂ miles W of the Cousane Gap leave car, go 250 yds (229m) up Maughanaclea Farm drive. Easy. Map F

Immediately to the east of the farm this is a ruinous but interesting recumbent stone circle. It lies on a mini-plateau with land falling to west, north and east. Of an original thirteen stones, seven remain standing, big and impressive pillars, five have fallen and one is missing. The stones are markedly graded in a circle 37ft 9ins (11.5m) in diameter.

The heights decline from 5ft 3ins to 2ft 8ins (1.6–0.8m) where the recumbent lies at the south-west, a fine long, low and level slab.

Inside the ring are two disturbed boulder-burials, one at the centre, the second to its east.

O'Nuallain, 1984a, 19, no. 23, *Plan*, 56

330 MAUGHANACLEA WSW (4)

Lat: 51°.8   W 080 556

9¹/₂ miles WNW of Dunmanway, 7 miles NE of Bantry. Walk. On the L40 at W 094 569 take the track leading south for ¹/₂ mile. At its end turn SW for a mile uphill. Not easy. Map F

In an elevated position at the west end of the hills this is a wrecked and 'christianised' Four-Poster. The three surviving stones stand at the corners of a quadrilateral 12ft 9ins ENE-WSW by 9ft 2ins (3.9 × 2.8m). The ENE stone, 5ft 3ins (1.6m) high, is split. The SSW and SSE stones are 4ft and 2ft 4ins (1.2, 0.7m) high respectively.

A hundred yards (90m) to the south is a radial-cairn.

O'Nuallain, 1984b, 69–70, no. 3, *Plan*, 70

331 MAULTANVALLY (3)
Lat: 51°.6   W 264 442
*6 miles SSE of Dunmanway, 5 miles
NNW of Ross Carberry. ²/₃ mile SE of
Kippagh Bridge. From the bridge take
the road S. The circle is visible from the
road, 150 yds (137m) to the E. Walk.
Awkward as in 2nd field with walls and
fences between. Map F*
In pasture at the edge of a terrace with
land falling to the south-west,
Maultanvally, 'the hillock of the old
place', is a ruined recumbent stone
circle with an internal stone. Of a
possible original eleven stones, four,
including the west portal, have gone.
The eastern, 4ft 6ins (1.4m) high, has a
sloping top.

The seven remaining stones surround
a circle 31ft (9.5m) across, and range in
height from 4ft 6ins down to the 2ft
(1.4–0.6m) of the recumbent at the
WSW, a large, level-topped block. A
misplaced heavy, flattish slab of quartz
lies just off the axis and well away
from the centre of the ring.

It is a pleasing site to visit but watch
out for bullocks who can be more than
curious.

Glanbrack Five-Stone ring (W 271
444) with its two outliers is ¹/₂ mile to
the ENE.

O'Nuallain, 1984a, 21, no. 30, *Plan*,
55; ibid, 44, no. 90

332 MILL LITTLE (3)
Lat: 51°.8   V 989 565
*15 miles W of Dunmanway, 5 miles N
of Bantry. From Coombola Bridge go N
for ¹/₂ mile, take lane to W ¹/₂ mile to
side-lane to N. Walk. At the small
Millbigg bridge over a stream the site is
W of ford 220 yds (200m) N of lane.
Easy. Map F*
This is an intriguing collection of small,
Bronze Age monuments. In a boggy
field is a Five-Stone ring with broken
radial portals. In the circle which is
about 10ft by 7ft 10ins (3.1 × 2.4m)
the recumbent at the south-west is 3ft
(1m) high.

Six feet (2m) west of the recumbent
is a well-preserved boulder-burial.
Fifteen feet (4.6m) to the south is

another boulder which may be the
capstone of a second grave although no
supporting stones are visible. A further
13ft (4m) to the south is a roofless
boulder-burial.

The complex is completed by a pair
of standing stones, 2ft 6ins (0.8m)
apart 53ft (16m) to the south-east.
Standing NNE-SSW they are 4ft and 2ft
6ins (1.2, 0.8m) high respectively.

Although the sites are hardly
megalithic the group has given artists
the 'feeling of a remote and special
place at which the echoes of long
forgotten rituals seem more vibrant
than at many more well known sites.'

O'Nuallain, 1984a, 40, no. 80, *Plan*,
69

333 OUGHTIHERY NW (3)
Lat: 52°.0   W 390 820
*9 miles SE of Millstreet, 6¹/₂ miles NNE of
Macroom. From Carrigagulla Bridge go
¹/₂ mile SE to Glenaglogh North. Walk.
150 yds (137m) S of junction of lane at
W 392 821. Easy. Map F*
This is a rather unappealing example of
a Five-Stone ring, crudely graded, the
south-east portal is almost prostrate
and not on the circumference.

The ring measures about 9ft 6ins by
8ft 10ins (2.9 × 2.7m). The recumbent
at the SSW is a level-topped, squarish
block which is only just smaller than
the other stones.

O'Nuallain, 1984a, 33, no. 57, *Plan*,
68

334 OUGHTIHERY SE (3)
Lat: 52°.0   W 413 801
*2 miles SE of Oughtihery. From Rylane
Cross at W 423 816 go SW to Sheskinny
Cross, turn SW for 1 mile past 2 lanes
to S. Walk. Just to the N of the lane.
Easy. Map F*
In rough pasture this is a ruinous and
overgrown recumbent stone circle. Of
an original seven stones two are
missing, including the eastern portal.
The grading from 3ft 3ins down to 2ft
3ins (1–0.7m) is feeble. The ring is
some 9ft 4ins (2.9m) across.

The recumbent at the south-west is
unmistakeable, 1ft 6ins and a full 6ft

Reanascreena, Co. Cork (335), from the wsw. *The recumbent stone is the flat-topped and lowest stone in the foreground.*

long (0.5–1.8m). Stones cleared from the field have been dumped inside the ring.

O'Nuallain, 1984a, 14, no. 8, *Plan,* 59

335 REANASCREENA (1)
Lat: 51°.6   W 265 410
7½ miles sse *of Dunmanway, 3 miles* nnw *of Ross Carbery, 1 mile* ssw *of Reanascreena. From there go* wsw *for ½ mile and turn* sse *onto straight lane for ½ mile into lane on* e. *Walk. Circle is 370 yds (338m)* wsw *across fields. Awkward. Ask if a better approach is available. Map F*
On the summit of a large hill to the south-west of the Creamery Reanascreena, 'the ring of the shrine' is at the south of a remarkable concentration of recumbent stone circles, Five-Stone rings and Four-Posters. No fewer than nine rings are known in a circle of land no more than three miles across, an average of only just over 500 acres (200ha) each, surely no more than family holdings.

This recumbent stone circle stands on a gentle western slope, half-hidden in

tall reedy grass. It is unusual in that it is surrounded by a wide ditch with an equally wide but low bank through which there is no gap for entry.

Within this enclosure twelve stones stand in a circle just over 30ft (9.1m) across. It is a diameter almost identical to that at Drombeg and only slightly smaller than that at Bohonagh. It is possible that a yardstick of a little over 3ft (95cm) was used when laying out the multiple-stone rings of this region, Reanascreena measuring 9.8 units, Bohonagh 10.4 and Drombeg 10.

The stones are irregularly spaced and not well graded. At the ene the flat-topped portals stand 4ft 9ins (1.5m) high. Opposite them the recumbent is 2ft high and 3ft 9ins long (0.6 × 1.1m).

Excavation in the summer of 1960 found a small, soil-filled pit near the centre. Ten feet (3m) to the north was a spread of charcoal. Below it was a pit in which there was a layer of soil and cremated bone. At the bottom a shale slab covered more burnt bone and charcoal.

The excavator believed that there had been a cremation pyre to the east of the

227

circle from which flecks of charcoal had been trodden into the ring on the feet of the circle-builders. Large stones in the ditch outside the portals and a thick dump of earth showed where renovation had been necessary to repair the damage caused by people treading and wearing away the earth near the entrance.

The azimuth of 258° marks no significant celestial event. Assays of 830±35 bc (GrN-17509) and 945±35 bc (GrN-17510), averaging c.1000 BC, suggest that like Drombeg (317) and Cashelkeelty (344) the ring is of Late Bronze Age date.

JCHAS 67, 1962, 59–69, Plan, 61

336 REANERRE (1)
Lat: 51°.9   W 203 729
12 miles SSW of Millstreet, 8¹/₂ miles W of Macroom. 330 yds (300m) NE of Reanerre church. Walk. In rough pasture 100 yds (90m) to E of lane from Reanerre NW towards Gortnascarty. Easy. Map F
There are two interesting sites here. At the edge of a terrace that falls abruptly to the north, and with long views to the south-east, there is a Five-Stone ring in good condition. The portals are about 3ft high (0.9m), the western wide and flat-topped, the east thinner and pointed. At the south-west of a ring some 8ft 6ins by 6ft 3ins (2.6 × 1.9m) the recumbent has a nicely level top.

A track just to the south leads westwards shortly to a row of six stones among trees, four to the north-east of a stone wall, two taller on the other side. Arranged NE-SW the stones have sloping tops angled upwards the tallest stone at the south-west, 5ft (1.5m) high.

O'Nuallain, 1984a, 37, no. 67, *Plan*, 68; Burl, 1993, 247

337 RYLANE (1)
Lat: 52°.0   W 438 813
13 miles SW of Mallow, 8¹/₄ NE of Macroom. ³/₄ mile E of Rylane Cross. Walk. The ring is 200 yds (180m) N of the lane to Donoughmore. Easy. Map F

Against a holly tree this is a Five-Stone ring 12ft 2ins by 9ft 6ins (3.7 × 2.9m). It is constructed of large slabs whose appearance is diminished by the dump of stones that reaches almost to their tops. In the litter is a pillarstone 6ft (1.8m) long that may be the outlier seen to the west of the site in 1916. Two portals at the north-east, the west 3ft (0.9m) high, the east a little lower, face a ragged-topped recumbent, equally high but almost 7ft (2.1m) long.

O'Nuallain, 1984a, 36, no. 65, *Plan*, 67

338 TEERGAY (5)
Lat: 51°.9   W 291 694
3¹/₂ miles SW of Macroom. Walk. 200 yds (180m) W of the L58 from Macroom to Dunmanway. Easy. Map F
The status of this overgrown ring is unclear. It could be a hut-circle, a boulder-circle of Kenmare, Kerry, type, or a variant recumbent stone circle. In its ruinous state only excavation might resolve the uncertainty.

Of an original nine or ten stones, seven survive with a gap at the north and a wider one at the south. If the stones are graded it was not well done. If a stone at the south-west is the recumbent it is flat-topped, level but higher than the 'portals' opposite it. The ring is about 25ft (7.6m) in diameter, 8 'Cork units' of 3.113ft (95cm).

O'Nuallain, 1984a, 15, no. 12, *Plan*, 54

339 TEMPLEBRYAN (3)
Lat: 51°.6   W 389 437
2 miles SSW of Ballinascarty, 1¹/₂ miles N of Clonakilty. Walk. Immediately W of the road from Clonakilty to Ballinascarty, just N of the junction of the road and a lane to its W. Easy. Map F
Well to the east of the major concentration of recumbent stone circles, this ring is to the south of the ruined Templebryan church. Also known as the Druid's Temple it stands on ground rising rapidly to the WNW and on a pronounced SSW-NNE slope.

It is wrecked. The western side of the

Beltany, Co. Donegal (340), *from the north-east.*

ring has one slab almost down and, of nine stones standing in 1743, only five remained in 1837. Of those five, four are erect today in a ring, as is common, about 31ft (9.5m) in diameter, or ten theoretical units.

The surviving stones are tall and very flat-topped, weathered vertically. Opposite the eastern portal the ssw recumbent is a thick, ovoid block with two thin bands of quartz running horizontally near its top and bottom. Its western side is vertical, its eastern convex, a shape repeated in diminutive form by the coarse, unshaped stub of quartz placed on the axis near the centre of the ring. It is about 2ft 6ins (0.8m) high.

260 yards (238m) to the north-west a 10ft (3m) high needle of stone with faint ogham markings on it stands in the abandoned churchyard. Christian burials have been found near it.

JRSAI 36, 1906, 262–4; O'Nuallain, 1984a, 22, no. 31, *Plan*, 55

Co. DONEGAL

The rings in north-western Ireland are few, large and of many stones. Except for Beltany they are in poor condition

340 Beltany, Tops (1, 5)
Lat: 54°.9   C 255 005
5 miles wnw of Strabane, 1 mile s of Raphoe. On the n slope of Tops Hill. Walk. From lane at C 259 001 ¼ mile w uphill. Easy. Map C
On the levelled top of a rounded hill this fine stone circle, one of the best in Ireland, stands around a platform 3ft to 4ft high (1–1.2m). There is a possible outer bank.

When Somerville saw the ring in 1909 it surrounded 'a flat circular space' but when Oliver Davies visited Beltany in the late 1930s 'the platform had been recently and unscientifically excavated, and had been left in dreadful confusion'. The chaos is still visible in the hummocks and hollows of turf.

Beltany, Co. Donegal (340), *the triangular cupmarked stone at the north-east of the circle.*

In a true circle 145ft (44.2m) in diameter some sixty-four stones remain of an original eighty or more, very closely-set in a style reminiscent of the circles in the Carrowmore cemetery, Co. Sligo (364), fifty-seven miles to the south-west. The comparison is made closer by the surging waves and troughs of small stones over the plundered interior. The platform, the kerblike circle-stones, the cairnstones inside can all be paralleled at Carrowmore and it is possible that Beltany is a ring transitional between late passage-tombs and early stone circles. If so it could be as early as 3000 BC.

The stones range in height from 4ft to 9ft (1.2–2.7m), the tallest a pillar at the WSW shaped like a grazing mammoth. It faces a triangular slab at the ENE, 4ft 6ins (1.4m) in height, whose inner face is lavishly decorated with cupmarks. At the north of the ring a large square stone stands 7ft (2.1m) high. There is a tall outlier, 67ft (20.4m) to the south-east. It is 6ft 3ins (1.9m) high.

It is for its astronomical alignments that Beltane is justifiably famous. Looking from a tall stone, 5ft 10ins (1.8m) high at the north-west, 'conspicuously greater and higher than its neighbours', the 'playing-card' outlier 212ft (65m) away stands side-on towards the midwinter sunrise over Betsy Bell mountain 28 miles away. Another less well-defined line looks WNW-ESE towards the hill of Croaghan seven miles away and the early November sunrise, the festival of Samain.

Unlike Caesar's wife neither of these sightlines is above suspicion. The orientation towards the outlier does not pass over the centre of the circle, and although the Samain line does there is nothing architecturally significant to define it.

The best and most persuasive alignment at Beltany is from the high south-western pillar to the cupmarked triangle whose pointed top provided a refined foresight towards 'the small but conspicuous hill-summit' of Tullyrap five miles away. It seems more than coincidence that the orientation is towards the May Day sunrise, the feast of Beltane, the modern name for the circle. Art in stone circles is repeatedly found on stones in line with a celestial event.

There are reports of a carved Celtic stone head being discovered in or near to the ring.

If returning to Raphoe visit the Druid Bookshop. The Stone Circle Restaurant is next door. Cupmarks on the tables?

Arch 73, 1923, 212–14; *UJA* 2, 1939, 293

341 BOCAN, Glackadrumman (4)
Lat: 55°.3   C 544 475
4½ miles ENE of Carndonagh, 1½ miles SE of Culdaff on W slope of Mass Hill. Just S of school and church on Culdaff-Moville road. Walk. 200 yds (180m) in junction of lanes just E of the road. Fair. Map 2

In pasture among rough moorland this exposed site offers extensive views. Also known as Culdaff it is in dreadful condition. There are conflicting claims that it once consisted of three concentric rings or was a devastated round cairn.

In 1816 twelve stones stood here in a 'circle' said to be about 60ft (18m) in diameter but today only seven remain in the north-west and south-east quadrants. They are between 4ft to 7ft (1.2–2.1m) high. Others lie prostrate and broken. There may have been an ellipse about 75ft SSE-NNW by 65ft (23 × 20m).

Boyle Somerville surveyed the ring in 1928. From a 5ft (1.5m) high stone at the south-east, on whose inner face he thought there might be very weathered cupmarks, to a higher at the north-west, 6ft 4ins (1.9m) in height, he deduced an alignment to the midsummer sun setting behind Farragan Hill five miles away.

Half a mile to the south-west, C 537 470, is the ruined court-cairn of Larraghirril, the 'Druid's Altar'. This, claimed John Toland in the early eighteenth century, was the grave of the druidess, Gealcossa, 'the white-legged', and not far away was the stone circle, 'her temple; being a sort of diminutive Stonehenge, which many of the Irish dare not even at this day in any way profane.' Things have changed.

JRSAI 29, 1929, 152–5, *Plan*, 153; Lacy, 71, *Plan*, 70

Co. DUBLIN

Although the county possesses some fine megaliths: Kiltiernan portal-dolmen with its great capstone; wedge-tombs at Ballyedmonduff and elsewhere; even a tall cupmarked standing stone at Rahee, it is not notable for its stone circles

342 PIPERSTOWN (5)
Lat: 53°.2   O 115 217 (approximately)
9 miles WSW of Bray, 7 miles SSW of Dublin, on the S slope of Spink Hill. The sites are about ¼ mile E of the road to the E of the reservoir. Walk. ¼ miles up slope in heather. Not easy to find. Map 2

In 1960 a fire destroyed much of the thick heather and peat covering the mountainside. Fifteen sites were exposed, eight of them burial cairns, the remainder dwelling places. Site K, at the north of the main group, was a small stone circle and cairn.

Excavated in September 1962, a low cairn, no more than 1ft 7ins (48cm) high had five small stones protruding through it. A sixth was discovered when the cairn was stripped. They formed a circle 9ft 6ins (2.9m) in diameter, and their average height was 1ft 5ins (43cm) with the two tallest at the south-west and west, 1ft 7ins and 1ft 10ins (48, 56cm) respectively. The south-west stone did not stand on the circumference and may have been a form of outlier.

At the centre was a pit in which cremated bone rested on charcoal which was interpreted as the disintegrated wood of a tray on which the hot bones had been carried from the pyre.

The circle-stones leaned outwards as though shifted by the cairn. 'These

231

orthostats appear to have served as buttresses rather than as kerbstones but their resemblance to a small stone circle with an outlier when the cairn was entirely removed suggests that they may have had a ritual rather than a functional significance.'

The sites have been badly preserved. They are hard to distinguish now that the heather has regenerated.

PRIA 64, 1964–6, 66–9, Plan, 67

Co. GALWAY
Like Co. Dublin this is not a region famous for its stone circles

343 MASONBROOK (2?, 6)
Lat: 53°.2   M 658 147
16 miles sw of Ballinasloe, 3 miles ESE of Loughrea. Immediately on the s side of the road from Loughrea to Tynagh. In the grounds of Masonbrook House. No walk. Map 2

Also known as The Ring and as the Seven Sisters this is a strange monument and may be partly or entirely of modern construction.

In an earthen bank some 70ft (21m) across and 3ft (1m) high seven stones stand, 4ft to 5ft (1.2, 1.5m) high. There is a single break in the earthwork. Local inhabitants believe that they have been re-erected.

Inside the ring there is a small mound, 12ft across and 3ft to 4ft high (3.7, 1, 1.2m). Excavation in 1916 found nothing prehistoric, but signs of marks caused by crow-bars led to the suspicion that the mound itself might have been no more than an Ordnance Survey cairn.

Four miles NNE of Loughrea is the Turoe Stone, M 630 223, on the lawn of Turoe House to which it was moved from just outside the now-destroyed rath of Feerwore.

PRIA 33, 1916–17, 505

Co. KERRY
Like Co. Cork to the east, this county contains a fine collection of recumbent stone circles, Five-Stone rings and Four-

Posters. There are also rings that appear to owe little to the recumbent stone circle tradition

344 CASHELKEELTY E (4)
Lat: 51°.8   V 748 575
8 miles NNE of Castletown Bearhaven, 2 miles WSW of Lauragh. On the L62 from Lauragh turn s (Lt) in ¾ mile just past the estuary. In ⅓ mile there is a track on the w (Rt). Walk. Follow track through trees NW and w for ⅔ mile to ford and stepping-stones. Circle is a further ½ mile to the W. Tiring. Map F

On a terrace overlooking Killmakilloge harbour this damaged ring was a Five-Stone circle with a diameter about 6ft (1.8m). Both of its portals have gone. Despite this loss Cashelkeelty is an important site in stone circle history because its excavation provided evidence of the age of the ring.

The recumbent is 1ft 6ins high and 5ft long (0.5 × 1.5m). The two circle-stones on either side of it are about 2ft 3ins (0.7m) high.

Excavation in 1977 revealed a central pit covered by a flat slab. In it were the cremated bones of an adult about twenty-five to thirty years of age. With the bones were six flints and a broken piece of sandstone which could have been the point of an ard.

Charcoal provided two radiocarbon dates of 970 ± 60 bc (GrN-9173) and 715 ± 50 bc (GrN-9172), the latter not being directly associated with the circle. The former date, if not from an intrusive burial, would suggest that the ring was in use around 1200 BC, not an impossibly late date for such a small ring so far to the west.

Just to its south is a Three-Stone row aligned W-E, the eastern stone being almost 8ft (2.4m) high. Close to it lay a leaf-shaped and a barbed-and-tanged flint arrowhead and a convex flint scraper. A large pit to the south of the row contained only earth but may have been a grave. Stratigraphical evidence suggested that the row was earlier than the circle and may have been associated with cereal cultivation in the years around 1250 BC.

A nearby recumbent stone circle, Cashelkeelty w, V 747 575, has been virtually destroyed, only three of eleven to thirteen stones surviving of a ring once about 56ft (17m) in diameter.

A. Lynch, *Man and Environment in S.W. Ireland*, Oxford, 1981, 65–9, *Plan*, 64

345 DROMATOUK (1)

Lat: 51°.9   V 953 714
4 miles WSW of Kilgarvan, 2¼ miles E of Kenmare. From Kenmare take the T65 S and shortly the L62 ESE towards Kilgarvan. In 1½ miles at V 934 718 cross the River Roughty. In 300 yds (275m) turn E and SSE and in ½ mile turn E. In ½ mile leave car. Walk. Follow track on N for 220 yds (200m) to field-walls. Walk NE, boggy ground to E. At end of walls ring is ¼ mile NE. Easy to miss as stones are hidden by the higher moorland. Map F
In a small green field, beyond overgrown walls after the awkward approach across sodden land this is a delightful Five-Stone ring about 8ft 10ins (2.7m) in diameter. The stones, blotched grey and white, are from 2ft 6ins to 1ft (0.8, 0.3m) in height with the recumbent at the SSW being the lowest. The portals are rather widely spaced.

Two small trees grow inside the ring.
O'Nuallain, 1984a, 45, no. 92, *Plan*, 66

346 DROMBOHILLY (3)

Lat: 51°.8   V 790 607
1¼ miles N of Lauragh. From there take the L62 E and N round Knockanouganish mountain for 2 miles to 1st lane on w. Follow it for 1¼ miles to T-junction. Turn S. In ¼ mile pass farm track on E. Leave car 150 yds (137m) up the hill. Walk. Ring is ¼ mile over fences, walls and rough ground. Well worth the effort. Map F
This is a fine recumbent stone circle at the edge of a terrace with magnificent views to the north-east and the estuary. The stones are very conspicuous against the skyline from the north. A low wall passes through the ring.

Of an original eleven stones the recumbent and one other have gone from a true circle about 28ft (8.5m) in diameter. The surviving stones are tall thin slabs with 7ft (2.1m) high radial portals at the NNE. The eastern leans towards its partner.

A lower but thicker, flat-topped block stands at the west opposite a broad, pointed slab at the east.

The recumbent may be the stone that now lies at the SSW just inside the circumference of the ring. If so, it has a peaked base and a flat top and would have stood about 2ft (0.6m) high. It is 3ft 3ins (1m) long.

With an estimated azimuth of 203°.1 and a declination of −29°.1 the recumbent would have been in line with the southernmost moonset.

O'Nuallain, 1984a, 30, no. 48, *Plan*, 53

347 DROMROE (3)

Lat: 51°.8   V 880 657
8 miles N of Lauragh, 3¼ miles SSW of Kenmare. On the L62 at Dawros Bridge, V 880 675, turn SE for almost 1½ miles. Pass a waterfall and a quarry. Where the minor road forks S and SW an inconspicuous farm lane also forks to the SW. It is not very obvious. Follow for ½ mile to farm. Walk. ⅓ mile WSW. Easy. Map F
At the edge of a terrace falling to the south-east, and in rough pasture, this is another fine recumbent stone circle. It has tall portals, good grading with stones sloping up towards the recumbent at the WSW.

Of its thirteen stones three are prostrate in a circle 31ft (9.5m) in diameter. The grading declines from the portals 5ft 3ins (1.6m) high to the stones against the recumbent, 2ft 7ins (0.8m) high. This stone is not the lowest but its level top has a noticeable depression at its centre rather like a gunsight.

The ring has a central boulder-burial with its heavy rectangular capstone along the axis of the ring. 6ft or so (2m) to its south is a flat-topped block 2ft 6ins (0.8m) high.

O'Nuallain, 1984a, 28–9, no. 45, *Plan*, 58

348 GURTEEN (1)
Lat: 51°.9   W 006 698
6 miles E of Kenmare, 2¼ miles S of Kilgarvan. On the Kenmare-Bantry road turn W at V 019 696. Go NW for ¼ mile. At T-junction turn SW. ¼ mile, park by house. Walk. Only 100 yds (90m) E but approach is awkward up bank, over barbed-wire. Not visible from lane. Fair. Map F
This fine recumbent stone circle stands on a ridge on rough ground vivid with yellow gorse. There are long views to the north but, paradoxically, the circle cannot be seen from anywhere farther than 120ft (37m) away.

It is an excellent site, 34ft 6ins (10.5m) across, of eleven stones, the easternmost fallen. There are some interesting features. The entrance is very unusual. Outside the circumference at the NNE are two, rather low and leaning radial portals but there are two others, circumferential and taller, in line with them in the ring itself. As is often the case, the north-eastern is wider and flat-topped. The radials, 3ft (1m) apart, are skewed to the major axis. It is a unique architectural feature in this type of circle.

The stones are well graded from 5ft in height down to 2ft 6ins (1.5m–76cm). At the SSW the recumbent is a massive block, domed, 3ft high and 8ft 3ins long (0.9 × 2.5m). It is not the lowest stone.

At the centre of the ring is a boulder-burial with a nicely-rounded capstone 8ft (2.4m) across. A thin sliver of stone against it may be a portion broken from the slab.

On the stones on either side of the entrance are possible cupmarks.

O'Nuallain, 1984a, 27–8, no. 43, *Plan*, 58

349 KENMARE (3)
Lat: 51°.9   V 907 707
In Kenmare itself. Walk. At Cromwell Bridge turn Lt down a short road. Before it turns Lt a gate on the Rt

opens onto a track. 100 yds (90m) the ring is on Lt. Very easy. Map F
Also known as the Shrubberies this is an ellipse 56ft E-W by 49ft (17 × 15m). It is probably the largest ring in south-western Ireland. Unlike most rings there the stones are not thin slabs but heavy boulders, thirteen standing with two prostrate at the north.

If there was an attempt at grading it was a feeble one and if there is a recumbent at the WSW it is a flat, very low stone.

At the centre of the ring is a boulder-burial with a monstrous capstone some 6ft 6ins long, 6ft wide and 2ft 6ins thick (2 × 1.8 × 0.8m). It must be almost seven tons in weight and would have demanded the strength of about thirty labourers to drag it into position.

O'Nuallain, 1984a, 26–7, no. 41, *Plan*, 57

350 LISSYVIGGEEN (1)
Lat: 52°.1   V 998 906
13½ miles NNE of Kenmare, 2 miles E of Killarney. On the T29 E from Killarney and 600 yds (550m) SSE of Woodford Bridge, V 991 904, turn NE. In 300 yds (275m) where road forks to the NE go straight on. Walk. In 200 yds (180m) ring is 150 yds (137m) to the W. Easy. Map F
'About two miles from Killarney, and half a mile from the mail-coach road from Killarney to Millstreet, at Liosviggeen is a very perfect but small stone circle.' Written in 1884 the words are still true. The lios, 'fairy fort', is unblemished.

Known also as the Seven Sisters, the ring is placed somewhat eccentrically inside an overgrown earthen henge which is about 51ft in across, its bank 6ft thick and 4ft high (15.6 × 1.8 × 1.2m). There is a probable entrance at the SSW and a possible at the NNE.

The seven stones of the ring are from 3ft to 3ft 9ins (0.9–1.1m) in height and enclose an area 14ft (4.3m) in diameter. There is a probable recumbent at the south distinguished by its lowness, its rectangularity and its flat top from the six other unshapely, peaked boulders.

It is reputed that some stone artefacts were found during some unauthorised excavation, but 'were thrown away'.

Outside the ring to the south, not in line with the SSW entrance, is a pair of big standing stones, E-W, 7ft 3ins (2.2m) apart. The east is the taller, 7ft 8ins (2.3m) high. Its partner, a thinner needle, 6ft 10ins (2.1m) high, has been thought to stand in line with the equinoctial sunsets but the grossness of the boulders prevents any accurate alignment. 'Some idiot tried to punch his name on one of the pillars.'

If the identification of the recumbent is correct then the fact that the pair is in line with the axis of the ring but not with the entrance of the henge makes it likely that the earthwork was a later addition to the site.

O'Nuallain, 1984a, 25, no. 38, *Plan*, 61

351 LOHART (2, 6)
Lat: 51°.8   V 824 663
6 miles SW of Kenmare, 5½ miles NNE of Lauragh. In the garden of a farmhouse on the L62 Kenmare-Castle Bearhaven road. Easy. Map F
Also known as Tuosist. In 1841 this site was described as a circle 35ft 6ins (10.8m) in diameter, composed of twelve stones from 4ft to 5ft 6ins (1.2, 1.7m) high. It seems to have had a central boulder-burial with a huge capstone 6ft by 5ft and 1ft 3ins thick (1.8 × 1.5 × 0.4m), weighing almost three tons.

The ring was allowed to fall into ruin and was then 'reconstructed' around 1964. A garden was planted in and around it and the place is now overgrown and unhandsome. Only six stones remain, three standing, loosely set, at the north, SSE and west. Three are already fallen at the east, south and SSW. Within them is a flat slab.

O'Nuallain, 1984a, 28, no. 44; Barber, 21, K2, *Plan*

352 REENKILLA (1)
Lat: 51°.8   V 768 577
9 miles N of Castletown Bearhaven, 1½

miles SSW of Lauragh. Walk. Not far but the site is on the wooded Knockacappul islet at the south-east end of Killmakilloge harbour. Approachable only at low tide. Map F
This is a good Four-Poster with an outlying stone. The four stones stand at the corners of an irregular trapezoid whose sides, from the north, clockwise, measure 11ft 6ins, ENE-WSW, 6ft 3ins, 8ft 10ins and 8ft 2ins (3.5, 1.9, 2.7, 2.5m). The tallest is at the north-west, 7ft 10ins high, the others being 1ft 4ins, 4ft and 2ft 3ins respectively (2.4, 0.4, 1.2, 0.7m).

44ft (13.4m) to the north is a standing stone 2ft 6ins (75cm) high.

O'Nuallain, 1984b, 71, no. 5, *Plan*, 70

353 SHRONEBIRRANE (3)
Lat: 51°.8   V 735 554
At Reenkilla, ½ mile W of Croanshagh Bridge, take the lane SSW at V 768 574. In 2 miles the circle is immediately N of the road in front of a farmhouse. No walk. Map F
Standing in the narrow Drimminboy valley in spectacularly mountainous terrain the only view from this dark recumbent stone circle is to the north-east.

Of an original thirteen stones five are missing from the north-east quadrant. Those that remain are starkly tall and impressive. The north-east portal is 8ft 6ins (2.6m) high, sharp-topped like a well-used gigantic wax crayon. Its partner leans deeply. From them the stones decrease in height down to the recumbent at the south-west, 2ft 3ins high and 7ft long (0.7 × 2.1m).

At the centre of the ring is a low mound.

O'Nuallain, 1984a, 29, no. 46, *Plan*, 53

Co. KILDARE
There are few stone circles here. Those that exist are very varied in form. According to legend most of them were created by playful pipers

Brewel Hill, Co. Kildare (354), from the west.

354 BREWEL HILL (4)
Lat: 53°.0　　　　　　　　　　N 833 013
*8¼ miles NNW of Baltinglass, 2½ miles
W of Dunlavin. On the low summit of
Brewel Hill. From Kilgowan take lane
SE at N 822 015. Walk. In ¾ mile a
track on the W leads ⅓ mile. Ring is on
hill just to the N. Easy. Map 2*
Popularly known as The Pipers' Stones,
today the site is in very poor condition,
overshadowed by trees and thick with
long grass. It is a ring for megalithic
aficionados only.

The four stones, none of them erect,
are inside a large circular deeply-
ditched and banked earthwork, 220ft
(67m) from crest to crest with entrances
at the east and west. Inside this is a
ploughed and weathered semi-circular
earthwork open to the north about 80ft
(24m) across. It is almost destroyed by
the planting of trees.

The southern half of what may have
been a complete stone circle is to be
seen inside this. They lie to the south of
an old field boundary. The ring would
have been 56ft (17m) in diameter.
Today there are two dark-grey granite
stones, 5ft 7ins and 2ft 6ins (1.7, 0.8m)
high, a red puddingstone, 5ft 6ins

(1.7m) high and a lower white quartz
block, about 3ft 3ins (1m) high. The
latter is the Piper's Chair.

Folklore has it that three giant pipers
and their young brother threw the slabs
from Knockadow Hill three miles to the
south. Two days later the pipers'
greyhound leapt from the hill onto the
stones and 'left the imprint of its toe
nails on each boulder'.
*JRSAI 61, 1931, 126–7; Churcher,
24, Plan*

355 BROADLEAS (3)
Lat: 53°.1　　　　　　　　　　N 931 075
*7½ miles SSE of Naas, 5 miles NE of
Dunlavin, 1½ miles S of Ballymore
Eustace. On the T42 S of Ballymore ¼
mile S of the Perrystreet crossroads the
ring is 50 yds (45m) W of the road.
Easy. Map 2*
In an open, level field on a low hill the
Pipers' Stones is a large ring similar to
the Athgreany circle, Co. Wicklow
(366), 2¾ miles to the south. Athgreany
also is known as the Piper's Stones
although there apparently only one
musician was responsible for the stones.

Broadleas is a large oval some 105ft
SE-NW by 92ft (32 × 28m). In it

twenty-seven stones stand and twelve more lie, some broken, of what may have been forty originally. In places they are almost contiguous and this has led to interpretations of the site as the kerbs of a demolished passage-tomb or of a vast ring-cairn.

It is quite possible that like Beltany (340) in Co. Donegal the site is a form transitional between kerbed chambered tombs and open stone circles, perhaps as early as 3000 BC.

A tree grew inside the ring. It has fallen but before then 'no one would have touched it'. Nor could the stones be counted.

South of Whiteleas House, at N 926 065, the Bracked Stones, a 78ft (23.8m) ring of fifteen stones, has been totally destroyed.

JRSAI 61, 1931, 130–1; Churcher, *Plan*, 24

Co. LIMERICK

There are few rings here but the scarcity is compensated for by the presence of the splendour of the Lough Gur sites

356 GRANGE, Lough Gur (1)
Lat: 52°.5   R 640 410
16 miles w of Tipperary, 11 miles SSE of Limerick, 2½ miles N of Bruff. Walk. Immediately E of the T50A. Easy.
Map 2
This immense, tree-shrouded ring, whimsically known as the Lios, 'fort of the fairies', is a megalithic wonder. Its excavation in 1939 revealed fascinating details of how it was constructed stage by stage culminating in the slab-lined earthwork that the visitor sees today.

It stands at the edge of one of the most important areas of prehistoric Ireland. Around the shores of Lough Gur in a landscape of forested limestone hills are the remains of a Neolithic village whose timber-framed houses decayed five thousand years ago. There are field-systems, a wedge-tomb,

Grange, Co. Limerick (356)

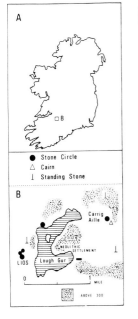

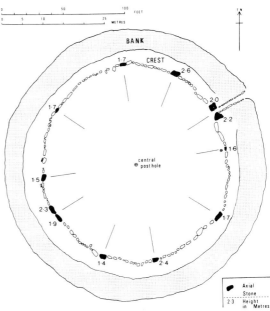

237

ring-cairns, standing stones, cairns, an island of the dead, a small stone circle and the great ring of Grange itself.

Here, among Neolithic stone-walled fields, its planners set up a slender post, and from it measured out a circle with a radius of 78ft (23.8m). On its eastern half they dug five holes, quite well spaced, and erected heavier poles in them. To the west they raised five more, opposite the first. One opposing pair stood in line with the November sunset, at that latitude, to the WSW, about 258°. The ENE end of the axis was to be the entrance to the ring.

Twelve heavy stones of local limestone and glacial volcanic breccia replaced the posts, two enormous slabs at the entrance, the northernmost 6ft 8ins (2m) high and flat-topped, its partner 7ft 2ins (2.2m) high and pointed. Facing them at the WSW two other great slabs, 156ft (47.6m) away, stood with tops sloping down to each other like an enormous v-shaped gunsight. Somerville calculated that it was aligned upon the early November sunset, the festival of Samain. The heaviest of the stones, a monstrous cube known as Rounach Croim Dubh, 'the prominent black stone', weighing over twenty tons, was set at the north-east towards the midsummer sunrise.

At that stage the site was a conventional stone circle but more was intended. A thick bank of cobbles and clay, up to 28ft (8.5m) wide and 8ft 6ins (2.6m) high was heaped up outside the circle, transforming it into a form of circle-henge. Characteristic of Irish henges it had no ditch. A gap through it, no more 3ft (1m) wide, lined with upright slabs, led to the massive portals at the ENE. To buttress the circle-stones from being forced inwards and dislodged by the weight of the bank more stones were laid along the ring's inner edge. A thick layer of gravelly clay was laid as a floor inside the ring. Very similar techniques were used at the circle-henge of Castleruddery (368) in Co. Wicklow almost a hundred miles to the east.

The work must have taken months.

Remains of food, rubbish, cooking-fires, coarse Knockadoon native ware, were found under the bank showing where the workers had squatted and sheltered as the earthwork was built stage by stage around the ring.

The Grange enclosure, however, was not only for local people. Inside it the excavation recovered 'foreign' sherds, Ebbsfleet ware from England, early and middle period beakers, grooved ware, suggesting that the great ring was in use around 2500 BC, a date in conformity with Somerville's Samain estimate. An S2/W beaker, lying smashed by the entrance, may have been fired as late as 2000 BC.

If this is not enough for the visitor there is a delightful Exhibition Centre with displays and literature on the far side of Lough Gur.

PRIA 54, 1951, 37–74, Plans; Clarke, II, 526, 1901F–1904F

357 LOUGH GUR C (3)

Lat: 52°.5   R 640 411
In next field, 130 yds (120m) N of the Grange circle. Fenced. Map 2
Difficult to visit because of the intervening fence, this is a small but attractive ring, its stones prettily varied in colour from reddish conglomerates to white limestones. They lie in an oval 57ft NE-SW by 53ft (17.4 × 16.2m). There are barely noticeable signs of an outer bank and the stones are problematically graded upwards to the south-west where there is a wide gap with the tallest stone of the ring, 4ft 8ins (1.4m) high at its west.

There is an unobtrusive central mound.

PRIA 54, 1951, 38

Co. LOUTH
Three sites only, all of them suspect

358 RAVENSDALE PARK (5, 6)

Lat: 54°.1   J 083 156
6¼ miles S of Newry, 1½ miles SE of Jonesborough. Walk. 200 yds (180m) E of minor road from Currahir Bridge to Marble Bridge. Up steep slope. In trees. Fair. Map 2

This is an oval, 23ft by 13ft (7 × 4m) of eight tall stones in a clearing in the woods. It was first exposed in 1840 and doubts have been expressed about its authenticity.

In 1907 five more stones were reported to just to the east, only one standing, lying concentrically with the oval. A firm opinion about the site was 'Almost certainly a bogus monument'.

There are other dubious rings at Bellurgan, J 090 097, and Shortstone East, H 982 110.

Arch. Inventory of Co. Louth, 1986, 18, no. 174

Co. MAYO

Not many circles but the group that does exist is fascinating

359 CONG, E, N, S, W (3, 1, 3, 1)
Lat: 53°.6   M 163 558
17½ miles WNW *of Tuam, 6 miles* SSW *of Ballinrobe, ¼ mile* NE *of Cong. Walk. Opposite Cong rectory on* E *side of road to Ballinrobe, immediately* N *of Deanery Place. Easy. Map 2*
Edward Lhuyd, the Welsh antiquarian,

visited Ireland in 1699 and saw this wonderful collection of rings the next year, his sketchy plans of them until recently being the only ones available. There are now detailed descriptions and good plans by Máire Lohan in *J. Westport Hist. Soc. 13*, 1993 [1994], 16–31.

The attractive small town of Cong, set in a lovely countryside of hills and streams near Lough Corrib, was a holy place from early times, a seventh-century monastery being replaced by a magnificent twelfth-century Augustinian abbey of which little remains today.

The area had been a religious centre long before then. Here there are four stone circles, all different, within 170 yards (155m) of each other like a pagan ecumenical Conference Centre. They lie in three separate fields and a paddock at the corners of a fairly symmetrical diamond.

A. *East* (3) M 164 558 This is the nearest to the road. It lies on ground falling gently to the ESE. It is a ruinous cairn-circle, covered in brambles, six thin hawthorns growing in the south-east quadrant and only four stones or

Cong North, Co. Mayo (359b), from the SSE. *The 'recumbent stone' and its flankers are at the far side of the ring.*

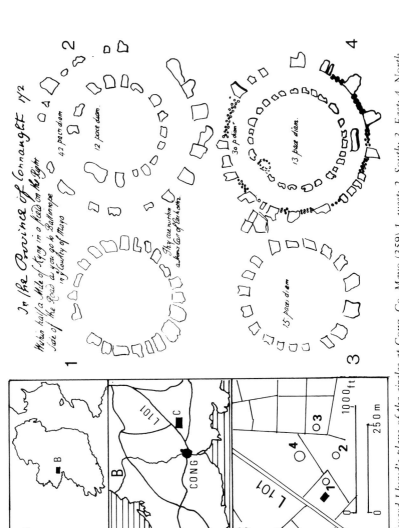

In the Province of Connaught 1½

Within half a Mile of Kong in a field on the Right side of the Road as you go to Ballinrobe in County of Mayo

42 pace diam

12 pace diam

They are within a bows cast of Each other.

1

2

30 p diam

13 pace diam

15 pace diam

3

4

Edward Lhuyd's plans of the circles at Cong, Co. Mayo (359) 1. west; 2. South; 3. East; 4. North

perhaps twelve originally, standing at the edge of a low cairn 46ft (14m) across. Lhuyd wrote, '15 paces'. Of the four stones between the north-west and south-west the tallest is no more than 2ft 3ins (69cm) high.

B. *North* (1) M 163 553 140 yards (128m) to the north-east is the finest, and most intriguing of the circles. It was erected on a low, presumably manmade, circular platform at the edge of a small spur falling to the north. The ring is a variant recumbent stone circle, 54ft (16.5m) in diameter, with an internal kerbed cairn 13ft (4m) across. Lhuyd recorded thirty paces for the ring and thirteen for the cairn, showing the rubbly edge of the platform around most of the site.

Once maybe of thirty stones eighteen remain, with a wide gap at the south-west where two tall and slender trees account for their absence. The flat-topped recumbent, slightly inclined inwards, 3ft high and 4ft 3ins long (0.9 × 1.3m), lies almost at due north, its possibly stunted west flanker 3ft 6ins high, its east 4ft 3ins (1.1, 1.3m). Both are level-topped.

At the south-east, opposite the three stones, is the surviving portal whose inner face has been weathered and pitted like a melting honeycomb. The pillar presumably was selected to stand there because of its 'cupmarked' appearance.

A few low kerblike slabs stand by some stones. More are shown in Lhuyd's sketchplan and they may be the survivors of a ring-cairn.

C. *South* (3) M 163 557 This wrecked and overgrown embanked stone circle, engulfed in trees and bushes, is 165 yards (150m) south of the north ring. Along the inner edge of a stony bank, 98ft in diameter, 6ft wide and at the east still 2ft high (29.9, 1.8, 0.6m) three or four stones remain standing at the east, the tallest 3ft 6ins high but broken (1.1m). There is one lonely stone at the west. Lhuyd, who saw the ring in a more open condition, recorded its diameter as forty-two paces with an inner ring twelve paces across.

D. *West* (1) M 162 558 In a paddock at Deanery Place, 130 yards (120m) north-east of the last ring, is a plain ellipse 54ft N-S by 53ft (16.5 × 16.2m). Lhuyd cited no dimensions for it. Its score of light-grey stones are flat-topped and are probably graded to the south-west, the northern stones averaging 2ft 6ins (76cm) in height whereas those at the south are up to 4ft (1.2m) high. There is a gap at the west and another at the south-east, although this 'entrance' is modern, caused by the presence of a collapsed stone wall.

The sites have been described as the surviving kerbstones of robbed cairns but only the eastern ring accords with this interpretation. The others are best seen as stone circles of differing regional architecture.

Earlier accounts explained that they were connected with the mythical first Battle of Moytura between the ingenious Tuath De Danaan and the small, dark Fir Bolg. The rings were erected by the Tuath to frustrate their enemies' champion, Balor of the Evil Eye, whose third eye, in the middle of his forehead, had the power to turn an adversary into dust. Disliking the prospect the Tuath set up the stones and painted figures of warriors on them. Balor's eye had no effect on the statues and, lamenting that he had lost his power, Balor abandoned the Fir Bolg to their defeat.

Evans, 162; *RCAHM-Pembroke*, 1925, xxxv, *Plans* (from Lhuyd, 1699)

360 INISHOWEN (5)
Lat: 53°.6   M 128 615
4½ miles SW of Ballinrobe, 1 mile SW of the ruined abbey. Walk. No information but should not be difficult. Map 2
William Stukeley, who had access to Lhuyd's notes, copied the plan of an apparent stone circle and inserted in it, 'On a mountain near the famous Fortification At Dynegeguill near Bellenrope in the County of Moyaw, but in Inys-Kynhairn Parish. 'tis 29 Paces diameter.'

On a flat-topped but overgrown

platform, 72ft (22m) across and 13ft (4m) high, some tall stones, up to 6ft (1.8m) high and almost contiguous, stand on the inner edge of an oval bivallate earthwork, 66ft (20m) along its major axis. Only excavation could determine whether this had been a genuine stone circle that had been incorporated into a rath.

According to Lhuyd it had two notably taller stones, but there is nothing to tell where they stood in the ring.

Stukeley, 1776, *Itinerarium Curiosum, II*, 84, 2nd, *Plan*; *Shell Guide to Ireland*. 1st ed., 1962, 74

361 ROSDOAGH, Rossport (5)
Lat: 54°.3   F 827 383
6 miles NNW *of Glenamoy, overlooking Sruwaddran Bay and Broad Haven. ¼ mile along untarred road. Walk. Over a ditch into the field. Fair. Map 2*
This monument, very close to a ruinous court-cairn, consists of two concentric circles, an outer, 54ft (16.5m) in diameter of thirty-three low stones, and an inner 30ft (9.1m) across, of sixteen. These 'Druidical Circles' are almost certainly the remains of a court-cairn.
Survey of the Megalithic Tombs of Ireland, II. Co. Mayo, 1964, 1–4, *Plan*, fig. 2

Co. MEATH
The county is more noted for its decorated Boyne passage-tombs and its huge unditched henges than for its stone circles

362 BALLINVALLY (4)
Lat: 53°.8   N 581 785
19 miles WNW *of Navan, 2 miles* ESE *of Oldcastle, 1 mile* NW *of the Loughcrew passage-tomb cemetery. From Oldcastle take the road* ESE *towards Patrickstown. In 2 miles turn* SSE *onto lane. In ½ mile there is a lane to the* SW. *Walk. ½ mile* W *of the junction. Fair. Map 2*
On the lower slopes of Slieve Na Callaigh of the nine stones of this ellipse, 95ft E-W by 88ft 6ins (29 × 27m) four remain standing. They may

once have surrounded a passage-tomb.
Archaeological Inventory of C. Meath, 1987, 40, no. 300. *No plan*

363 NEWGRANGE (3)
Lat: 53°.7   O 007 727
5½ miles WSW *of Drogheda, 2¼ miles* ESE *of Slane. Signposted. From Slane drive* E *, turn* SSE *past Knowth and follow signposts. In State care, charge. Walk. A few yards. Map 2*
Newgrange was seen by the Welsh antiquarian, Edward Lhuyd in the autumn of 1699. 'The most remarkable curiosity we saw by the way was a stately Mount at a place called New Grange near Drogheda, having a number of huge stones pitch't on end round about it.' This simple statement was the beginning of an unresolved argument. The ring is a conundrum. Nothing is certain about it, whether it was finished, its shape, its date and its relationship to the great passage-tomb it surrounds. All that is definite is that twelve stones exist today. And some of them are broken.

Around the magnificently decorated chambered tomb, with its midwinter sunrise roofbox at the end of a south-east facing passage, is an incomplete ring of stones of local Silurian grit. An arc of three, averaging 8ft 3ins (2.5m) high, stand outside the tomb's entrance. There are six more at the west, one at the north-west and two at the north-east. With an assumed spacing of 28ft (8.5m) the ring would have contained some thirty-five to thirty-eight uprights and, if circular, had a diameter of about 340ft (103.6m). Excavations between 1962 and 1975 came upon no conclusive proof of 'missing' stoneholes and the original number of stones remains unknown.

Claire O'Kelly, wife of the excavator, commented that 'it may be that, apart from the run of consecutive stones 9m [29ft 6ins] apart in the south, the remainder were more widely-spaced . . . and that no more than about half a dozen stones are missing.'

Adding to perplexity, the ring is neither circular nor concentric to the tomb. The north-west stone is about 28ft (8.5m) from the kerb and one at the north-east about 22ft 6ins (6.9m), whereas those outside the entrance are a full 53ft (16.2m) away.

Both the tomb and the ring are blunted ovoids, each with a flattened arc at the south-east. Analysis of the plan by Alexander Thom led him to the conclusion that the south-east was part of an ellipse, the north-west an egg designed from two circles drawn at the corners of right-angled triangles. The ring had diameters of 354ft SW-NE by 299ft (107.9 × 91.1m), the tomb 283ft by 196ft (86.3 × 59.7m). These lengths corresponded to multiples of his Megalithic Yard of 2.72ft (0.829): 130, 110, 104 and 72 respectively.

Claire O'Kelly was unconvinced, because to her there were too few points of contact between the suggested layout and the plans of the ring and the tomb to guarantee that the geometry was correct.

Even the age of the ring is controversial. Three radiocarbon assays from burnt material in the tomb: 2475 ± 45 bc (GrN-5462); 2465 ± 40 bc (GrN-5463) and 2585 ± 105 bc (UB-361) averaged 2508 bc, calibrated to 3250 BC. The ring may be much younger.

Excavations in 1982–3 confirmed the former presence of a huge concentric ring of postholes just to the south of Newgrange, some of which coincided with one of the three stones outside the entrance to the tomb and to a stonehole to the east. It is probable, though not positive, that the posts were earlier than the stones, the excavator, David Sweetman, believing 'that there were two distinct Beaker phases of activity, one associated with the large circle of pits' and a later which may have 'included the erection of the large stones of the so-called great stone circle.'

Twelve dates obtained from the pit-circle ranged from 2100 ± 65 bc (GU-1671) down to 1935 ± 70 bc (GU-1618), averaging around 2000 bc, the equivalent of 2500 BC, seven

centuries after the construction of the chambered tomb. Sadly, the stratigraphical relationship between the the pit- and the stone-circle could not be proved beyond question. As the excavator regretted, 'It would therefore appear that the great stone circle is later than the pit circle, though from this evidence alone one cannot be certain.' The stones remain a conundrum.

There is consolation. The admission charge includes entry to the tomb itself with its wondrous art, corbelled chamber and enigmatic stone basins.

M.J. O'Kelly, *Newgrange. Archaeology, Art and Legend*, London, 1982; P.D. Sweetman, 'A Late Neolithic/Early Bronze Age pit circle at Newgrange, Co. Meath', *PRIA* 85, 1985, 195–220. 208–9; E.W. MacKie, *The Megalithic Builders*, London, 1977, 182–3, *Plan*, 72

Co. SLIGO
Here may be the oldest 'stone circles' in Britain and Ireland, some of them surrounding cists and cremations dating back to 4600 BC

364 CARROWMORE (1, 3)
Lat: 54°.3   Centred on G 663 335
2½ miles SW of Sligo, 3 miles to E of Lough Gill and to N of Ballysadare Bay. From Sligo go WSW towards Magheraboy. In 1½ miles turn SSW. First sites are strung out mainly on W side of road, then a dense group in the triangle of small fields between junction of lane to Seafield, SW, and Kilmacower, S. Walk. Easy to most sites. Map 2
Once marked *Stone Circles* on the Ordnance Survey maps the early surveyors were percipient. Many of the so-called kerbed cairns and chambered tombs in this poorly protected megalithic cemetery are embryonic rings, forms transitional between the heavy kerbs of cairns and the true free-standing stone circle.

In 1983 F.T. Kitchin observed that 'Another feature of the Carrowmore tombs is the apparent absence of a

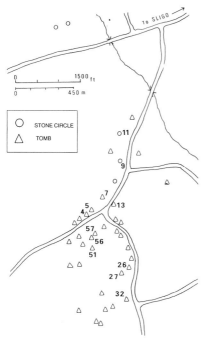

Carrowmore, Co. Sligo (364)

covering mound or cairn. It has
generally been accepted that the tombs
were originally covered and that the
boulder-circle acted as a surrounding
cairn . . . The writer's observation has
failed to discern any visible evidence of
cairn material within the circles . . . In
the four sites excavated recently no
evidence was found to suggest that a
cairn or mound either of stone or turf
ever existed.' To this should be added
the fact that the stones were either laid
on the ground or set in shallow hollows
with nothing to prevent them being
moved by a heavy internal cairn.

On a limestone plateau and in the
shadow of the towering Knocknarea to
the west, over sixty sites survive of a
hundred or more, others demolished
during the course of gravel-digging.
They concentrate in an area about 1½
miles from north to south and some ¾
mile wide. They are numbered from 1
to 65a.

The complex is a mixture of cairns,
dolmens, free-lying boulder-circles and
about thirty non-megalithic structures.
The only 'classic' passage-tomb
amongst them is Site 51, Listoghil, 'the
Giant's Grave', with eroded carvings on
its sill and capstone. It is a big cairn set
higher than the others and at the centre
of the major concentration. In contrast,
the metamorphosis from apparent kerb
to open circle is well illustrated by Site
26 at the south-east of the cemetery.

Excavations at Carrowmore from
1977 to 1979 suggested that the small,
simple tombs, lacking a passage, were
probably very early burial-places of
immigrant farming families who often
built the chambers of local gneiss on
low rises or knolls. From such
uncomplicated monuments, their central
burials spiritually protected by a ring of
contiguous boulders separating the dead
from the profane world, gradually
developed the idea of an open circular
enclosure.

A. It is not possible to describe all
the sites here. For the visitor with a day
to spare the following itinerary is
recommended. Start at the south with
Site 32, a boulder-circle alongside the
Kilmacower road. It lies strangely
situated on the curving head of a low
rise. Twenty-eight stones, shoulder to
shoulder, with three lying to one side
enclose an area 51ft E-W by 43ft (15.6
× 13.1m). A stone inside the ring may
be all that is left of a central dolmen.

B. Two hundred yards (180m) to the
north, *Site 27* on a little mound is
another boulder-circle, but with a
blotchy, despoiled cruciform tomb
inside it. It was excavated in 1978–9
when a series of C-14 assays provided
dates of 3090 ± 60 bc (LU-1698),
3050 ± 65 bc (LU-1808) and 2990 ±
85 bc (1818), with an average of 3043
bc, in real years about 3825 BC. This
was the latest of the Neolithic
determinations from Carrowmore,
causing the excavator to remark that 'It
is also likely that this may show the
end of the primary building of
megalithic monuments at Carrowmore.'
Enclosing the tomb but well spaced
away from it and with no sign of an
internal cairn is a ring of thirty-seven

boulders, heavy and close-set, 68ft N-S by 64ft (20.7 × 19.5m).

Above this ring, as with several others on the plain, the wide, smooth crest of Knocknarea mountain looms domineeringly with the nipple of Maeve's Cairn at its centre.

C. Against a quarry to the north-east is *Site 26* which was excavated in 1978. This is a completely free-standing circle of thirty large, rounded stones, originally perhaps thirty-eight, 53ft 3ins N-S by 47ft 10ins (16.2 × 14.6m). A central cremation was discovered. The ring was disturbed during the Iron Age.

D. Go north to the junction. Just to its north and right against the road is *Site 13*, for once a dolmen without a ring but with a monstrous capstone.

E. Return to the junction and go south-west. In 160 yards (146m) the overgrown *sites 56 and 57* are 125 yards (114m) to the east of the Seafield road. A little to their south is the passage-tomb of Listoghil. On a quiet slope *Site 56* has a ruined circle of eleven stones, with gaps at the north, north-east and east. With an estimated diameter of 32ft (9.8m) it stands on an artificial mound and surrounds an unroofed chamber or cist. The platform on which Site 4 stands is very obvious from this ring.

F. Just to the north is *Site 57*, a free-standing ring of thirty-three heavy boulders, eight of them in the next field, a big site 53ft N-S by 49ft 6ins (16.2 × 15.1m). They are massive stones, 6ft long, 3ft 6ins thick, 3ft high (1.8 × 1.1 × 0.9m), weighing four to five tons each. It would have taken perhaps a score of workers to move them into position. The interior is a platform of cobbles but inspection will show that the stones do not support, but lie on and against it.

G. Just WNW on the opposite side of the road *Site 4* is a boulder-circle excavated in 1979. It is the fourth of a line of increasingly spaced monuments extending to the NNE for almost ¾ mile. Its twenty-eight stones in an oval about 41ft E-W by 38ft (12.5 × 11.6m) surrounded a long cist from which an assay of 3800 ± 85 BC (LU-1840), c.4600 BC came. Such an early date is controversial. A second assay of 2370 ± 75 bc (LU-1750), c.3050 BC, came from contemporary material.

H. *Site 5* to the north stands on a

Carrowmore 4, Co. Sligo (364g), from the WSW.

Carrowmore 9, Co. Sligo (364j), from the south-west, a 'classical' stone circle.

conspicuously raised platform. Only one stone remains of the circle but standing within it is a 'Small but perfect cromleac consisting of five supports, still capped.'

I. It is essential to see *Site 7*. There is a small fee to be paid at the cottage behind which the site stands. Excavated in 1977–8 the dolmen had a polygonal chamber and 'Of the entire series this is indubitably the finest and best preserved cromleac and circle.' A central posthole, which may not have been contemporary with the chamber, gave a date of 3290 ± 80 bc (LU-1441), c.4050 BC.

The tomb stands on a manmade platform on the west-falling slope. The western stones of the encircling ring support the shelf but those at the east, although against the platform stand free of it. Thirty boulders, some of them fallen, surround the tall, capstoned chamber, the ring being 41ft 4ins E-W by 40ft 3ins (12.6 × 12.3m).

J. Well to the north, 285 yards (260m) away, is *Site 9*, a free-standing ring, with only eight of its exceptionally big and well-spaced stones surviving.

There is no trace of a platform on which the stones could have stood. The ring is 45ft N-S by 41ft (13.7 × 12.5m). It has a huge block at the south-west, 3ft high and 5ft wide (0.9 × 1.5m). Without doubt in any other county or country this setting would be called a stone circle.

K. *Site 11* to the north is another spacious ring, here with only five stones of which one is the adjacent field. The highest is at the WSW. It may be significant that the farther these open rings are from the megalithic tombs the more widely spaced are their stones and the bigger the rings become, Site 11 being no less than 70ft across E-W by 63ft (21.3 × 19.2m).

L. For additional interest there is a boulder-circle on the eastern outskirts of Sligo itself. Near St Anne's church is a christianised ring with crosses and a Madonna added. The ring now acts as a traffic island at Garravogue Villas.

PPS 49, 1983, 151–75, *Plan*, 154; G. Burenhult, *The Archaeology of Carrowmore*, Stockholm, 1984; *Archaeology Ireland 8 (1)*, 1994, 14–15; *ibid 8 (2)*, 1994, 34

Co. WATERFORD
There are a few questionable rings and one good Four-Poster

365 ROBINSTOWN GREAT (1)
Lat: 52°.4   S 811 291
16 miles WNW of Wexford, 5 miles ENE of New Ross. To the E of the road N from Old Ross to Palace. Walk. ¼ mile up hill. Fair. Map 2

Erected on a prominent hilltop this is a good example of a Four-Poster. It is far to the east of others in Co. Cork.

Its four stones stand at the corners of a rectangle about 14ft 9ins SW-NE by 11ft 6ins (4.5 × 3.5m). The north-west stone is the tallest, 5ft 3ins (1.6m) high. Clockwise the others are 3ft, 2ft 3ins but leaning and 4ft 7ins (0.9, 0.7, 1.4m). The ring is on a raised platform but this may be no more than the results of ploughing up to the stones.

Nearly 14ft (4.3m) to the south-west is a leaning 'playing-card' outlier once 2ft 8ins (81cm) high. Alongside it is a prostrate block of quartz.

O'Nuallain, 1984b, 71, *Plan*, 68; *JRSAI 42*, 1912, 15–16

Co. WICKLOW
There is a pleasing variety of spacious rings around the Wicklow mountains

366 ATHGREANY (3)
Lat: 53°.1   N 930 032
4 miles ENE of Dunlavin, 1½ miles S of Hollywood. Walk. 220 yards (200m) E of T42 from Hollywood to Baltinglass. Up gentle hillside. Easy. Map 2

Also known as the Piper's Stones, this collapsed ring stands on the soft north-eastern slope of a hillock with land falling away to the north-east before rising to the distant hills and mountains.

In a true circle 75ft 6ins (23m) in diameter fourteen stones of local granite remain of a probable sixteen, several missing at the north and west. Others lie at the south-west and south-east. In shape those that stand vary between rectangular and oval and may originally have been planned to alternate. The heights range from 3ft to 6ft (0.9 to 1.8m) where the tallest stands at the north-east. It is just

Athgreany, Co. Wicklow (366), from the SSW.

Boleycarrigeen, Co. Wicklow (367), *from the south-west.*

possible that it once formed one side of an entrance.

Down the slope, 132ft (40.2m) to the north-east, lies a big avocado-shaped boulder about 6ft long and broad (1.8m). With similar stones lying in the field the stone may be no more than a casual glacial erratic but it has been claimed to be an outlier.

If it once stood erect then it has fallen to the north from its pointed base. With an azimuth around 48° from the circle's centre it would have been in line with a low saddle between the hills and the midsummer sunrise. Because of this it is of interest that the field is known locally as 'Achadh Greine', Athgreany being a corruption, the 'field of the sun'.

Legend claims that the ring and the 'outlier' were dancers and pipers turned into stone for profaning the Sabbath. It is also said that fairies play the bagpipes there at midnight. Visit in daylight.

JRSAI 61, 1931, 128–30; Churcher, 8, *Plan*, fig. 1

367 BOLEYCARRIGEEN (1)
Lat: 52°.9　　　　　　　　　　　S 938 892
8¾ miles SSE of Dunlavin, 4¼ miles E of Baltinglass. ¾ mile S of Killybeg, S 941 903, turn W on lane to Boleycarrigeen. In 800 yds (730m) leave car at junction of lanes. Walk. Go back E 100 yds (90m) take track into forestry plantation S for 100 yds (90m), then ESE for 150 yds (137m) to ring. Easy to miss it, especially when the bracken is high. Map 2

This excellent embanked circle is spoiled by the high and thick bracken in and around it. Winter and early Spring are the best times to visit. It stands at the highest point of the pass between the Brusseltown Ring, 1329ft (405m) O.D. to the west and Keadeen Mountain 2146ft (654m) O.D. to the east.

Known as the 'Druidical Circle' and more evocatively as the 'Griddle Stones', the ring stands on a slight south-eastern slope. All around it high conifers conceal the skyline.

Of the ring eleven stones and a stump, all of local shale, remain of a hypothetical eighteen in a circle 45ft

Castleruddery, Co. Wicklow (368), from the north-east.

6ins (13.9m) in diameter. The tall pillars are quite evenly spaced about 4ft (1.2m) apart and are graded from the south-west, 3ft to 4ft 6ins (0.9–1.4m) high, up to the north-east where the tallest stands 6ft 3ins (1.9m) in height, a thin, pointed pillar.

Surrounding the ring is a substantial bank about 6ft wide and still about 3ft high at the south-east (1.8 × 0.9m).

In a ruinous mound 80 yards (73m) to the east the stones of a chamber or a cist are exposed. Folklore claims that it conceals a cave into which a local entered to discover a long hall with many small rooms on either side. Before he could explore further his candle blew out and could not be relit. He left.

PRIA 42, 1934, 39; Churcher, 10–11, Plan, fig. 2b

368 CASTLERUDDERY (3)
Lat: 53°.0　　　　　　　　S 916 942
17 miles SE of Kildare, 4½ miles NE of Baltinglass, 2½ miles NNW of Boleycarrigeen. 300 yards (275m) NE of Castleruddery House at the crossroads, S 914 943, take the ESE lane. In ¼ mile
the site is 75 yds (69m) S of the lane along a snaking footpath. Easy. Map 2

This circle-henge, once known as the Druidical Circle, surrounded by whitethorns and dense undergrowth, disproves the belief that what one sees is all that there is. A resistivity survey detected features not visible on the ground.

The site is an untidy circle of about forty lumpish grey stones with two of quartz at the NNE. The ring is surrounded by a well-preserved bank of soil and clay, still 4ft (1.2m) high, kerbed with low stones. About 15ft (4.6m) wide the bank is 115ft (35m) from crest to crest with an opening at the exact east.

Inside it the regular circle has a diameter of 100ft (30.5m). The two immense, coarse blocks of white quartz rest brilliantly at the entrance. They are huge. One is 9ft long, 6ft thick and 4ft high (2.7 × 1.8 × 1.2m). Its northern partner is as big, 10ft long by 4ft by 4ft (3.1 × 1.2 × 1.2m). Each must weigh in the region of fifteen tons. Beyond them a straggle of seven prostrate stones are all that remains of an approach avenue or row.

In 1970 aerial photographs of Castleruddery suggested that there may have been an outer ditch to the site and the resistivity survey of 1984 not only confirmed this but added to it.

Castleruddery's bank is thought to have been built of soil from an external ditch 24ft 3ins (7.4m) beyond the stone circle. Outside this there had been a second bank held in place by a timber revetment whose existence survived as a series of postholes. This bank had been formed from the material quarried from a wide ditch 200ft (61m) outside the circle.

In Isabel Churcher's words, 'The interpretation of this evidence gives a new picture of Castleruddery. A stone circle was embanked with an earth bank and kerbed with smaller stones. The soil for this bank was obtained from a ditch running concentrically outside the circle. A timber revetment was constructed, against which a bank, with material from an outer ditch, was placed. The outer ditch is double the diameter of the circle – thus showing a well planned structure.'

JRSAI 75, 1945, 266–7, *Plan*; Churcher, 27–33, *Plans*

France

Brittany; Southern France

BRITTANY

There are very few detailed accounts in English about the cromlechs in Brittany despite the importance of sites such as Er-Lannic and Kergonan. This is all the more surprising because rings like Île Béniguet seemed to have a clear affinity with stone circles in Cornwall.

The only published gazetteers are Bender (1986), and Burl (1985). Where other sources exist, for example the astronomical analysis of the Crucuno rectangle in Thom et al, (1973), they are quoted at the end of the site entry. Descriptions in French are included only where they are detailed. Readers are otherwise referred to more general books in which the cromlechs are mentioned such as Balfour (1992) and Service and Bradbery (1993).

CÔTES-DU-NORD

369 Tossen-Keler, Penvenan (2) Lat: 480.7, original latitude: 480.8
Originally just w of the Château d'eau, 13km (8 miles) NE of Lannion, 2km (1¼ miles) s of Penvenan. Now at Tréguier, 18km (11 miles) ENE of Lannion by the estuary on main road to Rt of the Place de Géneral de Gaulle. Map 4
Excavations in 1963–4 of an imposing mound revealed a multi-phase structure. On the old ground surface were two hearths containing charcoal, ashes and fire-reddened stones. A radio-carbon determination of 2550 ± 250 bc (Gif-280), c.3300 BC, was obtained from the charcoal.

The hearths had been covered by at least two, maybe even four rough, low cairns separated by narrow gaps in a manner reminiscent of the Neolithic Boghead mound at Fochabers, Moray, in Scotland, excavated in 1972 and subsequently by the writer in 1974 (*PSAS 114*, 1984, 35–73). The Tossen-Keler cairns lay under a large earthen mound. Many Late Neolithic sherds were found in its débris.

Almost enclosing the tumulus was a horseshoe-shaped cromlech, 31m wide and 29m long (102 × 95ft), open to the east. Its fifty-eight stones were mostly of local granite. The 'head' of the horseshoe at the west had an apparent entrance about 4m (13ft) wide, flanked by two heavy stones.

Three of the stones bore carvings: two opposed chevrons; a hafted stone axe; and an anthropomorphic figurine. As two of the blocks were upside down it is likely they were re-used slabs from a nearby but destroyed chambered tomb.

After the excavation the horseshoe was re-erected at Tréguier. The decorated stones were taken to the safety of a storeroom.
L'Anthropologie 72, 1968, 5–40, *Plan 8–9*

FINISTÈRE

*The cromlechs in north-western
Brittany are more lineally geometrical
than others to the south of the province*

370 BEG ROUZ VORC'H, Trégunc (3)
Lat: 47°.8
*5¹/₂km (3¹/₂ miles) ESE Concarneau.
600m (660 yds) NE of Trégunc. On
D122 at Beg Rouz Vorc'h hamlet turn
WNW onto lane for 200m (220 yds).
Walk. Standing stones and cromlech are
in fields to N. Fair. Map 4*
A cromlech in a ruinous circle about
30m (98ft) across. Twelve to fifteen
stones spaced 2m to 3m (6–10ft) apart.
A nearby menhir stands 7.4m (24ft
3ins) high. The rise on which the
cromlech lies is crowned with many
natural stones, mostly low but some
very large, up to 3m (10ft) long.
    Gilbert, 1962, 227–8, no. 22

371 PARC-AR-VARRET, Porspoder (3)
Lat: 48°.5
*500m (550 yds) NNW of Porspoder on
the D27a turn WNW (Lt) to the Saint-
Laurent peninsula for 500m (550 yds).
Walk. Cromlech is 500m (550 yds) on
NE coast. Fair. Map 4*
'Field of the dead'. A rectangular
enclosure, 40m N-S by 15m (131 ×
49ft). The south-west corner has been
eroded by the sea. At the south-east
corner is a menhir 1.5m (5ft) high. A
pair of standing stones 2m and 3m (6ft
6ins, 9ft 9ins) high and 5m (16ft) apart
can be seen 15m (49ft) from the south-
east corner.
    Gilbert, 1962, 224, no. 15

372 PEN-AR-LAN, Isle of Ushant (2)
Lat: 48°.4
*3km (2 miles) ENE of Lampaul along
D81. Walk. 1km (1100 yds) ESE of
Penn Arlan by the cliffs near the Croix
de Saint-Paul. Easy. Map 4*
A horseshoe open to the WSW,
measuring 13m by 10m (43 × 33ft)
with a central stone. Restored in 1988.
A Four-Stone row, N-S, stands alongside
it ending at a transverse E-W line.
150m+ (500ft) to the south is a quartz
block. The horseshoe's major axis is

aligned on the midsummer sunrise and
'each stone marked a different sunrise
over the course of the year, and also
lunar movements.'
    Briard, 1990, 50, *Plan*

373 PHARE DU CRÉACH, Isle of Ushant
(3) Lat: 48°.4
*2¹/₂km (1¹/₂ miles) W of Lampaul along
D81. Walk. Against the lighthouse on
the W coast. Easy. Map 4*
A megalithic rectangle divided by a
central line of stones. The shape is
characteristic of the angular cromlechs
of western Brittany.
    Briard, 1990, 50. *No plan*

ILLE-ET-VILAINE

*There are few cromlechs in this
département*

374 CHÂTEAU-BÛ, Saint-Just (1)
Lat: 47°.7.
*From Saint-Just take the lane to the W
for 1¹/₄km (³/₄ mile). Turn N. Pass
Alignements du Moulin to W in 250m
(275 yds). Continue N to next left (W).
In 600m (660 yds) the site can be seen
immediately to the S. Easy. Map 4*
On the Grée de Cojoux. On an oval
mound 35 × 26m, 2m high, (115 ×
85, 6ft), three tall stones stand at the
corners of a rectangle, 7 × 6m (23 ×
20ft). The tallest, 3.2m (10ft 6ins) high,
is at the north-east. The south-west is
the lowest, only 1.5m (5ft) high. The
north-west is a thick, leaning block,
about 2m (6ft 6ins) high. The missing
south-east stone may lie on the north
side of the mound. Three low stones
stand in line between the pillars on the
east side, and others lie broken at south
and west. The centre of the mound is
hollowed by a deep pit.
    The site is reminiscent of the Four-
Poster stone circles of central Scotland.
Excavations since 1991 have revealed
that its supporting mound covers a
transepted passage-tomb.
    Les Demoiselles, a pair of standing
stones with a fallen stone by them,
stand 400m (440 yards) to the ENE.
    Burl, 1988, 56–7, *Plan*

Château-Bû Four-Poster, Ille-et-Vilaine (374), during the 1990 excavation. The stones stand on top of the mound of a megalithic passage-tomb.

375 DEMOISELLES, LES, Langon (4?)
Lat: 47°.7
18km (11 miles) ENE of Redon. 200m (220 yds) W of the village just N of a minor road leading W by the sports field. Easy. Map 4
Until the nineteenth century there were six SE-NW rows on a slight slope with a concentric cromlech at its head. Today the rows are damaged and the cromlech has been partly destroyed. It lies among trees at the top of the rise 30m (100ft) to the north-west of the rows. Seven stones form an irregular oval about 10 by 6m (33 × 20ft). The rows are said to be girls turned to stone for dancing on Sunday.
    Burl, 1985, 82, no. 100. *No plan*

376 TRIBUNAL, LE, Saint-Just (1)
Lat: 47°.8
Walk. 100m (110 yds) W of the Château-Bû. Easy. Map 4
Among the megaliths of the Grée de Cojoux and just west of the Château-Bû 'Four-Poster', is a small horseshoe of nine low stones, the tallest 1.6m (5ft 3ins) high. Standing close to the road

the cromlech is no more than 16m (53ft) long and is open to the east. 45m (50yds) to the east, in line with the horseshoe's midpoint, is an isolated menhir, 1.3m (4ft 4ins) high, perhaps set in line with the equinoctial sunrise. To the west is the kerbed tertre of the Croix-Saint-Pierre.
    Briard, 1977, 64, 71. *No plan*

MORBIHAN
There are vast ruinous oval cromlechs and horseshoes here. That at Kerlescan West (384) is now closed to the public

377 CHAMP DE LA CROIX, Crucuny (3)
Lat: 47°.6.
4km (2¹/₂ miles) both N of Carnac-Ville and E of Plouharnel. From Carnac-Ville take the D119 N for 4km (2¹/₂ miles), turn W to Crucuny. In 400m (440 yds) the cromlech is behind the wall of a farm garden just S of the junction. Easy but ask. Map 4
In Breton, 'Parc-er-Groez' or 'field of the cross', all that remains is the south-west arc, 45m (148ft) long, of a ruined

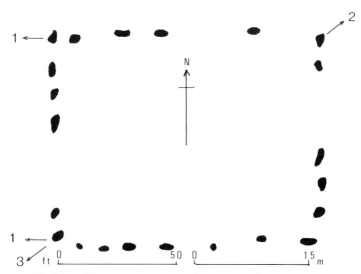

Crucuno, Morbihan, Brittany (378). 1. To the equinoctial sunsets; 2. To midsummer sunrise; 3. To midwinter sunset

horseshoe that is now part of the garden wall. Its stones are about 2m (6ft 6ins) high. Modern drystone walling fills gaps between them. The stones were re-erected, by Le Rouzic in 1926–7. In the same garden a 2m (6ft 6ins) high menhir stands 78m (255ft) to the north-east.

Thom and Thom, 1978, 119–20, *Plan*, 119

378 CRUCUNO, Plouharnel (2)
Lat: 47°.6.
3km (1¹/₄ miles) NNW of Plouharnel, 400m (440 yds) E of the dolmen in Crucuno hamlet. From Plouharnel take the D781 NW for 3km (1¹/₄ miles). Turn NE. Crucuno hamlet is ³/₄km (800 yds). Walk. 370m (400 yds) down track to E (Rt) of the dolmen. The 'quadrilateral' is in a field to the E (Rt). Easy in dry weather. Map 4A
Approached by what is often a discouragingly muddy lane the cromlech is also often fearsomely thick with spiky gorse.

Also known as 'Parc Vein Glass' or 'field of the blue stone' Crucuno is a symmetrical rectangle, arranged almost perfectly E–W. Its sides measure 33.2 by 24.9m (109 × 81ft 8ins), a ratio of 4:3. The diagonals are 41.5m (136ft) long. The tallest stone stands at the south-east corner. Only nine stones of twenty-two stood before Gaillard's restoration in 1882. The astonishing precision of the layout led to criticism of the reconstruction but its accuracy is confirmed by a survey by Dryden and Lukis fifteen years earlier in 1867.

Sightlines seem to have been part of the design, the long sides directed neatly towards the equinoctial sunsets and, because of a different horizon height, less well to the sunrises. The NE-SW diagonal points to the midsummer sunrises and midwinter sunsets.

The Crucuno cromlech has affinities with other 'astronomical' rectangles such as the destroyed site of Lanvéoc, Finistère; King Arthur's Hall (7d) on Bodmin Moor, Cornwall, SX 130 777; and, of course, the Four Stations at Stonehenge (84) in which the long and short sides as well as the diagonal are associated with solar and lunar events.

A. and A.S. Thom and R.L. and A. Merritt, 'The astronomical significance

Er-Lannic, Morbihan (379), the northern ring from the east.

of the Crucuno stone rectangle',
Current Anthropology 14, 1973, 450–
4, *Plan*; Burl, 1987, 141–9

379 ER-LANNIC, Gulf of Morbihan (3)
Lat: 47°.6
*Very private. Motor launches from
Lamor-Baden, 14km (8³/₄ miles) SW of
Vannes take visitors to the
magnificently decorated chambered
tomb of Gavr'inis and also
circumnavigate the nearby islet of Er-
Lannic for photographs to be taken.
No walk possible. Map 4*
A sub-rectangular cromlech with an
adjacent but sea-covered horseshoe to
its south. They had been erected on a
low hillock that became partly
submerged when the sea-level rose in
Roman times.

A. *The flattened circle*, with a long
axis NW-SE, measures about 72 by 54m
(236 × 177ft), a 4:3 ratio like
Crucuno. The stones are almost
contiguous, ranging from 2m to 5.3m
(6ft 6ins to 17ft 4ins) in height. There
are two tall outliers now hidden below
the water at the east and west of the
cromlech.

Excavations between 1923 and 1926
by Le Rouzic recovered Middle
Neolithic Chasséen ware from an
earlier occupation site and Late
Neolithic Conguel ware directly
associated with the circle which
probably dates from about 3300 BC.

The stones stand in a rubble bank. At
their bases were cists containing animal
bones, flints, quartz and other artefacts.
Two stones at the north-west and one
at the east bear carvings of stone axes
and a 'yoke'. There were cupmarks on
a packing-stone.

B. The southern site is *a horseshoe*,
open to the east with a major axis 61m
(200ft) long. It was first noticed in
October 1872, when Closmadeuc, an
archaeologist from Vannes, visited the
north ring at very low tide and saw
seven or eight stones exposed in the sea
with tips of others apparent.

Like Crucuno (378) and many early
stone circles in Britain, Er-Lannic
contained lines to cardinal points and
to astronomical events. East-west was
marked by the two huge, now-fallen
outliers, the eastern 50m (165ft) from
Stone 14 at the north-west of the

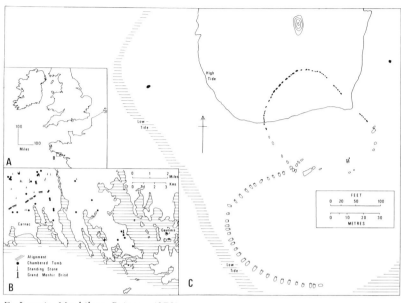

Er-Lannic, Morbihan, Brittany (379)

cromlech, the western, 90m (295ft) from it, a great block weighing some twenty tons. At due south in the horseshoe was a gigantic pillar called by fishermen 'men-ar-gou' or La Roche du Forgeron, 'the blacksmith's stone'.

The possible astronomy is lunar. The long SE-NW axis, determined by what may be a three-sided and unroofed Cove below water at the south-east of the cromlech and Stone 14, 5.4m (17ft 9ins) high to the north-west, appears to be in line with the major northern moonset. Approximately at right-angles to that line an observer at the centre of the cromlech would have seen the major northern moon rise over the eastern outlier. These are conjectures rather than certainties. Available plans of Er-Lannic are poor, many of the stones are fallen and as many are under the sea. Even the Cove is questionable. But the astronomical interpretation of the two cromlechs may well reflect the preoccupation with the moon and the rituals of life and death of people 5000 years ago.

Rouzic, Z. Le, *Les Cromlechs de Er-Lannic*, Vannes, 1930; Burl, 1976, 130–6, *Plan*, 131

380 JARDIN AUX MOINES, Néant-sur-Yvel (5) Lat: 48°.0
In Brocéliande Forest, Paimpont, 21km (13 miles) s of St Méen-le-Grand. 2³/₄km (1³/₄ miles) ENE of Néant-sur-Yvel. Walk. 250m (270 yds) w of crossroads in woods between the D141 and the lane from Le Pertuis Néant to Néant-sur-Yvel. Easy with persistence. Map 4
'The monks' garden'. Restored. Probably a cromlech, but the site has similarities to other rectangular enclosures such as Notre-Dame-de-Lorette, Pontivy.

To the west of the Butte aux Tombes is an oblong of standing stones, NE-SW, 25m by 6m (82 × 20ft). Quartz and white puddingstones transported from a source 3km (2 miles) away alternate with local red schist. At the south-east end two internal cross-walls form separate compartments like the terminal cells of allées-couvertes. Excavations in 1983 uncovered a pile of red and white stones covering two Late Neolithic pots.

A legend claims that the stones are wicked monks and seigneurs petrified for their misdeeds.

Briard, 1989, 41–56, *Plan*, 43

381 KERBOURGNEC, Saint Pierre-Quiberon (3) Lat: 47°.5
9km (5¹/₂ miles) SSW of Carnac-Ville, 4km (2¹/₂ miles) N of Quiberon. In Saint-Pierre Quiberon follow the rue del'Église to the rue de Marthe Delpirue. The complex of five rows of stones is 300m (330 yds) down road on the W (Rt). Walk. Easy. Map 4
From the far end of the rows a narrow footpath leads west and south for 120m (130 yards) to a western arc of stones, all that remains of a cromlech originally perhaps either ovoid, 96 by 76m (315 × 250ft), or a horseshoe open to the east. Some forty high and thin slabs remain, several of them covered in ivy. The arc is broken by gaps. The relation of the cromlech, whatever its original shape, to the rows is unclear. The truncated rows once extended at least 150m (165 yards) eastwards down to the sea.

Lukis, 1875, 29, 35; Thom and Thom, 1977, 7, 22, *Plan*

382 KERCADO, Carnac (3) Lat: 47°.6
2¹/₂km (1¹/₂ miles) NE of Carnac-Ville in the grounds of the château. Open to the public. From Carnac take the D119 1¹/₄ km (1³/₄ mile) and turn E onto the D196. The Kermario rows are on the N side of the road. In 1km (1100 yds) the château road is signposted S (Rt). Walk. 500m (550 yds) to the site along drive. Easy. Entrance fee. Map 4A
An incomplete ring of twenty-seven standing stones surrounds a passage-tomb with a large carving of a hafted stone axe on the underside of the chamber's capstone. There are faint engravings on four other sideslabs. The tomb was excavated in 1863, again in 1924 and restored in 1925. As well as burnt human bones many artefacts were recovered. Finds of Middle and Late Neolithic pottery, Grand Pressigny

flint, diorite and jadeite axes and callais beads can be seen in Room 2 of the Carnac museum.

Surrounding the mound is a misshapen stone 'circle' measuring 18 to 19m (59–62ft) in diameter, its irregularity suggesting that the ring was a later addition to the tomb, the positions of the stones being casually offset from the kerb. They are graded in height, the tallest, 1.8m (6ft) high at the ESE outside the tomb's entrance. The best-preserved arc is at the south. No stones survive at the north.

Charcoal from the tomb provided a determination of 3890 ± 300 bc (Sa-95), around 4675 BC. It is likely that the ring belongs to a much later period.

Daniel, 141–2; Burl, 1985, 137–8, no. 176, *Plan*

383 KERGONAN, Gulf of Morbihan (1 for stones, 4 for misuse) Lat: 47°.6
On the Île-aux-Moines. 10km (6 miles) SW of Vannes. Ferry from Port-Blanc 3km (1¹/₄ miles) NE of Larmor-Baden. Cromlech is 1¹/₄km (¹/₂ mile) S of landing-stage and Locmiquel on W (Rt) alongside of road towards Nioul. Bicycles can be hired near the quay. Quite easy. Map 4
Capable of containing a thousand comfortably-spaced participants the well-preserved megalithic horseshoe of Kergonan should be one of the showplaces of prehistoric Brittany. It is not. It is a disgrace.

Also known as the 'Cercle de la Mort', 'circle of death', and 'Er Anké', 'the goddess of death', dirges should be keened here for the neglect of the finest cromlech in Brittany. Lovers of wild flowers will enjoy the wilderness of thistles, mallows, dandelions, poppies, clover, head-high burdock and wild roses. Enthusiasts for megaliths will be saddened by the tangled barbed-wire, overgrown gardens, ugly footpath, shabby houses, walls that bar access to parts of the cromlech, hedges, intrusive, closely-planted trees and abandonment.

Kergonan is a vast U-shaped cromlech, open to the south-east, 70m deep, 95m wide (230 × 312ft) at its

Kergonan, Île-aux-Moines, Morbihan (383), *the north-east arc of stones in a wilderness of undergrowth.*

mouth. Of its thirty-one remaining stones, twenty-four still stand. They are thin flat-topped slabs 1 to 3m (3–9ft 9ins) high, almost contiguous, their smoother sides facing inwards. The majority are linked by a low drystone wall. There are reports that the mouth of the cromlech, now open, was once lined with small stones side by side with a tall terminal menhir at each end, 2.5m to 3m (8ft 2ins–9ft 9ins) high. That at the north-east is known as the Pierre de Moine because in outline it resembles a cloaked monk.

Other stones are much lower except those at the north-western head of the horseshoe that stand 3m to 5m (9ft 9ins–16ft) high.

The astronomy of the design is debateable. Previously it was deduced that to the south-east end of the axis, 126°, the featureless midpoint of the mouth was in line with the midwinter sunrise. But there was no foresight. More probably it was the opposite end to the north-west that was the target where the tallest stones stood in line with the midsummer sunset. It is a belief given some support by the

observation that the north-west gap in the cromlech, where a footpath leads to some houses, may once have been filled by the Pierre Colas, a massive stone, possibly a gnomon. It is now part of the foundation of a house 30m (100ft) WSW of the cromlech's western side. The stone that stood alongside it is named 'Pierre de Sacrifice'.

An avenue of small stones may have led to the cromlech from the south. In the early nineteenth century an English antiquarian, the Rev. Bathurst Deane, wrote that its course from Penab 'was formerly traceable in the direction of the island from south to north; but when we saw it there were very few stones remaining; sufficient, however, to convince me of the nature of the temple.'

An axe-carving on one of the stones reported by Le Rouzic is almost impossible to find because of the weatherworn condition of the uprights and the engulfing vegetation. Recently a rectangle, probably anthropomorphic, has been noticed on another stone.

Excavations in 1864 recovered a quartz borer, and in 1877 flint flakes were found at the bases of the biggest stones.

The cromlech's associations with funerary rites are attested by its art, its solar alignment, and its other name of Er Anké, 'Er Ankeu the notorious harbinger of death who usually appears as a skeleton in a white shroud and driving a cart with squeaky wheels.'

Merlet, 1974, 7–19, *Plan, 9*

KERLESCAN NORTH, Carnac, see after Kerlescan West

384 KERLESCAN WEST, Carnac (1)
Lat: 47°.6.
3km (2 miles) NE of Carnac-Ville, 8¹/₂km (5¹/₄ miles) SSW of Auray. From Carnac take the D119 1km (1100 yds) and turn E onto the D196 In 1³/₄ km (1 mile) the cromlech is by the road to the N (Lt). Easy. Map 4A
Just west of the thirteen Kerlescan rows of 555 stones, the tallest about 4m (13ft) high, is a 'rectangle', 78m by 74m (256 × 243ft), of tall granite pillars, its long sides arranged N–S.

Some eleven stones stand in a shallow convex arc along the short south side by the road. An equally shallow convex arc of eleven stones forms the long western side. A straight line of eighteen stones stands on the east. Despite gaps where that row has been robbed, its stones are close-set, unlike the well-separated stones in the rows to the east. Such contiguity is typical of cromlechs, as though their builders wished to conceal the interior from the profane world.

There are no stones along the cromlech's north side where, between it and the trees to the north, is an overgrown 98m (322ft) long mound of a tertre in which Neolithic axes and sherds were found. At its western end is a 3.7m (12ft) high menhir, an 'indicateur', perhaps sighting-device, common to many Breton burial-places.

The absence of stones from the northern side of the 'oblong' is unlikely to be the result of robbery. Stones taken from the cromlech would have been removed from the south side

against the road. Instead, with its curved sides and open north end Kerlescan West is best interpreted as a horseshoe to whose north-eastern corner and open mouth an avenue of two lines of standing stones led from the ESE before the accretion of extra rows obscured its existence.

This hypothetical avenue is detectable. From the north-east stone of the cromlech the avenue's south side contains eighteen stones stretching ESE over a distance of about 90m (295ft). The stones beyond that point are probably later additions. Some 10m (33ft) wide over most of its course the 'avenue' characteristically narrowed to about 6m (20ft) as it neared the cromlech, its great stones rising in height as they approached the enclosure.

Thom and Thom, 1978, 92–7, *Plan 94;* Burl, 1993, 140–3, *Plans*

385 KERLESCAN NORTH, Carnac (3)
Lat: 47°.6
In the wood immediately N of the Kerlescan rows. Easy. Map 4A
Lost among trees and undergrowth are the ruins of an enormous megalithic horseshoe of which forty-two stones remain, thirty-six still standing. Open to the ESE the cromlech is 200m long and 235m wide at its mouth (220 × 255 yards). The first stones of its western arc are about 100m (110 yards) north of the tall, isolated menhir that stands just north of the Kerlescan West cromlech.

The spacing of the horseshoe's stones is very irregular, and the wilderness of vegetation renders it impossible to comprehend the size or layout of this great setting, most of whose stones are no more than 1.5m (5ft) high. To have planned it, as the Thoms did, was a masterpiece of surveying.

Thom and Thom, 1978, 96, *Plan*

386 KERZERHO, Erdeven (5) Lat: 47°.6
From Plouharnel take the D781 NW towards Erdeven. In 5km (3 miles) the rows are on the E (Rt) of the road opposite a house. Easy. Map 4A

Ménec West, Carnac, Morbihan (388), *the western arc of closely-set stones in the cromlech.*

Here there are ten parallel rows of numerous stones, their western end interrupted by the dangerously straight D781. The majority of the stones are to the east of the road.

There are a few on the other side. In the first row, by the house, the east face of the second stone from the south-east has two or three large cupmarks near its base and some smaller above them. The stones of this line, however, are as widely spaced as their companions across the road and there are the remains of other rows behind them. Despite the cupmarks, therefore, and the reports that there had been a cromlech at Kerzerho the gaps between the decorated pillar and its partners make it unlikely that, unless moved from behind the house, the stone was ever a member of the lost enclosure.

In the mid-eighteenth century it was claimed that there were trilithons at Kerzerho like those at Stonehenge (84), but there is nothing comparable in Brittany. It could have been imagination or self-deception or even a vanished megalithic mystery. 'En tout cas il y a là une énigme.'
Lukis, 27–8; Giot, 1960, 124; Bender, 1986, 141

387 Ménec East, Carnac (4)
Lat: 47°.6.
1¼km (¾ mile) N of Carnac-Ville, Just E of the D119 in the junction between that road and the D196. Easy. Map 4A
Only twenty-two stones remain of this egg-shaped cromlech, the majority along its western arc. They are on level ground at the head of a gradual rise up which twelve ragged rows meander. The cromlech was once about 108m long, SE-NW by 90m (355 × 295ft).

Midwinter sunrise and midsummer sunset were indicated by the longer axis.

Thom and Thom, 1977, 1B, 14; *ibid*, 1978, 64, 70, *Plan*, 64

388 Ménec West, Carnac (3)
Lat: 47°.6
1km (1100 yds) NNW of Carnac-Ville, 2km (1¼ miles) ESE of Plouharnel. From Carnac take the D781 NW for 375m (400 yds). Turn N onto the D196.

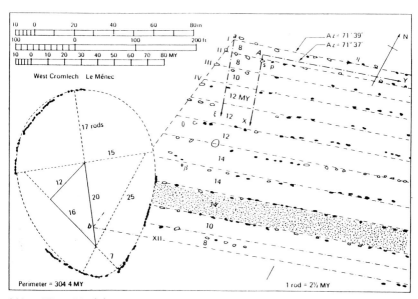

Ménec West, Morbihan, Brittany (388)

In *½km (650 yds), where a carpark is on the Rt and the road curves away to the E, take the short lane directly ahead to the N. Arcs of closely-set stones of the cromlech enclose the hamlet. Easy. Map 4A.*

Although similar in shape to its counterpart at the east of the rows, the western cromlech was an inverted egg with its narrower tip to the south-east near the modern road. It was built around a wide, gentle knoll at the head of land declining to the east.

Badly disjointed by stones being taken for the houses of Le Ménec hamlet, the finest arc is to the north-west of the buildings. Another good stretch can be seen at the south-east. The local granite stones are heavy and stand tightly shoulder to shoulder.

Once about 91m by 71m (300 × 230ft) the ring enclosed a space of some 5075m² (1¼ acres) and could have accommodated a thousand people without discomfort.

Twelve rows crawl uphill to it from the east. It is noticeable that the two most parallel, lines nine and ten from

the north, the third and fourth from the south, have stones rising in height towards the cromlech, the tallest abutting a 10m (33ft) wide gap in the ring's east side between a run of seven stones to the south and three to the north. As the central axis of the two rows bisects the gap and points to the peak of the knoll and the cromlech's centre it is possible that it is the central line of a former avenue 11m (36ft) wide and some 120m (390ft) long that over the centuries was both lengthened and engulfed in a plethora of later, less well-laid out rows on either side of it.

Such an avenue would have provided a controlled approach to the cromlech, perhaps at seasonal times of the year. Unlike Ménec East (387) it is the shorter SW-NE axis here that appears to contain solar sightlines to the midwinter sunset and midsummer sunrise, solstitial events opposite to those of Ménec East.

Thom and Thom, 1978, 62–77, *Plan*, 63; Burl, 1993, 135–40, *Plans*

261

SOUTHERN FRANCE

There are other prehistoric stone circles in France. One or two are worth mentioning here, a full 650km (400 miles) south-east of Carnac and 45km (28 miles) north-west of Montpellier.

389 LE PLANAS, Perrarines, Gard (2)
Lat: 44°.0.
A. *14km (8¼ miles) wsw of Ganges, 9km (5½ miles) sw of le Vigan. Just w of side-lane N immediately w of the junction of the D113 Montdardier-Blandas road and the D513. Easy. Map 4B*
On a flat saucer of land between the hills this is an enormous oval some 104m E-W by 88m (340 × 290ft) of thirty-nine impressive stones. In height they range from 1 to 1.5m (3–5ft). Near the centre of the ring is a tall pillar 2.3m (7ft 6ins) high. The site was restored in 1975.

Not having seen the ring the writer can vouch for its existence, but not its authenticity. Paradoxically, it is much more like the great ovals of north Britain than the egg-shaped cromlechs and horseshoes of Morbihan and Finistère.
B. *Le Can de Ceyrac*, Lat: 43°.7
14km (8½ miles) south-east of Lodève, 32 km (20 miles) ssw of le Planas. Another huge ring, 95m (312ft) in diameter is reported here.
F. Niel. *Connaissance des Mégalithes*, 1976, 113

390 PUY DE PAULIAC, Aubazines, Corrèze Lat: 45°.2
10½km (6½ miles) ENE of Brive-la-Gaillarde A ring, about 35m (115ft) in diameter of some forty gneiss blocks up to 1m (3ft) high.
F. Niel, *Connaissance des Mégalithes*, 1976, 118; J.M. Geneste et al, *Les Hauts Lieux de la Préhistoire* en France, 1989, 109

GLOSSARY

ALLÉE-COUVERTE   A rectangular megalithic tomb in Brittany with no passage or covering mound.

ARD   A primitive plough with a single blade and stone share which scratched the ground but turned no furrow.

BLOCKING STONE   A heavy pillar standing at the end of a stone row, usually at right-angles to the line.

BOULDER-BURIAL   A shallow Bronze Age grave in Ireland, lined with low blocks and covered with a massive capstone.

BOULDER-CIRCLE   A small Bronze Age ring of thick stones almost touching each other.

BRONZE AGE   A period from about 2200 to 800 BC in western Europe which saw the development of metalworking and an increasing stratification of society.

CAIRN   A burial mound, long or circular, composed of a mass of small stones.

CIRCLE-HENGE   A henge containing a stone circle.

CIST   A slab-lined grave with a covering stone.

COURT-CAIRN   A megalithic tomb of south-west Scotland and northern Ireland with a markedly concave forecourt.

COVE   A Late Neolithic setting of two sidestones and a backstone like a roofless porch. Coves are thought to be imitations of Early Neolithic megalithic burial chambers.

CROMLEAC   Literally a curved or bent stone, the word once signified a megalithic tomb but is now archaeologically obsolete except in Wales.

CROMLECH   Derived from 'crom leac' the word is used in Brittany to denote a geometrical or ovoid megalithic enclosure akin to the stone circles of Britain.

CUPMARK   A small manmade circular hollow ground into a stone. Its significance is unclear but may be related to the sun or moon.

CUP-AND-RING MARK   A cupmark with an artificial groove around it.

DOLMEN   'Dol-maen' or table-stone is a term appled to an elementary form of megalithic tomb with a small chamber and large flattish-topped capstone.

ERRATIC   A rock moved some distance by glaciation.

FLANKER   One of two tall standing stones on either side of the recumbent block in a Scottish stone circle.

FOUR-POSTER   A small Bronze Age stone circle of four stones that only rarely stand at the corners of a rectangle.

GNOMON   A pillar or rod that shows the time by the shadow that it casts on the ground.

HENGE   A Neolithic or Bronze Age earthen circular or ovoid banked enclosure with inner ditch and one or more entrances, the equivalent of a stone circle.

KERB   A stone on the circumference of a mound.

KERB-CIRCLE   A little ring of very closely-set stones, sometimes with a central cist.

MEGALITHIC 'Mega-lith', big stone.

MENHIR 'Maen-hir', stone-tall, a Breton term for a standing stone.

NEOLITHIC New Stone Age about 4500 to 2200 BC which saw the introduction of farming, pottery and the building of megalithic tombs in western Europe.

OUTLIER A standing stone outside a stone circle or henge.

PASSAGE-TOMB A Neolithic megalithic tomb, usually circular, with a stone-lined passage leading to a burial chamber inside the mound.

PLAYING-CARD A stone, rectangular in outline, with one broad face, the other very narrow.

PORTAL An entrance stone. In some stone circles, particularly in north-western England, a pair of stones form portals just outside the circumference to define an entrance.

POSTHOLE The earth-filled hole where a post once stood.

RADIAL-CAIRN An Irish cairn in which, instead of kerbs, slabs lie just inside the circumference at right-angles to it.

RATH Sometimes a pre-Roman but more often an early Christian banked-and-ditched sub-circular enclosure. Most raths were family farmsteads but some were small defensive sites.

REAVE One of a series of parallel Later Bronze Age stony walls meandering for miles across the Dartmoor countryside demarcating wide areas of land.

RECUMBENT STONE A huge block laid flat between its flankers somewhere between the SSE and south-west of stone circles in north-eastern Scotland. In south-west Ireland the 'recumbent' is often a thin slab opposite the tallest stones of the ring.

RING-CAIRN A circular cairn with an open-air central space in which human cremations were buried.

TERTRE French 'mound' or 'hillock'. A burial-place.

TRAPEZOIDAL Wedge-shaped.

TRILITHON 'Three-stone', two tall stones supporting a lintel, a feature best-known inside Stonehenge.

WEDGE-TOMB A long trapezoidal tomb in Ireland whose entrance is at the higher, wider western end.

ABBREVIATIONS

Ant	Antiquity
Arch.	Archaeologia
Arch Ael	Archaeologia Aeliana
Arch Camb	Archaeologia Cambrensis
Arch J	Archaeological Journal
CBA	Council for British Archaeology
DAJ	Derbyshire Archaeological Journal
GAJ	Glasgow Archaeological Journal
JBAA	Journal of the British Archaeological Association
JCHAS	Journal of the Cork Historical and Archaeological Society
JHA	Journal for the History of Astronomy
JRIC	Journal of the Royal Institute of Cornwall
JRSAI	Journal of the Royal Society of Antiquaries of Ireland
PDAS	Proceedings of the Devon Archaeological Society
PDNHAS	Proceedings of the Dorset Natural History and Archaeological Society
PPS	Proceedings of the Prehistoric Society
PRIA	Proceedings of the Royal Irish Academy
PSAL	Proceedings of the Antiquaries of London
PSAN	Proceedings of the Society of Antiquarians of Newcastle
PSAS	Proceedings of the Society of Antiquaries of Scotland
PSNHAS	Proceedings of the Somerset Natural History and Archaeological Society
RCAHM	Royal Commission for Ancient and Historical Monuments
TBFC	Transactions of the Berwick Field Club
TCWAAS	Trans. Cumberland and Westmorland Antiquarian and Archaeological Society
TDA	Transactions of the Devonshire Association
TDGNHAS	Transactions of the Dumfries and Galloway Natural History and Archaeological Society
TLCANHS	Transactions of the Lancashire and Cheshire Archaeological and Natural History Society
TPPSNH	Transactions and Proceedings of the Perthshire Society for Natural History
TSANHS	Transaction of the Shropshire Archaeological Society and Natural History
TTB	Thom, Thom and Burl, 1980
UJA	Ulster Journal of Archaeology
VCH	Victoria County History
WAM	Wiltshire Archaeological Magazine
YAJ	Yorkshire Archaeological Journal

BIBLIOGRAPHY

TECHNICAL AND PRACTICAL

Atkinson R.J.C., *Field Archaeology*, London, 1946

Coles J., *Experimental Archaeology*, London, 1979

Curtin W. & R.F. Lane *Concise Practical Surveying*, London, 1978

Farrar R., *Survey by Prismatic Compass*, C.B.A., 1987, (2nd ed)

Hogg A.H.A., *Surveying for Archaeologists and Other Field-Workers*, London, 1980

GENERAL

Not every reader of this Guide will be a devotee only of stone circles, fascinating though they are. Many visitors will wish to know what else there is of megalithic interest in the vicinity. For those enthusiasts the following books are recommended.

EUROPE IN GENERAL

Balfour, M. *Megalithic Mysteries. An Illustrated Guide to Europe's Ancient Sites*, London, 1992

Service, A. Bradbery, J. *The Standing Stones of Europe. A Guide to the Great Megalithic Monuments*, London, 1993

GREAT BRITAIN

ENGLAND

Dyer, J. *The Penguin Guide to Prehistoric England & Wales*, London. 1981

Thomas, N. *Guide to Prehistoric England*, London, 1976

SCOTLAND

Feachem, R. *Guide to Prehistoric Scotland*, London, 1977

MacKie, E.W. *Scotland: an Archaeological Guide*, London, 1975

WALES

Dyer, J. *The Penguin Guide to Prehistoric England and Wales*, London, 1981

Houlder, C. *Wales: an Archaeological Guide*, London, 1974

UNITED KINGDOM

CHANNEL ISLES

Johnston, D.E. *The Channel Islands. An Archaeological Guide*, Chichester, 1981

Bender, B. *The Archaeology of Brittany, Normandy and the Channel Islands*, London, 1986

ISLE OF MAN

Kermode, P.M.C. and Herdman, W.A. *Manks Antiquities*. Liverpool, 1914
Manx Museum. *Prehistoric Sites in the Isle of Man*. Douglas, 1973.

NORTHERN IRELAND

Evans, E.E. *Prehistoric and Early Christian Ireland. A Guide*, London, 1966
Harbison, P. *Guide to the National and Historic Monuments of Ireland*, Dublin, 1992

REPUBLIC OF IRELAND

Evans, E.E. *Prehistoric and Early Christian Ireland. A Guide*, London, 1966
Harbison, P. *Guide to the National and Historic Monuments of Ireland*, Dublin, 1992

BRITTANY

Bender, B. *The Archaeology of Brittany, Normandy and the Channel Islands*, London, 1986
Burl, A. *Megalithic Brittany. A Guide to Over 350 Ancient Sites and Monuments*, London, 1985
Scouëzec, G. le and Masson, J-R. *Bretagne Mégalithique*, Paris, 1987

SITES IN THE GUIDE

Aubrey, J. (1665–1693) *Monumenta Britannica, I*, Milborne Port, 1980
Barber, J. (1972) 'The stone circles of Counties Cork and Kerry. Part I'. Unpublished MA dissertation, University of Cork
Barnatt, J. (1978) *Stone Circles of the Peak*, London
— (1982) *Prehistoric Cornwall. The Ceremonial Monuments*. Wellingborough
— (1989) *Stone Circles of Britain. Taxonomic and Distributional Analyses and a Catalogue of Sites in England, Scotland and Wales. Parts i, ii*, Oxford
Bender, B. (1986) *The Archaeology of Brittany, Normandy and the Channel Islands*, London
Bowen, E.G. and Gresham, C.A. (1967) *History of Merioneth, I*, Dolgellau
Briard, J. (1987) *Mégalithes de Bretagne*, Rennes
— (1989) *Mégalithes de Haute Bretagne*, Paris
— (1990) *Dolmens et Menhirs de Bretagne*. Rennes?
Browne, Rev. G.F. (1921) *On Some Antiquities in the Neighbourhood of Dunecht House Aberdeenshire*, Cambridge
Bryce, J. (1910) *The Book of Arran, I. Archaeology*, Glasgow
Burl, A. (1976) *The Stone Circles of the British Isles*, New Haven and London
— (1979) *Prehistoric Avebury*, New Haven and London
— (1985) *Megalithic Brittany. A Guide to over 350 Ancient Sites and Monuments*, London
— (1987) *The Stonehenge People*, London
— (1988) *Four-Posters. Bronze Age Stone Circles of Western Europe*, Oxford
— (1993) *From Carnac to Callanish: the Prehistoric Stone Rows and Avenues of Britain, Ireland and Brittany*, New Haven and London
— (1994) 'The stone circle of Long Meg and her Daughters, Little Salkeld', *TCWAAS 94*, 1–11
— (scheduled for 1996) *The Stone Circles and Cromlechs of Britain, Ireland and Brittany*, New Haven and London
Butler, J. (1991) *Dartmoor Atlas of Antiquities, II. The North*, Exeter
— (1993) *ibid. IV. The South-East*, Exeter
— (1994) *ibid. III The South-West*, Exeter
Chart, D.A. (1940) *A Preliminary Survey of the Ancient Monuments of Northern Ireland*, Belfast
Churcher, I. (1985) 'Form and function, comparisons and contrasts. A survey of stone circles in southern Leinster',

unpublished BA dissertation, University of Durham

Clarke, D.L. (1970) *Beaker Pottery of Great Britain & Ireland*, I. II, Cambridge

Cleal et al (1995) *Stonehenge in its Landscape*, London

Daniel, G. (1963) *The Hungry Archaeologist in France*, London

Davies, O. (1939) 'Stone circles in Northern Ireland', *UJA 2*, 2–14

Dymond, C.W. (1879–81) 'A group of Cumberland megaliths', *TCWAAS V (O. S.)*, 39–57

Evans, E.E. (1966) *Prehistoric and Early Christian Ireland. A Guide*, London

Feachem, R. (1977) *Guide to Prehistoric Scotland*, London

Gilbert, M. (1962) *Pierres Mégalithiques dans le Maine et Cromlechs en France*, Guernsey

Giot, P-R. (1960) *Brittany*, London

— l'Helgouac'h, J. and Monnier, J-L. (1979) *Préhistoire de la Bretagne*, Rennes

Grimes, W.F. (1963) 'The stone circles and related monuments of Wales', in: (eds. Foster, I. Ll. and Alcock, L), *Culture and Environment. Essays in Honour of Sir Cyril Fox*, London, 93–152

Grinsell, L.V. (1976) *Folklore of Prehistoric Sites in Britain*, Newton Abbot

Henshall, A.S. (1963) *The Chambered Tombs of Scotland*, I. Edinburgh

— (1972) *ibid*, II, Edinburgh

Johnson, N. and Rose, P. (1994) *Bodmin Moor. An Archaeological Survey. Volume I. The Human Landscape to c.1800*, London

Johnston, D.E. (1981) *The Channel Islands. An Archaeological Guide*, Chichester

Lockyer, Sir N. (1909) *Stonehenge and other British Stone Monuments Astronomically Considered*, 2nd edition, London

Longworth, I. (1984) *Collared Urns of the Bronze Age in Britain and Ireland*, Cambridge

Lukis, W.C. (1875) *A Guide to the Principal Chambered Barrows etc. of South Brittany*, Ripon

McConkey, R. (1987), 'Stone Circles of Ulster', unpublished MA thesis. The Queen's University of Belfast

Merlet, R. (1974) *Exposé du système solstitial néolithique, Reliants entre eux certains cromlechs et menhirs dans le Golfe du Morbihan*, Rennes

Murray, J. (1981) 'The stone circles of Wigtownshire', *TDGNHS 56*, 18–30

O'Nuallain, S. (1978) 'Boulder-burials', *PRIA 78*, 75–114

— (1984a) 'A survey of stone circles in Cork and Kerry', *PRIA 84C. 1*, 1–77

— (1984b) 'Grouped standing stones, radial-stone cairns and enclosures in the south of Ireland', *JRSAI 114*, 63–79

Pontois, B. le. (1929) *Le Finistère Préhistorique*, Paris

RCAHM-E Royal Commission for Ancient and Historical Monuments, England

RCAHM-S ibid, Scotland

RCAHM-W ibid, Wales

Ruggles, C.L.N. and Burl, A. (1985) 'A new study of the Aberdeenshire recumbent stone circles, 2. interpretation', *JHA 8*, S27–S60

Stuart, J. (1856) *The Sculptured Stones of Scotland*, I, Aberdeen

— (1867) *ibid*, II, Edinburgh

Thom, A. (1967) *Megalithic Sites in Britain*, Oxford

Thom, A. and Thom, A.S. (1977) *La Géométrie des Alignements de Carnac. (Suivi de Plans Comparatifs)*, Rennes

— and A.S. (1978) *Megalithic Remains in Britain and Brittany*, Oxford

—, A.S. and Burl, A. (1980) *Megalithic Rings: Plans and Data for 229 Monuments in Britain*, Oxford

Waterhouse, J. (1985) *The Stone Circles of Cumbria*, Chichester

Worth, R.H. (1967), (eds) Spooner, G.M. and Russell, F.S. *Worth's Dartmoor*, Newton Abbot

INDEX

The site's Guide number is bracketed. **Major entries are in bold type.** *Illustrations are italicised*